W9-BCU-432

NARRATIVE TECHNIQUE
in the
ENGLISH NOVEL

NARRATIVE TECHNIQUE

in the

ENGLISH NOVEL

Defoe to Austen

IRA KONIGSBERG

Archon Books
1985

First published 1985 as an Archon Book
an imprint of The Shoe String Press, Inc.
Hamden, Connecticut 06514

The paper in this book meets the guidelines
for performance and durability of
the Committee on Production Guidelines for Book Longevity
of the Council on Library Resources.

Library of Congress Cataloging-in-Publication Data

Konigsberg, Ira.
Narrative technique in the English novel.

Bibliography: p.
Includes index.
1. English fiction—18th century—History and
criticism.   I. Title.
PR851.K66   1985   823'.009'23   85-15669
ISBN 0-208-02081-0 (alk. paper)

Printed in the United States of America

For
Anna, Peter, and Sasha

Contents

CHAPTER THREE

TOM JONES:
The Novel as Art

CHAPTER FOUR

TRISTRAM SHANDY'S
Anatomy of the Mind

CHAPTER FIVE

HUMPHRY CLINKER
and Parallactic Narration

CHAPTER SIX

PRIDE AND PREJUDICE:
The Paradigmatic Novel

Preface

Literary criticism and scholarship seem to be, at least for the present, in a state of relative calm. The flurry of activity during the past two decades in critical theory and the resulting anxieties for anyone engaged in practical criticism seem to have subsided. The writer of a literary study need no longer feel the pressure of considering whether he or she might belong to this or that camp, or the unhappy frustration of trying to figure out exactly what each camp represents. Having survived the recent wars, we are now free to pick from the spoils and to pursue our own destinies, somewhat richer from the battles for truth which have been so earnestly and, at times, so brilliantly fought.

There are those who would argue that the war continues, and I would not deny that in various locations and publications skirmishes still occur. But certainly all the fury about structuralism and poststructuralism has diminished considerably. Those who have recently rallied around the flag of the resurrected Russian critic Mikhail Bakhtin do not seem certain in which direction to proceed. And supporters of reader-response criticism seem less to be converting us than making us aware of what we have already dimly perceived.

My own approach in this book is to be as independent as possible, but at the same time to look for help from whatever source seems applicable and prudent. My general thrust is traditional and practical. I have examined a group of early prose narratives that are responsible for establishing in England what we refer to as the modern novel. My study concludes with Jane Austen, because in her works we see the culmination of this early development and a paradigm for future writers in the genre. I relate the five authors represented in this book more closely than have previous scholars, and seek to show that in their fictional concerns and the narrative techniques they developed they were frequently guided by similar moral and aesthetic goals. One of the ways I seek to accomplish my own goals is by relating these novels to significant intellectual ideas and trends in the period in order to show how these works were partly shaped by similar forces. Another is by applying narrative theory as it has developed in our own century to these novels in order to place them in a larger generic context. My final method is to integrate into these other approaches, as subtly and inobtrusively as I can, some ideas I have collected from the recent debates in critical theory. Except for the introductory chapter, where I outline some of my theoretical concepts, the bulk of this book is primarily about the novels and the way they are written. It is my hope that the reader will come away from this book with a greater sense of why and how the modern novel emerged from earlier fictional forms, and with a greater understanding of the contributions and unique achievements of the major writers within this development.

I want to express my gratitude to those who helped me see this book into final form and into print. I am grateful to my colleagues Sheridan Baker, Lincoln Faller, and Robert Weisbuch, who read this work in its early stages and gave needed advice and encouragement. Ian Watt has been a constant support in the later history of the manuscript. Not only has his own writing been of significant help, but his kindness and generosity have been a source of strength and hope for me. Russell Fraser has consistently been for me a model colleague, a good friend, and a sage counselor. I express immense gratitude to James Winn, who came riding in on a white charger and gave the final push to send this work into daylight. I shall always be in his debt. At a very crucial time, my colleague and chairman, John Knott, came forth with sound advice and productive assistance. I also wish to thank the Rackham School of Graduate Studies, at the University of Michigan, which supplied financial aid for writing this book and bringing it into print.

Introduction

THE READER'S EXPERIENCE

Defoe, Richardson, and Fielding, the first major novelists,[1] proceeded in new fictional directions, but they made their advances with the support of literary precedent. Defoe, who was mostly concerned with his fiction as an economic venture, began working with established materials, even though he soon discovered that he was also doing something new that made his works eminently appealing to the reading public of his time. *Robinson Crusoe* was a combination of make-believe and travelogue, a commercial product to make some money by capitalizing on already-developed interests in the audience. The response to Robinson Crusoe the man, however, was overwhelming—it was no longer the adventures nor the unusual life alone that provoked reaction, but the sense of the character behind the events, making the events themselves significant, that gave the work its impact. And so Defoe went on to write a series of narratives, frequently developing with each a major character who seemed more credible and lifelike than any of the adventurers, rogues, or criminals who had appeared before, but still writing his works within the older molds of pseudo-biography, criminal fiction, adventure book, and travelogue. Richardson and Fielding were more aware of their works as literary endeavors, as ventures in a new art form, though they disagreed about their goals and means. Yet both of them, like Defoe, used traditional literary elements—Richardson subtly and skillfully, Fielding openly and brilliantly.[2] All writers begin with the literary tradition they inherit, no matter what they do to it, and they write for an audience educated to respond in particular ways. What is significant about the first novels is that writers used materials and techniques from older literary forms to provoke new kinds of responses. Later in the genre's development, when the audience knew how to respond in the new way, elements from more traditional kinds of literature generally disappeared, and earlier novels became the chief influence on new works. Literature radically new takes a while to be accepted or even understood, since an audience must have some degree of preparedness in the reading process, and even though the earliest novels offered something very new, they did so in a way that seemed neither radical nor upsetting because of this manipulation of traditional elements.

But the impact of the new reading experience upon the public is evident from the very beginnings of the genre. One correspondent, signing herself "Philopamela," wrote to Richardson after the publication of *Pamela* (1740): "I entirely agree with her in every thing, sympathize in all her Distresses and Misfortunes, feel Pleasure or Pain only when Pamela does."[3] We can relate this correspondent's involvement with Richardson's heroine partly to the nature of the novel's subject matter. Philopamela cares about Pamela because the heroine and her situation have some kind of meaning in the immediate context of her own world and her own experience. It is one thing to feel an occasional vicarious thrill from the exploits of literary figures in earlier fiction, but quite another to be involved with the happenings of characters who have some resemblance to people whom one imagines to inhabit the real world. Certainly Pamela's sexual adventures might offer such thrills, but they seem stronger because the girl herself belongs to the servant class, comes from respectable folks, and is threatened in a not uncommon domestic situation. If Defoe, Richardson, and their successors met a receptive and ready audience, it was because they were able to offer them a world relevant to their own at the same time that they gave them the opportunity to escape their own. This aspect of the novel's subject matter was clearly recognized in the eighteenth century. Hugh Blair, in his *Lectures on Rhetoric and Belles Lettres* (1783), saw the novel as beginning in England after the Romance and during the age of Charles II, but he claimed the following important development:

> Since that time . . . somewhat better has been attempted, and a degree of reformation introduced into the Spirit of Novel Writing. Imitations of life and character have been made their principle object. Relations have been professed to be given of the behavior of persons in particular interesting situations, such as may actually occur in life. . . . [4]

I confess that I am talking about the novel's "realism," even though the concept has been subject to much critical disputation. By now we are well aware that there is no monolithic interpretation of the term, and that different novelists create different kinds of reality.[5] At this point, I am using the term only in a general sense, referring to the novel's capacity to create a fictional world with proximity to the reader's idea of his own reality. As much as the novel may open to us new vistas and experiences, its capacity to interest and convince us is dependent upon its creation of the probable and relevant. I have also made my definition relative because fictional realism varies according to prevailing philosophic and cultural notions about reality itself,[6] which influence both the writer and the reader. But we still must go further if we are to understand the novel's "realism" in any meaningful way.

Ian Watt is of assistance in my investigation with his definition of "formal realism" as the "premise, or primary convention, that the novel is a full and authentic report of human experience, and is therefore under an obligation to satisfy its reader with such details of the story as the individuality of the actors concerned, the particulars of the times and places of their actions, details which are presented through a more largely referential use of language than is common in other literary forms."[7] Watt identifies some basic ways in which writers made their "realistic" subject matter "realistic," but certain questions are left unanswered here. Why does the reader respond so strongly to this material? How does he respond to it—what is his moment-to-moment relationship to this "authentic report of human experience"? Something happened to fiction in the eighteenth century that made the reader respond to narrative as never before, something more than an inclusion of "details" and "a more largely referential use of language," something that involved the reader deeply with the characters and their world—and it is here, in the nature of the reader's involvement, that we must seek to learn the true nature of the novel's "realism."[8]

Norman Holland, in his psychoanalytical examination of literary response, sees our "identification" with characters as "a complicated mixture of projection and introjection, of taking in from the character certain drives and defenses that are really objectively 'out there' and of putting into him feelings that are really our own, 'in here.' "[9] Holland sees introjection as the basic or ultimate psychic act, and he finds this true of our response to drama and film as well as literature.[10] But I think we have to make a distinction between our responses to characters in externalized and internalized art forms. When responding to a play or film, the images appear outside of us; when reading a novel, we create the images and assemble the pictures from the signs which the writer has given us—the visual dimension is internalized and personalized. At the same time, the act of reading forces the character's thoughts through our mind, makes us repeat them to ourselves, so that to some degree they seem to be our own thoughts. The inner world of character is shut off from us when we view a performance on stage or screen, and we can only surmise what the characters think and feel from the external behavior and speech of the actors. Since we are always cognizant that what we are seeing and hearing is going on outside of us rather than inside, the characters of drama and film seem more distanced than those we respond to in the novel. For these reasons, I find the nature of our identification with those characters different from that which we feel toward characters in the novel—it is one of projection and not introjection, a state where we send out our needs and desires to the figure who appears before us in an external, physical reality. We project our aggressive instincts, our fears, even our guilt, but we also project our better nature, our hopes for our own joy and happiness. The second type of projection is one which Anna Freud describes as a "surrender of one's own wishes to another person...comparable to the interest and pleasure with which one watches a game in which one has no stake oneself."[11] In this sense, much of our identification is a form of wish-fulfillment. When reading novels, however, because the character is literally created within us, because his thoughts project themselves into our own, the identification takes possession of us and must be seen as one of introjection.[12] There is something libidinal about this relationship, in that we seek to take the character into ourselves and possess him. What we actually desire is to introject the character's qualities or emotional experiences into ourselves. We can say that this introjection also satisfies our narcissistic impulse in that we accrue to ourselves the virtues or accomplishments of the character. The nature of our feelings, of the experience we undergo when responding to the two distinct and different types of art—one performed outside of us and one inside—must be seen as distinct and different also.

The kind of experience that I am describing in relation to the novel was not possible with earlier fiction for a number of reasons, three of which I have already implied: such works did not (1) deal with concerns and a fictional world realistic and credible enough to relate to the reader's own life, (2) depict events and characters with sufficient specificity to allow the reader an internal visual experience, or (3) describe psychological states in a credible way that permitted the reader to internalize the thought processes of the character.[13] Such elements are certainly missing from the fiction of Mrs. Behn, published in the late seventeenth century. Even such an epistolary work as Tom Brown's *Lindamira* (1702), with its love and courtship theme, contemporary settings, and dramatic secondary figures, suffers from a superficial hero and heroine, a lack of dramatic immediacy, and a plot that dwindles into mere intrigue. Some kind of vicarious experience is at times possible with early fiction, but generally events and characters are presented in such a superficial or typed way that there is little but the most general feelings and experiences to relate to. Since whatever projecting we do is into the adventure itself instead of the characters, we tend to fantasize about ourselves, with our own identities, in such a situation, rather than identify with the central character. But even these moments are not frequent, and we must often wade through pages of uninvolving incidents and artificial introspection which we tend to read from a distance and with minimal interest.

But looking at Philopamela's statement again, what we sense is a very different reading experience, one that would hardly be possible with most of the heroines of earlier fiction. I do not deny that a certain amount of fantasizing is evident in her words, but I also claim that she is fantasizing herself as Pamela, and that when she reads the novel she not only puts herself in the shoes of Richardson's heroine but, to a significant extent, loosens her hold on her own identity. It is not her own thoughts and feelings were she in Pamela's situation that she imagines; as she reads the novel, it is the heroine's thoughts and feelings that pass through her brain and evoke within her a sense of being Pamela—not completely, of course, for at the same time she still maintains a sense of her own person, of watching Pamela as a separate entity.[14] When the character's thoughts pass through our minds, and we feel to some degree what the character feels, we are always, as Dr. Johnson tells us in relation to drama, in our "senses."[15]

In the drama, as I have already asserted, the characters are external to us, and their inner thoughts do not pass through our minds. Dr. Johnson is less certain that we are always in our senses, however, when reading fiction, where sometimes "the power of example is so great, as to take possession of the memory by a kind of violence, and produce effects almost without the intervention of the will...."[16] For this reason, "the best examples only should be exhibited...."[17] Memory was considered by the major philosophers of the period to be the basis of personal identity,[18] and it seems clear to me that Dr. Johnson is seeing the faculty in the same way. Fiction was a threat for him because the reader's mind and imagination were filled with experiences and thoughts not his own, allowing memory and hence identity to be too easily exchanged for those of the fictional character. Memory, however, was a sufficient safeguard against the loss of identity when viewing drama, which did not involve such an internalized experience: "Imitations produce pain or pleasure, not because they are mistaken for realities, but because they bring realities to mind."[19] I would argue at this point that memory also helps to keep us in our "senses" when reading fiction, though in a somewhat different way. When reacting to the novel, we put together responses from our emotional memories, since we have not in fact undergone the fictional experience and can only imagine reactions that to some degree and in some variation we have already felt. The fact that we must construct this experience from our emotional memories keeps us at least partly rooted in our own lives and self-awareness. Of course, we also maintain some self-awareness because the experience we construct within us is an imagined one, and the emotions we feel are imagined also since they are not in reference to an actual event. Hence, what we feel can only be an imitation of the subjective state of the character. But still we are compelled to put together our feelings in a new way and for a new situation—in other words, through our involvement and responses, we are allowed to extend our experience even if we do so only in our imaginations. This may be the ultimate value in reading a novel, the development we achieve through personally relating to the work of art and undergoing what seems to us a new experience.

This self-awareness, inherent in the process of our identification, is also reinforced by our own conscience and system of values, which we can never ignore no matter how much our egos allow us to relate to the character. At the same time that we are identifying with the character, we are judging him and ourselves as well. The novel, by having us relate to the character while we maintain our own "senses," by allowing us to be aware of our relating to the character, also allows us to understand ourselves better: we are able to consider the reasons for our involvement, and we are able to compare our own probable behavior in the same situation to the ways the character responds, to experience the character's responses and our own likely responses. The novelist can determine how deeply we are to be involved and how much our self-awareness and judgment are to operate through the amount or texture of descriptions of internal states. The novel's achievement is in allowing us to be in someone else's "senses" and our own at the same time, and it is in relation to this dual purpose that narrative technique must be understood.

We must go further now and establish more specifically how the novel in the eighteenth century allowed the reader the kind of relationship with the characters that I have been describing. The novel's subject matter, visualization, and internalization were crucial, but there was one additional factor, a focus on all these elements that offered the reader an inroad to both the fictional world and the psyches of the major characters. Scholes and Kellogg refer to a popular critical concept in a way particularly helpful for my argument:

Anything significantly new in realistic narrative must correspond to something significantly new in actuality. And this can be achieved only through a new way of looking at life. Technically, the requirement of a new vision throws heavy emphasis on narrative point of view—perhaps, more accurately, on the relationships among point of view, subject, and audience.[20]

To make my point in the boldest and simplest way, a radical alteration in point of view changed everything else in a number of eighteenth-century narratives—character, action, setting, and even language. Point of view became a means not merely to allow the reader to see what a character sees but also to perceive with the character, to have his mind filled with the character's sights, ideas, and responses. Perception, then, became the goal of point of view, and it was a major concern of the new fiction. Perception is the basic act of awareness in the human mind, and it derives from all our senses. But its chief source is sight, and I shall be mostly using the term in this context throughout my study. The novel allowed the reader to perceive the fictional world as did the character, and hence brought him closer to experiencing with the literary figure than ever before in fiction. I would even go so far as to say that all the major novelists from Defoe to Austen, in one way or another, are concerned with perception—technically, thematically, and aesthetically. In this way the novel was the art form that best satisfied both a growing interest and a cultural need in the period. Watt has argued that the novel was a response to the growth of post-Renaissance individualism in its presentation of individual characters in an individual and specific way.[21] My argument is that the novel was a response to a new awareness of individual perception and to the growing sense that this was the domain of art. One of the reasons for the frequent use of first-person narration in the novels of the eighteenth century was the interest in individual perception; the chief breakthrough at the end of the century was the development of a third-person style of narration that allowed the reader to perceive the action with a character, and also allowed the control and manipulation of traditional third-person voice. Since perception in the novel from Defoe to Austen will be a major concern of this study, we must briefly examine the intellectual and cultural background to the subject during this period.

PERCEPTIONAL PSYCHOLOGY

Locke's exploration of the human mind, especially of the way in which the individual perceives the external world, in his *An Essay Concerning Human Understanding* (1690), was a direct confrontation with the

7

whole problem of knowledge that was to have a decided effect upon both philosophic speculation and general thought during the next century.[22] Descartes had gone inside the human mind to discover reality, but he saw there innate ideas of the empirical world that derived from the same divine source as that reality.[23] Locke put the burden of knowing reality on man's shoulders. Sensations and reflections lead to perception, which gives rise to ideas:

> PERCEPTION, as it is the first faculty of the mind exercised about our *ideas*, so it is the first and simplest *idea* we have from reflection, and is by some called thinking in general. Though thinking, in the propriety of the *English* tongue, signifies that sort of operation in the mind about its *ideas*, wherein the mind is active, where it, with some degree of voluntary attention, considers anything. For in bare naked *perception*, the mind is, for the most part, only passive; and what it perceives, it cannot avoid perceiving.[24]

Locke goes on to build his theory of knowledge upon this basis, and the reader begins to suspect that individual views of external reality vary greatly with the senses and mental capacities of the perceiver:

> the fewer senses any man, as well as any other creature, hath; and the fewer and duller the impressions are that are made by them; and the duller the faculties are that are employed about them: the more remote are they from that knowledge which is to be found in some men.[25]

Though Locke is still confident in the similar perceptual abilities of all men—"I am nevertheless very apt to think that the sensible *ideas* produced by any object in different men's minds are most commonly very near and undiscernibly alike"[26]—he does leave the door open for a relativistic explanation of reality, one which saw reality dependent upon the nature of the individual observer:

> we, having but some superficial *ideas* of things, discovered to us only by the senses from without or by the mind reflecting on what it experiments in itself within, have no knowledge beyond that, much less of the internal constitution and true nature of things, being destitute of faculties to attain it.[27]

The next step is Berkeley's "subjective idealism,"[28] a theory put forth in *A Treatise Concerning the Principles of Human Knowledge* (1710), where he claims that "all those bodies which compose the mighty frame of the world, have not any subsistence without a mind—that their *being* is to be perceived or known."[29] Hume was considerably influenced by Berkeley, and joined with him in taking away from external reality its objectivity and autonomy:

we never really advance a step beyond ourselves, nor can conceive any kind of existence, but those perceptions, which have appear'd in that narrow compass. This is the universe of the imagination, nor have we any idea but what is there produc'd.[30]

I have cited these philosophers to demonstrate their concern with perception, a concern which permeated the general culture of the time. Reality, the world outside us, was to become dependent upon the individual confronting it. The advance of science, the investigations into the natural world, were not to shake loose the notion of man as the perceiver and subjective center of the world.[31] The significance of the individual as the central focus of the universe, as the all-seeing eye whose mind perceived and shaped external reality, was felt in the literature of the day, and we can easily mark the path to the subjectivism of the Romantics. In eighteenth-century poetry we can find a development leading towards Wordsworth's *The Prelude* (1799-1805; 1850), a poem which deals with two perceptional levels—the hero of the work growing into the man through his perceptions of external reality, and the writer himself perceiving both that world again and himself originally learning to perceive it. The subject of perception and imagination was dealt with specifically in Akenside's *Pleasures of Imagination* (1744), and the act of perception itself became dramatized in works like Thomson's *The Seasons* (1727-1746) and Gray's *Elegy in a Country Churchyard* (1751), a poem about the poet perceiving the world around him and then imagining his own life perceived by another. Cowper's *The Task* (1785), a long, discursive, meditational, and autobiographical poem, in its subjective nature and focus on the individual poet perceiving external reality puts us right on the threshold of Wordsworth's poem. In criticism as well the shift is evident, with Addison's papers on the imagination (1712) popularizing Locke and bringing to the study of literature an emphasis on the reader as perceiver of the work of art.[32] Longinus, with his discussion of our responses to the sublime, also had his effect on Addison and the period in general—the *Essay on the Sublime* was the source of numerous treatises.[33] Even Dr. Johnson, with his belief in a verifiable reality and the immutable laws of nature, puts the focus of his criticism right in the head of the perceiving reader.[34]

The novel became the major literary form during this period, not because it embodied certain philosophical notions but because it literally dramatized a significant awareness of the individual's relationship to reality developing in the culture of the time: the novel most directly confronted the problem of perception in both its narrative technique and its subject matter. Most writers dramatized the perceptional dimension of their major figures and enticed the reader into perceiving with them. The novel more than satisfied the reader's need to know and learn about other people; it satisfied his interest in how others thought and felt by allowing him the illusion of seeing and responding to external reality with them. The reader was allowed a perspective on reality which the novel suggested was the only meaningful perspective—the subjective and individual. But this new kind of fiction also allowed the reader the opportunity to expand his own perceptions and experiences through involvement with fictional characters. Fielding, who did not recreate his character's inner worlds at length nor with much specificity, developed the perceptional dimension of his narrator, as much a character as any figure in the book, and allowed the reader to perceive the fictional world with him. Indeed, in Jane Austen's third-person narrations, the reader was allowed to perceive with the characters and, in varying degrees, with the narrator.[35] Perception was of such fundamental significance to the novel that the subject was even confronted head-on and made a major thematic concern in works by Fielding, Sterne, Smollett, and Austen. Events like the changing composition and growing middle-class sensibility of the reading public[36] and the decline of the theater were, of course, instrumental in the development of the novel, but they can hardly explain the revolution that took place in English fiction. I would argue, then, that the novel was largely the creation of the sensibility and metaphysical direction of an age—an age coming to believe that reality was inside the individual and the universe was an extension of the inner world—and that if we examine the novel in light of this perceptional dimension, we can better define and understand many of the narrative techniques developed by the earliest writers in the genre.

VISUALIZATION IN THE NOVEL

Since perception is largely dependent on seeing, it is logical to find also in the period a strong interest in visualization and visual form. Certainly the Restoration and the eighteenth century saw a heightened awareness of the visual arts and the decorative aspects of everyday life. Portrait painting, architecture, furniture, china—all pleased the eye and developed the perceiving minds of the public. More significant to my point are such studies as Newton's *Opticks* (1704), which focused on light and color; Berkeley's *An Essay Towards a New Theory of Vision* (1709) and *The Theory of Vision...Vindicated and Explained* (1733), which were directly concerned with visual perception and both psychological and metaphysical in their approach; and Dr. R. Smith's ambitious *A Compleat System of Opticks* (1738). Locke's *Essay*, in its analytical investigation of the human mind, is, of course, also concerned with sight and its impact on the thinking process. More than that, Locke even suggests that thinking itself is a visual process. Ernest Tuveson sums up this aspect of Locke's *Essay* in the following way: "Since ideas are images, since even complex ideas are multiple pictures, and since understanding itself is a form of perception, the visual and the intellectual world tend to become amalgamated. Abstraction is only one sense impression isolated from the others."[37] According to Locke, "the soul comes to reflect on and consider" mental operations that "furnish the understanding with another set of *ideas*, which could not be had from things without. And such are *perception, thinking, doubting, believing, reasoning, knowing, willing*, and all the different actings of our own minds; which we, being conscious of and observing in ourselves, do from these receive into our understandings as distinct *ideas* as we do from bodies affecting our senses."[38] Tuveson, quoting Locke, develops this point: "The mind, then, is always the observer, even when the object is its own actions, which 'pass there continually, ... like floating visions.'"[39] Thoughts were discussed in largely visual terms by many of the period's major philosophers, and David Hartley even argued that "The Names of intellectual and moral Qualities and Operations" themselves "suggest certain associated visible Ideas" in our minds.[40]

Visual thinking, however, is a subject not confined to a past age. In our own century, Freud has warned that "we must not ... forget the importance of optical mnemonic residues, when they are of *things*, or to deny that it is possible for thought-processes to become conscious through a reversion to visual residues, and that in many people this seems to be the favoured method."[41] But Freud found this method of thinking incomplete and inferior to verbal thought because it fails to deal with relationships between things. More recently, Rudolf Arnheim has written a sustained and persuasive study on visual thought in which he states that "no thought processes seem to exist that cannot operate, at least in principle, in perception. Visual perception is visual thinking."[42] Arnheim argues that "Man can confidently rely on the senses to supply him with the perceptual equivalents of all theoretical notions because these notions derive from sensory experience in the first place." The visual medium, offering "structural equivalents to all characteristics of objects, events, relations," can represent "shapes in two-dimensional and three-dimensional space, as compared with the one-dimensional sequence of verbal language." Arnheim argues against thinkers like Cassirer and Sapir who see language as primary to visual elements and as the molds in which the stuff of visual experience is poured. For Arnheim, language "assists the mind in stablizing and preserving intellectual entities." But verbal statements themselves "refer to imagery in some other medium. . . . they all need a mental realm to exist in." Arnheim even answers Freud's argument that images can not represent the "important logical links of reasoning" by claiming that conjunctions and prepositions, for example, are "represented by highly abstract, topological shapes."

I have cited Arnheim's study and given certain details of his argument to support what I believe is a necessary critical approach to the novel, especially if we are to understand its development in the eighteenth century. I have already claimed that Locke saw thinking largely in terms of visual perceptions, and if he did not directly influence the novel in this respect,[43] his thoughts were pervasive and had an effect on the general thinking of the time. In any case, the novel, from its earliest inception, seems to work according to the same premise—that thoughts are visual, and that the experience of reading a novel, of thinking about the characters and thinking with them, is a visual one. Of course, the novel's medium is language, but the words are the meeting place between the writer's visual conceptions and those images developed in the reader's mind. The writer finds the necessary linguistic signs to communicate perceptions about the characters and their world, and from these signs the reader creates an internal visual experience.

I am talking about much more than a detailed description of setting, since writers like Jane Austen achieve a visual dimension through other techniques.[44] One of the innovative elements in the novel from Defoe to Austen is visual narration, as if the writers want to encourage the reader to see exactly what is going on, even in those passages which describe internal states and reactions: when the character observes the external world, we are not only to see him perceiving but also to perceive that world with him; when the character thinks and feels, we are to have an external image of him, but at the same time we are to visualize his internal drama. By making thought visual—perceptions, reactions, and reflections—the novelist transposes this level more easily and fully into our imaginations, thus increasing our involvement with the character. The character's thoughts are described not in any abbreviated or condensed linguistic form but as he himself visually experiences them. Because thinking is visual, the character's thoughts pass into our own minds easily and readily without the necessity of our finding visual equivalents for them. Since our own thinking process is not fully activated, the character's ideas pass through our minds as our own visualizations. Of course, the images are conveyed in words and hence require that we fill them out from our own past visual experience. But such a process is not conscious and rather tends to personalize the images for us and even involve us more with the character. The fact that the character's appearance and behavior may also be described by the narrator does not necessarily externalize him for us, since we generally have a visual sense of our own appearance and behavior in the world even in the midst of conscious thought. But a sufficient amount of external description can also be useˈ as a control in our identification with the character and allow us both the involvement and judgment that I have already discussed.

Most novelists have sought to make their novels visual for the reader's imagination, and critics have hardly been oblivious to this fact. Joseph Conrad's famous statement on the subject from the preface to *The Nigger of the Narcissus*—"My task . . . is, by the power of the written word to make you hear, to make you feel—it is, before all, to make you *see*"[45]—and Henry James's criticism well document my point. Indeed, as Leon Edel has reminded us, James, who was preoccupied with the visual dimension of the form, continuously used "the terminology of painting . . . for the discussion of the novel."[46] The purpose of my discussion is to point out that visualization is a concern of the novel in more ways and on more levels than is generally recognized, and that it was a prime concern of our earliest novelists, who first developed basic techniques to create this dimension.

We must consider further how the reader's own mind contributes to the images suggested by the text. The reader is given hundreds of pages of words which he must continuously translate into mental pictures. The fullness of each mental picture depends upon both the amount of words and their denotations and connotations. Yet it is obvious that no writer can give us all the details for either an external situation or a mental state. Even Smollett, who expertly details his settings, is still dependent upon the reader's capacity to fill in the blanks—what he actually gives is a series of specifics that suggest in our mind a more detailed and larger picture than he presents.[47] Jane Austen, on the other hand, is not specific in her description of the external world, yet she suggests to us this world, provokes us into imagining it through her depiction of her characters' interplay and dialogue as well as their internal reactions to the world outside them. By filling in the blanks, the reader becomes more involved in both the external world and the character's reactions to it. Forced to call upon his memories, he recreates a reality and an experience which are partly his own.[48] It is this personal collaboration that allows for variation among readers in their experience and interpretation of fiction.[49]

But people read novels in a sufficiently like manner to allow them to experience and talk about the same novel in similar ways, and to allow the writer the possibility of manipulating readers in a similar manner. We must dwell for a while on the similar experiences, the common responses, the writer can count upon before we can properly understand the variation and uniqueness in each reader's involvement with the novel.

E.H. Gombrich, in *Art and Illusion*, demonstrates that each viewer is trained to interpret the paintings of the time into what passes as an image of reality in his own mind.[50] A painting is not a photographic representation of reality but a configuration of signs which we have been taught to interpret in our minds as reality. A similar kind of relationship takes place between the reader and the text of the novel. The writer puts together signs in such a way that the reader can visualize them mentally as a reality.

I have already stated that novelists generally write within the context of earlier novels and can anticipate readers who to some degree are educated to the kind of works they are writing; and that without earlier novels from which to develop their own works, the authors of our first modern novels utilized traditional subject matter and techniques from different kinds of literature to help the reader intuitively fill in the gaps and achieve a picture which the text could only suggest. Moll Flanders belongs to a tradition of rogue and criminal protagonists who prepared the reader of Defoe's time to see and understand her. Richardson's Clarissa had been prepared for in the conduct book, religious confessions, and drama. When enough novels had been written, the reader could rely upon such earlier fiction to help in visualizing the characters and action of each new work. Placed within a somewhat familiar context, the reader was not only able to operate as a trained participant but also brought a little further, given a newer view of character and somewhat different or developed experience, and thus prepared for the fiction to come. I am not claiming that there is a steady progression of any kind, or that a single kind of novel develops. The road from Defoe to Austen is neither straight nor easily discernible. I am claiming that we find in each succeeding major writer some new or developed approach to the fictional world that extends the reader's capacity and broadens the future possibilities of the form.

We have been examining throughout this introduction the ways in which the reader's mind activates and contributes to the fictional world, but there still remains one last aspect of the subject to discuss before we turn to our study of the individual novels. As well as perceiving separate images, the reader must also assemble them, as the novel progresses, into some kind of order—into a developing form. He must have a sense of how the separate frames fit together into a sequence, and how all the sequences form the plot.[51] The order in which the mind arranges images as the novel progresses may be the total view that the protagonist holds, but more often the protagonist's visual comprehension of these events is seen as part of the work's action. As we read the novel, we may perceive with the character the individual events and the recall of past actions, but we also perceive the character and his perceptions as part of the work's totality. This sense of the whole, this larger view, is one of the reasons why our involvement with the character is always partial and controlled.

The reader's mind has the capacity to remember and order images, altering this temporary design with each new image; it also has the capacity to anticipate future actions which will further or complete the design,[52] and to respond to each new image according to what has gone before and the reader's past anticipation. Sometimes the reader anticipates with suspense and pleasure several possible future actions, and hence several possible future designs.[53] The mind, then, functions diachronically and synchronically at the same time: it visualizes a sequence of passing images while arranging them in the larger context of a temporary order. Finally, of course, at the conclusion of the work, there is only the completed spatial and visual image of the entire work of art.

At various points in our reading, then, we are aware of the work's temporary gestalt, just as at the conclusion of the work we are aware of the finished and total gestalt. As Wolfgang Köhler points out several times in *Gestalt Psychology*,[54] temporal experiences follow the same organizing principles as spatial ones. The dynamic force which pulls together all the events of the novel in our minds, as we read and after we have completed the text, is plot. We can understand how our final perception of the work is organized by plot with the help of Köhler once again: "Association is necessary for recall, and association presupposes a sufficient degree of unification in the sense of organization."[55] Our recall of the novel's entirety is dependent upon the association of the parts achieved through the work's plot. Gestalt psychology explains, I believe, how we can perceive a work's totality synchronically in our minds instead of having to recall it diachronically, episode by episode. As teachers and critics, we often feel a sense of dissatisfaction when we break down a text, when we discuss the individual parts or themes— certainly we notice the anxiety among our students as the work's totality is shattered for them. The problem is, of course, that we cannot communicate verbally, in temporal language, the totality that we can perceive spatially in our minds. If thought is visual, then it follows that the knowledge we have of an entire work is visual as well. In Boethius's *The Consolation of Philosophy*, Lady Philosophy explains to the narrator God's capacity to see past, present, and future simultaneously. It is that kind of expansive vision that the novel creates in the vast space of the reader's mind.

We have established, then, four influences on each image: (1) the words themselves, with all their connotations, which create the image; (2) literary traditions that force us to see character, setting, and action partly in typed ways; (3) the context of the novel itself, the past actions and anticipation of future ones which add a resonance to each image; and (4) the reader himself: his own personality, which colors the image, and his past experiences and memories, from which he constructs the visual image itself. We must emphasize though, in relation to the last influence, that the successful novelist is specific enough in the use of signs and skillful enough in provoking us to call up certain images from our memories to control what we see and how we respond. But, as we have said before, readers' minds vary and perceptions differ, and no two readings of a novel are ever quite the same. Responses to older works also vary from age to age because of the impact of changing cultural and social forces on readers' personalities and sensibilities, each age evoking somewhat changed perceptions of older works and hence the possibility of finding new values in them.

A SYNOPSIS OF THIS STUDY

We have not wanted for technical discussions of the novel in general, nor is it still possible to say that any of the major novelists treated in this work has received scant critical attention. What I have attempted to write, however, is the first study which focuses largely on narrative technique from Defoe to Austen.[56] In the following pages, we shall examine the ways in which the first major English novelists developed the form of the novel and, within that form, the techniques that produced in the reader the kinds of responses and experiences I have been discussing. We shall see the way these writers extended earlier literary techniques and created new ones to establish narrative methods basic to future novelists. We shall also relate these developments to certain aspects of the period's intellectual background, some of which I have already discussed. Inseparable from these subjects is thematic interpretation, an analysis of the writer's moral concerns as well as his attitudes towards his characters and their world, which he seeks to communicate in large part through the reader's experiencing of the novel. Narrative techniques are not used merely to give us an emotional experience but to have us learn by extending our own experience and hence broadening our awareness about human nature, about the world in which we live, and about ourselves. All of these goals will be accomplished, I hope, through an examination of one novel by each author that best demonstrates the concerns I have been discussing and makes the most significant contribution to the art of the novel.

The path was neither straight nor smooth, and certainly these works were not equally successful, but the novelists, even though they sometimes focused on different aspects of the fictional world or went about their business in somewhat different ways, were all concerned with exploring similar kinds of human problems and creating within the reader similar kinds of experiences. Without discounting the enormous range and variety in future fiction, I think it fair to say that by the beginning of the nineteenth century, with the works of Jane Austen, the basic aims and techniques of novel-writing had been explored, developed, and well established.

CHAPTER ONE

MOLL FLANDERS
and the Pattern of Character

Defoe's brief but remarkable fictional career began with *Robinson Crusoe* in 1719, a work of immediate popularity and one with sufficient technical achievement to put us into a new age of prose narrative. But for several reasons I have chosen to examine a later work by Defoe, *Moll Flanders*, which appeared in 1722. *Robinson Crusoe* has a powerful mythic appeal to us because in a direct way it deals with universal situations and needs[1]—the individual confronting the universe, taming nature, asserting total independence and self-reliance—but it also borders on fantasy with its capacity to satisfy our dreams about faraway places and extraordinary adventures. Even though Robinson's internal dimension is consistently dramatized and his religious and moral development portrayed with care and detail, the very nature of the book's subject matter creates an individual isolated from the real world and hence limited in his psychological concerns. Moll's psychology is somewhat contradictory and certainly uneven in its depiction and development, but she lives in a world recognizable to the reader, her perceptions respond more subtly to external reality, and her internal drama, because of the world she confronts, is more varied and complex. For these reasons *Moll Flanders* is more novelistic in both subject matter and technique, and more related to the other works we shall discuss.

THE PREFACE TO *MOLL FLANDERS*

Defoe argues for authenticity in his preface to *Moll Flanders*—he claims that the work presents the story of a true person. With this argument, Defoe defends his work against his period's suspicion of fiction—for at this point the novel is not yet an established literary form, and the various types of fiction are merely vehicles for entertaining stories.[2] The serious reading public of the eighteenth century seems to have had a mania for punishing itself with didactic and moral literature; and even when it was allowing itself pleasure, the pretext for edification had to be there. Made-up stories had no relevance to life; there was nothing to learn from them.[3] Many people thought of fiction in terms of the romance, with its superhuman characters and incredible situations.[4] There was no mimetic theory to justify fiction in the way both comedy and tragedy could be justified. True stories, lives of real people, on the other hand, were valuable since they were applicable to real life. If the novel were to make a start, it would have to do so in disguise, pretending to be what it was not—pretending to be true.

Right at the very inception of the novel, then, there was a demand for narrative form dealing with real material. Of course, this demand also led Defoe, and especially later writers, to authenticate their novels by developing narrative techniques which would present this material realistically; and ultimately it would not even be necessary to claim that the material was taken directly from life so long as it was presented as true to life, so long as it gave the illusion of reality. But Defoe must now pretend that *Moll Flanders* is true; that the characters and actions are authentic; that the work is not madeup and therefore negligible; that, being based on life, it has value as a practical moral lesson. Yet Defoe admits that the narrative cannot be completely authentic: "It is true that the original of this story is put into new words, and the stile of the famous lady . . . is a little alter'd, particularly she is made to tell her own tale in modester words than she told it at first; the copy which came first to hand having been written in language more like one still in Newgate . . . " (p. 3).[5] Some concessions have to be made to our sensibilities; there has to be some alteration in the telling. Defoe is having both sides of the argument: by letting us know that the original manuscript was too real for our eyes, he is arguing for the authenticity of his source; on the other hand, he is explaining that some concern for our responses, aesthetic as well as moral, has to be shown.[6] The future of the novel lies in that concession, a concession which will be made more readily and fully by those writers who follow Defoe.

But Defoe cannot admit the concession so fully because of the moral demands of his public:

> the moral 'tis hoped will keep the reader serious, even where the story might incline him to be otherwise. To give the history of a wicked life repented of necessarily requires that the wicked part should be made as wicked as the real history of it will bear. . . . (Pp. 3-4)

19

It seems plausible enough to deal with wicked events if a moral lesson is to be drawn from them—but their presence is argued for by another telling reason, one that underscores his concern with responses from his readers other than moral: "There is in this story abundance of delightful incidents, and all of them usefully apply'd" (p. 4). Clearly he means us to consider the "wicked" incidents as delightful: "The first part of her lewd life with the young gentleman at Colchester has so many happy turns given it to expose the crime . . . that it abundantly attones for all the lively description . . . " (p. 4). Does a conflict already seem to appear in his intentions? Is it possible to describe immoral actions and make them "delightful" for the sake of morality? Defoe is arguing that he intends to purge us of bad inclinations through our association with his heroine. He goes on to tell us that he will show wicked actions only to render them finally "unhappy and unfortunate" (p. 5). He will show the villains "brought to an unhappy end, or brought to be a penitent" (p. 5). The significance of this dual purpose should not be underplayed. A staunch Puritan would say that one does not entertain with delightful events, many of them wicked, to make a moral point. But Defoe *is* writing fiction, with all his pretenses not to be doing so, and he is writing fiction to sell copies and make money.[7] To do so he must be entertaining, and he must be concerned with his reader's responses to his work. There is no irony here. The preface is both a defense of his work and a job of advertising. Its contradictions are consciously, though not cynically, made. Defoe would like to be moral, and he knows that his work must appear to be moral. But he also knows what his reader wants beyond the appearance of morality.[8]

Defoe is writing in the tradition of rogue biography; like Kirkman and others, his major concern is to present a multitude of interesting and exciting events.[9] Moll has been chosen not so much because she will present an interesting character for study as because of what she has done. The emphasis of the book, as the full title tells us and the preface implies, will be on her actions, not her character. Not once in his preface does Defoe mention character study as one of his aims in writing. But he had already learned from his writing of *Robinson Crusoe*, and to some extent from *Memoirs of a Cavalier* (1720) and *Captain Singleton* (1720), that a developed character was also a source of interest for the audience and gave an authentic perspective to the adventures, hence making them more credible. For these reasons Defoe created a character as real as the actions she engaged in and as valid in her own right as the moral lessons she espoused, but this was not the basic intention of his work.

Defoe, then, has defined for us his novel: it is the first-person narration of an authentic life, somewhat rewritten by the editor for reasons of propriety and pleasure, with an emphasis upon action, much of it wicked, though all of it entertaining and morally useful.

MOLL'S VOICE

Knowing Defoe's intentions in writing this work, and knowing the tradition of criminal fiction in which he is writing, we must be impressed by how much characterization of Moll we do get. From the first page of the novel there is a voice speaking to us, and it is a convincing, lifelike voice. We are listening to someone talk to us, telling us about herself and her adventures. I have already suggested that first-person narration not only satisfied a growing interest in the individual by emphasizing the distinct presence and personality of the hero or heroine but also manifested the age's concern with the individual's perception of reality.[10] More significant in *Moll Flanders* than the presentation of objects and settings is the relation of the main character to the real world; there is a dynamic interplay between the two that gives both a tension and a cohesiveness to the entire created world of Defoe's novel. First-person narration directly showed the central character responding to external reality. Third-person point of view dramatizing the internal perspective of the character may do the same, as I have mentioned earlier, but such a narrative method was not a developed or a consistent technique at the time—most third-person narration was omniscient, and distant from the characters and their perceptions of the world. There is another reason for the wide use of first-person narration, one that relates to my opening discussion about authenticity: if fiction had to seem authentic, then it had to imitate the most authentic and authenticated kinds of writing—autobiography, memoirs, and letters. Narratives told in the third person, even though they may claim to be histories, have the aura of storytelling, of something made up. In part, this is because the narrator does not directly partake in the actions, and much of what he describes either has come to him indirectly or must be imagined by him. First-person narration seems to be authentic because here is the person who was engaged in the action, actually telling us his experiences. We believe in the existence of the voice talking to us because we hear it; if the person in the story is the same as the person describing the story, then we are more ready to believe in him as well.

Because an actual person must be doing the telling, we believe in the existence of that person even when the language may be ostentatious or simply awkward; we may even think the language is an indication of the teller's personality.[11] But it is unlikely that we are able to take seriously what the narrator is telling us about himself, nor is it possible for us to believe in the authenticity or reality of his characters within the narrative so long as his language stands in the way. Moll's language seems to us real in that it is close to speech and not at all "literary." For this reason we are more ready to believe what Moll has to say about herself at the time of the writing and about herself when she engaged in the action of the novel. But Moll's language is also suffi- ciently real to create for us the character and her world within the narrative, and sufficiently transparent to allow us to see into that world without being distracted by the voice of the speaker.

A revolution had taken place in English prose style, and Defoe is the first major writer of fiction to show this. Gone from fiction is the rhetorical and often artificial prose of the seventeenth-century writers of romance. In 1667, Bishop Sprat had argued that one could not communicate the realities of the natural world without precise and accurate language.[12] The modern novel, dependent upon creating a semblance of the real world, could not develop until there was a prose precise and accurate enough to convey the world's reality.

Defoe's education for writing was in journalism, where he learned to write clearly and with immediacy; where his prose had to communicate a good deal of information with an aura of truth; where his sentences had to move fast, not confusing the reader but introducing him to fact after fact.[13] Here is a good example of the direct and functional style that Defoe developed for his fiction:

> I was continu'd here till I was eight years old, when I was terrified with news that the magistrates (as I think they call'd them) had ordered that I should go to service; I was able to do but very little wherever I was to go, except it was to run of errands, and be a drudge to some cookmaid, and this they told me of often, which put me into a great fright; for I had a thorough aversion to going to service, as they call'd it, tho' I was so young; and I told my nurse that I believ'd I could get my living without going to service if she pleased to let me; for she had taught me to work with my needle, and spin worsted, which is the chief trade of that city, and I told her that if she would keep me, I would work for her, and I would work very hard. (Pp. 11–12)

Defoe's prose runs on, doing several things at once: giving us information, creating Moll's world with a number of concrete details, dramatizing her situation by suggesting a particular scene with her nurse and her general emotional reactions throughout the episode. At times in the novel there is some confusion as to whether the point of view or attitude belongs to Moll when she participates in the action or when she is writing about the action years later. In this passage, the general attitudes and feelings clearly belong to the young Moll, and they are reinforced by the unsophisticated language and sentence structure. The journalistic freedom of Defoe's prose allows him this flexibility, allows him to shape what is basically a free-flowing prose style with a high accumulation of facts into a language that reflects the lack of sophistication and emotional insecurity of a young girl. But we are still aware that the mature Moll is writing the paragraph when she tells us that she thinks "they call'd" the men "magistrates" and that spinning worsted is "the chief trade of that city." These details also begin to develop for us a sense of the older Moll's pragmatic and literal nature. The accumulation of details, the collapsing of time, are logical in the memory of the woman who is writing the book; and it is this constant relating and synthesizing of past events that often gives the novel one level of reality—through the narrating, the storyteller, Moll herself, is created for us. But these events of the past also have the objective of explaining both the development of Moll's general situation in life and the development of the character of the women who will be engaged in the various exploits which the older Moll will relate.

We are learning now what crucial experiences in her early life helped form her character—but we are also seeing that character take shape before our eyes:

> As for my money, I gave it all to my Mistress Nurse, as I call'd her, and told her, she should have all I got when I was a gentlewoman, as well as now; by this and some other of my talk my old tutoress began to understand what I meant by being a gentlewoman; and that it was no more than to be able to get my bread by my own work....(P. 14)

The simple language, the short clauses in the first half of the sentence, convey to us the simple, naive nature of the girl, but the sentence also conveys to us Moll's desire for independence, her early preoccupation with being a "gentlewoman," and her early knowledge that "money" is the key to being independent and a "gentlewoman."[14] Though Moll's definition of a "gentlewoman" will change, she will never lose this preoccupation with money. Her preoccupation with money, and her habit of valuing objects according to their cash worth, is a motif that runs throughout the book and a means by which Defoe creates Moll's character for us.

There is some concern for Moll's physical appearance a few paragraphs later, and this aspect of her being is also related to the character that Defoe is developing for us:

> I was now about ten years old, and began to look a little womanish, for I was mighty grave, very mannerly, and as I had often heard the ladies say I was pretty, and would be very handsome, you may be sure it made me not a little proud. However, that pride had no ill effect upon me yet, only as they often gave me money, and I gave it to my old nurse, she, honest woman, was so just as to lay it out again for me, and gave me head-dresses, and linnen, and gloves, and I went very neat.... (P. 15)

Defoe never fully describes characters; he always seems to work with generalizations. Indeed, the other figures in the book receive even less description than Moll, and this is one of the reasons, along with other deficiencies in characterization, why we have such difficulty seeing them. But Moll's physical attributes are important because, through at least half the book, they will be the source of her survival. Already here, as early as her tenth year, we are told of her attractive appearance; and although we are never given much more detail than that, it is sufficient, along with the data we are given about the responses of others to her charms, to contribute to a visual picture of Moll. But other traits are added here to Moll's developing character, traits that will remain with her throughout her life and be part of her general pattern of character. Her early "womanish" appearance and the fact that she is "pretty" may not indicate an erotic nature in Moll, but they do tell us that Moll values herself in these terms and already sees the usefulness of her appearance; they also begin to suggest that we understand Moll's position in her world as an attractive object for others. Her gravity and manners, also mentioned in the passage, suggest to us Moll's seriousness as she confronts life, as well as that distance and superiority she maintains throughout most of the book. Again we are told of the importance of money for Moll, the realization of what it can do for her—and clearly the money referred to in the passage is very much related to her appearance, since it is her physical characteristics and demeanor which have earned her the financial reward, and it is the reward which allows her to dress "very neat." Earlier, Moll told us that she wished to be a "gentle-woman," which for her meant a self-employed individual. Here she also shows an aspiration to appear genteel, a concern she will maintain throughout the work and which she will have to satisfy, for much of her life, with her physical person.

CHARACTER IN THE NOVEL

The emphasis in these passages has been upon Moll's isolation in the world, something she will feel until the very end of the book, and the habits of mind developed from that isolation—her fear of poverty and a demeaning life; her growing sense of self-dependency; her financially oriented sensibilities; her defensive sense of superiority; and her desire to achieve the state of what she calls "a gentlewoman." Once these ideas are established in the early pages, they become the major forces in her entire life and thread together all the episodes of the work. There are, of course, other characteristics in Moll which later will be developed, characteristics which we need for a fuller and more satisfying portrayal, but already here, at the beginning of the novel, we have the pattern of a person emerging, one with a consistency and unity sufficient to make her interesting and engaging.

The creation of character is a dynamic process and one of the chief sources of pleasure we feel when reading a novel. Indeed, it is probably the primary distinction between the novel and the myriad of fiction written during the seventeenth and early eighteenth centuries.[15] The romances, the fictitious histories and biographies, the novels of manners, are all singularly united in their emphasis upon action and in their lack of characterization. *Moll Flanders* is in a unique transitional position: consciously written for the sake of its actions, it also creates a character that at times seems to overpower its primary intention. Defoe develops in the pages of his novel the pattern and shape of a character who evokes in our imagination the sense of seeing and knowing a person named Moll Flanders. We are now engaged in tracing the development of that character, but it would be well to make some generalizations on the process itself before we go any further so that we can better understand Defoe's achievement and his failure with Moll, and so that we can establish some principles of characterization for our discussion of future novelists.

Character in the novel is the result of a cohesion of traits or qualities, both personal and physical, which we assign to a single name—we might even say that it is the accumulative effect of the author's language or verbal signs which refer to that name.[16] In the case of first-person narrators, it is the accumulation of both what the character tells us about himself, directly and through others, and what we assess ourselves from the character's attitudes—in other words, it is the accumulative effect of the narrator's conscious and unconscious use of language. My emphasis here is on the word "accumulative": since language is temporal and gives us over a period of time the traits or qualities which we assemble in our mind into the pattern of character, what we really have is a series of temporary patterns which develop, generally early in the work, into the total one. The various stages of the pattern are responsible for the various stages of our mental image of the literary figure; hence, our final visual perception of the character is dependent upon the accumulation of partial visual perceptions.

In the case of Moll Flanders, where we are given only some generalizations about her physical appearance, our visualization develops largely from traits of character and thus tends to be subjective in nature; we all vary to some degree in the visual associations we have for different psychological or moral attributes. But though Defoe leaves us free to assign our own physical details to his literary figure, such details can all be reduced again to the same basic elements of personality—though we may all see Moll somewhat differently, our understandings of her should not vary by much. Even in those cases where we are given considerable physical detail, our visual associations for psychological and moral qualities have a direct input into the figure's image, and thus our perception of the character is still somewhat subjective. I would even argue that the image we hold of a character is as dependent on the basic kind of person he is as on any given physical details. Once the pattern is formed, though, when we have enough personal and physical traits to assemble the whole, we perceive the visual shape and features of an individual presence and personality. Of course, the density in pattern differs from author to author, and so does the intensity of our sense of character.

The total pattern of the character, once we perceive it, need not be finished or static. Personality traits might still be added, but added in the continuum of time within the world of the novel. Such an extension of pattern is what creates a sense of developing character, where the fictional person actually undergoes growth while still holding on to the basic shape of his personality. Or the pattern might actually be altered— certain personal traits might be substituted for others—to create a sense of changing character. Such a change is only acceptable when the entire pattern still maintains enough of its original qualities so that we know we are dealing with the same character. Some development or change seems a good idea, because the novel imitates life and we all undergo some development or change in life; because the novel, like life, is defined by time, which itself necessitates growth or alteration. But the pattern must also have the definite, continuing shape that we have in real life and that we call personality. As the novel continues, the reader holds in his mind a visual realization of the character, but a realization of a character who is flexible and lifelike, even when he is not undergoing development or change. This effect is achieved because different elements of the pattern, certain qualities of character, are emphasized from time to time, each brought forward against the background of the entire pattern. The changing focus on traits emphasizes the variability and complexity of character and gives to the entity a dynamic quality.

MOLL'S CHARACTER

We have been examining in Defoe's novel the emerging pattern of Moll's character. But so far it has only been the young Moll we have seen, and not the adult woman whose adventures we follow through most of the work, and we still do not have the final shape of her adult personality. The Moll we are to know throughout the book finally emerges from the next block of action, which deals with her seduction at the age of seventeen or eighteen and her relationship with the seducer and his brother. Defoe works into this first block of action with some subtlety, gradually lessening the movement of time and filling us in, as he goes along, with the necessary details of Moll's character at this point in her life and the situation in which she finds herself. Her middle-class preoccupation with being a "gentlewoman" is further developed as we are told of her receiving an education beyond her station in life. Moll continues to persist in her superiority: "I learned to dance and speak French as well as any of them, and to sing much better . . . " (p. 18). But Moll never appears to us as one who can speak French or even sing and dance, for Defoe has no concept of this kind of character, and Moll's overwhelming materialism and pragmatism quickly suppress such qualities. But her desire to be considered a "gentlewoman" and her insistence on her superiority are very much in keeping with her general character. The word "gentlewoman" keeps reappearing in Moll's vocabulary and begins to take on special connotations. It accumulates meaning and becomes a sign for us of some of Moll's important attitudes and specific limitations. The concept of being a "gentlewoman" is no longer limited to earning one's own keep without being a servant. Economic independence becomes more and more tied in with the appearance of gentility, and the appearance of being a "gentlewoman" (or "gentleman") becomes a sign of individual superiority. It is in this context that Moll begins to make her assessment of other people and to judge the success or limitations of her own life. There is no question that part of her fascination with the man who seduces her has to do with his station in life and his manners: he was "a gay gentleman that knew the town, as well as the country . . . " (p. 19). Except for this, and the fact that "tho' he had levity enough to do an ill-natured thing, yet had too much judgment of things to pay too dear for his pleasures . . . " (p. 19), we never discover anything more about him. Indeed, the quality of appearing and behaving like a "gentleman" is the only one we ever discover about all Moll's men, so persistent is she in her own attitude toward others and so desirous is she to affirm her own superiority.

Human beings are social animals; their psychology is developed in large part through the influence of others, and they define themselves through others. Moll lives off others and at times with others, yet these people are never fully presented. We are told about them in general terms, and we rarely see them as individual living creatures. Failing to see her in relation to others, failing to create other characters to develop her further, Defoe makes Moll a terribly isolated and, in this respect, a strangely incomplete figure. Like a true criminal figure, she remains alone and in competition with the remainder of the world. Her attitudes toward others give us necessary information about Moll, but what they do not tell us seems more significant and explains some of her failures as a character. Defoe gives us enough in Moll's character to make her more than a literary rogue, more than a device for portraying exciting adventures, and for that reason the absence of other humans with whom she can sufficiently relate, while still maintaining her independence, is all the more felt.

I do not wish to belabor this point, but there are those who claim that Moll's failure to give us a sense of the other people in her life is a manifestation of her independence and isolation, that this failure is really a legitimate part of her character.[17] My own feelings are that this failure to create secondary characters is a result of Defoe's emphasis on the action—what happened to Moll or what she did—and his preoccupation with Moll as the central agent of the action. Moll is not supposed to be isolated or coldhearted in a number of her relationships. She is very much emotionally involved with the older brother, but the emphasis is on her unnatural situation, the adventure in which she is engaged. In these adventures, the secondary figures are only agents, catalysts for the action. The same can be said of Moll's own brother, with whom she lives in incest for several years. All we ever know of his personality, before Moll's discovery of their true relationship, is that he is good-tempered (pp. 70 and 74) and above thirty (p. 75). The emotional impact of Moll's change of attitude toward him, which he does not understand, is so overwhelming that he makes two attempts at suicide, but his emotional reactions are described in the most stereotyped way (p. 90). The focus of this whole section is not on the characters but on their unnatural situation (p. 78). All we know of Jemy's personality, who is the true love of Moll's life and who appears several times in the novel, is that "He had, to give him his due, the appearance of an extraordinary fine gentleman; he was tall, well-shap'd, and had an extraordinary address..." (p. 124). That he has the appearance and manner of a gentleman is, of course, significant, but this information reinforces our knowledge of certain of Moll's attitudes without telling us very much about him and without developing further any deeper aspects of her character.

I have gone into the problem of secondary figures in the novel to clarify the nature of Moll's character, both the way in which it is developed and the way in which it is not. Moll's character is developed largely in terms of her self-awareness and not through her awareness of others; even her minimal relationships with other people serve only to reinforce her personal, intrinsic qualities. From Defoe's preface we know that the emphasis in his book was to be on the adventures in which she was engaged. So strong is Defoe's concern with Moll as the center of action that all other figures in the book are minimized almost to insignificance. His advancement in fiction was in the creation of his central figure; the next advancement was to come with Richardson and his creation of a fuller fictional world.

At this point in the novel there is an apparent separation between the older and younger Moll. The older woman can look back upon her behavior years before and understand it from a maturer and more worldly-wise position. Moll can say of her younger self:

> I had a most unbounded stock of vanity and pride, and but a very little stock of virtue.... Thus, I gave up myself to ruin without the least concern, and am a fair memento to all young women whose vanity prevails over their virtue. (P. 24)

We may be somewhat dubious about Moll's moralizing here, but unquestionably there is a difference between the character of the young girl, driven by vanity into a precarious relationship, and the woman who censures this youthful behavior. The real distinction becomes clear when Moll continues:

> On the other hand, if I had known his thoughts, and how hard he supposed I would be to be gain'd, I might have made my own terms, and if I had not capitulated for an immediate marriage, I might for a maintainance til marriage, and might have had what I would; for he was rich to excess, besides what he had in expectation. (Pp. 24-25)

Moll is not behaving with financial prudence in this early affair—she has not yet learned the way of her world—and the older woman condemns her younger self for this. The girl is too taken up with her own beauty and its immediate—not long-range—rewards: "I... was taken up only with the pride of my beauty ... as for the gold, I spent whole hours in looking upon it ... " (p. 25). The point here is that Moll sees the gold only as a gift for her beauty, almost as a symbol of her physical excellence. This is vain, and stupid, because gold must also represent sustenance and survival. Moll loses sight of this because she is too young and inexperienced. She does not see that her beauty is being used, and she is not using her beauty.

In the seduction scene, however, Moll's vanity seems to be pushed aside by the basic appeal of the money, and here she behaves true to form, that is, her action is verified by everything we know of her up till now—by her life of dependency, her insecurity, and her fear of poverty. When the elder brother pulls out the bag of money, Moll is persuaded to submit. Her concession is briefly told and her emotions are not very detailed. Yet the description of the seduction is powerful, because it is consistent within the developing pattern of Moll's character and develops that pattern even further; because everything in the narration— the eroticism and the real "moral" lesson—are absorbed into the economic psychology of Moll's character:

> My colour came and went at the sight of his purse, and with the fire of his proposal together, so that I could not say a word, and he easily perceiv'd it; so putting the purse into my bosom, I made no more resistance to him, but let him do just what he pleas'd, and as often as he pleas'd; and thus I finish'd my own destruction at once, for from this day, being forsaken of my virtue, and my modesty, I had nothing of value left to recommend me, either to God's blessing, or man's assistance. (P. 27)

Moll can look back and remember this event with a pathos and understanding she could not possess then; and yet there is also a convincing emotional reaction on the part of the young girl, one properly directed toward the money. When Moll puts the purse into her bosom and lets the man do what he will, economics and eroticism come together in an action that seems inevitable: the purse and the bosom, especially in conjunction, carry more meaning than a page of description. The rhythm of "but let him do just what he pleas'd, and as often as he pleas'd; and thus I finish'd my own destruction at once ... " conveys Moll's utter abandonment, her transition to an object being used, and the final collapse of her innocence. The word "value" in the final sentence has been so prefaced in the book that it conveys a wealth of meaning beyond the information of the single sentence. The value of something is what the world will pay for it. Having lost her virtue and thus becoming secondhand goods, Moll's value in terms of an honest marriage is now virtually nonexistent. In a world which judges people and things by their economic value, and in the mind of a character who always sees herself and the world in economic terms, the loss of her value is a personal tragedy. This is Moll's turning point, and years later, when writing her memoirs, she realizes it. She will now have to pretend to have value. The status of a "gentlewoman" will now have to be earned in a painful and dangerous way. The young Moll does achieve this insight by the end of the episode with the two brothers, and the distance between her and the older narrator is considerably closed. Moll is flagrantly misused by her lover when he forces her into marriage with his younger brother. Her protestations of love are to no avail; her lover is quick to point out his precarious financial situation, and Moll must give in to economic realities. The lesson will not be lost on her. Moll lives in marriage with the younger brother for five years but feels little affection for him. His death leaves her free to face the world, a more experienced and a smarter person: "I was now, as above, left loose to the world, and being still young and handsome, as every body said of me, and I assure you I thought myself so, and with a tolerable fortune in my pocket, I put no small value upon myself" (p. 53). This is the Moll we have known—attractive and proud, thinking of herself in economic terms (the words "fortune" and "value" stand out)—but she has grown up and matured; her pattern has developed: "I had been trick'd once by that cheat call'd love, but the game was over, I was resolv'd now to be married or nothing, and to be well married or not at all" (p. 53). She is now worldly-wise, but still she has a craving to be a "gentlewoman," still there is this need or lack in her which forces her to wish for stature: "I was not averse to a tradesman, but then I would have a tradesman, forsooth, that was something of a gentleman too . . . " (p. 54). Moll's greater experience and her distrust of "love" have developed within her a core of cynicism. Moll's realistic assessment of herself and her life, her pragmatism, her sheer practicality, are now fully developed, as is her new unromantic attitude: "I kept true to this notion, that a woman should never be kept for a mistress that had money to make her self a wife" (p. 54).

When Moll says "Thus my pride, not my principle, my money, not my vertue, kept me honest" (p. 54), she makes a moral and rather pathetic statement that seems accurate and totally in keeping with her character. She is not rationalizing her behavior; she is not drawing an extended moral lesson which the situation cannot support; she is making a statement about her motivations from a moral but realistic point of view. The Moll who writes her memoirs presents her own wisdom and attitudes as a character and forces us to understand them as they developed in the younger Moll: "[I] sold my self . . . to a tradesman that was rake, gentleman, shop-keeper, and beggar all together" (p. 54). But the younger Moll was still capable of mistakes which the present Moll looks upon with some contempt: "But I was hurried on (by my fancy to a gentleman) to ruin my self in the grossest manner that ever woman did..." (p. 54). At such moments as these, we have the two Molls, with enough similar characteristics to suggest that they are the same person but with sufficient differences to suggest their different ages. But these occasions will appear less frequently in the book, for now we have Moll basically as she will be the rest of her life and with much the same awareness as the woman writing the book. We have really been watching, so far in the novel, the development of two character patterns, and gradually they have begun closely to approximate each other. This is a crucial point, since a number of critics have sought to explain the novel's ambiguities and contradictions as the result of Defoe's consciously playing off the older Moll against the younger, of his having the older woman unaware of the motivations in her earlier self and the implications of her activities and thus filling the book with bogus rationalizing and moralizing.[18] The only problem with this theory is that from this point in the novel both characters mouth such statements and both seem to understand Moll's experiences in much the same way. For example, even though the younger Moll forgets that she is still legally married and committing adultery, her moral reactions to her long affair with the married man is much the same as when she is older:

> But I never once reflected that I was all this while a marry'd woman, a wife to Mr. —— the linnen-draper, who, tho' he had left me by the necessity of his circumstances, had no power to discharge me from the marriage contract which was between us, or to give me a legal liberty to marry again; so that I had been no less than a whore and an adulteress all this while. I then reproach'd my self with the liberties I had taken, and how I had been a snare to this gentleman, and that indeed I was principal in the crime; that now he was mercifully snatch'd out of the gulph by a convincing work upon his mind, but that I was left as if I was abandon'd by heaven to a continuing in my wickedness. (Pp. 108-9)

Certainly both Molls have a propensity for moralizing throughout the book that most often seems to miss the point of the episodes just described. At the same time, both Molls *are* aware of what necessitates the younger woman's immoral life:

> I wanted to be plac'd in a settled state of living, and had I happen'd to meet with a sober good husband, I should have been as true a wife to him as virtue it self could have form'd. If I had been otherwise, the vice came in always at the door of necessity, not at the door of inclination.... (P. 112)

It is not a case, then, of the older Moll being ignorant or hypocritical about her former situations and motivations, nor of the younger one being unaware of the life she was living and its moral problems. At this point in the novel, in spite of the older Moll's occasional expressions of hindsight, both women respond in much the same way, and there is no evidence in the text that Defoe consciously or consistently uses the distance between his two Molls for ironic purposes. Nor does it seem plausible that Defoe ironically intended the older Moll to create her former self in her present image, filled with the same delusions and moral hypocrisy. Again, there is no evidence within the text to support this, no way in which we can see this double level of irony. Such a complexity in narrative technique, where the created world reflects the distortions of the narrator's own psyche, would be unique for Defoe in the entire body of his prose narratives, and unique in fiction at least until *Tristram Shandy*.[19] So long as there is no indication that the author intends an ironic interpretation of any level of his work, so long as there is no clear "handle" for such an interpretation, I see no point in making one.

At this point in the novel, though, we are not yet disturbed by any moral confusion. We are still close to the sources of Moll's particular development, and we are willing to understand and accept both her position in life and her personality. Though Moll's stay in the Mint adds little action to the novel, it underscores the amorphousness of both her personal and social identities (she assumes the habits of a widow and the name "Mrs. Flanders") and emphasizes her precarious situation in life: "I knew I had no friends, no, not one friend or relation in the world; and that little I had left apparently wasted, which, when it was gone, I saw nothing but misery and starving was before me" (pp. 58–59).[20] The long section which follows, on the position of women in society and the importance of a good marriage, though at first focused on the relationship of an acquaintance of Moll with a young captain, is significant because it places Moll's situation in a larger social context and crystallizes in her mind the necessity for certain attitudes towards men and marriage. Both Molls see this, and both understand it.

All of this background and social context have been carefully worked out, and Moll appears to us very much a product of her world. Her natural abilities had been encouraged in her early life and allowed to progress beyond those suitable to her station; her self-consciousness about her superiorities had been increased by her difficult position in life and the threat of a demeaning existence. Her belief in her superiority and her sense of herself as a "gentlewoman" have given her not only a means of maintaining her dignity but, more important, the drive to survive and maintain that dignity with all the weapons at her command. Her relationship with the older brother has taught her not to trust others, but to use them instead of being used by them. Men and marriage now become for her a means of survival—but survival on her own terms. At the same time, Moll's uncertain birth and early life with the gypsies, the precariousness of her early life, and the fact that she seems to have no real social context leave her in a constant quandary about who she is and what she is: with all the strength and solidity of the various qualities that make up her character, Moll also suffers from a dreadful uncertainty about her identity.

These are the distinctive elements of Defoe's characterization that give her a real presence in our minds, but also evident are those elements missing from the real Moll—normal human feelings of love and compassion. I am not willing to accept the argument that this insufficiency is a conscious part of her characterization. Defoe does give Moll opportunity for such relationships and does call upon us to accept Moll's humanity in them. I have already discussed Defoe's failure with his secondary figures, and there is no doubt that Moll's human insufficiencies are in part a result of the lack of developed characters in her world with whom she can convincingly relate. But there are other significant reasons. Once Defoe finishes the first part of the book, in which he relates the early events in her life to the development of her character, the remainder of the work becomes largely episodic— picaresque—and each episode functions more for its own sake than for any further development of character. Defoe now fulfills the promise of his title page and preface, giving the reader a series of entertaining and edifying adventures. Each episode functions separately from the others, contributing little to any developing pattern of either character or plot. It was necessary to develop Moll this far, to give us the basic ingredients for a personality that could be involved in these kinds of actions, but further than that Defoe seems unable or unwilling to go. From this point the focus is more on the action—the unusual adventures—and Moll's emotional responses to these events. Some episodes call for Moll to show emotions that do not even seem part of her character as it has been developed. A good example of this is the episode dealing with the delivery and disposal of her child when she is alone in London. The emphasis is clearly on the situation and not on Moll, but Moll must show the correct emotions, and so here we have the heroine displaying maternal feelings painfully missing up to this time. Once the episode is over and the baby disposed of, maternal feelings disappear from Moll's character until the very end of the book, even though other children are mentioned from time to time. The event does not influence Moll's character or her future. In Moll's relationship with Jemy, it is again the situation that is emphasized, and Moll's emotions are of secondary importance. Once Jemy disappears, this emotional side of Moll disappears with him. These are not inconsistencies or contradictions— they are simply anomalies, elements of behavior that have no real part in the consistent and dominating patterns of Moll's character.

Part of the problem may also be that the Moll within the narration has virtually no memory: she is a person nearly always responding to the immediate situation in an immediate way. Granted that the novel is supposedly written by Moll remembering her earlier life, the dramatic focus is nonetheless on the character within the narration, on her actions and mind, enough to make us realize that memory and reflection play no part in any kind of development or change within her, and that past relationships and events rarely reoccur in her mind to influence her present character or behavior. Once Moll's character has been shaped by the early events of her life, it becomes stabilized; her responses and attitudes are both instinctive and unchangeable. Defoe's first-person narrator works back in time, remembering what she thought and felt during the narrated event, but she does not remember herself remembering, something which future writers of first-person narratives would achieve. Most first-person narration during this period was limited in this respect. The narrator remembering his own past was as far as the writer could go into time consciousness.[21]

Defoe's first-person narrative technique, his sense of Moll remembering her past life, limits the time dimension of that past existence in another significant way. Though Moll has traced for us the early development of her character, from this point in the novel she remembers herself in a stable and unchanging way. In only fifty pages, we discover that fifteen years have gone by and Moll is now forty-two (p. 111). She tells us that she has aged in her appearance, but this is about the only indication we have of any change in her. Indeed, her attitudes, her sentiments, and her character in general are the same as they were twenty years earlier at the end of her first marriage. She is acting, thinking, and even talking at forty-two as she did at twenty-two. Moll's age does eventually catch up with her in one sense, when later in the book she tells us that she is now too old "to be courted for a mistress ... " (p. 164). Too old to survive by selling her body, she becomes a criminal. But only Moll's way of life, not her character, is changed by the ravages of time. It is the same person, behaving and thinking in the same way but engaged in different kinds of adventures. Moll's character is not altered or developed in any way to suggest the passing of years, and her static personality within the actions of the novel makes the temporal dimension of her past existence also seem static.

This sense of a static character in a static time dimension is reinforced by the way in which Moll, the first-person narrator, neglects transitional time periods between the events of her past life which she describes. The five years of Moll's marriage with the younger brother are left a total blank for us. Moll lives as wife to her own brother in Virginia for eight years, but it seems to us that their life together might just as well have been for eight weeks. What has happened to her during all that time? How did events affect her? Once Moll discovers the nature of her relationship with her brother, in spite of her horror and the realization that she must act, she lives in that state of sin for three years! We have no idea what happened during that specific period or how Moll survived her loathing for the relationship through such a long duration. Indeed, the action resumes immediately as if there had been no three years. Moll's selection of disparate events for narration, with a disregard for interlinking periods of time, and Defoe's use of what seems to be an arbitrary chronology destroys any sense of time passing, and this reinforces our sense of the static and unchanging nature of Moll's character.

Even without a sense of past in Moll's mind, or a continuum of time within the narrative itself, Defoe could still suggest a development or change in his character by adding to or altering her pattern in each new episode. That Moll does not seem to develop or change is, of course, primarily the result of Defoe's unconcern with that aspect of her life and personality. His concern is with the individual event and his character's responses to that event. Moll's characterization is more than sufficient for that purpose, and it also unifies these episodes into a fictional whole through the consistency of the basic personality that it creates. Throughout the book, Defoe wishes to present a series of difficult, challenging, exciting, and often unusual adventures, and he wishes to show us his character in those situations, struggling to survive, but struggling to survive on her own terms. To survive continuously in this way she must have certain qualities throughout the book, and so these remain constant. The problem of aging is only a concern insofar as it changes the nature of the circumstances, making Moll a thief instead of a whore, but the character remains the same in order to overcome the circumstances in the same way.

CONFLICTS IN IDENTITY

It is the consistency and strength of Moll's character that also works against much of Defoe's moralizing. One of the book's contradictions that Defoe never resolves is in the conflicting arguments for necessity and morality. Defoe many times emphasizes Moll's social and economic situation, blaming it for her vice,[22] but throughout the book, Moll also blames herself. It is a back-and-forth argument, but one senses consistently that Defoe's instincts are to put the blame on necessity, that, in spite of his Presbyterian background and moral compunctions about her actions, he forgives and admires Moll. What we have, then, is not a character with a realistic moral ambivalence but one whose platitudes and contrition often ring false. Moll's actions seem true to both the demands of the situation and the nature of her character. She is in a situation where she must struggle to survive, even if it means performing "morally" unacceptable acts—and Moll's character demands that she survive. Note how unconvincing seems the following moral passage, taken from the episode where she is being courted by the banker, especially in the context of the entire scene:

> Then it occur'd to me, What an abominable creature am I! and how is this innocent gentleman going to be abus'd by me! How little does he think that having divorc'd a whore he is throwing himself into the arms of another! that he is going to marry one that has lain with two brothers, and has had three children by her own brother! one that was born in Newgate, whose mother was a whore, and is now a transported thief; one that has lain with thirteen men, and has had a child since he saw me! Poor gentleman! said I, what he is going to do! After this reproaching myself was over, it followed thus: Well, if I must be his wife, if it please God to give me grace, I'll be a true wife to him, and love him suitably to the strange excess of his passion for me; I will make him amends, by what he shall see, for the abuses I put upon him, which he does not see. (P. 158)

Why does this sudden burst of morality fail to convince us? Why does it seem largely an insertion to make Moll and Defoe feel good? Because at the same time she is condemning herself, Moll is also giving us a résumé of the events which have forced her into this life of deception; as a result, *we* find it difficult to condemn her. Because this résumé also seems to point out the extraordinary aspects of her life, lest we have forgotten, and brings us up to date by informing us that she has now "lain with thirteen men." Because the sentiments seem to have no effect upon Moll's actions even at the time she is expressing them. Right after this insertion, Moll is acting her true self and, amidst her moral protestations, carrying out her scheme to trap the man: "I was a great while before I could be perswaded, and pretended not to be willing at all to be married but in the church; but it was all grimace . . . " (p. 159). There is no evidence here that Defoe is being ironic with Moll's passage of moral introspection or that he sees her as a moral hypocrite. If he won't let her live honestly, he wants her at least to feel "honestly." The end of the passage states that Moll would live honestly and behave decently to her husband if she were allowed to do so. It is fate, or rather the demands of Defoe's plot, that does not allow her. This husband will die in five years, and once more she will have to resume her wicked ways in order to survive. That Moll so far is not inherently bad is evident from the fact that at no time when she is married and cared for is she actually sinful. While she is married to her first husband, she may lust for his elder brother, but she commits no adultery. And though she may legally commit adultery against her linen-draper husband, it is only because he has fled the country and she is once more on her own, forced to use her person for survival. Only later in the novel does she commit crimes compulsively, and that is finally a result of her constant life of struggle and worry: she simply cannot stop fending for herself, even when the need is temporarily gone (p. 192). What I am saying is that these passages ring false mostly because such morality doesn't matter, and we want Moll to know that it doesn't matter. It is not that she uses this morality to hide her dishonest nature—to us, she has no dishonest nature which she need hide. Such qualities are not part of her character; her tenacity, intelligence, and will to survive are. Most of the book shows Moll forced into these situations—Defoe tells us this often enough—and responding in a necessary, consistent, and believable way. The morality, then, seems false because it is not needed; it is untrue to the situation, and at times it hides the truth. Catering to the moral demands of his audience as well as to his own ambivalent feelings about the character, Defoe is not letting Moll be true to the real human dilemma he has created for her, nor is he letting her be true to her real self. Moll isn't a hypocrite, but when she says these things she sounds hypocritical. The point is that Moll remains faithful to her men while they survive and look after her. That Defoe dispenses with them so readily makes her self-condemnation and moralizing gratuitous, not hypocritical. Moll puts the case truthfully at the end of this adventure when she says:

> But there are temptations which it is not in the power of human nature to resist, and few know what would be their case, if driven to the same exigences. As covetousness is the root of all evil, so poverty is the worst of all snares. (Pp. 163–64)

That is all that need be said. The sociological truth of the statement is borne out by the action of the novel; the morality mouthed earlier is not.

I think that we can also understand the failure of Defoe to create a consistent and credible moral pattern within Moll by examining another aspect of the larger character pattern that he has succeeded in creating. Throughout the book we have the sense that Moll, made insecure by her enigmatic birth in Newgate and her early life as an orphan, has a problem with her social and personal identities.[23] One manifestation of this problem is her continuous concern with appearance and her perennial desire to be treated like a "gentlewoman." She constantly asserts to us her sense of superiority, especially in the section where she associates with the criminal class. Indicative of her dubious identity is Moll's dubious name. We never know her real name, and sometimes we wonder if she has any:

> These [the criminals] were they that gave me the name of Moll Flanders: for it was no more of affinity with my real name, or with any of the names I had ever gone by, then black is of kin to white, except that once, as before, I call'd my self Mrs. Flanders, when I sheltered my self in the Mint; but that these rogues never knew, nor could I ever learn how they came to give me the name, or what the occasion of it was. (P. 186)

In her life of crime, she changes not only costumes but her sex as well: "As my governess had disguis'd me like a man, so she joyn'd me with a man. . . . And as we kept always together, so we grew very intimate, yet he never knew that I was not a man" (p. 187). After this adventure, Moll leaves off her male disguise, but she still remains a shadowy figure among her companions: "yet I never let them know who I was; nor could they ever find out my lodging. . . . They all knew me by the name of Moll Flanders, tho' even some of them rather believ'd I was she than knew me to be so. . ." (p. 193). All those who know her by the name of Moll Flanders are either killed or transported; thus, "if I should have had the misfortune to be taken, I might call myself any thing else as well . . ." (p. 194).

The elusiveness of Moll's personal and moral identities is never clearer than in the episode with the drinking baronet. Moll is supposed to be older now, but there is some hedging even about that: "I did not indeed look so old as I was by ten or twelve year; yet I was not a young wench of seventeen, and it was easie enough to be distinguish'd" (p. 196). Moll neither acts older nor is responded to as an older woman by the baronet, even when he is not drunk. Her attitude in the episode shows not only a moral confusion imposed upon her by Defoe's anger at drunkenness and lechery but a confusion about who she is and what she is. How old is she? Is she attractive or not? Moral or immoral? How responsible is she for her relationship with the man? Throughout the episode her piety is never directed at herself, as if she herself is not so much a moral being as a scourge against vice. The point is that Moll simply has no personal identity, and as a result she has no moral or ethical identity. As a creature shaped by a competitive and economic world, she assumes mostly competitive and economic characteristics and as a result has no capacity for independent moral judgment of that world or her role in it. Valid moral judgments require a knowledge of self and some inner core of certainty from which one judges. If Moll's moral judgments sound false to us, it is because they do not come from an internal ethos. They are arbitrary, often clearly imposed upon the character by Defoe. The qualities we do recognize in Moll—her insecurity, sense of superiority, pragmatism, shrewdness, acquisitiveness, genius at survival—can be successful only without moral values in Defoe's own world and in the one he creates for Moll. Indeed, they are qualities that result from her failure to have a real identity and sense of self that could produce an honest moral response to the world and her actions in the world.

We want Moll to be more than she is because we can see qualities in her pattern, confusions and problems beyond the moralistic ones, that Defoe could not see. Moll is a character who succeeds for the modern reader because of her personal limitations. In her character we see implicit what will become explicit in future heroes and heroines of the novel: the problem of identity, and the search of a character for self-realization. Self-realization will be sought, of course, in a social context, but the focus of the search will be on individual achievement. This concern in the novel, already evident in *Moll Flanders*, is not only a manifestation of the age's developing interest in the individual, but also an indication of the individual's struggle to free himself from restrictive modes of thought and behavior as well as restrictions in the social structure.[24] I think we can see in *Moll Flanders* two basic cultural modes of thought: a religious and moralistic one that is basically the product of traditional belief; and a pragmatic and empirical one that sees the character both in relation to the real physical world and as the creator of his own destiny within that world. Moll is caught in a conflict between the two, and as a character she never survives it. Defoe was a Presbyterian, and the religious and moral belief at his disposal was Calvinistic. We can apply Rudolf G. Stamm's statement about Defoe's beliefs in general to *Moll Flanders*, and understand from another perspective why so much of the religion and morality in the book seems hollow:

He [Defoe] lacked the sense of sin, of a need for salvation, of the insignificance of things earthly, of the weakness of human reason unaided by the grace of God, even of the reality of the powerful Calvinistic God, whose will was destiny. . . . It is certain that the new optimistic faith in the power of human reason to discover the laws of nature and to regulate human affairs got a strong hold of him.[25]

The conflict is never seen by Defoe, and so Moll is not allowed to work out a solution. The morality in the novel is to be taken at face value. But it is the real, empirical world, not the religious, moralistic one, that interests Defoe, and it is the force of that world on his character and Moll's response to it that should be the real "ethical" core. Moll is forced to make specious moral judgments about her life and hence is never allowed to work out the problem of her identity, never allowed to realize herself in terms that are meaningful in relation to the world outside her and her own experiences. That adventure must still remain for the heroines of *Clarissa* and *Pride and Prejudice*.

NEWGATE AND AFTER

In Moll's Newgate experience and her flight to freedom and prosperity with her Lancashire husband, we see manifest the pull between her actual character and the character Defoe sometimes thinks he has created. Here we see the confusions and inconsistencies in Moll's character—but we also see, in spite of this, the final triumph of the force of her character, of the basic pattern which we have recognized throughout the novel as the "real" Moll.

Newgate is the place Moll dreads throughout the book, yet all her actions lead her there. The place means death to this character who has struggled all her life for survival; it also means the ultimate humiliation, the crushing of her notions of superiority. Newgate becomes for Moll "an emblem of hell itself": "I look'd on my self as lost, and that I had nothing to think of but going out of the world, and that with the utmost infamy; the hellish noise, the roaring, swearing and clamour, the stench and nastiness, and all the dreadful afflicting things that I saw there, joyn'd to make the place seem an emblem of hell itself, and a kind of an entrance into it" (pp. 238-39). It is in such a place that Defoe wishes to show Moll's moral conversion and her repentance for a life of sin.

After having established Moll's basic character for us and then kept it relatively constant through some two hundred pages, Defoe will find it difficult to change or develop that pattern. Indeed, alteration will have to come from within the pattern itself; the seeds that lead to Moll's conversion will have to be there already—certain qualities within her will have to expand and suppress other qualities that have long held them in abeyance. By now we have been shown so much of Moll's criminal life, and the personal qualities which have allowed her to survive in that life have been so strongly drawn, that we shall also need evidence for the change. We shall have to see the conversion; it will have to be convincingly drawn for us—it can't be briefly sketched or summarized.

Moll realizes that her first repentance in Newgate is bogus and has resulted from her fear of death. Again she tells us of the horror she feels for the place, of her humiliation at being there and at her ill-treatment by the inmates. This is all within character, but the problem is that we are being told Moll's experience instead of being made to see it. With all her hatred for Newgate, the place is never described, nor can we see Moll actually there, living there: Moll tells us that "no colours can represent that place to the life; nor any soul conceive aright of it but those who have been sufferers there" (p. 240). When true repentance comes, we are also cut off from hearing what the minister says to Moll and from seeing her reactions with any specificity: "those impressions are not to be explain'd by words, or if they are, I am not mistress of words to express them . . . " (p. 251). Not allowed the words which could describe Moll's repentance, we must believe in it solely on the basis of our knowledge of her character as it has been developed in the book up to this point. But we have seen that life for Moll has been a struggle, and necessity rather than inherent evil has forced her to commit her whoring and stealing. We have never seen within her character the self-knowledge or self-awareness that would allow her to see herself as a moral agent and one capable of sin. The repentance, then, seems inconsistent or unnatural. We neither see it nor believe it.

Two other problems undermine Moll's repentance for us. The first is the very general and typical confessional language which describes her conversion. She seems to be playing a role here, the role of the professional penitent, whose words we may read in a whole school of confessional literature[26] but whose voice is not that of the real Moll either as character or narrator. Secondly, and more importantly, Moll goes back on the words she speaks here, contradicts her "conversion," and ends up right where she was at the beginning, with the same values and character. How seriously can we accept her conversion when on the one hand she tells us, "how absurd did every pleasant thing look (I mean, that we had counted pleasant before) when I reflected that these sordid trifles were the things for which we forfeited eternal felicity!" (p. 250), and then, having been transported to the colonies, reaps more rewards with more relish than at any other time in the book? Moll's penitence is never put to the test, and her very language as a penitent is soon contradicted. This contradiction is never more evident than when Moll describes her husband's reactions to their sudden acquisition of wealth:

> ...and then I pull'd him out the hundred pound in silver, as the first year's produce, and then pulling out the deer skin purse with the pistoles, And here, my dear, says I, is the gold watch. Says my husband, So is heaven's goodness sure to work the same effects in all sensible minds, where mercies touch the heart; lifted up both his hands, and with an extasy of joy, What is God a doing! says he, for such an ungrateful dog as I am! Then I let him know what I had brought over in the sloop, besides all this; I mean the horses, hogs, and cows, and other stores for our plantation; all which added to his surprize, and fill'd his heart with thankfulness; and from this time forward I believe he was as sincere a penitent, and as thoroughly a reform'd man, as ever God's goodness brought back from a profligate, a highwayman, and a robber. (P. 294)

Moll is certainly not being condescending about this. The attitudes her husband expresses clearly match her own. Once Moll repents, God makes his appearance in the book as the great source of earthly delights. Defoe's Calivinism leaves its imprint on the book as Moll and her husband become part of the elect, and upon them rain gifts from heaven. Until now Moll did not have these gifts, and their absence was a sign of her damnation. This Calvinistic drift is certainly not worked out with any conscious intention and, like all the religion and morality in the book, it sits uneasily with the other elements. Defoe's Calvinism and his secular and empirical interest in man's life on this earth synthesize with a good deal of moral confusion: salvation and damnation take place here and not in the hereafter; they become significant not in God's eyes but in man's eyes.[27] Of course, this synthesis in Defoe's thinking is similar to that which took place in society in general.[28] As did the world around him, Defoe saw economic success as a special kind of election and was willing to be less concerned about the moral value of the deeds which lead to that success. Moll's religious conversion and sporadic morality throughout the book seem less responsible for her rewards than her work as whore and criminal. One even senses Defoe's uneasiness about his facile religious rationalizations at the end of the novel when in his preface he tells us that after the adventures described in her book, Moll "was not so extraordinary a penitent as she was at first..." (p. 7).

The repentance, then, like the moralizing, is beside the point, especially since it suggests that the individual is responsible for his situation in the world and hence morally responsible for his action, and that the things of this earth are negligible compared to eternity. Moll's world puts the lie to this, and so does her true character. Moll acts, and usually thinks, as if this were not true. She knows that she is placed as a victim in this world and that her circumstances are stacked against her; that not only to achieve an economic status of which her world approves but even to survive, she must beat the world. She does this with an intelligence, shrewdness, and awareness which we admire. She does this because she knows she has to do it. Predestination and necessity are both involved here, but God is not responsible for them—society is. Nor do they rule out the possibility of a person's succeeding through his own individual efforts: social necessity determines the game one must play— the starting position, the rules, the moves necessary to win—but one plays the game and determines himself if he will win or lose. Moll's world will crush her if she lets it. In this context, we can see another reason for Defoe's failure to create secondary figures. Feelings for others, for husbands and children and brothers and governesses, are not part of that game, and Defoe mostly sees Moll in terms of that game. He rarely allows her to stop playing, even at the end of the book when she seems to be victorious. Defoe permits Moll a single sentence to describe her parting with her governess. Moll goes off with her Lancashire husband, whom she has found again in Newgate, but we know as little of him as a character at this point as we did earlier in the novel. He is overshadowed by Moll and her activities to such an extent that he now seems weak-minded and weak-willed; he appears to be one of the many objects which she is so busily accumulating. Moll's sheer triumph over her world is what really concerns Defoe, and as a result his heroine seems isolated from others and is denied meaningful repentance. But this is also the triumph that Defoe makes us admire and feel throughout much of the book. It is the triumph of a strong, successfully drawn character who defies the contradictions imposed upon her by both her author and his age.

SCENIC TECHNIQUE

Moll Flanders is written as a first-person narration, and thus we have an awareness of the narrator perceiving both her world all over again and herself in that world perceiving. But Defoe is only sporadically interested in this level of perception, and rarely exploits it. At times, however, he creates for us a vivid sense of the Moll within the novel living in and perceiving her world—and this is narrated for us by the older woman. The point here is that we see the world as Moll saw it: we see her seeing it, and we see it with her. Defoe achieves this effect on a number of occasions in his novel, creating a visual external scene and keeping it within the circumference of Moll's perceptions.

Narration has traditionally been divided into the two basic techniques of telling and showing, although much narration is a combination of the two.[29] The first technique synopsizes large periods of time, generalizes actions, and frequently emphasizes the narrator's own presence. The second dramatizes individual actions in a context of space and time, creating for us a detailed visual illusion of what happened. Earlier fiction relied more on simple, historical summation, on telling, but the novel developed with a greater emphasis on scenic presentation, on showing.[30] What is not often realized is that scenic presentation in the novel developed largely as a technique for expanding the perceptional dimension: as writers became more concerned with the world as the individual sees it, that world had to be more graphically portrayed. Already in Defoe's novel we find a greater movement towards scenic presentation, even though Defoe neither relies consistently on the technique nor creates a scene as visual and dramatic as those created by future novelists. Frequently we sense that once in a scene, Defoe does not know how to proceed, that he switches from direct to indirect discourse, from particularlized to general action, from details of setting to general description, without any real purpose. Often, unimportant events are given detailed and dramatic presentation, while important ones receive hurried attention and are briefly summarized. I must emphasize again that Defoe is not working in a fixed tradition and cannot be criticized for doing half-well what others had scarcely done at all. It is significant enough that even with his continuous emphasis on the exciting or unusual, he is also at times interested in the way his heroine perceives both the situation and her role in it, and that from this impulse he attempts to give the reader a vivid sense of the world in which Moll acts as well as of her own actions.

The first time we see Defoe slowing down to give a more detailed scenic job of narration is during Moll's adventure as servant in the home of the two brothers. Moll, ill and lying upstairs in her chamber, overhears the family while they are at dinner (pp. 38-42). The visual image we have of the scene includes the two levels of action, one juxtaposed against the other. Moll overhears what takes place below and does not see it, yet the visual force of our imagination immediately dramatizes that level of action for us—but as Moll would visualize it, since we are hearing the characters through her ears as she lies upstairs. We are still a long way from the fully developed dramatic scene, and

Defoe's limitations are evident. His deficiency with secondary characters prevents the scene in the dining room from coming fully to life because we cannot conceptualize these people in any detail. Moll herself stays out of most of the scene, reporting directly what she heard, not integrating her own point of view into the episode—that is, neither asserting nor developing her characterization by the way she describes the scene. At one point, the mother leaves her family, walks up the stairs, and comes into Moll's room to talk with her. Moll reports the confrontation in indirect dialogue, distancing it from us and breaking the steady flow of dramatization. After the mother's return to her family, the scene ends with a nice bit of dramatic interplay as Robin innocently suggests that Moll is in love with his older brother and the latter responds with feigned virtue. The real irony should come from the knowledge of what Moll must think when she hears this upstairs, but Defoe does not dramatize this level of response.

The scene in which Moll is married to the banker is similar in its spatial structure, but it presents Moll's perceptions of and responses to external reality in a fuller way. The scene itself also receives considerably more dramatization. It happens in a particular place (the inn at Brickhill) and at a particular time (in July or August). The characters are in a room that contains a bed, and physical objects abound throughout the scene—the great bundle of papers, including the banker's deed of divorce; his wife's certificate of burial; the "little chagreen case" from which he gives Moll a "fine diamond ring"; and the marriage license. The room is spatially placed in relation to other parts of the house, and its upstairs location is emphasized several times. Moll and the banker move in and out of the room—he speaks to the landlord and minister downstairs, she speaks to him on the landing—so that the concentricity of the scene is broken. Other people play a part in the scene—the landlord, the minister, the wife and the daughter of the landlord. The two main characters exchange a considerable amount of dialogue. Indeed, some of the dialogue and action is vividly real:

> No, No, says he, I must not be deny'd, I won't be deny'd, I can't be deny'd. Well, well, said I, and giving him a slight kiss; then you shan't be deny'd, let me get up. (P. 157)

The action of the scene is continuous and natural. Moll's character is consistent for most of the episode, and we are constantly aware of how she is then seeing the scene and how she is responding. She is still impressed by the banker's "gentlemanly" behavior (he had met her with a coach and four, he has given her the ring, he has offered her no offense);

she is somewhat cautious about his divorce but "not so scrupulous" as she pretends, for she would take him without the documents; and she plays with him magnificently, leading him right into the jaws of marriage. But the scene seems only half-realized, caught somewhere between summary and full recreation. As usual, the narrator does not draw any of the secondary characters: Moll's "husband" remains only a good-natured, gentlemanly person (as have been most of her men); the innkeeper is merely "an officious, tho' well-meaning fellow" (p. 158); and the parson is a "merry good sort of gentleman" (p. 159). Moll as narrator interrupts her story on occasion to get in the way of the scene, and the long moralizing passage, which we have already discussed,[31] does not seem justified in the context of the episode or in the context of her character.

It is Moll's perception of the world itself, not of her relationships, that often seems valid. She may never fully describe that world, but she describes enough of it, and we further know that world through her responses to it. The scene in which Moll receives a farewell letter from Jemy is brief and narrated as if being recalled by her older self—it is half retold and half dramatized—but it achieves a dimension of reality because Moll's past perceptions and responses are extensions of her true character:

> Nothing that ever befel me in my life sunk so deep into my heart as this farewel. I reproach'd him a thousand times in my thoughts for leaving me, for I would have gone with him thro' the world, if I had beg'd my bread. I felt in my pocket, and there I found ten guineas, his gold watch, and two little rings, one a small diamond ring, worth only about six pound, and the other a plain gold ring. (P. 133)

Even when Moll is in love, the economic way in which she sees reality must impose itself upon her feelings. It is not enough to say that her Lancashire husband left her some money and jewelry, but each piece of jewelry must be itemized. In the middle of describing her sorrow for his departure, in the midst of the second narration of genuine love in the book, Moll must not only itemize, she must tell us the value of the rings, conveying the significance of these items to her both when she participates in the scene and now.[32] The small diamond ring "worth only about six pound" emphasizes the consistency of Moll's basic character that paradoxically both limits the range of her human capacity and also stamps that definite and indestructible personality on our mind. We do not doubt Moll's love, but we realize that in the scene, the money and jewelry are as important as her lover. So consistent is Moll's attitude that the money and jewelry are associated with the man and almost become symbols for him—Moll has succeeded in synthesizing, in her singular world vision, everything which means the most to her: "I sat down and look'd upon these things two hours together, and scarce spoke a word..." (p. 133). It is the extraordinary depth of Moll's acquisitive feelings, the fact that they manage to shape her vision of the world and even seem to define all her emotional responses, that makes her character and the world in which she lives come alive. Merely to praise Defoe for his presentation of a world of real physical objects is not sufficient.[33] His reportorial instinct for fact brings a dimension of verisimilitude to the novel, but he also makes that physical realism a manifestation of his character's personality: we see and assess the physical world in terms of his character's vision and judgment of it; we see it and feel it as does Moll.

The novel creates a reality, but it can never be the reality of the physical world that surrounds us, made up of countless objects, places, and people. How then to suggest the real world within the confinements of the novel form? By depicting the way in which the individual sees and responds to the real world, through the selective process of the character's mind and personality. Such a reality is close to our own concept of reality, since we know the external world only as it is filtered through our consciousness. The use of details and facts is only the beginning of narrative technique, and to credit Defoe merely for that achievement is to undercut what he actually accomplishes and what makes *Moll Flanders* an extraordinary work. Realism in the novel, to be more than reportorial writing, must be synthesized with character. The world of *Moll Flanders* is the world of the heroine; it is when Defoe breaks that vision, when the world he creates becomes a manifestation of concerns not intrinsic to Moll's character, that the novel appears inconsistent to us.

The scene in which Moll commits her first crime (pp. 166-67), like several of the scenes in the criminal section of the novel, shows Defoe in his most novelistic form, successfully creating a world through the perceptions and responses of his heroine. Here we have no problem with Moll's personal relationships, since Defoe is concerned only with her and the adventure. He makes us understand why she acts as she does and how she acts, as well as her responses to her actions. Her personal state and motivations are well documented: her poverty, her desperation, her confusion, and her instinctive struggle for survival. Throughout the scene, Moll repeats such statements as "doing I did not know what" (p. 166) to remove the blame from her conscious will, and at one point she even blames the devil for her actions. In spite of her confused state, we are given an accurate description of the scene of the crime so that we can see exactly what happens, so that it is visual and real to us, so that we can see it the way Moll immediately sees it. The stool before the counter, upon it a little bundle wrapt in white cloth; the maid servant beyond, with her back to Moll, looking up towards the top of the shop; the apprentice upon the counter reaching up to a shelf—all of this gives us an actual scene, with real objects and people, spatially ordered, and it allows us to see the place as does the heroine. Moll as narrator describes the way in which she backed into the shop and took the bundle, her flight through the streets of London, her examination and description of the loot, so that we have an immediate sense of what she saw and felt, of her perceptions and responses to the reality which surrounded her and in which she acted. The entire scene is within the context of her own lived experience.

This is what the art of the novel is all about. Defoe creates a character who comes immediately alive in her situation. We endure the situation, are made to see it and feel it as does the character, because she is vivid enough for us to see and associate with, and because the scene is real enough to absorb us into it with her. No writer of prose fiction before Defoe is able to involve us in such scenes, and no future writer can create a similar kind of fictional experience for the reader until Richardson appears on the scene with *Pamela*, and especially *Clarissa*, some two decades later.

CHAPTER TWO

CLARISSA:
Private Vices and Public Virtues

Who therefore so fit for an example to the rest of the sex? At worst, I am entirely within my worthy friend Mandeville's assertion, *That private vices are public benefits.*   (III, 145)[1]

RICHARDSON'S FICTIONAL WORLD

From the first page of Richardson's *Clarissa* (1747-1748), we are aware of being in a different world from that of Defoe. In spite of some unpleasant happenings, this is the more normal world of everyday England, where parents worry about whom their children will marry and where children worry about the interference of parents in their private lives. Richardson not only made it acceptable to write about a more normal, everyday world in fiction—he made such a world the concern of most future novels. By doing so, he significantly extended the reader's emotional and intellectual relationship to the world of fiction. One no longer read only to be excited or to escape from his own reality. One now empathized, felt, and identified with fictitious characters because they were more like himself; one was more absorbed into the world of fiction because it was more like his own world. And because of this, because the distance between the reader's and the writer's world was lessened, one could now test the characters and their experiences against one's own reality. In spite of the stunning fictional moments that we share with Moll Flanders, we probably will not experience anything like her adventures in our own lives; indeed, at times we feel no more than vicarious thrills when reading about her. But with Richardson's characters, our involvement is more sustained and frequently deeper; hence we may more vehemently disagree with his portrayal of their behavior, since the issues are more pertinent and understandable to us.

What also allows us to slip into Richardson's world is its completeness and autonomy. There appear to be no blank areas: personality, emotion, thought, behavior, action, and location are sufficiently documented so that the whole world appears before us with a fullness not known in earlier fiction, and this fullness creates for us a sense of completeness and independence, as if the world of the novel had all the elements needed to exist as a reality within itself. There is, of course, much to argue with in Richardson's novel, but it is a work we argue with in different terms; we argue with it because it gives the illusion of being definitive. *Clarissa* is the first example in fiction of the completely autonomous world, the self-contained illusion of reality that the modern novelist creates.

From the very beginning, almost as soon as we are aware of the novel's autonomy, of its complete and self-sustaining illusion of reality, we must break through the wall of language that separates us from the author's world even while creating it, and involve ourselves in that world and become part of it. In the act of reading, the novel must lose its separateness for us; it must draw us in from our own world. The means by which we enter that world, the doorway for us, is, of course, character. There must be someone in the novel, or some few characters, with whom we can associate, inside of whose skin we can be, and through whose eyes we can see.[2]

CLARISSA'S PRIDE

From the very beginning of *Clarissa*, we are aware of another difference from *Moll Flanders*: the novel contains developed characters besides the heroine—in fact, a large number of them—and it deals with their interrelationships. Though many of these characters are not complex, each has a specific personality. The book does not even begin with the voice of the heroine but with that of a friend, writing to Clarissa, questioning her, and evoking from her an immediate answer. There is only one central rhythm in *Moll Flanders,* and that is the single voice of Moll, but in Richardson's novel we sense the symphonic interplay of numerous voices. Richardson introduces the social dimension and thus expands the spatial perimeter of fiction. Moll, in spite of her desire for a place in society and her few close relationships, is basically asocial; she is the outsider—and it is her voice alone that we hear in the wilderness of commercial civilization. But Clarissa is a character very much part of her social world: her personality is shaped by it, her values developed from it, and the events of her life caused by it.[3] From beginning to end she is in constant interplay with the world of characters which surrounds her. Here is the crux of the whole book, and, in a sense, of what so much English fiction will be about: Clarissa is an individual, feels herself an individual, and it is the conflict between her sense of self and the world to which she so inextricably belongs that is the real drama of the novel. Ironically, as individualism begins to develop in Western civilization, as the older confining systems of belief continue to disintegrate, the individual finds himself more and more dependent upon society at large. The economic network becomes more complicated as one economic entity becomes dependent on another and another. Capitalism is based not only on the interdependence of different phases of production and trade, but on the incorporation of more and more people for both labor and consumption. A money economy depends upon the interchange among large groups of people. As the economic structure becomes larger, incorporating more people, its success becomes more dependent on the ordered relationship of these people. As the old religious structure of the universe and religious view of the world breaks down, people are left free to choose their own beliefs. Society must therefore rephrase and realign its values, structure a new code of behavior to keep its people together, and prohibit rampant individualism, which will tear asunder the new economic and political structure.

Much picaresque fiction had been anti-feudal by implication and thus had also dealt with the individual and his conflict with society.[4] But in the novels of Defoe, the conflict had become much more explicit and its nature had changed—for one thing, society had become capitalistic and was becoming bourgeois; for another, the individual had begun to reach for a sense of personal identity in a world of sometimes ambivalent or even corrupt values. As we have already seen, the problem of identity was central to Moll's situation, though it was neither explored at any length nor resolved in the novel. In *Clarissa*, the problem of identity becomes not only central to the plot of the novel but also one of the chief thematic concerns. Richardson's novel is the first frontal attack against the dehumanizing forces in society that attempted to minimize the responsibility and sanctity of the individual; it is the first exploration of the new relationships forming between the individual and his world; it is the first fictional study of a character largely concerned with her own personality, and exploring her identity in more than religious terms; and, lastly, it is the first work that displays an array of narrative techniques to present these themes.

In the opening letter of the book, Anna Howe begins the development of Clarissa's characterization and emphasizes the heroine's virtues and superior qualities. In the very next letter, the heroine herself underscores these elements and through her own voice dramatizes her character. Her letter is filled with reasoned judgment and moral sentiments, but it contains one disturbing note—Clarissa is willing to censure people, and her portrait of her sister, though perhaps true, is not kind. Throughout the novel, she blames others, especially Anna, for their condemning attitudes, but Clarissa is herself the worst perpetrator of this fault in the book.[5] Granted, she is superior—we have enough reports from other characters and her own letters to affirm this—but her treatment of others and her own sense of superiority make us aware of pride in this moral figure, a pride which allows her to seem something less than a paragon. Clarissa must be aware of her superiority if she is to withstand the attacks of her family and Lovelace, if she is to be steadfast in adversity, but this constant awareness on her part and the resulting downgrading of others, as well as the lecturing tone of so much of her correspondence, makes her seem flawed to us. In *Pamela*, the heroine's moral superiority made her often appear ludicrous, but Richardson has learned a great deal since that book, and he has learned how to use the difficulties in moral characterization to advantage. In his second novel, recognizing the inevitable sense of her own superiority that his heroine must give when describing other characters from a moral point of view, he extends this quality into a pride in self, and uses it to show even further the heroine's morality by having her recognize her fault and laudably condemn it. The result is that Clarissa is able to present realistic portraits of others, censure herself for these portraits, and then be praised for censuring herself. Richardson goes even further than this: he takes this fault of his heroine and uses it for purposes of plot. Clarissa's pride in her own abilities, her sense of superiority, allows her to carry on a correspondence with Lovelace against the warning of her relatives and to grant him a secret rendezvous in which she is tricked away. Hence, the pivotal action in the novel, the heroine's departure from her family, is made the result of a flaw in her character. But Richardson wishes us to see continually the genuine superiority of his heroine and to understand this fault only in the context of her entire pattern of behavior:

> The principal of these two young Ladies is proposed as an Exemplar to her Sex. Nor is it any objection to her being so, that she is not in all respects a perfect character. It was not only natural, but it was necessary that she

should have some faults, were it only to show the Reader how laudably she could mistrust and blame herself, and carry to her own heart, divested of self-partiality, the censure which arose from her own convictions....[6]

Clarissa's pride also functions in a more positive way. When she utters her powerful line *"That the man who has been the villain to me you have been, shall never make me his wife"* (III, 222), we hear perhaps the clearest statement of a significant aspect of her personality developed throughout the book—her deep sense of her individualism and her human rights, a sense that is a result of her pride in self. She may at times be censorious, superior, and self-righteous, but when Clarissa stands up against family, lover, and her entire social world, we have the most striking literary example of individual dignity in the entire century. Clarissa can make such a statement because she is proud, because she is strong, and because she is earnestly right in her action. When her pride in self prohibits her from accepting Solmes for a husband and giving in to her family, she is right. She is equally right when she refuses the man who has defiled her body and attempted to control her soul. Pride has many facets, negative and positive, and the pattern of traits which make up Clarissa's character includes both.

Clarissa's pride, as well as her moral sense, explains a good deal about her behavior to Lovelace before the rape and establishes a context in which we can better understand her feelings for him during that period. Her feelings for Lovelace, though never fully admitted, are hinted at numerous times by Clarissa herself, and directly stated, also numerous times, by Anna. As a decorous, virtuous female of the eighteenth century, Clarissa cannot openly admit that she is in love. To admit it would be to admit that she has the capacity for passion and sexuality. Her love for Lovelace is also in conflict with her pride: marriage would mean for her the subjugation of her individual rights (as both Solmes and Lovelace make clear), and it would also mean the subjugation of her physical body. Note, for example, Clarissa's comment on the subject:

> Oh, my dear! were but a woman, who gives reason to the world to think her to be in love with a man [and this must be believed to be my case; or to what can my *supposed* voluntary going off with Mr. Lovelace be imputed?], to reflect one moment on the exaltation she gives *him*, and the disgrace she brings upon *herself*; the low pity, the silent contempt, the insolent sneers and whispers, to which she makes herself obnoxious from a censuring world of both sexes; how would she despise herself! And how much more eligible would she think death itself to such a discovered debasement!
>
> (II, 230)

Clarissa, then, in the eyes of her world and in her own eyes, can never admit her love for this man (or any man), at least until she is married to him. Pride as well as sexual morality prohibit this. Once under Lovelace's protection, her dilemma is that she should operate as if she loves him and openly encourage their marriage, yet she is incapable of doing so lest he discover that she does love him. Clarissa's love for Lovelace, then, is part of her characterization during the first half of the work, but not an overt part—it is rather an underlying feeling which she seeks to hide from, but which affects her behavior.[7] This love must also be seen as influenced and controlled by other elements of her character. Clarissa's feeling for Lovelace and her inability to operate on the basis of these feelings for personal and social reasons are the cause of much of her difficulty. Trying to hide her feelings from herself and others, she still is swayed by them; unable to admit them, she allows herself to be manipulated by Lovelace. Individualism has not yet reached a point where one's passions are sacrosanct; it now functions to keep one from losing oneself to the passions. Benevolent feelings are different, for they are ordered and controllable, but passions are neither.[8] If she gives in to her passions, Clarissa must lose what is most important to her—her independence and her sense of herself as a sacred and private being. Though *Clarissa* is sentimental in its belief in benevolent feelings, it is still neoclassic in its distrust of the passions. Richardson makes love an important part of his novel, but he is hardly romantic about the subject.

THE TRIUMPH OF PRIVATE VIRTUE

We can understand a great deal about Richardson's concept of his heroine, the character he tried to achieve, and the techniques he used to do so, by examining Clarissa as a social figure and as an individual. From the very first page of the novel, it is evident that Clarissa is intended to be a model for her society, an example of virtuous and moral behavior. This is an intention that never disappears in her characterization, even when she is beset by the problem of pride and even in her worst sufferings. The lecturing tone of many of her letters, her discourses, and her frequent analyses of her behavior from a moral point of view, as well as the fact that the plot is clearly a vehicle by which she can manifest her virtuous behavior, all make us aware of her moral function in the work. But Clarissa's morality is given wider and more significant ramifications in the novel: it is frequently indicated that she is a moral exemplum for her entire social world. Clarissa is a figure who manifests the best virtues of her society and, as a result, takes on gigantic proportions in the eyes of that society—she becomes a public figure, watched, examined, and analyzed by all. Most of the characters in the novel see her this way, and many function to test her as a moral exemplum. We can even say that the entire action of the novel takes on the importance of a public ritual by which society tests and manifests its own values through Clarissa Harlowe. This moral and public dimension of Clarissa's character is introduced in the first paragraph of the novel by Anna Howe:

> I am extremely concerned, my dearest friend, for the disturbances that have happened in your family. I know how it must hurt you to become the subject of the public talk; and yet upon an occasion so generally known, it is impossible but that whatever relates to a young lady, whose distinguished merits have made her the public care, should engage everybody's attention. I long to have the particulars from yourself. . . . (I, 1)

Because of her "distinguished merits," whatever Clarissa does is known to her world—"mother and all of us, like the rest of the world, talk of nobody but you on this occasion" (I, 2)—and, by embodying the best values of her society, better than anyone else, Clarissa becomes a model for that society and answerable to it: "You see what you draw upon yourself by excelling all your sex. Every individual of it who knows you, or has heard of you, seems to think you answerable to *her* for your conduct in points so very delicate and concerning" (I, 2-3). Of course, Clarissa is an example especially to her sex and must uphold the honor of that sex, but by doing so, she satisfies the expectations—indeed the needs—of her entire society. Throughout the work, one senses that because society has placed so much upon her shoulders, it fears and is even obsessed with the fact that Clarissa might crack beneath the strain. Because she represents what that world most esteems in itself, her failure would be the world's failure. For these reasons the concern for and attention given to Clarissa are extraordinary: "write to me therefore, my dear, the whole of your story. . . . And pray write in so full a manner as may satisfy those who know not so much of your affairs as I do" (I, 2).

Since Clarissa is such a public figure, since she must always feel accountable to her society, she must act in light of what people will think, and she must analyze her behavior in that light. This public awareness makes her more than an exemplum, gives tension to her inner, virtuous being, and allows her morality to influence plot in more than an exemplary way. We can go further than this: if the values of her society, the values that she must uphold, are in any way corrupt or contradictory, contradiction will be manifest in the heroine's behavior, or she will be aware of those unreasonable values in her society and be paralyzed in her action. Both of these happen in the novel and add further confusion and tension to the conflict between Clarissa's individualism and the demands of her social world. In presenting an exemplary character in his novel, in writing a didactic work, Richardson was forced to consider the problems of being a paragon in a world not made for paragons. He could not merely present a superior person; he had to show what it was like to be a superior person, what the personal pitfalls were in a society not itself superior or always virtuous.

Clarissa's mother says to her, early in the novel, "I cannot but say that you have hitherto behaved extremely well; but you have had no trials till now: and I hope, that now you are called to one you will not fail in it" (I, 78-79). The heroine's first test takes place when she confronts her entire family in their attempt to sell her in marriage to the odious Mr. Solmes. Here Clarissa seeks to respond to the dehumanizing economic values of her social world with the values of personal worth and dignity also fostered by that world.[9] Clarissa achieves a temporary victory in her resistance to an alliance with Solmes, but the threat remains. The only permanent solution for her is to free herself from the confines of the family, but by doing this she would deny familial loyalty to affirm loyalty to herself. The situation is even more complicated because Clarissa's only means of escape is through Lovelace, an upper-class libertine whom she should distrust in spite of his attractive qualities. Her aunt states what appears to be Clarissa's real test: "If you can forbear claiming your estate, and can resolve to avoid Lovelace, you will continue to be the greatest miracle I ever knew at your years" (I, 237). A better statement of the test would begin: "If you can avoid Lovelace and still not give in to the demands of your family. . . ." It is clear from the start that this is what she should do, but her family's pressure is great, and Clarissa's pride, as well as her initial attraction to Lovelace, is sufficient to allow her to do just what she should not do—put herself within the grasp of a recognized libertine. From the start, Clarissa knows that she is playing with fire, that she is acting presumptuously in corresponding with Lovelace:

> O my dear! what is worldly wisdom but the height of folly? I, the meanest, at least the youngest, of my father's family, to thrust myself in the gap between such uncontrollable spirits!—to the interception perhaps of the designs of Providence, which may intend to make these hostile spirits their own punishers. If so, what presumption! Indeed, my dear friend, I am afraid I have thought myself of too much consequence. But, however, this be, *it is good, when calamities befall us, that we should look into ourselves, and fear.*   (I, 413)

Pride, then, plays a key role in her corresponding with this man, and hence pride leads to her being tricked away by him. We are to censure this pride, but even Richardson felt that in such circumstances the heroine could not be condemned:

> Clarissa might have been excused, if anybody. But I made her *appoint, repent,* and *resolve against* going off; Yet tricked away; and this, as a Consequence of her first Error, of Corresponding with Lovelace against Prohibition; tho' at first doing it on Motives not illaudable.[10]

The test, indeed, is not reasonable, and soon it appears that Lovelace himself is to be her real test:

> Then who say Miss Clarissa Harlowe is the paragon of virtue?—is Virtue itself?...Has her virtue ever been *proved?*...To the test then—and I will bring this charming creature to the *strictest* test...*that all the sex*, I say, may see what they *ought to be....*   (II, 36)

Belford tells Lovelace that the test he will offer Clarissa is not fair, "Considering the depth of thy plots and contrivances; considering the opportunities...considering how destitute of protection she is..." (II, 158-59). Belford is right: the test is not fair, but only because Lovelace does not have a chance. Clarissa may love him, but with her sense of morality, her pride, and her repressed nature,[11] there is not a possibility in the world that she will succumb. There is never a point in the novel when she seems even tempted to succumb. If chastity were the real issue of the book, there is no contest, and the sex is vindicated.

Lovelace uses the subtitle to Mandeville's *Fable of the Bees*, "Private Vices, Publick Benefits," in his ironic argument that by seducing Clarissa, he will be performing a public service in warning other women against such rogues as himself (III, 145). But Mandeville's words have wider and more serious implications in the novel. First, Lovelace's vice establishes the situation where Clarissa's real test can take place, a test that will ultimately serve as a public display of true virtue. Second, the heroine's own vice, if we may call it that, will be found to be pride in her role as a public exemplum. And third, Clarissa's victory over her vice, especially when it will be known through the publication of her letters, will serve as a moral lesson to all her world. What is the real test, then, and where is the battle fought? The test may come from the outside, but the battle is fought *in* Clarissa. The heroine's personal dignity and her worth are tested by the demands of her society, and the struggle within her is against her pride in her public image. The struggle is actually for a true and nobler pride, one that transcends the limits of her public self and the demands of her world. In achieving this better self, in rising above her society, the heroine demonstrates to that society the deepest values and most moral conduct.

Clarissa desires to appear virtuous to her world, and she takes great pride in her public reputation. She goes out of her way, too much so, to be a paragon. Anna, at one point, says, ". . . you wish to be thought superior to all our sex in the command of yourself . . ." (I, 362). A short while later Clarissa writes, "I am afraid I am singled out (either for my own faults, or for the faults of my family, or perhaps for the faults of both) to be a very unhappy creature!—*signally* unhappy!" (I, 419). She realizes her own responsibility for her situation and acknowledges her flawed character: "My calamities have humbled me enough, to make me turn my gaudy eye inward; to make me look into myself! And what have I discovered there? Why, my dear friend, more *secret* pride and vanity than I could have thought had lain in my unexamined heart" (I, 419-20).[12] All this is within the context of Clarissa's virtuous behavior: she is still moral, chaste, and an example to her sex; she is an example to her sex also in the way she discovers her fault and repents of it. Clarissa behaves admirably as she examines and analyzes herself and comes to certain realizations about her true nature.

It is in the presentation of the heroine as "penitent" that the private figure begins to transcend the social-ritual figure, though Clarissa never entirely frees herself from a concern for society and its judgment of her behavior until the end of the novel. But while she is successfully performing the ritual role for her public, upholding their values and being a penitent for their sins as well as her own, her inward eye is divorcing herself in large part from that society—she removes herself more and more from its false values, as she sees her salvation more and more dependent upon her own inner spirit. Clarissa, in the extremity of her suffering, may say that the cause of God's punishment is "impenetrable" to her (III, 232), but she more often recognizes the true experience she is undergoing. She sees her pride as having caused more than her presumptuous behavior in associating with Lovelace; she sees it as the source of much of her conduct and her desire for public acclaim. But still she bemoans the loss of that reputation. She is disconsolate because she remains, at least partly, a social creature:

> What a pride did I take in the applause of every one! What a pride even in supposing I had *not* that pride! Which concealed itself from my unexamining heart under the specious veil of *humility*. . . .
> So desirous, in short, to be considered as an *example*! A vanity which my partial admirers put into my head! And so secure in my own virtue!

I am punished enough, enough mortified, for this my vanity.... I more despise myself for my presumptious self-security, as well as vanity....
But I was very young. . . .
What strange imperfect beings! But *self* here, which is at the bottom of all we do, and of all we wish, is the grand misleader.
. . . who, from such a high reputation, left to proud and presumptuous self, should, by one thoughtless step, be brought to the dreadful situation I am in? (II, 378–79)

Anna, in spite of her independent voice, supports the cause of society throughout much of the book, and urges Clarissa to see to her reputation: "I think your reputation in the eye of the world, though not your happiness, is concerned, that you should be his" (III, 11–12). It is a striking statement from such a woman, but Anna knows that if one is to live in this world, she must recognize the values and demands of society. Clarissa's eyes, having recognized the vanity of this world, now turn to the next: "as I have escaped with my honour, and nothing but my worldly prospects, and my pride, my ambition, and my vanity have suffered in this wreck of my hopefuller fortunes, may I not still be more happy than I deserve to be? And is it not in my own power still, by the divine favour, to secure the greatest stake of all?" (III, 18).

The rape sends Clarissa into a state of shock, confusion, and then clear-sightedness. In her suffering, she gains a greater understanding of her own independence, of her own value, of the futility of keeping credence in the world. Clarissa could marry Lovelace; she could save her good name; she could once more appear in the eyes of the world. Anna advises her to do so, as do all her friends, but to do so would be to sell herself cheaply: to accept Lovelace after what he has done to her would be to deny her personal integrity and the sacredness of her individual being.

Still not free from guilt and suffering, she judges herself from an inner morality: "Ruined me in my *own* eyes; and that is the same to me as if *all the world* knew it" (III, 232). Clarissa still wishes that she could have saved her reputation, but she now knows unequivocally that she must rise above her society; to give in to it at this point would be to debase herself entirely. She may think herself ruined in the eyes of the world, but her pride and superiority still exist, though now they are channelled in proper directions, and what before was the cause of her downfall becomes the source of her dignity and strength:

I have a mind that cannot be debased, in *essential instances*, by *temporal calamities*. Little do those poor wretches know of the force of innate principle (forgive my own *implied* vanity, was her word). . . . (III, 503)

What ultimately happens in the novel is that Clarissa, through her internal struggle, sufficiently transcends her society so that her ordeal becomes a test undergone not for the sake of her world but for the sake of herself and her God.[13] Richardson's didactic impulse ultimately gets the best of him, and his heroine becomes a perfect moral exemplum and is sanctified in the last act of her drama. This final development has been prepared for throughout the work. Lovelace suggests earlier that Clarissa is a modern Job, while he himself performs the role of the archtempter: "Satan, whom thou mayest, if thou wilt, in this case call my instigator, put the good man of old upon the severest trials. 'To his behavior under these trials that good man owed his honour and his future rewards'" (II, 40). In Sally's hands, Clarissa's Bible opens naturally to this story:

> ... I make no doubt but you have doubled down the *useful places,* as honest Matt Prior says.
> Then rising, and taking it up—Ay, so you have. The *Book of Job!* One opens naturally here, I see.... *Ecclesiasticus* too." (III, 439)

Clarissa is tested and tested again—by her family, by Lovelace, and by her society. She is Job-like in her resistance to evil and Job-like in her refusal to turn from God. In her eyes, her afflictions have been approved by God:

> "Great and good God of Heaven," said she, "give me patience to support myself under the weight of those afflictions, which Thou, for wise and good ends, though at present impenetrable by me, hast permitted! (III, 232)

Lovelace himself finally realizes the higher level of meaning in Clarissa's test: "Your cause, madam in a word, I look upon to be the *cause of virtue,* and, as such, the *cause of God*" (IV, 91). In the last part of the book, Clarissa, having been punished for the sins of her world and waiting to join God in Heaven, parallels Christ rather than Job.[14] Her paternal father, the symbol for her of social authority on this earth, is replaced in her system of values by her Father-in-Heaven:

> SIR,—I have good news to tell you. I am setting out with all diligence for my father's house. I am bid to hope that he will receive his poor penitent with a goodness peculiar to himself; for I am overjoyed with the assurance of a thorough reconciliation, through the interposition of a dear, blessed friend whom I always loved and honoured. (IV, 157)

Richardson's infatuation with his heroine's greatness, as well as his didactic impulse, gets the better of him, and Clarissa becomes an example of absolute virtue on the threshold of eternity. But by turning her back on the world, by refusing the "honorable" way out, by dying rather than selling herself cheaply, she fulfills the whole movement of the novel that takes her from social pride to pride in self—the pride in self when one is beholden only to God. At the end of the novel, Clarissa achieves that superiority which she desired all her life by rising above the world into the hands of her Redeemer.

CLARISSA'S VOICE

Clarissa is as much aware of herself as she is of the society which claims her allegiance, and gradually she must come to know herself as an entity separate from that world. In *Moll Flanders* were the first seeds, the basic situation of a woman separated from a stable environment and undergoing the problem of coming to grips with who and what she is. But Defoe substituted for an honest self-awareness and analysis a traditional morality that was itself crushed by the more realistic and instinctive nature of his character. Clarissa's self-examination has some of its roots in the same kind of Puritanical confessional literature as Moll's[15]—though we can also say that both are influenced by the general Protestant emphasis on the individual's inner state as he travels the road to salvation or damnation.[16] But the inner struggle of Richardson's heroine, until the end of the novel, has been secularized and more directly integrated into her social situations. We can also see the self-awareness of the heroine and the emphasis in the work on this inner dimension of her character as part of the empirical thrust of the entire century, which also influenced Defoe's novel, though to a lesser degree: in Richardson's novel is the realization that reality is centered in the individual consciousness; that the external world has meaning only as the individual perceives it and as it relates to him; and that the drama of our existence is largely played out in the arena of our own inner world.

Richardson and, to some extent, Defoe mark the beginning of an important development in the eighteenth-century novel: the presentation of self-aware characters who satisfied a growing interest in individual psychology and in reality as seen from an individualized perspective. But their novels offer more than such a view of reality: they offer a means by which the reader can experience that reality. The novel as it develops in the eighteenth century differs from earlier fiction because (1) it presents a more normal social reality, (2) which is experienced by self-aware characters (and sometimes narrators), (3) through whom the reader can see, experience, and respond to the people and events of the created external world. Most novels develop a focus through at least one character who presents us with a viewpoint to the created world, a viewpoint through which we can experience that world. A more centralized focus allows a sustained and hence intense involvement for the reader, as well as a larger, more nearly complete, and more unified experience from the work's totality than can be achieved by multiple focuses. Once we establish our position in the novel, once we can enter the skin of one or two characters, we are reluctant to be moved. Not only will our interest and loyalty be spread too thin if we are confronted with too many internalized characters but so will our emotions. Multiple points of view, a larger variety of central figures, will work better in novels that are less psychological and that require a different kind of perception, an association with the implied author's judgmental and comic point of view.

But as the novel develops in England and satisfies the reader's desire to perceive and experience through character, it will also have to allow him to perceive and judge more clearly than the character so that he can achieve a wider and richer understanding. That is, we must be able to experience with the character and experience the character as part of the created whole; we must have our emotions and instincts satisfied through a more knowledgeable perspective than the character can offer. Richardson achieves this to some degree through his use of multiple perspectives. Later in the history of the novel, the development of a flexible third-person point of view that dramatizes and distances the character's inner world will allow both a sustained focus on fewer characters and the larger view.

But first-person narration is a necessity at this stage in the novel's history. In the eighteenth century, the reader was being developed to the point where he would be able to accept the novel as art and still respond psychologically to it; at such a point, first person narration for authenticity and as a scaffold for character would no longer be necessary. At the beginning of the novel's development, however, though Richardson was willing to have his reader accept his works as fiction, first-person narration was the only technique he had with which to create the immediacy and reality of the characters through whom the reader could experience the novel—the authentic voice still had to support the "illusion of reality":

> Will you, good Sir, allow me to mention that I could wish that the *Air* of Genuineness had been kept up, tho' I want not the letters to be thought genuine; only so far kept up, I mean, as that they should not prefatically be owned *not* to be genuine: and this for fear of weakening their Influence

where any of them are aimed to be exemplary; as well as to avoid hurting that kind of Historical Faith which Fiction itself is generally read with, tho' we know it to be Fiction.[17]

In *Clarissa*, the major characters directly create their own realities for us. From Clarissa's first letter (I, 3-8), we hear her distinctive voice and imaginatively re-create her, as one by one her traits are revealed:

> How you oppress me, my dearest friend, with your politeness! I cannot doubt your sincerity; but you should take care that you give me not reason from your kind partiality to call in question your judgment.   (I, 3)

Not only do we have here two elements of her personality—her humility and her propensity for judging others—but we also have a relationship between the two which puts each element in a particular and personal light. The complexity of the pattern of traits which creates Clarissa for us is the result of such elements playing off and defining one another. Clarissa's humility often seems to be used as a defense when judging others, and judging others is a means by which she points out her own humility. She knows how to behave and speak humbly, but she also possesses a pride in that humility and a sense of superiority from it. But more is at work in these first lines to help characterize her. Her first words in the novel, "How you oppress me," suggest the way in which she reacts to external events—with a sensitivity and, even to such a minor occurrence as receiving a compliment, with a sense of suffering. The exclamation point at the end of the sentence adds that emphasis, that note of drama, with which she highlights the slightest event. "But you should take care. . ." suggests the censorious way in which she responds to others, that sense of superiority which is reinforced by the remainder of the sentence, "that you give me not reason . . . to call in question your judgment." These basic responses to the external world will be repeated throughout the novel in a myriad of ways. In the remainder of the paragraph, Clarissa manages to take Anna's praise of her and turn it into an example of self-praise by her friend, not only an illustration of the way in which she is constantly judging others but also an introduction into the book of two major concerns that more directly involve Clarissa herself: self-analysis (Anna, you should look into yourself and see what you are really doing when you praise me), and pride (You are really praising yourself). We must also note Clarissa's diction, the words she uses which identify her interests and further establish her character— words like "politeness," "art," "animated," those qualities Clarissa respects in behavior; "sincerity," "kind partiality," "judgment," "love," the internal qualities which she admires; and "judgment," "distinguish," "lessons," "observes," "knowing," "confession," "suspect," "secretly intend," words which by their accretion suggest her basic concern and constant propensity for analyzing and discovering others as well as herself.[18]

The next paragraph, a brief one—"Our family has indeed been strangely discomposed.—*Discomposed!*—It has been in *tumults* ever since the unhappy transaction; and I have borne all the blame; yet should have had too much concern from myself had I been more justly spared by everyone else" (I, 3–4)—shows us how from the start, through the use of punctuation, italics, and sentence structure, Richardson reinforces the conversational tone of these letters and creates for us a sense that we actually hear one character speaking to another.

In the next paragraph, some of Clarissa's traits are developed and a few new ones added:

> For whether it be owing to a faulty impatience having been too indulgently treated to be *inured* to blame, or to the regret I have to hear those censured on my account whom it is my duty to vindicate; I have sometimes wished that it had pleased God to have taken me in my last fever, when I had everybody's love and good opinion; but oftener that I had never been distinguished by my grandfather as I was: since that distinction has estranged from me my brother's and sister's affections; at least, has raised a jealousy with regard to the apprehended favour of my two uncles, that now and then overshadows their love.   (I, 4)

Clarissa at first suggests that she might have acted from pride, but then offers loyalty as a possible source of her behavior, her feeling of responsibility and duty to those who had been loyal to her. "Indulgently treated" is an example of Clarissa's humility and superiority once more clashing. Her wish that she had died when she had everyone's favor suggests an inclination towards martyrdom, a concern with death, and the high value Clarissa places on other people's opinion of her in spite of her earlier comments to Anna on praise. Indeed, the next statement, her humble wish that she had never been favored, is undercut by what we sense to be a pride in that favor. In addition, the statement about dying also suggests the self-centered and dramatic way in which Clarissa sees herself and her situations: as if, more than anyone else, she is aware of her own significance and willing to perform accordingly. The diction in the paragraph, the moral language—"faulty impatience," "indulgently treated," "*inured* to blame," "censured," "good opinion"—clearly belong to Clarissa in both the moral framework of her thinking and her continuous concern for her public relations.

This kind of diction, these concerns, the interplay of traits, her moralistic and dramatic tones, are the data which fill our minds and assemble for us an image of the heroine. This data comes directly to us from the character herself; it is communicated through her own language as she writes her letters. As we continue to read the novel, the pattern of Clarissa's character further develops through her epistolary voice, a voice we can recognize anywhere in the book.

Like Moll Flanders, Clarissa receives only the most general kind of description. Her physical appearance comes to us largely through Lovelace, who sees her most often in the following romantic and erotic way: "such a constant glow upon her lovely features: eyes so sparkling: limbs so divinely turned: health so florid: youth so blooming: air so animated . . ." (I, 148). Much of our visual impression of the heroine derives from two sources: detailed descriptions of her actions and behavior that appear in her own letters as well as in those of Lovelace and Belford; and the pattern of her personality established for us through her own epistles. Right now, in the early part of the novel, Clarissa describes her behavior in a number of scenes, but these seem only to reinforce the picture we already get of her through our perception of the personality writing the letters. Indeed, in these earlier epistles, Clarissa is as much summarizing past events in which she had no part and describing the morals and behavior of others as she is telling us about her own personal experiences. What is achieved is an immediate presence, with very specific personal qualities and a very definite style of writing. Her pride, her extreme and sometimes specious humility, her propensity for suffering, her strength, her intelligence, her capacity to see into others, and her extraordinary moral bent are important elements that go into the composite picture we form of her. Almost from the start, we know Clarissa to be an attractive young woman—we find this out indirectly from her own letters and from Anna's—and into this general shape we funnel the details of personality and behavior that develop and animate the image, or continuous series of images, that we have of the heroine.

As in the case of Moll Flanders, our picture of Clarissa tends to be subjective, since the physical details are general and we are left to make our own visual associations with the various personal elements of her pattern. But for several reasons we generally have a greater awareness of Richardson's heroine and see her more vividly and in more detail. Of course, the physical references we do receive are more frequent and somewhat more substantial, but, as I have said before, the image we have of characters in the novel is more dependent on their personal traits than on their physical ones—indeed, we often tend to distort or simply ignore detailed external descriptions to allow our own imaginations the freedom of seeing the character according to our own private associations and experiences. This is a level of imaginative involvement which the novel, by its verbal nature, allows us: one picture may be worth a thousand words, but a thousand words permit us our own unrestricted and personal visual experience. The more vivid and nearly complete sense we have of Clarissa, compared to our awareness of Moll Flanders, is in part dependent on the more numerous and detailed elements of her personality. Clarissa has more facets to her character and more variability in her behavior. At the same time, her contradictions are an integral part of her personality and not simply imposed upon her from time to time. For these reasons, her pattern is more complex and yet more integrated, her presence more vivid and immediate.

This vivid sense we have of Clarissa is, of course, dependent on her personal and evocative style of epistolary correspondence. Defoe's journalistic prose leaves him relatively free of restrictions and allows him a certain amount of flexibility, but, in the long run, the style he creates for Moll is basically factual and reportorial, impersonal and detached. Clarissa writes her letters "wholly engaged in...[the] subject,"[19] when she is still emotionally involved in the narrated event, and her style conveys and defines her responses and her personality. But her letters are also at times individual dramatic situations, communicating in an immediate and personal way her present thoughts and feelings in response to the correspondent with whom she carries on an epistolary dialogue. Such letters are more than narratives or monologues: they convey not only what the writer is remembering and feeling but also an independent situation, a moment of pure drama in which the character in her performance manifests her own personality. In other words, there is the drama of the individual letters as well as the drama of past events described within the letter. Later in this chapter, we shall examine more closely how individual letters become an independent dramatic event, creating with immediacy the personality of the writer, and also how they recreate past dramatic episodes. But now we shall examine a little further the language of Clarissa's letters, and the way it contributes to our understanding and visual sense of her.

It is necessary to point out that the heroine and all the major correspondents in the novel are literate and somewhat self-conscious about their letter-writing.[20] Epistolary correspondence in the eighteenth century was more than a simple and direct means of communication; it was an expression of literacy and manners, a way of conveying who and what a person was. Letters were often written as first drafts and then polished in final copy to exhibit one's learning and style. In Richardson's novel, characters are generally writing in response to an immediate situation and scarcely have the time for much conscious literacy, but we still sense in their epistles something of the formality and grace that we associate with the best letter-writing of the period. Richardson's achievement was to make the letters of his novel a dramatic and flexible means of creating character and situation while still conveying the conventions and formal elements of the mode of communication. What we generally have is the distinct and individual voice of the writer, as it addresses the other correspondent, imposing itself upon the letter form itself. Lovelace's comment, *"familiar writing is but talking"* (III, 241), is to be taken with considerable seriousness.

The very form of the novel, then—characters writing letters to one another, especially in the midst of immediate and pressing events— creates a prose that approximates the normal language of speech. But I make such an assertion only to qualify it again, since no literary language is ever free of the influence of past literature. Clarissa's flexible and relatively realistic prose style not only shows certain formal elements of letter-writing in general but also reflects at times the linguistic structure and diction of the literature of Richardson's period, especially the conduct book, religious confession, and drama.[21] The overlaying of these linguistic patterns[22] is neither obvious nor forced for two reasons: (1) their elements are integrated into the character's personality (i.e., Clarissa is moralistic and censorious, hence the codebook is a proper idiom for her; she is much concerned with the state of her soul, hence confessional prose is an ample vehicle for her self-examination; and she has a sense of her own importance that compels her to dramatize her situation in the language of the theater); and (2) their language and sentence structure, at least in the cases of the confession and drama, are not in themselves artificial and are flexible enough for creating character. Such traditional linguistic elements made Clarissa somewhat more understandable and visual to the readers of Richardson's time. Here was a character who, in her situation and psychological complexity, seemed new and compelling, yet also at times seemed to have the sound and image of other literary types.

The most popular form of reading during this period was of a religious and moral nature. Richardson read a number of these books which embodied the ethical code he accepted. His earliest writings, including his volume of model letters, were primarily didactic,[23] and once he embarked as a novelist, his expressed goal was to be a moral teacher. Clarissa is the vehicle for his teaching in his second novel.

Sometimes in the first part of the work, she even resembles the harassed but moral daughter, debating with her parents for participation in the choice of husband, who appeared in such works as Defoe's *The Family Instructor* (1715). But it is her general moralistic and didactic nature throughout the work, the fact that she takes upon herself the image of paragon and teacher, that best shows the shaping influence of these works. Her concerns, viewpoint, and language are at times those of such conduct books as Samuel Pufendorf's *The Whole Duty of Man* (1658?) and Defoe's *Religious Courtship* (1722).[24] Especially interesting, however, is the way in which traditional sources are transcended: so much of Clarissa's moralizing becomes confused, contradictory, and dramatic in the context of her own situation and character development. This is evident in the passages I have already analyzed: her strictures on humility grow into assertions of pride; her belief in duty is contradicted by a struggle for independence; her judgments against others imply judgments of herself. The clarity and certainty of the heroine's moral code fall victim to the confusion and complexity of her own psyche. At the same time, Richardson places Clarissa in the uncertainties and contradictions of the external world, where moral codes are inadequate and dangerously confining. While creating his heroine according to certain preconceived notions and with corresponding linguistic patterns, Richardson's own sense of the complexities of human personality and existence transcends the controls of his conscious beliefs and gives a remarkable depth and verisimilitude to her character.

Clarissa's concern with her own culpability, her penchant for self-analysis, and her introspective passages have the impression of another kind of moral writing: the confessional autobiography, wherein the writer delved into the motivations behind his actions and the nature of his spiritual state.[25] Although from a strongly religious point of view and within the structure of a preconceived moral order, the focus of such works was on the individual fighting for salvation within his own soul. The language and tone of these autobiographies is at times evident in the voice of Clarissa, and creates for us an introspective and struggling figure:

> Let me, however, look forward: to despond would be to add sin to sin. And whom have I to raise me up, whom to comfort me, if I desert *myself*? Thou, O Father! who, I hope, hast not yet deserted, hast not yet cursed me! For I am Thine! It is fit that mediation should supply the rest.   (II, 378–79)

In Richardson's work, the confessional element has been secularized and fully integrated into the narrative. The impulse for self-analysis from a moral viewpoint that we get in confessional writing is evident in the novel, but the nature of the introspection is less religious and more personal, less pietistic and more human, less confined to the self and more immediately concerned with the pressing events of social life. We are confronted with the dramatic conflict of a soul responding to external actions and relationships, concerned with good and evil and torn between certainty and doubt, between pride and humility—and it is this internalized conflict that is so unique in fiction up to this point.

Equally as pervasive, and more evident, is Clarissa's dramatic voice, her frequent speeches and declamations, which have the language, tone, and rhythm of the drama. We know of Richardson's interest in the theater and his knowledge of contemporary plays.[26] Several times in the work, characters compare one another to dramatic figures,[27] and Lovelace himself is fond of quoting from the drama. Clarissa's dramatic idiom is from the heroic tragedy and she-tragedy of the period.[28] I would go so far as to say that Richardson often seems to visualize Clarissa, with her prolonged suffering, as the heroine of one of these tragedies. Entire scenes display her with great emotion (even histrionics) and with highly theatrical behavior. Nowhere is this more clear than in her major confrontations with Lovelace:

> "Thou, woman (looking at the mother), once my terror! always my dislike! but now my detestation! shouldst once more (for thine perhaps was the preparation) have provided for me intoxicating potions, to rob me of my senses——
>
> "And then (*turning to me*), thou, wretch, mightest more securely have depended upon such a low contrivance as this! . . .
>
> . . . "Stop where thou art, O vilest and most abandoned of men! Stop where thou art! Nor, with that determined face, offer to touch me, if thou wouldst not that I should be a corpse at thy feet!" (III, 288)

As she then brandishes the penknife in the air, we most certainly are reminded of the tragic heroines that held the stage in Richardson's time. But it is especially in her speech, in its slightly formal and archaic sentences, in its formal second-person pronouns, in such dramatic language as "terror," "detestation," "intoxicating potions," "wretch," and "corpse at thy feet," that one senses the extent of this influence. Compare this passage in attitude, tone, and diction to the following one uttered by a heroine of heroic tragedy:

> *Statira.* No barb'rous woman! though I durst meet death
> As boldly as our Lord, with a resolve
> At which thy Coward heart wou'd tremble:

> Yet I disdain to stand the Fate you offer,
> And therefore fearless of thy dreadful threats,
> Walk thus regardless by thee.[29]

Clarissa's dramatic language, however, is integrated in a far more subdued way in her commentaries and responses to her correspondents:

> And now to give me cause to apprehend *more evil from him, than indignation will permit me to express!* O my dear, perfect your scheme, and let me fly from so strange a wretch!   (II, 378)

It is more than the italics and exclamation marks that bring to life Clarissa's voice here: it is the dramatic rhythm, diction, and sentiments of her sentences. Clarissa's dramatic language functions both to give immediacy to her feelings and to give the reader a visual impression of her distraught and worried state. As this letter continues, we see the way in which the dramatizing impulse, so clear in her characterization, synthesizes with the moral and confessional aspects of her thoughts— indeed, how the theatrical element integrates and dramatizes these two traditional chords.

But here also Richardson does more than borrow a developed literary idiom for his character's speech: Clarissa's very use of this idiom is a manifestation of her personality and psyche, a means by which we see and understand her better. We have already noticed in Clarissa's early letters a propensity for self-dramatization, a trait which results from too strong a sense of self-importance and from an awareness that the world is always watching her and that she must respond accordingly. Clarissa as a letter-writer has the divided personality of the performer—she is both the person involved in the action and a person watching herself perform. But even in her reflective letters, when the heroine directly communicates her present state of mind, we often feel that she is still the self-conscious performer. The dramatic idiom, then, becomes the natural language of the woman who senses herself acting an important role before an attentive world. I do not wish to overstress this point; Clarissa is not as conscious a role player as Lovelace.[30] Much of her behavior is sincere and instinctive: self-dramatization is not her major difficulty; it is only a symptom of her internal flaw, which is an acute pride in herself and in her public reputation.

LOVELACE'S VOICE

Lovelace's voice, no less clear and sharp than that of Clarissa, creates a distinct though complex figure, one we are continuously seeing in a series of immediate and dynamic images. His voice also acts as counterpoint to that of the heroine, establishing a rhythmic and tonal contrast which both helps to define hers and to establish for it an ironic and dramatic context. A good example of the counterpoint of voices, the separate rhythms of those of Lovelace and Clarissa playing against each other, comes just after the rape. Lovelace answers Belford's letter of recrimination in his usual dramatic and flamboyant style: "Let me alone, you great dog, you!" (III, 199). He follows this with a letter in which he suggests his diabolical methods: "Thou wilt say I am a horrid fellow! As the lady does, that I am the *unchained Beelzebub* . . ." (III, 202). In his next letter, pity and guilt are evident, but in the context of the same energetic and irreverent style: "I pity her with all my soul; and I curse myself, when she is in her wailing fits . . ." (III, 204). He copies Clarissa's delirious and pitiful letter which begins "MY DEAREST MISS HOWE,—O what dreadful, dreadful things have I to tell you! . . ." (III, 205), against which he then plays his own voice: "Plague on it! I can write no more of this eloquent nonsense myself . . ." (III, 205). Unable to copy further, he includes Dorcas's transcripts of Clarissa's pitiful ramblings, made to seem all the more pitiful by contrast to his own frenzied style: "And can you, my dear honoured papa, resolve for ever to reprobate your poor child?" (III, 205). Her last letter is a condemning, though pathetic, complaint against her rapist: "Ah! villainous man! what have you not to answer for!" (III, 213). Lovelace's response is equally dramatic: "I will not hear thy heavy preachments, Belford, upon this affecting letter. So, not a word of that sort! . . ." (III, 213). From this point the voices are heard to play against each other within the letters of Lovelace as he describes in detail his confrontations with the heroine. Not only do their two voices clash as they confront one another, but Lovelace's voice as narrator also clashes with Clarissa's voice as performer within the scene.

In their contrasting letters, which are normally written to someone else, we also see Richardson building dramatic irony and tension through a juxtaposition of voices that emphasizes each character's separate qualities, and each character's obliviousness to those qualities expressed in the other's voice. This kind of irony is particularly evident in the earlier parts of the book, when Clarissa is largely unaware of Lovelace's true character and his plans concerning her. We hear the counterpoint of their voices as Clarissa writes to Anna and Lovelace to Belford, but we also hear the clash of their voices, as two distinct, unintegrating rhythms, in those scenes where they face one another. Clarissa's voice is made to seem much more pathetic and misguided because of what Lovelace's voice has already communicated to us and because of what it must now represent for us.

Lovelace's voice is more flexible, vigorous, and personal than that of Clarissa. It is the voice of the lover, intriguer, showman, artist, intellectual, and cynic. Whereas Clarissa uses the epistolary form to explain, dramatize, and analyze, Lovelace uses it as an extension of his own energetic and demonic personality. From Lovelace's first letter we become aware of his distinct voice, and we also become aware of the literary traditions behind it and behind his character in general:

> In vain dost thou and thy compeers press me to go to town, while I am in such an uncertainty as I am in at present with this proud beauty. . . .
>
> This man has by his proposals captivated every soul of the Harlowes—*soul!* did I say—there is not a soul among them but my charmer's. . . .
>
> . . . And, the devil of it, that love increasing, with her—what shall I call it?—'tis not scorn: 'tis not pride: 'tis not the insolence of an adored beauty—but 'tis to *virtue.* . . .
>
> . . . I was led by the blundering uncle . . . to the *divinity* as I thought; but, instead of her, carried me to a *mere mortal.* . . .
>
> . . . I must needs try my new-fledged pinions in sonnet, elegy, and madrigal. I must have a Cynthia, a Stella, a Sacharissa, as well as the best of them: darts, and flames, and the devil knows what, must I give to my Cupid. I must create beauty, and place it where nobody else could find it. . . .
>
> But to return to my fair jilt—I could not bear that a woman who was the first that had bound me in silken fetters . . . should prefer a coronet to me: and when the bird was flown, I set more value upon it, than when I had it safe in my cage, and could visit it when I pleased.
>
> But now I am *indeed* in love. I can think of nothing, of nobody, but the divine Clarissa Harlowe. Harlowe! How that hated word sticks in my throat—but I shall give her for it the name of love
>
> CLARISSA!—O there's music in the name,
> That, soft'ning me to infant tenderness,
> Makes my heart spring like the first leaps of life!
>
> But couldst thou have believed that I . . . could adopt those over-tender lines of Otway? . . .
>
> This it is that makes my pride mount above my resentment. By this engine, whose springs I am continually oiling, I play them all off. (I, 144-47)

Lovelace is magnificently artificial, literary, and theatrical, but somehow he brings it all off; somehow that energy in him, that monomania, cunning, and penchant for self-dramatization creates a character larger than life but still credible within the context of Richardson's illusion of reality. It is, in fact, the literary clichés, the dramatic and poetic rhythms of his lines, that create his character, that

make him appear vivid to us, that make him seem a man lost in his
distorted self-awareness, in his self-deception, in his constant role-
playing.[31]

Within Lovelace's letters we hear the rhythm and diction of (1) the
drama, especially heroic tragedy and a number of plays with villainous
rakes; (2) the courtly letter; and (3) love poetry such as the sonnet and
Cavalier lyric. The above quotation, with its self-analyses,
declamations, theatrical poses, and manifestation of rage and pride,
clearly shows its dramatic antecedents.[32] Compare it to the following
passage from Lee's *Mithridates* (II.i.104–12):

> *Mithridates*: She must be mine, this admirable Creature,
> Her Charms are now inevitable grown;
> And, while I seem to fright her from my Son,
> I talk, and gaze, and dote, to my undoing.
> See her no more; lose her with weighty thoughts,
> And drown her in the Ocean of thy Power:
> In vain I strive with cares to keep her down,
> In vain does business sink her to the bottom;
> This Bladder Love still bears her up again.[33]

Elements of the courtly letter and love poetry are seen in Lovelace's
attitudes towards Clarissa, the stock treatment of her divinity, and his
language of "soul," "virtue," "adored beauty," "fair jilt," and "silken
fetters."[34] The quotation from Otway's *Caius Marius*, where Marius
junior rhapsodizes over Lavina (I.i.); the mention of sonnet, elegy, and
madrigal; and Lovelace's reference to poetic names and images suggest
more than his literacy, more than the fount of much of his dramatic,
poetic, and often bizarre language: they suggest the context in which he
sees much of his own behavior and many of his attitudes, and the context
in which the reader of Richardson's time saw him as well.

Lovelace's language is literary because he constantly sees himself
and others in a literary framework: reality for him is the make-believe
world of his reading. His penchant for self-dramatization forces him to
place everyone else in a role and to see them only as a part of his grand
drama; indeed, it also forces the reader to visualize the characters in part
as their literary prototypes and frequently as dramatic performers.
Lovelace is like a schoolboy with his games and "let's-pretend"
obsession. His roles as actor and director prevent him from feeling
compassion for the heroine's suffering and make him wish to control her
struggle for individuality and independence. When he is not
worshipping Clarissa in the language of the courtly letter and love
poetry, he is engaged in the role of heroic tyrant and villain, seeing her in

the traditional role of the fallen woman of the drama: "And should not my beloved, for her own sake, descend by *degrees* from *goddess-hood* into *humanity*?" (II, 477). Lovelace has the pride of the dramatic tyrants, a pride that forces him to see *his* Clarissa both as superior to all women and, like all women, as victim to his prowess. It is this pride and his quest for superiority that motivate his machinations against the heroine, that allow him to plot against the proud Anna, that fill his letters with stories of sexual triumphs and adolescent views about the weakness of women and his own irresistible power. What all this leads to is a great deal of confusion on Lovelace's part, confusion because he is awed by Clarissa and also in love with her. Yet his awe must be overcome. His stances, defined by the artificial language in which he seems trapped, force him to act against the very creature he loves; the fixed way in which he must think causes him ultimately to destroy Clarissa and himself. What at times seems monomania forces him into the most outlandish deceptions and intrigues. His efforts to get at Clarissa are incredible: the "elopement," the rented house of Mrs. Sinclair, the hiring and disguising of Tomlinson and the harlots, and his own disguises make him seem like a man driven—driven by the roles he feels compelled to play.

The fire scene is an example of Lovelace's being carried away by his vision of Clarissa as the desirable innocent of the drama, and of himself once more as potentate and villain:

> Wicked wretch! Insolent villain!—Yes, she called me insolent villain, although so much in my power! And for what? —only for kissing (*with passion indeed*) her inimitable neck, her lips, her cheeks, her forehead, and her streaming eyes, as this assemblage of beauties offered itself at once to my ravished sight; she continuing kneeling at my feet, as I sat.
> If I *am* a villain, madam—And then my grasping, but trembling hand—I hope I did not hurt the tenderest and loveliest of all her beauties— If I *am* a villain, madam—   (II, 503)

Lovelace's role-playing, his pride and vanity, his sexual nature, and his love for Clarissa lead to a considerable amount of confusion in him, and this ultimately is what makes him succeed as a character. All of these qualities play against each other and lead to a chaotic, driven character, to a man who seems out of control, to an inner world of uncontrollable conflict. It is all dramatically stated and dramatically developed in the energetic but conflicting rhythms and diction of Lovelace's voice. He seems real because the various pieces do not fit together, and hence he escapes the straitjacket of a single role. He achieves a greater reality by the end of the book because he possesses an ego which finally realizes what is going on inside of him, and a consciousness and conscience that come to the forefront of the character and ultimately transcend the roles he has felt compelled to play.

What we have, then, is the character Lovelace talking aloud ("Now I talk [*familiar writing* is but *talking*, Jack]" [III, 241]); engaging in the roles of lover, villain, potentate, poet; responding to Clarissa's voice always in the context of his own immediate role; and feeling his various roles play against one another and work against the real feelings he has for the heroine. Lovelace constantly seems to be talking himself into one role or another:

> And what will be my subject, thinkest thou? Why, the old beaten one, to be sure; self-debate—through temporary remorse. . . .
>   . . . I don't know what it is that gives a check to my revenge. . . . Conscience is dead and gone. . . .
>   Well then, it must be love. . . .   (III, 155)

His role-playing and self-debate go on and on as he fluctuates between states of mind until, driven by his desperate pride, he commits the act that shatters the whole drama, that brings reality crashing down upon his head. Clarissa at this point refuses to play the role of the fallen woman, and Lovelace discovers that he has played away his last hand and lost what he so ardently desired, that the drama—his drama—is over, and that he can no longer write the script. In a sense, Clarissa now becomes fixed in her role, but it is a role of her own making, one absolutely apart from the world of Lovelace's drama. He is suddenly faced with the drama of moral virtue, a drama in which he has no part:

> Strange, confoundedly strange, and as perverse [that is to say, as *womanly*] as strange, that she should refuse, and sooner choose to die [O the obscene word! and yet how free does thy pen make with it to me!] than be mine, who offended her by acting *in* character, while her parents acted shamefully *out of theirs*, and when I am now willing to act *out of my own* to oblige her: yet *I* not to be forgiven!   (III, 508)

At first there is frenzy and theatricality, but then Lovelace's temper seems to grow calmer, his language less artificial. There are still the passages of role-playing, of self-celebration, but "although I put on these lively airs, I am sick at my soul! My whole heart is with my charmer!" (III, 511). Now there is a more serious note throughout, one of self-realization that keeps breaking through—"I am *not* the savage which you and my worst enemies think me. My soul is *too much* penetrated by the contents of the letter . . ." (IV, 303). In such passages, Lovelace's language has become more natural, the theatrical stances have diminished. He is groping for reality, and such language shows this. Still, he is not a new man—"How daredst thou (though unknown to her) to presume to take an apartment under the same roof with her?" (IV, 303)—for what we have here is a character not changed but changing.

Clarissa's death capsizes Lovelace and he finds himself torn loose, without any moorings; he tries to take safety in his earlier role-playing, but the situation is now different and the role-playing can function only to express a man lost, threatened, on the edge of extinction. The new vein of language keeps reappearing to show us that Lovelace is not, and can never again be, the man he was. Even when he assumes a theatrical stance, his language is less artificial and shows the change that has already taken place within him.[35] He may struggle and regress, but just as his language manifests new elements, so does his personality. On a separate sheet he writes:

> Let me tell thee, in characters still, that I am in a dreadful way just now. My brain is all boiling like a cauldron over a fiery furnace. What a devil is the matter with me, I wonder! I never was so strange in my life.
> In truth, Jack, I have been a most execrable villain. And when I consider all my actions to this angel of a woman, and in her the piety, the charity, the wit, the beauty I have *helped* to destroy, and the good to the world I have thereby been a means of frustrating, I can pronounce damnation upon myself. How then can I expect mercy anywhere else!   (IV, 378)

There are still fragments of Lovelace's old prose style here—"cauldron," "fiery furnace," "devil," "execrable villain"—and he still sees himself in an over-dramatic way. But mitigating this is the new language in his letters—"piety," "charity," "good to the world," "mercy"—the language of Clarissa and her world, of the moral and religious writers, and it is this diction which seems to be triumphing over his older language. The struggle of his moral conscience for dominance, the battle between two prose styles, is overcoming him, and though he can finish the letter with a quotation from Lee's *Mithridates*, the flame finally seems to go out within him, his ego appears defeated, and the self-creator stops creating himself: no more role-playing, just self-realization and the threatening emptiness that always lay behind his created self: "And is it so? Is it *indeed* so? Good God? Good God!" (IV, 378).

What makes the novel end so powerfully is not merely the pathos of Clarissa's death, but also the fact that Lovelace achieves a self-realization that is more noble than any role he has feigned in the past. By the end of the novel, Lovelace is no longer a figment of his own imagination, a created thing of clichés and quotations: he is a real man. Clarissa's sanctification is matched by Lovelace's humanization, and we finish the novel with the knowledge of his tragedy as well as hers. Lovelace's final letters are written by a person who has achieved self-awareness and hence a state of calm—it is his awareness of personal guilt and his own human insignificance that raises him to nobility. There is still pride in Lovelace, a pride that drives him to his destiny with Morden. Tension exists between his pride—"And in this respect only I am sorry for his skill, and his courage, lest I should be obliged, in my own defense, to add a chalk to a score that is already too long" (IV, 522)—and his guilt— "Indeed, indeed, Belford, I am, and shall be, to my latest hour, the most miserable of beings" (IV, 522). It is this guilt that undermines his pride and prepares us for his demise. All these letters move on, with an air of inevitability, to the tragic denouement, and the servant's letter describing Lovelace's death, the fact that it is written by a servant, adds both pathos and irony to his ending. But Lovelace's final words, though noble and generous, though suggestive of his self-realization, are once more dramatic, almost theatrical, as if the old spirit is still within him— but this time it is a spirit necessary to the occasion, one that asserts his manhood and supports the dignity of the proceedings. After his mortal wound, he cries, "Oh, my beloved Clarissa! Now art thou—" (IV, 529) but is unable to finish. A little later he says,

> There is a fate in it! . . . a cursed fate!—or this could not have been! But be ye all witnesses that I have provoked my destiny, and acknowledge that I fall by a man of honour!   (IV, 529)

Fatalistic and grandiose, he goes to his grave—but also acknowledging his guilt and the force of virtue that has defeated him.

Clarissa and Lovelace write letters that are remarkably visual and keep the reader continuously involved with the mind of the writer as well as the action of the novel. We shall see that both characters are especially visual in their narration of past events, though Clarissa is so to a greater degree. But the heroine's normal conversational and discursive style, where she conveys her present responses and internal state, is not as imagistic as that of Lovelace, though, like all speech, it too depends upon the reader's visual perception of thoughts and feelings:

> How soothing a thing is praise from those we love! Whether conscious or not of deserving it, it cannot but give us great delight, to see ourselves stand high in the opinion of those whose favour we are ambitious to cultivate. . . .   (I, 287)

Clarissa's moralizing, her conduct-book mentality and language, rely upon the reader's capacity to see what she is saying, to translate the signs into a series of pictures that convey the meaning of her discourse and help establish her personality. But Lovelace's voice is more strikingly imagistic in these passages that create for us the immediate psychic state of the writer.[36] It is this imagistic style that not only animates the pages of his letters but graphically and solidly conveys his thoughts and personality to us.

We have just examined Lovelace's literary imagery, the way in which he expresses his concept of himself as well as his relationship to the heroine through the images of drama, courtly letter, and poetry. We should also notice at least one more of the various imagistic strands that appear in his letters to emphasize this aspect of his writing. The animal imagery in his letters, for example, expresses Lovelace's proud and ruthless self, his fear of others, and his contempt for mankind in general:

> Thou knowest nothing, Jack, of the delicacies of intrigue . . . of the joys that fill the mind of the inventive or contriving genius, ruminating which to use of the different webs that offer to him for the entanglement of a haughty charmer. . . . Thou, Jack, who like a dog at his ease, contentest thyself to growl over a bone thrown out to thee, does not know the joys of the chase, and in pursuing a winding game. . . .   (II, 30)

Lovelace first sees himself as a crafty spider, selecting a web with which to entrap his victim. Then, while seeing Belford as a dog growling over a bone and Clarissa as "a winding game," he makes himself, by implication, an energetic and joyful hunting dog. Lovelace often uses animal imagery in relation to entrapment or the chase in order to assert his own superiority and power over others. But I said before that this particular strand of imagery indicates not only the way Lovelace sees his relationship to others, but also the fear and contempt he feels in relation to people in general. It seems evident that anyone who spends so much time conquering women and asserting his superiority over the individuals of both sexes finds human relationships a constant threat to his freedom and ego. Lovelace must reduce others to animals in order to prove himself to himself. The contempt he wants to feel for others is a means of avoiding self-contempt. Yet the fact that he often sees himself as an animal, albeit a superior one in craft or strength, indicates that his Hobbesian cynicism about human nature is all inclusive: deep down, Lovelace senses that he is no better than the rest of his species.

SCENIC TECHNIQUE

The epistolary form itself is responsible for the distinctive voices of the heroine and villain, and also allows for the work's more striking narrative techniques. The popularity of epistolary literature during this period has been sufficiently documented and some of the reasons for that popularity explored.[37] But the most significant aspect of the subject is the dexterity and versatility that Richardson brought to epistolary fiction: no work before his novels comes anywhere near the artistry of his individual epistles or their interplay within the work's structure.[38] We must, of course, acknowledge that though Richardson brought epistolary fiction to such a high point, his type of narrative was not to flourish after him.[39] Many of his narrative accomplishments were to continue, but without the external trappings of the letter form. The epistle allowed Richardson developments in narrative technique which were themselves to become independent of the very form responsible for their existence.

As we have already seen, Richardson wanted his reader to realize his work was fiction, but he wanted his letters to appear sufficiently genuine to support the reader's "Historical Faith" in the characters and actions of the book.[40] Letters are something we all write in real life, and their very appearance in a fictional work seems like an extension of part of our own world. It is hardly an overstatement that one of the chief preoccupations of the characters in *Clarissa* is letter-writing, and correspondence plays a crucial part in the development of the work's plot.[41] We can go even further and say that the very form of the novel, letters written by the characters, is so integrated into the plot, is such a part of the characters' actions and needs, that there is no separation between the world of the novel and the mode of narration, that what happens and the way it is told are inseparably entwined. There is no sense of story-telling in the traditional way—the story is as much in the telling as it is in what is told.

Letters are a natural form for presenting Clarissa's personal dilemma as she seeks to free herself from the dictates of her social world. From the very beginning of the novel, we are aware of the letter's public nature. Not only are all the epistles eventually made known to the public, but as the novel progresses copies of individual letters are read by all sorts of people. It was not unusual at the time for people to keep duplicates of their own letters, but in *Clarissa* characters make copies both for themselves and for the eyes of others. Equally significant is their practice of copying other people's letters. Lovelace, at one point, writes: "For, on reperusal of a copy of my letter, which fell into my hands by accident, in the handwriting of my Cousin Charlotte, who, unknown to me, had transcribed it, I find it to be such a letter as an enemy would rejoice to see" (IV, 442). Clarissa frequently records or cites passages from letters she has written to others, but she also includes either copies or summations of letters written by Lovelace and members of her family. When Clarissa is in the house of Mrs. Sinclair, Lovelace secretly has a group recording the heroine's letters—"Dorcas no sooner found them, than she assembled three ready writers of the *non-apparents*; and *Sally*, and *she*, and they employed themselves with the utmost diligence, in making extracts . . ." (II, 362).

More and more we realize how much letters are seen as public statements of private thoughts. Clarissa assesses the personalities of others through their letters; she does this frequently to Anna, and, on one occasion, she analyzes a letter written by Lovelace passage by passage, basing upon it a full and detailed description of his character (III, 462-64). Clarissa's own letters are public confessions, manifestations of her personal qualities that are intended to be read by more than the recipient of the epistle. Her virtue and honesty are apparent in the open way in which she analyzes and exposes herself. Epistolary writing should be from the heart, we are told time and time again, and it is the heart of the letter-writer, or his lack of it, that is to be assessed by a host of readers.

But letters also function for the public disclosure of what happens to the correspondent, and this is made clear in the first letter of the novel when Anna asks Clarissa to write letters of considerable detail because, as an example and a public figure, she must give a public account of everything she does. But she must also show with specificity the conduct of others to her so that we can properly judge her responses. Clarissa realizes that the way people conduct themselves in public offers an insight into their personalities and attitudes. Therefore, it is incumbent upon her to describe characters not only with details of what they say but with details of how they act:

> and then you will always have me give you minute descriptions, nor suffer me to pass by the air and manner in which things are spoken that are to be taken notice of; rightly observing that air and manner often express more than the accompanying words. (I, 5)

Richardson generally does not describe the physical appearance of his secondary characters in any detail:[42] he sees them externally as types, not as specific individuals, and he sees them as stage figures, as general, distanced shapes. Interestingly, he depicts characters by those qualities which are most discernible in the theater—speech, manner of speech, movement, gesture. The lack of detailed physical characteristics for the secondary figures allows us the same private visualizations that we perform for the major figures, though their simpler and less-developed patterns force us to see them more as types, as cartoon figures, who in our minds are emblematic of certain dominating personal and moral traits. But the details of behavior are necessary for us to see them acting and interacting in specific ways that establish their personalities and personal relationships, and for developing the novel's plot in a predetermined way. In *Moll Flanders*, we have seen how secondary figures are never presented with any detail or specificity and thus scarcely make an impression upon us. In Richardson's novels, most secondary characters are presented with sufficient details of behavior to allow us to see them as well as the heroine; thus we have a world fuller, spatially larger, and more visual than any yet to appear in fiction, a book richer and denser in texture.

Clarissa's description of Mr. Solmes is a striking example of secondary characterization: "[He] approached me as soon as I entered, cringing to the ground, a visible confusion in every feature of his face. After half a dozen choked-up madams—he was very sorry—he was much concerned. . . . He hemmed five or six times, as I had done above; and these produced a sentence—that I could not but see his confusion . . ." (I, 377). Poor Solmes is documented for posterity. Each of the details in his description adds to the clear visual image we have of his behavior and to our comprehensive understanding of his character. That Solmes approaches Clarissa immediately upon her entrance suggests his nervousness and anxiousness; that he cringes and is confused suggest his uncertainty, insecurity, and guilt, causing the following "choked-up madams" and expressions of sorrow and concern to seem all the more insincere; that he stops and is unable to complete a sentence emphasize his inadequacy in the presence of the virtuous Clarissa, while making his efforts seem all the more futile. Solmes's behavior, his obsequiousness in front of the heroine, his uneasiness, all manifest an ungainly, inferior, and even devious person, while they increase our sense of Clarissa's superiority and plight. Of course, the correspondents who write these letters are still emotionally involved in the event, and so their descriptions of secondary characters tend to be subjective; part of the impact of Solmes's behavior, for example, is in our seeing him the way the heroine saw him. But such descriptions are to be taken as substantially accurate, even when Lovelace is doing the narration.

A sense of their letters being written for the public eye is true of all the major correspondents in the novel, and the result is the same kind of detailed presentation of external events. Lovelace's letters seem written for more than Belford; they seem written for the world at large so that his own behavior, especially in the context of the behavior of other characters, can be measured and appreciated. He is constantly exhibiting himself and describing others in relation to himself, though his descriptions of other characters tend to be briefer, more subjective, and more ridiculing than those of the heroine: "He was devilish ceremonious, and made a bushel of apologies for the freedom he was going to take; and, after half a hundred hums and haws, told me that he came—that he came—to wait on me—at the request of *dear Miss Howe*, on the account—on the account—of Miss Harlowe" (III, 485). The description is effective, though not quite as full and fully dramatized as those in Clarissa's letters, drawn with her serious and moral public eye.

The characters described by Clarissa and Lovelace, though presented with much detail of action and behavior, remain static and unchanging throughout the work. The book's explicit didactic function is in part responsible for this—by seeing Clarissa as an exemplum and by presenting the people who surround her in terms of their moral relationships to her, Richardson permanently fixes these figures in the moral pattern of the work. The fact that he has only one way of presenting most of these secondary figures—from another character's point of view—also prevents us from seeing internal complexity or fluidity in them. But even Anna and Belford, who themselves write letters, concentrate so much on Clarissa and her problems that they are largely seen in their unchanging relation to her. Since most of these characters are fixed in the moral pattern of the work and are seen from an external viewpoint, their contours are simplified and their traditional source shows clearly. Here is a description of Clarissa's family in confrontation with her:

> Such a solemnity in everybody's countenance! My mother's eyes were fixed upon the tea-cups, and when she looked up it was heavily, as if her eyelids had weights upon them, and then not to me. My father sat half-aside in his elbow-chair, that his head might be turned from me; his hands clasped, and waving, as it were, up and down; his fingers, poor dear gentleman! in motion, as if angry to the very ends of them. My sister sat swelling. My brother looked at me with scorn, having measured me, as I may say, with his eyes as I entered, from head to foot. My aunt was there and looked upon me as if with kindness restrained, bending coldly to my compliment to her as she sat; and then cast an eye first on my brother, then on my sister, as if to give the reason (so I am willing to construe it) of her unusual stiffness.   (I, 35)

The visual sense of the characters is strong; their details, specific and functional. As in the description of Solmes, Richardson sees these figures dramatically, theatrically, as if they are posturing, as if they are displaying the external signals used by figures on the stage to convey their personalities and emotion.[43] As we have seen, this is not the only literary tradition evident in Richardson's novel, but it is the one he most often uses to present the public appearance of his characters. The same kind of characterization appears in Clarissa's deathbed scene, where the figures all seem caught in some theatrical stance, where the entire scene seems taken either from the stage or an illustration in a playbook.[44]

Clarissa discusses and describes her family in a number of letters during the first part of the novel, but she does not tell us more than we see of them in the above-quoted scene. Their character patterns are established from the start, and in spite of their reappearances and the detailed dramatizations of their actions and behavior, they never change or develop. The results are twofold: we tire of them soon and begin to doubt their credibility; and we become infuriated by their immobile behavior and Clarissa's unwillingness to renounce them. There is a Dickensian dimension here, as Clarissa finds herself trapped in a world of fixed types. This may add to the frightening pathos of her situation, but it also adds to the sense of frustration we so often feel—a frustration, I might add, equally created by the limitations and repetition of even the complex and developing Clarissa, limitations and repetition caused by her insistent demand that she behave morally and remain an exemplum to all in a world of such ogres.

We have already seen that *Moll Flanders'* visual dimension is best created in scenes describing the heroine's crimes. Detailed presentation, especially of spatial relationships in the world of places and objects, creates a sense of what Moll sees and experiences as she performs her exploits. Richardson also creates his external world through spatial arrangements, but he does so with both his characters and his physical reality in order to increase our sense of Clarissa's confrontation with the social world outside her, and he does so far more consistently than Defoe. The elements which each writer emphasizes reinforce the general function of his work: the spatial ordering of the physical world in *Moll Flanders* to develop our sense of Moll's interesting actions; the behavior of characters and their spatial interactions in a spatially defined world in *Clarissa* to emphasize the private-social concerns. Our perception of reality is contingent upon spatial awareness, and from the beginning, in the novel's attempt to create an illusion of reality for the reader, writers developed spatial as well as temporal dimensions to a greater extent than did the authors of earlier fiction.[45] It was necessary to extend the spatial dimension of a scene and put more emphasis on the arrangement of details and physical relationship between characters and the external world in order to create a greater visual awareness and hence involvement for the reader, in order to allow him to perceive and experience the fictional world as did the major characters.

In an early episode in *Clarissa* concerned with the heroine's struggle against her family, we can see Richardson using the spatial dimension of his scene to increase both our visual awareness and our understanding of what takes place. The room in which the central action occurs is like a traditional theater setting, with means of access on stage right and stage left, but we are also able to visualize an adjacent enclosure with the Harlowes crowded together and listening at the door to the heroine's confrontation with Mr. Solmes.

> There are two doors to *my* parlour, as I used to call it. As I entered at one, my friends hurried out at the other. I saw just the gown of my sister, the last who slid away. My Uncle Anthony went out with them; but he stayed not long, as you shall hear: and they all remained in the next parlour, a wainscot only parting the two.   (I, 377)

What is most impressive about the scene, however, is the physical interplay of characters, the way we see them responding to one another in a definite spatial context. Mr. Solmes has little success, and Clarissa's uncle soon joins the fray:

> And, Mr. Solmes, turning to him, take notice of what I say: *This* or *any* death, I will sooner undergo (that will soon be over) than be yours, and for *ever* unhappy!
>
> My uncle was in a terrible rage upon this. He took Mr. Solmes by the hand, shocked as the man seemed to be, and drew him to the window. Don't be surprised, Mr. Solmes, don't be concerned at *this*. . . .
>
> Then coming up to me (who had thrown myself, very much disordered by my vehemence, into the most distant window) as if he would have beat me. . . .   (I, 380)

The spatial context of the scene, the arrangement and rearrangement of characters, allows the novelist a full development of dramatic actions and allows the reader a full visual perception of what takes place, a perception that includes the heroine within it and yet is seen from her point of view.

Richardson's *Clarissa* creates for the reader a sense of specific and continuing locales, of action taking place within an actual physical context. More than any earlier work of fiction, it gives us an awareness of the characters living their day-to-day lives in the spatial context of buildings and rooms, of upstairs and downstairs, of interiors and exteriors.[46] We get detailed descriptions of settings only on occasion, though one of these is worth noting—the picture of the officer's house where Clarissa is kept prisoner after her rape and second escape from Lovelace:

> A horrid hole of a house, in an alley they call a court; stairs wretchedly narrow, even to the first-floor rooms: and into a den they led me, with broken walls, which had been papered, as I saw by a multitude of tacks, and some torn bits held on by rusty heads.
> The floor indeed was clean, but the ceiling was smoked with variety of figures, and initials of names. . . .
> A bed at one corner, with coarse curtains tacked up at the feet to the ceiling; because the curtain-rings were broken off; but a coverlid upon it with a cleanish look, though plaguily in tatters, and the corners tied up in tassels, that the rents in it might go no further. . . .   (III, 444)

Belford's description goes on for more than a page, graphically and specifically painting the hellhole to which Clarissa has been driven by Lovelace. I am unaware of any similar description in earlier fiction, and it is not until we come to the works of Smollett that we again find such a conscious and dramatic use of physical setting.

But such detailed descriptions cannot be used often, lest the progress and the pace of the novel be seriously impeded. We generally see the physical world of *Clarissa* in the same unspecific and vague way that we see our own. Like our physical world, that of the novel has meaning mostly in terms of the perceiver's movements and activities, of his relationship to it and the people that surround him. We see the rooms in *Clarissa*, then, generally without detail of decor but as specific spatial contexts for action, affecting the movement and interaction of the characters. We also see each room as part of an entire building in order to understand the way in which the larger structure and the arrangement of its parts affects the action as well. During the first part of the novel, action is dependent upon the design of the Harlowe home. Clarissa generally remains in her own room, virtually a prisoner, and on occasion visits the rooms below or walks in the garden. Characters enter and leave her room, and, all the while, Clarissa is aware of what is going on downstairs. After her departure with Lovelace, she is given a description of the arrangement of Mrs. Sinclair's "respectable" dwelling: "She rents two good houses, distant from each other, only joined by a *large handsome passage*. The *inner house* is the genteelest, and is very elegantly furnished; but you may have the use of a very handsome parlour in the *outer house* if you choose to look into the street" (II, 110). What we see is really a blueprint of Clarissa's prison, the inside house shut off from the world by a passageway and another house. While Clarissa is in Mrs. Sinclair's home, we are continuously aware of the spatial arrangement of each room and of the room's relationship to the other parts of the building because all this is meaningful in terms of the heroine's closeness to or distance from the other characters and the outside world. Richardson generally seems to forget the two houses, and presents the location as a single dwelling. But note how the entire house and all the rooms become suddenly alive, how the entire physical setting becomes a dynamic spatial entity, when the heroine escapes before the rape:

> "About half an hour after, Dorcas, who had planted herself where she could see her lady's door open, had the curiosity to go to look through the keyhole . . . and finding the key in the door . . . she tapped at it three or four times. . . .
>
> "Having no answer she stepped forward, and was astonished to find she was not there. She hastily ran into the dining-room, then into my apartments, searched every closet. . . .
>
> "Not finding her anywhere, she ran down to the old creature and her nymphs, with a Have you seen my lady? . . .
>
> "They were sure she could not be gone out.
>
> "The whole house was in an uproar in an instant; some running upstairs, some down, from the upper rooms to the lower; and all screaming. . . ."   (II, 522)

Novels have the capacity to manipulate visual images, perspectives, and distances. They can focus on portions of rooms, on whole rooms, and even on all the parts of a building simultaneously. Although the novel is a temporal form, developing its narrative through the sequential ordering of words, it can achieve all these effects because it registers images on the reader's mind which can perceive spatially. The reader's mind can hold at once a series of related images, can see simultaneously various relationships in a total vision. It can also see each new image in the context of past images, giving each scene a wider frame of reference and a deeper significance. This retentive and spatial capacity of the mind is one of the reasons why we always possess a greater awareness of the novel's action than any single character, and why our identity with any character can only be partial.

Paradoxically, by emphasizing the spatial dimension of his scenes, Richardson slows down the pace of the novel, fixes us in time, and makes us aware of the slow ticking of the clock. For this reason the novel has a sense of time and a time scheme more detailed and realistic than those we find in earlier fiction. In *Clarissa*, characters function in a world of time as well as space, and it is the temporal dimension which allows us a visual sense of both external and internal action, of the continuity of things happening. It is the temporal dimension which also allows our involvement with the characters as they live through the events and our awareness of their development or change throughout the book. In earlier fiction, events and the characters' responses are summarized; a myriad of adventures are quickly disposed of; and designation of duration has no significance to us as readers because we cannot sense the time passing. *Moll Flanders* suffers from a lack of an overall temporal dimension—Defoe creates no carefully developed temporal context in which to place his heroine and the novel's events. The duration of his work is a lifetime that has no meaning in terms of years passing and personal development or change. But in a number of the individual scenes we do have a partial awareness of Moll acting in a continuum of time, and this increases our involvement with her. One of Richardson's most significant achievements is to decrease considerably the pace of fiction, to slow down the rush of events, thus giving the reader a greater sense of time passing and of the action of the novel taking place within a continuum of real time. Fiction moves from the simple picaresque structure, the narration of many events that supposedly fill a whole lifetime, to a detailed and controlled presentation of a series of related events that take place within a limited temporal span. Involved here is a change from a narrative emphasis on summation to techniques that dramatize in detail a character's experiences—for the reader, it is a change from watching at a distance the rush of general events to becoming involved in the denser texture and time scheme of the created reality. In the confrontation between Clarissa and her family discussed above, behavior is presented with such detail, conversation is recorded so faithfully, that we have the sense of seeing everything exactly the way it happened—minute by minute, second by second.

By giving us a greater sense of spatial and temporal realism within each scene, Richardson must narrate fewer actions and events and confine his entire work to a briefer span of time: he must give us a shorter and more cohesive plot. Richardson's dramatic focus within each scene is related to his sense of his entire work, with all its repetition and slowness, as a dramatic entity. The action of *Clarissa* takes place within one year, the first letter dated January 10 and the last December 18. Richardson documents each letter with a date and frequently with the hour or part of day to give us more than a sense of time passing; he does so also to give us a sense of the order and relatively brief duration of events. With his awareness of dramatic theory and practice, Richardson seems to be applying the neoclassic rule for unity of time—that tragedy should take place within the span of a single day—to his work, but he has made his temporal unity one year in accordance with the greater length of the novel form.[47] Richardson's temporal unity, however, is in fact temporal realism. His novel recognizes the unalterable effect of immediate time on human destiny: it is a statement, in one sense, that fortunes change and lives complete themselves not in the passing of years but in the passing of each year.

PSYCHOLOGICAL LETTER-WRITING

To satisfy the letter's public function in describing the conduct of the writer and that of the characters he or she confronts, and to involve the reader more fully in the created world, Richardson developed the letter form's inherent capacity for communicating information, for telling us what the correspondent saw and experienced. But the reader's involvement was also furthered by the development of another capacity inherent in the letter—the creation of the writer's inner state. As well as communicating to the recipient information concerning past events, the letter-writer is also conveying feelings and states of mind even when not consciously doing so—in the manner of describing what already has taken place. We can say that the letter form in general, allowing a free-flowing, associational, and personal method of discourse, is a natural vehicle for creating characters internally.[48] Richardson's impact on his own century was largely in his extension of the internal dimension in fiction, in his expansion of mental space. His major impact on the novel was in developing a propensity in epistolary writing for conveying psychological and emotional states into a narrative technique for characterization that later in the history of fiction would not be dependent on letter form. Helping to develop this technique were the confessional element within his heroine—the fact that she was operating at times in a particular tradition that emphasized an internal morality—and the dramatic element within both his heroine and villain—the fact that, like a playwright, he portrayed them expressing verbally their own thoughts and feelings in an immediate and dramatic way.

Clarissa constantly describes her internal responses during narrated events: "I therefore paused, hesitated, considered, and was silent for some time. I could see that my mother hoped that the result of this hesitation would be favourable to her arguments" (I, 100-101). Unlike Moll, Clarissa's feelings and behavior within the narration are often affected by her memory of past events: "But then, recollecting that all was owing to the instigations of a brother and sister, wholly actuated by selfish and envious views... that my disgrace was *already* become the public talk...and then Mr. Solmes's disagreeable person. ... All these reflections crowding upon my remembrance..." (I, 101). Her role as a moral exemplum and the public nature of the letters requires that she present her feelings and thoughts for judgment. This presentation of her internal state, depicted dramatically and with great detail, allows the reader to do more than judge: it allows him to experience with the heroine her past actions and responses and her moral dilemma. Clarissa often conveys her present responses to earlier events when writing her letters, thus somewhat controlling our involvement in the narrated action and allowing us some detachment and her own hindsight for our judgment of her past behavior:

> He took the removed chair and drew it so near mine, squatting in it with his ugly weight, that he pressed upon my hoop. I was so offended (all I had heard, as I said, in my head) that I removed to another chair. I own I had too little command of myself. It gave my brother and sister too much advantage. I dare say they took it. But I did it involuntarily, I think. I could not help it. I knew not what I did.   (I, 68)

What we often receive from such scenes is a double image of the heroine, first involved in the narrative event and then responding to it once again as she writes her letter. Sometimes she dramatically sustains her present mood and state of mind throughout a series of paragraphs and even letters while conveying information about past actions.[49] An example of this comes early in the novel, when she writes about the letter she has left for Lovelace, in which she promises to go off with him:

> And now, that I am come to this part, my uneasy reflections begin again to pour in upon me. Yet what can I do? I believe I shall take it back again the first thing I do in the morning—yet what *can* I do?...
> Yet why should I be thus uneasy, since, should the letter go, I can but hear what Mr. Lovelace says to it?... Twenty things may happen to afford me a suspension at least: why should I be so very uneasy? ...
> The man, my dear, has got the letter! What a strange diligence! I wish he meant me well, that he takes so much pains! Yet, to be ingenuous, I must own that I should be displeased if he took less. I wish, however, he had been a hundred miles off! What an advantage have I given him over me!   (I, 432-34)

In such narrative passages we are constantly aware of the heroine's voice as a dramatic presence.[50] The focus is less on what has occurred and more on her present responses to the event; in other words, the drama is largely played out in the act of writing.

Sometimes Clarissa focuses almost entirely on her present state and dramatizes at length her immediate thoughts and feelings. What we visualize on these occasions is the dramatic scene at that moment. Such epistles are themselves dramatic events. After her rape, Clarissa returns to the pen and through her writing dramatizes her present emotional crises (III, 205-13). Some of her papers are unfinished letters; others are moral exhortations to herself or others. In all of these papers there is a sense of delirium, hysteria, self-pity, and melodrama; they resemble the rambling of an emotionally distraught person (though each of Clarissa's statements has some obvious meaning in the larger context of the work). The section ends with a letter to Lovelace (III, 210-13), one that is more controlled and that gives evidence of her returned senses, but one with enough disorganization, rambling, exclamations, and apostrophes to recreate her immediate confused and self-pitying state of mind. Even during the long process of dying, when Clarissa's letters display her in her most moralistic and superior way, when the strength of her will contrasts with the pathos of her situation—especially as it is described by others—there are those paragraphs in her letters which remind us of her immediate state and dramatize her condition:

> *Mamma,* I would have wrote—is the word distinct? My eyes are *so* misty! . . .
> Another breaking off! But the new day seems to rise upon me with healing in its wings. I have gotten, I think, a recruit of strength. . . .   (IV, 302)

All this is skillfully done and creates for us a vivid awareness of the character just at the moment of writing the letter. Clarissa, through the manipulation of sentence rhythm, punctuation, and paragraphing, and the careful selecting and placing of words, becomes a living presence for us as she narrates and discourses at length.

Lovelace is also adept at psychological letter-writing. Like the heroine, he can convey in a single narration his thoughts and feelings both during the scene and at the time of narrating the scene. Like Clarissa, he too can make the epistle itself into a dramatic event, creating for us an awareness of his state of mind when writing and a visual perception of him at that very moment:

> Well, but now let's try for't. Hoy—hoy—hoy! Confound me for a gaping puppy, how I yawn! Where shall I begin? At thy executorship? Thou shalt have a double office of it: for I really think thou mayst send me a coffin and a shroud. I shall be ready for them by the time they can come down.   (IV, 113)

Lovelace, in general, displays more versatility and flamboyance in epistolary writing than the heroine. His letters range anywhere from strict playscript form, where he sees himself as one of the performers, to those where he displays his present psychological state. The common aim in all his writing is to dramatize—to dramatize especially himself in the past or present scene, or both. Lovelace, like Clarissa, writes close to the event, when he is emotionally involved in what has taken place or will take place—as he tells Belford, "I love to write to the *moment*" (II, 498).[51] One of Lovelace's unique capacities is to bring together the narrated scene and present moment, to merge the two into a striking projection of his own warped personality and present state of mind:

> There! Begone! Be in a plaguy hurry running upstairs and down to fetch from the dining-room what you carry up on purpose to fetch, till motion extraordinary put you out of breath, and give you the sigh natural.
> What's the matter, Dorcas?
> Nothing, madam.
> My beloved wonders she has not seen me this morning, no doubt; but is too shy to say she wonders. Repeated What's the matter, however, as Dorcas runs up and downstairs by her door, bring on, O madam, my master! my poor master!
> What! How! When!—and all the monosyllables of surprise.
> [*Within parenthesis* let me tell thee, that I have often thought that the little words in the republic of letters, like the little folks in a nation, are the most significant. . . .]   (II, 435)

In the episode he describes, Lovelace has taken ipecacuanha and tests Clarissa's affections with his self-induced illness. At the moment of writing to Belford, he seems to throw himself into the scene—or, rather, to re-create the scene as a projection of his present erratic state of mind. This part of the episode is told in present tense to break down the time distinction between then and now. The narration itself seems a combination and, sometimes, confusion of past dialogue and thoughts, and of the writer's present monologue. The sudden exclamations and speeches, the erratic rhythms, the melting of time present and past, create for us the rush and energy of the action as well as the rush and energy of Lovelace's mind in the act of narration. At the end of this passage, he breaks the scene with a sudden interjection, a witty but calm observation on "little words" that is meant to show his absolute control over both the material he is narrating and the characters within the narration, but that demonstrates instead the schizophrenic state of mind Lovelace's constant performing and role-playing often force upon him.

But Richardson's general tendency throughout the book is to emphasize and dramatize the characters' responses during the narrated scenes more than their later responses. This is crucial, I believe, for an understanding of both Richardson's fictional techniques and the general development of the eighteenth-century novel. Richardson clearly states what for him is the focus of his work:

> All the Letters are written while the hearts of the writer must be supposed to be wholly engaged in their subjects (The events at the time generally dubious): So that they abound not only with critical Situations, but with what may be called *instantaneous* Descriptions and Reflections. . . .
> "*Much more* lively and affecting, says one of the principal characters . . . must be the Style of those who write in the height of a *present* distress; the mind tortured by the pangs of uncertainty (the Events then hidden in the womb of Fate). . . .[52]

He frequently attempts to minimize the time gap between experiencing and relating so that the emotions and thoughts involved in the event are not lost, nor the memory of details insufficient to create a fully dramatized scene. Richardson wants the reader to experience what Clarissa experienced, to perceive the event and feel it as did she, and not to lose the fullness of the aesthetic experience in the time lag caused by first-person narration.

Paradoxically, in Richardson's efforts and accomplishments, we see one of the major reasons for the eventual demise of the epistolary novel and for the development of third-person point of view as the major vehicle for narration. There are, of course, several reasons why novels stop being written in letters, including the limitations of time and place in the fictional world caused by the act of writing epistles, and the incredible epistolary skill and time for correspondence which the characters must possess. But more important, I believe, is the limitation evident in all first-person narration: that our sense of the character in the act of writing to some extent works against the dramatic immediacy of the character's experience in the narrated event. Richardson overcomes this limitation to an extraordinary degree, describing past events with much detail or using the present responses of the character for contrast and dramatic irony. But on those frequent occasions when he strives to immerse us in time past, both the few observations by the "I"-narrator, as natural as they may be, and the "I" pronouns are there to remind us intermittently of the time lag between the described event and time of writing and to pull us out of the scene. In Clarissa's long passages of introspection, however, when she is not narrating a specific event, there is no pull for our involvement between two levels of action, and we respond fully to the heroine at the time she writes her letters; her state of mind at that point becomes the immediate dramatic reality for us. The problem here, however, is that such long, introspective passages tend to move us away from the central events of the novel and suspend for us the forward movement of the narration.

Jane Austen, who apparently wrote her first versions of *Sense and Sensibility* and *Pride and Prejudice* in letter form,[53] ultimately would make the breakthrough in technique by the simple expedient of changing first-person narration into an internalized third-person point of view. As a result there would be no "I"-narrator existing on a later time level to draw our attention from the novel's central action and movement; the character's perspective through which we view the events would be fully integrated into the dramatic action itself, and the character's responses, including long passages of introspection, would fit into the single linear development and time flow of the work's plot.[54] We can see this technique already embedded in Richardson's novel: there are numerous sections where present responses are minimal and could easily be omitted, and where first-person pronouns could be changed to third, hence removing any distractions from the scene's dramatic immediacy and the central narration. Some future writers will consciously break the novel's linear time scheme and create several temporal levels, but they will do so for thematic reasons and sustained special effects. Richardson does not consciously break the linear time scheme with such artistic intentions but rather inherits the two temporal levels as an inherent part of first-person narration. The interplay he achieves between the time levels is often skillful, but its function is always for immediate effect, not for any larger structural or thematic concerns, and for minimizing the disruption in the reader's involvement caused by the two levels of action. Sterne is the only major figure of the eighteenth century to make a virtue of the novel's capacity to deal with multiple time levels; the main development in the novel's time scheme during this period is towards a single linear flow. I do not wish at this point to go any further into the development of internalized third-person point of view: such a discussion must wait for Jane Austen's *Pride and Prejudice*, and it should come after an analysis of Fielding's omnipresent third-person narrator. What I have tried to emphasize is Richardson's achievement with first-person narration, and the fact that some of his developments could go further only in third-person narration. The reader's involvement with the character's perceptions, responses, and experiences would have to be provoked by a more sustained dramatic immediacy, even if it meant losing the kind of interplay that Richardson at times achieved between the two time levels.

On both time levels, however, Richardson's internal dramatization is considerable and allows the reader a degree of identification with his two major characters not possible with any of the protagonists in earlier fiction.[55] Characters' minds, both during the event and in the act of writing, are filled with complex and conflicting feelings, with different levels of response, with past and present images: as well as expanding the spatial perimeter of his social world and individual scenes, Richardson spatially developed the perimeters of human consciousness. Indeed, his dramatization of his heroine's interior world on both time levels is so detailed and sustained that we still associate with her and project our thoughts and feelings through her even when the scene is described from someone else's point of view. This is true to some degree when Lovelace describes their confrontations, although we frequently are forced to see the scene from his point of view and with his reactions, and it is more often true when Belford describes her noble and suffering behavior. Our identification with Clarissa is, of course, controlled by our own self-awareness and by the fact that much of our imaginative experience must come from our own resources; and it is controlled within the novel by the separation of the two time levels; the multiple points of view; a wider view of the heroine's situation than she herself possesses; and, at least for the first part of the novel, the depiction of her personal shortcomings. But the main force of Richardson's novel is certainly to involve us deeply in Clarissa's plight and to have us experience it as much as possible with the heroine herself.

The reader's identification with Richardson's heroine should also be examined in relation to sentimentalism, a significant literary and cultural force in the period but one that is still hard to pin down and understand fully. R. F. Brissenden, in his study of the "novel of sentiment," points out that the reasonable nature of one's better feelings and their role in forming moral judgments were emphasized in the first part of the century, and it was only as the century progressed that reason and feeling began to part company.[56] We shall certainly see the ramifications of this split in the later novels of the period. But Brissenden goes too far in arguing that "Sentiment for him [Richardson] did not have a great deal to do with feelings. . . ."[57] The following statement by Clarissa, concerning her sister, is one of several that appear in the novel and argues for the importance of feelings:

> Bella has not a *feeling heart*. The highest joy in this life she is not capable of: but then she saved herself many griefs, by her impenetrableness. Yet, for ten times the pain that such a sensibility is attended with I would not part the pleasure it brings with it.   (I, 218-19)

Clarissa acknowledges here both the pain and pleasure that a "feeling heart" brings, but she also suggests the moral nature of such feelings. The capacity to react emotionally to the experiences of life makes one sensitive, responsive, and alive. But Bella has not "a feeling heart," the heroine tells us, because she also refuses to respond to Clarissa's plight— she shuts herself off from feeling for others even though such an emotion might bring joy through the shared grief. We are really concerned here with sympathy and benevolence, two major components in both eighteenth-century ethics and sentimental literature. Lord Shaftesbury had written that pleasure and virtue were to be found in "THE NATURAL AFFECTIONS (such as are found in Love, Complacency, Good-will, and in Sympathy with the Kind of Species)."[58] Sympathy was the affection emphasized in sentimental literature, a sympathy for those in distress which was both pleasing and virtuous. Not only the characters within the work but the audience as well were supposed to feel for those in distress, and feel with them. Although benevolence was often seen as a means of demarcation, of separating those who gave from those who received, in ethics and literature there was a movement that emphasized the common experiences we all share, that saw suffering as a possibility for everyone. It was upon this foundation that a number of playwrights and novelists appealed to their audience. Sympathy led to empathy, which led to identity. Richardson's novel, in its attempt to have the reader perceive reality with Clarissa and identify with the heroine in her suffering, reflects both the developing perceptional psychology we have already examined and the new cult of sensibility.

But what of Lovelace? What do we say about the letters in which his complex and evil mind is the dominating concern? Certainly Richardson wants us to understand from these letters what a reprobate he is and to appreciate the challenge Clarissa faces. And certainly Lovelace's private story and development, as we have already seen, is of dramatic and moral significance. But we sense that more is involved here, that his attractive but invidious mind is given more documentation and credibility than these functions require. The temptation is to talk about Richardson's fascination with the character and to see Lovelace as a projection of the author's own fantasies. Richardson himself said that he identified with the characters of his novels when creating them: "I am all the while absorbed in the character. It is not fair to say—I, identically, am any-where, while I keep within the character."[59] Unquestionably Richardson's identification with Lovelace is responsible for the remarkable immediacy and energy of the character's letters, an immediacy and energy which make the reader in turn associate with the character. The direction of my study, however, is to understand why and how *we* do the associating, and my present concern is to understand *our* relationship to Lovelace.

Our identification with the characters of a novel extends our own experience in a positive way and broadens us as human beings, but there is another side to the issue, another kind of experience we enjoy. Clarissa is a paragon and a victim, and though we relate to her at her best, see ourselves behaving in her noble way, we also relate to her when she suffers and associate with her victimization. We enjoy more than feeling pity for her and for ourselves; we find pleasure in the imagined pain. Lovelace is an attractive figure, one who himself undergoes a process of self-realization, and certainly we associate with this aspect of his character. But he also is a libertine, an intriguer, a tormentor, and ultimately a rapist, and some part of us responds to this side of him. Lovelace at times satisfies the aggressive and even sadistic part of us. The sexuality in Richardson's novel is not concerned with love but with violence and destruction. There is a pornographic element in *Clarissa*, a particular focus that shows in great detail and at great length the mental and physical torture of a virtuous and attractive woman. Clarissa and Lovelace are inseparably connected in the novel and satisfy within us both our masochistic and sadistic needs.[60]

But I would not argue that such an identification with Lovelace is pervasive or intense enough to suffice throughout the novel—we must see more in him and more through him. It would be impossible for us to identify with any character from such a limited point of view for any length of time; and this is one of the reasons why any work of hardcore pornography, after a short while, becomes insufferably dull. The novel's form and techniques, its dramatization of human psyches, its perspectives into and through the mind, demand characters worth caring about. A good part of our attention in *Clarissa* goes to the heroine; our sustained involvement with her is the result of her complexity, her humanity, and her strength. Sometimes we become involved with Lovelace's psyche and begin to identify with him: a complex creation, he displays for us a debased and violent human nature, but a human nature with some virtue and with the capacity for change and growth. As complex creatures ourselves, we respond to both sides of his character.

REPETITION AND STASIS

All of this discussion of Richardson's techniques, the examination of his achievement in individual parts of the work, cannot hide the fact that ultimately one finishes the novel with much respect for the author but also with a sense of exasperation. In its entirety, as a complete work of art, the book is not a success.[61] We must acknowledge, though, that Richardson never considered his novel as a "work of art," as an organized and shaped literary entity: in his time, there were no standards, no established tradition for what a novel should be. What he attempted to achieve was a species of writing that gave the reader a particular kind of experience when he was reading the work—emotionally and morally. Richardson's only concerns with the novel's wholeness, its finished state, were that all the letters be related to the major plot, and that the work's moral function be fulfilled.[62] For this reason, it seems to me, Richardson worked piecemeal: there are effective, even astonishing, sections of the book, but not a sufficient regard for how all the pieces fit together.

Watt claims that Richardson caused a "revolution" in fiction when "he avoided an episodic plot by basing his novels on a single action, a courtship."[63] The step was significant, but it was hardly the entire journey. If the problem in *Moll Flanders* was too many individual episodes, that in *Clarissa* was a slender story line spread over seven volumes.[64] Richardson's novel suffers from its great length, from the fact that too little seems to happen to warrant that much prolificacy. Many of the individual sections are fine, the action dramatic, the characters compelling, but often one feels that these sections are too much the same and that the forward thrust of the novel is not sufficiently evident. The development in Clarissa's character is scarcely discernible at times in the multitude of letters and scenes; the key events—the rape and the heroine's death—are so delayed that they lose their impact; scenes often explore the same problems with little advance; and the heroine and villain repeat too often the same attitudes, reflections, and responses. The novel's two temporal levels—the fact that they divide our attention or that the later time level, when the correspondent is writing, occasionally disengages us from the narrated action—also add to this sense of paralysis.

The very effects that Richardson sought to achieve—a visual and detailed presentation of external events, the full and minute description of reflection and emotion—work for the immediacy of the reading experience and against a sense of development and wholeness. Within the individual sections of the novel, there are different intensities of dramatization, a movement between internalization and externalization, and shifting points of view. But often we sense that one technique or a focus on one character has continued too long; often we feel as if we have returned to where we had started, and that the drama has been played for no reason beyond its immediate effect. The point is this: the novel creates for us a psychological and emotional involvement, but it must also satisfy that involvement, seem to control and order it, and finally complete it. We must be involved and at the same time feel that our involvement is bringing us somewhere. The needs and desires that compel our involvement must finally themselves be satisfied. The novel as art should impose upon the raw materials of life the shaping vision of the author, and through that shaping vision bring to resolution and completion what we experience as readers. At the end of the work, we must feel not only that we have experienced with the characters but also that we have sensed at the same time a direction and control imposed upon their experiences. The novel must finally affirm an order and harmony we long for in our own existence, but which we may never achieve.

Richardson's novel does not achieve this, nor, as we read the work, do we often feel that we are moving in that direction. A fuller plot, more intricately developed, though working towards a final point of resolution, would help; yet there would still have to be a greater mastery over the individual parts of the novel: the author would have to play one against the other and relate them all into the final accumulative effect of the work, varying his narrative techniques with mastery and with the purpose of reinforcing the work's development and overall structure. I am, of course, describing a goal toward which all novels move but which not many achieve. In the next chapter, we shall see how Fielding moves in this direction with *Tom Jones*, especially through his stylistic achievement and plotting of the novel. But I must reaffirm at this point that Richardson's accomplishment was still remarkable. He established the basic relationship between the reader and the author's illusion of reality that was to be fundamental to the future novel; he expanded the perimeters of the social world, individual scene, and human psyche; and he developed many of the basic narrative techniques that were to be the tools of future writers. He is both the dinosaur and the father of the English novel, and without him it is inconceivable that by the end of the century Jane Austen could have been writing such a work as *Pride and Prejudice*.

CHAPTER THREE

TOM JONES:
The Novel as Art

FIELDING'S "REALISM"

In spite of the publisher's preface to *Moll Flanders*, the novel is written as an authentic document, the autobiographical, true-life account of the "I"-narrator. Although Richardson claimed that he wanted his reader to be partly aware that the letters in *Clarissa* were not "genuine," and even included an author's preface and postscript with his novel, he also wanted to maintain the reader's "Historical Faith" in the work by creating an "Air of Genuineness."[1] To achieve the "Genuineness," he made the novel appear as a collection of real letters written by actual people; and to emphasize the authenticity of the letters, he had an editor, not an author, occasionally intrude in the course of the collection to explain the deletion and arrangement of epistles. *Tom Jones* (1749), however, neither appears to be, nor reads as, an authentic document or series of documents. It is a created work of art from beginning to end, and to remind us of this, Fielding divides his novel into discrete books, and each of these books into individual chapters, frequently with humorous or fictional headings. More significantly, the author himself, or the supposed author, writes a discourse on his plan of operation or on human nature before each book and interjects his own voice and commentary throughout the story itself.

We have, then, a discernible and operating literary framework, within which and through which we see the characters, action, and setting of the novel. But though this literary framework minimizes the authenticity of the mode of telling and reminds us that the characters are created by the writer, it also develops and even emphasizes the reality of the characters. *Tom Jones* makes us perceive and respond to its world in ways true of the novel form, but to do so it employs a variety of techniques that at first seem inappropriate to this new type of fiction.

Fielding's literary self-consciousness is also evident in his reliance on traditional literary materials and techniques. Although Defoe and Richardson rely on earlier literary models, they do so in ways that seem unobtrusive and hardly disturb the innovative and novelistic elements of their works. Fielding uses traditional literary models in a far more conscious and manipulative way, but he does so to achieve his own kind of fictional realism. To appreciate Fielding's fictional achievement, to assess his role as an eighteenth-century novelist, we shall have to understand the term "realism" in a more extensive and even more meaningful way than we normally do when discussing the novel. Fielding, unlike Defoe and Richardson, is clearly a transitional figure, bridging both literary tradition and the novel as well as traditional cultural attitudes toward human nature and attitudes toward human nature developed in the new fiction. He is, if I may use what at first seems a contradictory term, a neoclassic novelist—contradictory if we limit our notion of the novel to a literary form that depicts a particular kind of reality, one that emphasizes individuality in characterization and specificity in description. Fielding's neoclassicism has, of course, been pointed out by other scholars, but often to the detriment of his accomplishments as a novelist.[2] What has not been sufficiently recognized is the way his neoclassicism is shaped and modified to fit the aesthetic requirements of the new fiction—indeed, the way it opens up and extends possibilities inherent in the novel form. Fielding's neoclassicism is evident in his use of traditional literary materials and notions of character, but he employs these to create a particular kind of realism, one that depends on the reader's capacity to respond to and perceive the fictional world. We can understand Fielding as both a neoclassicist and a novelist, then, if we focus on the fictional experience *Tom Jones* creates and the modes of perception it offers, instead of looking for a kind of subject matter and narrative exposition that may appear in many novels but that are by no means the *sine qua non* of all novels.

In *Shamela* (1741), Fielding began to develop his own kind of realism in response to what he considered the unnatural and unrealistic assessment of human behavior in Richardson's first novel, *Pamela*. Fielding's initial literary response was parody and burlesque, but both imply a superior moral vision and a more realistic attitude about people than those in the work attacked—by substituting material that at first seems incongruous to the literary form and by exaggerating the literary techniques to emphasize this incongruity, the writer turns the subject he ridicules inside out and creates a world that seems funny because, in comparison, it seems so much closer to reality. *Shamela* is a very funny work; it is funny because it exposes the sham in *Pamela* and presents to us a view of life far more akin to the world we see around us. Parody and burlesque, then, depend upon the subject and style ridiculed; they gain impact only by comparison—*Shamela* is meaningless without *Pamela*. *Joseph Andrews* (1742) seems to begin in response to *Pamela*—it first suggests the falsity of Richardson's values by transferring them to an unlikely person and exploring them in a context that more accurately resembles the world around us[3]—but a number of crucial changes that make the work neither parody nor burlesque soon become evident. First, the values Richardson had eulogized in *Pamela* and Fielding had mocked in *Shamela* are transformed into larger and more admirable qualities in the person of Joseph Andrews. Second, the more realistic world has taken over with its multitude of separate and individual characters. Third, the action of the novel moves in its own independent direction. And fourth, Fielding no longer burlesques Richardson's literary techniques and unreal assessment of character but presents his own comic and neoclassic realism. This last point is what is most significant in relation to *Tom Jones*, for this is the impetus that Fielding follows in writing his larger and more ambitious novel.

Fielding's movement from fictional parody and burlesque to his comic novel *Joseph Andrews* seems a logical and even necessary one, just the way the movement from that novel to *Tom Jones* also seems inevitable. In *Shamela*, his attack against a false view of human nature results in a more realistic, though highly comic and exaggerated, fictional world, one dependent on Richardson's novel. The impulse to present a true depiction of human nature gets the better of him in *Joseph Andrews*, and he creates an autonomous fictional world, one that is then further developed and amplified in *Tom Jones*.[4] The comic perspective itself remains the arbiter of truth in both novels, but instead of exposing another author's false assessment of his characters, it exposes characters' false assessment of themselves. The comic writing in *Shamela* exposes the author who is not on the scene, while the comic writing in the novels exposes the characters who are on the scene and hence puts its focus on the immediate fictional reality. But an exposing comic perspective in a fictional world necessitates a different kind of realism from that which we found in *Moll Flanders* and *Clarissa*. Fielding's comic realism deals with typical and recognizable human fallibility and weakness, not with specific people and individual character traits or personal dilemmas.

His characters are typical both of certain groups of people but also of human nature in general. We laugh, or at least are amused, because we recognize the same failings in people around us and, to some extent, in ourselves, but we are relieved because we find ourselves free from such extreme states. In other words, Fielding's comic perspective is related to his larger neoclassic vision; his comic exposure of human fallibility necessitates the generalized and universal human traits of neoclassicism.

We can better understand Fielding's notion of fictional realism if we look at *Shamela*'s burlesque of verisimilitude in *Pamela*:

> Mrs. Jervis and I are just in bed, and the door unlocked; if my master should come—Odsbobs! I hear him just coming in at the door. You see I write in the present tense, as Parson Williams says.

> Mrs. Jewkes went in with me, and helped me to pack up my little all, which was soon done; being no more than two day-caps, two night-caps, five shifts, one sham, a hoop, a quilted petticoat....[5]

In the first passage, Fielding makes fun of Richardson's attempt to create dramatic immediacy and credibility through present-tense narration; in the second, he ridicules Richardson's use of common details to create an air of probability and authenticity. Fielding's point is that realistic techniques of narration cannot substitute for the truth about human nature. In Fielding's eyes, Richardson presents an illusion of reality— but not reality itself, not the way people act and think. True realism exposes human nature as we all know it. We can project this attitude into Fielding's *Joseph Andrews* and *Tom Jones*, where his realism is not in narrative technique but in the interpretation and exposure of human motivation which he achieves through a comic, not realistic, mode of presentation. Fielding therefore refused Richardson's epistolary form, which seemed only to give an appearance of authenticity to his work, and his realistic narrative techniques, which involved the reader in a particularized and dramatized world that seemed only to hide a false assessment of character and fallacious system of values. Fielding, on the other hand, used nonrealistic techniques to present what seems to us a realistic assessment of character—if we allow ourselves to believe that it is possible to state universal truths about human behavior and create characters in a general mold.

Our response to Fielding's realism, to his depiction of human nature, is complex: we respond with both involvement and understanding as we do when reading most novels, but here our understanding of character is more related to our awareness of people in our own world and to ourselves as well. Fielding's comic techniques function (1) to generalize characters; (2) to expose them beyond their own awareness; (3) to bring us to an understanding of the world in which we live; (4) to make us aware of ourselves as related to the characters of the novel; and (5) to make us aware of ourselves through the manner in which we respond to the characters. The literary framework of the book and the traditional styles are all part of the comic technique and means by which the author guides and manipulates our responses. I will go further than this and say that even what are often considered rudimentary narrative techniques—the generalized presentation of characters, the stylized or incomplete depiction of inner states, the half-developed dramatic scenes—are all part of the comic perspective and a means of shaping the reader's aesthetic experience.

In my discussion, I shall not be distinguishing between the actual reader and the "implied reader" as have several critics.[6] I realize that the distinction is sometimes a useful one, that the narrator on occasion seems to address a fictional reader of his own creation, but my analysis is based on the conviction that throughout the work, the two merge and the actual reader plays the role of the "implied reader" as it is laid out by Fielding. Indeed, I would even argue that the guise of the "implied reader" is a mere convenience to allow the author directly to address the real reader, that it is a transparency that disappears from the reader's mind as he responds to the narrator. My discussion of *Tristram Shandy* will also be predicated on the same belief.

A more basic reason limits the usefulness of talking about an "implied reader" in *Tom Jones*. While directing the reader's perceptions, Fielding, far more than Defoe or even Richardson, calls upon the reader's own experience and depends upon him to fill in the blanks and supplement the created world itself. Like Sterne after him, though not to the same extent, he develops an interplay between the narrator of the work and the reader. But Sterne develops this relationship in a work primarily psychological and epistemological; Fielding develops his narrator's relationship with the reader primarily for moral purposes: the reader is to fill in the blanks so that he is forced to perceive and judge matters partly on the basis of his own experience, and the validity of his perceptions and moral judgments is tested against the ultimate exposure of character and development of plot. As we read the work, then, we generally do not see the narrator addressing an "implied reader" whom we perceive as another fictional creation; the narrator establishes a pattern of interplay between ourselves and the text that forces us to respond even at those moments when he refers to the reader in a personal, comic, or even ironic manner.

Fielding's realism is not on the page; it is achieved in the mind of the reader as he is manipulated and led to see through the behavior of characters and perceive them in a fuller way than their speech, actions, or even thoughts allow. Their behavior achieves significance as we are made to understand their true motivations, and as we are also made to see these figures in the larger context of universal behavior. We have the character on the page performing in a certain way and pretending to act for certain reasons, but, at the same time, the episode is described by the narrator in such a way that we are forced to see the figure's behavior in a truer perspective. What we have are two images of the character—the way he seems to himself and the way he should be accurately perceived— and it is the incongruity between these images which causes much of the book's humor. Of course, the narrator does at times come right out and tell us how to interpret behavior, but often the perspective is only suggested by the literary framework, the manner of narration, or the literary echoes we hear.

Sometimes our understanding of a character or action becomes more accurate or nearly complete further on in the work, when we receive new information, and in such cases our perception is dependent upon the novel's development of plot. For this reason perception is always uncertain or relative, and we are warned time and again not to be simplistic and make snap judgments, even when the narrator has already suggested to us a fairly accurate view of matters. Reality, the way things are, is at times not perceived until all the facts are in, and until we free ourselves from our own prejudices and limited vision. We can interpret much of the action of the novel as being concerned with the problem of perception: Tom must learn to perceive others correctly and act accordingly, and others must learn to perceive him correctly so that he can achieve his just and happy rewards.[7] One of the significant aspects of the new kind of fiction written during these years was the writer's awareness of the reader's relationship to his work, and his development of narrative techniques to foster an intense concern with the world of his novel. We see in *Tom Jones* this same kind of awareness on the part of the writer: his recognition of the reader's responses to his work and his constant attempt to manipulate and develop those responses. Fielding tries to involve the reader less emotionally than Richardson and less psychologically than Sterne, but he demands responses equally complex and every bit as moral. As the characters in the novel must learn to perceive reality more accurately, as judgment must be suspended until all the facts are in, as Allworthy must learn to be less blinded by his moral principles and Tom less gullible about people in general, so must the reader learn to see the world of the novel with accuracy and judiciousness—and by doing so perceive it with the truer perceptions and greater wisdom of his friend, the narrator.

THE LITERARY FRAMEWORK IN *TOM JONES*

The full title of Fielding's novel is *The History of Tom Jones, A Foundling,* and throughout his dedication to George Lyttelton, the novelist claims that as a history his work is to be seen as very much related to the real world.[8] The character of Allworthy, for example, is based upon no less than three living people, including Lord Lyttelton. That Fielding claims to base Allworthy on more than one person suggests his desire to depict in his character general human characteristics and not the specific traits of a single person. This kind of general realism functions "to recommend Goodness and Innocence," which is the author's "sincere Endeavor in this History" (p. 7).[9] But Fielding does not intend to fulfill this endeavor in a dry narrative style. Like the other novelists of the period, he is cognizant of the visual capacity of his fictional form:

> This honest Purpose...is likeliest to be attained in Books of this Kind; for an Example is a Kind of Picture, in which Virtue becomes, as it were an Object of Sight....(P. 7)

Fielding asserts not only the moral value of his book but the fact that his lesson will be taught through the reader's perception of the visual dimension of his work. Allworthy as a character will efficiently serve as an example because he will be a "picture" of the kind of man we ought to emulate. Fielding's characters may be typical in behavior and general in significance, but they are drawn with sufficient specificity in personality, action, and dialogue to evoke within our minds a series of mental pictures. They are visual illustrations of various moral points, even though the reader must penetrate their surface to understand them fully.

Fielding goes on to assert in his dedication that his plot will also illustrate the moral lesson of his work: "Besides displaying that Beauty of Virtue...I have attempted to engage a stronger Motive to Human Action in her Favour, by convincing Men, that their true Interest directs them to a Pursuit of her" (p. 8). He makes one further point in his dedication worth noting: "For these Purposes I have employed all the Wit and Humour of which I am Master in the following History; wherein I have endeavoured to laugh Mankind out of their Favourite

Follies and Vices" (p. 8). Our perceptions and understanding of the narrative must be directed by the "Wit and Humour" of the author—the visual images of the characters and actions will not suffice to convey the truth by themselves. The work is a history, but it is a comic history. The term "History" tells us about the kind of novel we will read, its relevance to our own reality; the author's statement about "Wit and Humour" tells us something about the literary techniques to be used and the narrator's perspective of his created world.

The same juxtaposition between history-as-reality and comedy-as-perspective is evident in the novel's table of contents. The title to Book I—"*Containing as much of the Birth of the Foundling as Is necessary or proper to acquaint the Reader with in the Beginning of this History*"— asserts that the work is a history, a narration of the hero's life, and that it will start right at the beginning with an account of his birth. The title also emphasizes, as does the full title of the novel itself, that the subject of the history is a foundling and not a prince or some such aristocratic figure. But there is also a touch of facetiousness here in the way the reader is told that he will receive only as much information as necessary; the comic tone and the easy yet manipulative relation between narrator and reader are thus immediately established. There is a touch of facetiousness also in the titles to the next two books, which introduce the sections dealing with Bridget's marriage and Tom's youth, but this quality is not evident in the remaining titles, which take on the sole function of giving us the temporal sequence of the events in each book. Indeed, all the book titles emphasize the historical nature of the work— much as does the dating of the letters in *Clarissa*—by giving the reader a detailed and realistic chronology of the narrative.[10]

The titles to Fielding's chapters are more frequently facetious and manipulative than the book titles. Throughout the work, there are headings which merely suggest the subject of the chapter, and, at the end of the novel, titles only seem to mark time until the work's conclusion. But especially in the first five books, and intermittently throughout much of the novel, chapter headings establish our attitude towards the subject which is about to be described, and keep us somewhat detached and amused through their comic tone. In other words, chapter titles often help manipulate our response to the mimetic material itself. Sometimes titles reflect on character in a straightforward way: "*A childish Incident in which, however, is seen a good-natured Disposition in Tom Jones*" (III, viii); in an oblique manner: "*A short Hint of what we can do in the Sublime, and a Description of Miss Sophia Western*" (IV, ii); and in an ironic way: "*The Character of Mrs. Western. Her great*

Learning and Knowledge of the World, and an Instance of the deep Penetration which she derived from those Advantages" (VI, ii). Sometimes titles will seem to say nothing in particular, while they are actually directing our attitude to the material: *"A little Chapter, in which is contained a little Incident"* (V, iv). This title, along with the following one—*"A very long Chapter, containing a very great Incident"*—suggest Fielding's method of juxtaposing and contrasting chapters for variety as well as development of theme; and the very next title—*"By comparing which with the former, the Reader may possibly correct some Abuse which he hath formerly been guilty of in the Application of the Word Love"*—forces an even more significant comparison of chapters in order to develop one of the narrator's points about human nature.[11] There are a number of titles stressing the basic theme or concept to be drawn from the chapter, reminding us that for all the fun to be derived from the scene, the author's intention is didactic, and the episode itself fits into a larger, all-encompassing moral vision. Character and incident, therefore, often seem to be illustrative, and the chapter can be seen as a dramatized essay manifesting the title's observation as well as the commentary of the narrator interjected in the episode itself. The introductory chapters to each book are, of course, essays, and as well as developing the narrator's ideas about novel writing, they discuss the various moral points to be drawn from his narrative. In this way, these opening chapters often function like the titles themselves, preparing us for what is to come and predisposing our responses to the material.

In many of the chapter titles, the narrator asserts his role as author, reminding us that we are to be led by him because he is creator of all that takes places—*"A Picture of formal Courtship in Miniature, as it always ought to be drawn, and a Scene of a tender Kind, painted at full Length"* (VI, vii)—and because he is also a wise and learned person, writing for the education of mankind—*"Containing infallible Nostrums for procuring universal Disesteem and Hatred"* (X, iv). From time to time, he reminds us of our role as reader, asserting our inferior position to his more sagacious and knowing self, relating us to the characters within the chapter, yet also putting us on the spot and making us cautious and wise in our judgments about what will take place—*"Containing such grave Matter, that the Reader cannot laugh once throughout the whole Chapter, unless peradventure he should laugh at the Author"* (I, vii).

Chapter divisions themselves, the way the action is broken into segments, function to contrast and juxtapose episodes while they also control the development of plot and hence the reader's involvement with and awareness of the characters and events.[12] Thus, the chapters also function organically throughout the work. I do not mean to belabor the point about these chapter titles and divisions, but we make a serious mistake if we dismiss them as conventional paraphernalia[13]—if we dismiss anything as conventional paraphernalia in this novel. Fielding is the first of our novelists to emphasize his work as created art and to exploit the nonmimetic elements of the novel form itself. And yet he does so without minimizing the seriousness of his created world, or its relationship to our own reality. Indeed, Fielding substitutes for the facade of authenticity we find in the novels of Defoe and Richardson a literary facade which actually functions to reinforce and develop our sense of the novel's reality while we read. He creates a carefully wrought literary framework, one composed of a dedication, introductory essays to each book, a prominent narrative voice, and book and chapter divisions and titles. This literary framework (1) guides and controls our perceptions and understanding of the created world; (2) acts as a buffer, keeping us from an intensely emotional or psychological involvement with the characters and fostering a more comic and cerebral response; (3) helps develop another level of reality, that of the narrator, who is himself part of the framework which he has created and who through it demonstrates his superior learning and perspective; and (4) brings, if not another reality to the work, at least another context and even another world, the artificial world of books and literary conventions which actually exists outside the novel and which here serves not only as a means of manipulating our responses but also as a contrast to the mimetic reality within the novel. In other words, the artificial world of literature contrasts with and underscores the reality of the characters and their world within *Tom Jones*.

LITERARY TRADITION

As well as reminding us that his work is art by creating a literary framework, Fielding also emphasizes this aspect of his novel by using traditional literary models and techniques to give us specific perspectives on the characters and action. Fielding's literary heritage has been noted in various ways by various scholars. It is not my intention to rehash or summarize old arguments but rather to discuss his literary background within my own context and show the way in which he uses these traditions in the new fiction. Fielding brings his literary background into a work that is unequivocally a novel; he imposes upon *Tom Jones* a vast array of traditional voices, echoes, and techniques to develop and highlight the realistic aspects of his mimetic material.

One of the pervasive literary voices we hear throughout the work is that of the Augustan essayist. This is evident not only in the introductory chapters to each book but in the very narration throughout much of the work. Fielding himself was an essayist,[14] and in his earlier essays we can already hear intimations of the narrative voice in *Tom Jones*. In general, there is a strong relationship between the narrative voice in *Tom Jones* (and these essays) and the voice used by such successful periodical writers as Addison and Steele. It is not an exaggeration to say that the novel's narrator speaks, thinks, and makes his points like an essayist, and that he has a personality with the same kind of intelligence, judgment, wit, and taste as the voice in the Augustan essay. Like these figures, Fielding's narrator is a repository of humanistic values, a depiction of the kind of man, with all his idiosyncracies, that the educated person admired.

In some ways our relationship with the narrator of *Tom Jones* substitutes for our relationship with the figures in the novel: we have as good a sense of his personality as of any within the fictional world, and, undoubtedly, a much more extensive view of the way in which his mind works and the way in which he perceives reality; we even soon begin to associate with his responses and judgments, to see the created world of his novel and our own world much as he does. Fielding's narrator is the kind of person we wish to be, and some of our enjoyment arises from flattering ourselves that we are in complicity with him, seeing and thinking as he does.

Instead of having a first-person narrator who gives credibility and authenticity to the story through his involvement in the action, we have, then, a distinct middle and transitional level of reality between the novel's fictional world and that of the reader—the world of the narrator himself. Often we find ourselves in this in-between world, where both our own and the novel's fictional realities face one another. We are suspended and held here by the narrator, aware of his voice, his values, his control, and his literary techniques; at times we watch him instead of the reality within his book. When he wishes to do so, he will guide our attention either way, most frequently to the world of *Tom Jones*, yet not infrequently to our own. But our vantage point spatially is often between: distanced to some degree from direct involvement with the characters and still aware of our own reality, we are frequently forced to compare the moralities of both worlds, but only to find the proper values with which to judge both these spheres in the narrator himself.

Although the Augustan essayist voice is strong throughout much of the work, it is only one of many styles which the narrator uses.[15] At the beginning of *Tom Jones*, the narrator is quick to assert his presence and acknowledge the various literary roles he will perform throughout the work. When we start reading the first chapter, we assume his role as novelist and await the appearance of his characters, but instead he first establishes his role as essayist: "[We] shall prefix not only a general Bill of Fare to our whole Entertainment, but shall likewise give the Reader particular Bills to every Course which is to be served up in this and the ensuing Volumes" (p. 25). The voice of the essayist will, of course, appear in more than the introductory chapters; it will appear throughout the work, interrupting with short commentaries whenever the writer sees fit. After the novel's plot has begun and we have met some of the major characters, the narrator often speaks to us as novelist, describing to us his created world and discussing with us his problems as a writer of fiction (p. 41); and, at other times, he is the historian, narrating to us the events in the life of Tom Jones from birth to fortune and emphasizing that "Truth distinguishes our Writings from those idle Romances which are filled with Monsters, the Productions, not of Nature, but of distempered Brains..." (p. 113). But the narrator also tells us that to make sure his work is not "likened to the Labours of ...[dull] Historians," he has "taken every Occasion of interspersing through the whole sundry Similes, Descriptions, and other kind of poetical Embellishments.... Without Interruptions of this Kind, the best Narrative of plain Matter of Fact must over-power every Reader..." (p. 114). Putting "Similes, Descriptions, and other kinds of poetic Embellishments" in a work already established for us as comic suggests that they will function satirically[16]—not that Sophia will be satirized in the description that follows the introductory essay to Book IV, but that this kind of writing will be satirized to show its insufficiency in describing the heroine. More often, however, it is the characters within the work who are the victims of the narrator's satiric voice.

But *Tom Jones* is a novel and not a satire; therefore, its general form and function cannot be related to any traditional satiric work or even type. Fielding uses satire as only one of his fictional perspectives, and he draws his satiric techniques from a variety of sources to make the perspective accurately and properly relate to the matter at hand. We shall refer to several of these satiric techniques—to Fielding's narration of farcical actions, his mock-heroic descriptions, and his comic characterizations, for example—when we discuss the more general influence of their individual sources on his work. Right now I want to continue my discussion of narrative voice by emphasizing the following points: the narrator's role as satirist is only one of several roles he assumes; the satiric voice itself, deriving from a number of literary traditions, is variable in tone and approach; and the satiric voice is primarily a means of provoking in the reader realistic assessments of mimetic material.

Within Fielding's narrative prose we can discover several traditional satiric strands. As well as the ironic and mildly satiric tones of the voice in Addison and Steele's essays, we also at times hear the somewhat more condemning and morally righteous Augustan voice in Dryden's political satires and Pope's *Moral Essays.* There is also on occasion the same authorial self-mockery that we hear in such comic romances as Cervantes's *Don Quixote* and Scarron's *Roman comique,* a self-mockery that at times even becomes the self-directed irony developed in Swift's satiric essays.[17] Nor should we fail to identify the mock-epic tones that we hear not only in the comic romance but also in the works of the Augustan poets. Each of these strands to some degree associates the object of Fielding's attack with the object attacked in the original literature, and each strand resonates with the moral values upheld in the earlier works. Fielding's satiric voice has an enormous flexibility and range that moves easily from the controlled irony and shrewdness of Sir Isaac Bickerstaff and Mr. Spectator to the outward invectiveness of Dryden's and Pope's speakers, from the charming self-deprecation of Cervantes's narrator to the more stringent, self-directed irony in Swift's narrative voices. In relation to this last point, I would add that the self-mockery and irony in Fielding's narrator is clearly a guise, an obvious pretense not only to show his own self-awareness and the strength of his ego but also to prod the reader into thinking for himself. Fielding's satire and irony, however, function primarily to undercut the characters within the fictional world and also the reader's insights into their behavior and his own values. His satiric voices are always controlled and morally directed. In their variety and variability they are a compendium of techniques from the great age of satire, and they help place Fielding's work in a larger cultural context than that of the novel.

The narrator, then, suggests to us at the start a number of literary roles that he will assume—novelist, essayist, historian, and satirist. He will use each role, with its own kind of style, to achieve a different response within the reader, to have him perceive the characters in a specific way, but the narrator will still appear to us as a composite whole, a very specific and definite person, one to be admired for, among other things, the dexterity of his literary manipulations and the learning which they manifest.

Fielding's literary sources are evident in more than his narrative voice. The discussion of *Joseph Andrews* as a "comic epic-poem in

prose" in the preface to that book, and the reference to *Tom Jones* as a
"prosai-comi-epic" in the text of that novel (p. 158), have evoked much
discussion, though the tendency in criticism has been to deny epic
influence on either work.[18] My own feeling is that *Tom Jones* derives a
considerable amount of its basic conception from the epic, that we are to
have in mind some of the great epic heroes when we read about Tom as
well as other epic qualities and techniques when we perceive certain
events. Fielding keeps reminding us of this relationship by his references
to or quotations from specific epics in the text of his work. The epic
analogies in the novel function sometimes as a contrast for both
thematic and comic purposes, but more often as a positive context. The
fact that the novel is composed of eighteen books suggests to us that it
has epic largeness. When we see that the work describes a journey, with
the hero progressing through a full and representative landscape of his
time, we are reminded of the classical journeys of Odysseus and Aeneas.
Indeed, the epigraph on the title page of the novel, "Mores hominem
multorum vidit," is Horace's paraphrase of the opening three lines of
the *Odyssey* in his *Ars Poetica* (11. 141–42).[19] Like the travels of Odysseus
and also Aeneas, Tom's journey takes him through a multitude of
adventures and introduces him to a myriad of places and characters. We
do not have here a reflection of the journeys of such comic-romance
figures as Don Quixote or Gil Blas, for Tom is closer in character to the
epic heroes, and his adventures take on a corresponding significance. He
is a great warrior, a passionate lover, and fundamentally he represents
the best qualities of his time. Tom's imprudence, gullibility, and
passionate nature are more than concessions to realism: they are flaws in
his nature which must be corrected so that he can become a true hero,
and they are flaws related to weaknesses in the epic heroes—Achilles'
pride and anger, Odysseus' imprudence with Polyphemus and the
Sirens, and Aeneas' sexual weakness for Dido. Like Odysseus and
Aeneas, Tom must learn wisdom by experience and suffering, but in this
respect he is closest to Virgil's hero, the way Fielding's values, as those of
his era, are closest to the values of the ancient Romans. The resemblances between Tom and Aeneas transcend sexual activity. Tom's
benevolence, his basic goodness, his healthy human nature, his
charitable sensibility, are the eighteenth-century equivalents to Aeneas'
piety, his loyalty to his country, his family, his gods. And, like Aeneas,
Tom must pass through a series of tribulations, must indulge the sexual
passions only to be cleansed of their excess, must travel from place to
place, must suffer and almost be brought to the brink of despair, must
finally perform a feat of arms in which he is triumphant, and must from

a low point be brought high once more. Tom's epic journey is clearly more related to that of the epic hero than it is to that of the picaro or the hero of the comic romance.

And the world through which Tom passes, realistic and everyday as it may be, is as vast and varied as the epic world, as fraught with challenges, adventures, and violence, and as populated with diverse characters. The epic dimension of the novel functions in more than a structural way: it allows the infusion of epic values, not only to elevate Tom but also at times to denigrate the host of real English types, as when Tom's virtues as an epic warrior make the fisticuffs of the innkeeper, his wife, and Betty seem all the more unseemly at the Upton inn; and when, in the same scene, mock-epic descriptions are used to describe directly and undercut the behavior of these comic figures. But for all its normality and even commonness, the world of *Tom Jones* is not divorced from the strange and supernatural events that occur in the epic. In his introductory chapter to Book VIII, Fielding attacks the use of the "Marvellous" in both the epic and modern writing, but what he succeeds in doing in his own novel is to rationalize and make comic the strange and supernatural. Tom himself appears as a ghost the night he stalks Northerton; the Man of the Hill, in his strange location and with his strange garb, appears at first as an unholy apparition; Partridge, who lives in constant fear of the supernatural, finally confronts the ghost of Hamlet's father in the playhouse. The world of *Tom Jones* also contains a supernatural power within it, one similarly unhuman, divine, and all-powerful as the deities in the epic. "Fortune" is used countless times by Fielding to explain the happenings of his novel; it is a supernatural agent that is felt in the lives of almost all the characters. This force in the novel, however, is more than an equivalent to the supernatural agents in the epic: as scholars have demonstrated, Fortune is for Fielding attributable to his Christian God, and a convenient way to communicate to the reader the ordering and harmonizing force within the Christian universe.[20]

But in spite of all this epic influence, Fielding lived in an age which could not take a straightforward epic. Eighteenth-century England might have admired this earlier literary form, but it no longer believed in great heroes or the possibility of a heroic world: it was an age of scepticism and reason, an age of reality and "truth." The epic had to be translated into the period's own terms and infused by the period's own spirit; it had to be freed from the limitations of its own genre and opened up by the form and techniques of the major eighteenth-century narrative, the novel. But in *Tom Jones* we can still see the submerged form of the epic giving an extra dimension to our perception of the hero and, in a comic way, to other characters as well, and bringing literary authority, a universality of theme, and a basic narrative structure to the novel.[21] At the same time, the moral values of the classical world and its literature reinforce and integrate with Fielding's own benevolent and Christian ethic. Unlike Dryden and Pope, who also employ epic analogies and techniques in their work, Fielding employs the old tradition less to humble his own period than to reinforce his literary work and give moral significance to his own world. Even behind the comic use of this technique is a fundamental belief in order and the correctibility of mankind.

Fielding's use of the epic is primarily serious because of his esteem for the genre and many of its values; yet *Tom Jones* is pervasively a comic work, and for this reason we also find comic-romance techniques in the novel. The argument for this influence on Fielding's first two novels has been made by Sheridan Baker,[22] and Homer Goldberg has written an entire book on *Joseph Andrews* as a comic romance.[23] Some of the influences of this earlier literature that Goldberg sees at work in Fielding's first novel are to some degree observable, I believe, in *Tom Jones*, and function much as his other literary borrowings. To begin with, *Tom Jones* has the same emphasis upon physical action, frequently of a violent nature—Molly's fight in the graveyard (pp. 135-37) and the battle in the Upton inn (pp. 379-83) are reminiscent of similar comic struggles in the pages of Cervantes and Scarron. Perhaps we can make a more sweeping statement and say that like the comic romance, *Tom Jones* has a number of scenes of a rambunctious nature, in which the depiction of character is almost always sacrificed to action, where the intention seems largely comic, where a mock-epic technique is at times used, and where the episode basically functions to debunk human pretense. Indeed, within such a scene as the fight at Upton, we hear the echoes of similar struggles in the works of Cervantes and Scarron, and we place the characters within the same context of human absurdity. Fielding's scenes are, however, more developed and skillfully drawn, his characters more realistically presented, and the individual episodes fit more logically and dramatically into the work's context. But in their kinds of action, emphasis, and even tone, they are still of a piece with similar episodes in the earlier fiction. In these scenes, we also see something true of Fielding's novel in general: he brings to his work for the development of his concepts of human nature a host of "low" figures—his servants, innkeepers, and soldiers, for example—that also fill the pages of the comic romance. The relationship between

Cervantes's Sancho Panza and Fielding's Partridge is obvious, but what must also be appreciated is the way in which the comic romance influenced Fielding in the scope and depth of his social world, allowing him to bring to his work, within its epic framework, a wider variety of character than had yet appeared in the novel.

The comic romance, of course, satirizes elements of the romance and sees this literary form as sometimes pretentious and silly, as an example of human delusions and vanity. In *Tom Jones*, the unrealistic romance is a perfect context for the reader to understand the sometimes silly, though amusing, behavior of Tom in his relationship with Sophia. But like Cervantes's and Scarron's works, Fielding's novel shows an occasional relationship to the serious romance which is not one of parody or comic intention.[24] Not only is this evident in some of Tom's heroic or chivalric actions, in the handsome appearances and larger-than-life virtues of Tom and Sophia, but one can hear in a number of the book's romantic passages the language of the romance.

In general, however, the comic romance seems to have influenced Fielding in a deeper and more pervasive sense: such works did not merely debunk the romance but used the material of these books to debunk human pretense and folly. Tom Jones is a modern epic hero and not a comic-romance protagonist, but like the major figures in Le Sage's *Gil Blas* and Marivaux's *Le Paisan parvenu*, he moves through a world of pretension and hypocrisy, where false values are exposed by a sudden confrontation with reality. Fielding's comic-romance techniques define and develop his characters for the reader; they deflate and expose people who are blind to virtue in others and who have conceded their own virtue behind masks of foolish and grotesque deceit.[25]

Fielding also employs comic elements and techniques from the drama to present his characters and guide our responses to them. Having worked so long in the theater, he could not turn to the new art form without bringing to it some of the skills he had learned as a playwright. Certainly his dramatic training had an impact on his plotting of the novel, but where the influence of the drama is most obvious is in the masterly presentation of comic figures through dialogue. The language of characters like Honour, Squire Western, Mrs. Western, and most of the innkeepers is the forceful, immediate, exaggerated, and highly amusing language of the theater, a language Fielding had developed in such characters as Puzzletext in *The Grub-Street Opera* (1731) and Squire Badger in *Don Quixote in England* (1734). Some of Fielding's best scenes in the novel are those where little is dramatized but in which we hear the distinct and powerful comic voices of these characters. Also significant about the dramatic dialogue is the way in which it focuses on particular works and mannerisms of speech which give the individual character a specific and yet illustrative nature. We are dealing here with a comic speech, developed in the theater and evident in Fielding's plays, that makes a number of his fictional characters into recognizable human types. Fielding's theatrical dialogue, then, functions for more than comic effect: it allows the reader to relate these figures to various types in the drama and understand them in a larger illustrative context, hence reinforcing the author's neoclassic view of his characters as representative types of human nature. Fielding's fictional form and his narrative techniques allow him to give many of these characters a complexity in their typical behavior and a universality beneath their stereotypic dialogue that he could not achieve with his comic dramatic figures. We can make the same general comments about the less comic voices of his upper-class characters in London, namely Lady Bellaston and Lord Fellamar, but their voices convey to the reader a more specific dramatic background and system of values. Fielding originally developed such characters in those of his own plays that resemble the earlier comedy of manners—for example, there are significant resemblances between Lady Bellaston and Mrs. Modern in *The Modern Husband* (1731), and between Lord Fellamar and Captain Spark in *The Universal Gallant* (1734). The dialogue of these London figures in the novel, as well as their general behavior, suggests to us the world of the comedy of manners with its pervasively decadent morality, and this in turn influences the way in which we see and judge these characters.

I have been trying to demonstrate not that Fielding's work is derivative and a pastiche of earlier traditions, but that he uses his literary background in a conscious and carefully wrought way. Fielding employs literary tradition as a rhetorical device, as a means of manipulating and guiding our responses to the characters and their actions, of allowing us to see them more clearly and, at times, to see with them, and of allowing us to perceive his point of view and come to his moral conclusions. His use of earlier literature relates him to the entire Augustan tradition, especially to poets like Dryden and Pope, who employed this technique in a less psychological and perceptional way but used it for similar moral and comic purposes.[26] There are other reasons for Fielding's use of literary tradition, more general reasons related to the nature of the new kind of fiction. First, Fielding's conscious use of various traditions functions in large part to show that he belongs to his age, that this new literary form which he pretends to be inventing is actually supported by the literature of his time as well as by that earlier literature which his age admires. Second, since the novel is a new form, without a traditional background to give it authority, Fielding's learning establishes for his narrator an authority in the novel and brings his contemporary reader to a point of acceptance not only because the narrator knows so much but also because he can write with such diversity. Third, Fielding in this new fiction seeks to reaffirm what is basic and universal in human nature and what values have best stood the test of time, and to do this he employs those literary traditions which also have stood the test of time and which have supported the same basic human values.

All of this literary tradition is used in neither a pedantic nor a deadly-serious way, but with subtlety, wit, or comic gaiety. For the reader, there is always a delight from watching Fielding's kaleidoscopic vision and the variety of his techniques. Fielding's vision is comic, and his multiple approaches help present his material in a comic light. His assortment of literary techniques, his variability and flexibility, his sudden shifts in style, and the different combinations of approach and subject matter create a work that is singularly alive and dynamic. All of this opens up the reader to a rapid series of impressions and insights, to a deepening awareness of human diversity and even complexity, and to a developing and more encompassing view of human nature.

IDENTITY IN THE NOVEL

Having established the cultural context for the narrator's self-conscious literary techniques, we must now do the same for his concept of character before we can proceed to a closer examination of the novel's text. We have already spoken of Fielding's neoclassic aim to have us see his figures as types and also as indicative of general human behavior—but this is hardly a new insight, nor does it allow us to see with any precision the nature of his characters and his method of characterization. We must place Fielding's characters in a larger cultural context, while seeing more accurately how they differ from figures we confront in works of other novelists. To do this we must again return to Locke, whose concept of human identity, in *An Essay Concerning Human Understanding*, gives us further insight into the new focus on character and methods of characterization in the novel in general and helps us to understand Fielding's different accomplishment.[27]

Consciousness, for Locke, is the center of personal identity, our way of knowing both that we are and who we are: "For since consciousness always accompanies thinking, and it is that that makes everyone to be what he calls *self*, and thereby distinguishes himself from all other thinking things: in this alone consists *personal identity*, i.e. the sameness of a rational being."[28] Fiction in the eighteenth century begins to work with this consciousness, this cause of personal identity, as the focus which orders all action and gives significance to what takes place in the external world. *Moll Flanders* is about the consciousness of the heroine, and that consciousness is the organizing principle of the whole work and at times the real dramatic center of the action. The same kind of focus is true of *Clarissa, Tristram Shandy, Humphry Clinker,* and the third-person narrative *Pride and Prejudice*—the point of view, chronology, and structure of these works are all related to the consciousness of characters. *Moll Flanders* and *Clarissa* are, in a sense, modern fictional histories because the consciousness of their heroines in time present is the unifying element of all the actions that fit into the sequential plot and have taken place in time past. In relation to this point about time past, the following statement by Locke is significant: "And as far as this consciousness can be extended backwards to any past action or thought, so far reaches the identity of that *person*."[29] A significant shift in the novel from earlier fiction is that the relationship and arrangement of past actions receive significance and meaning from the present consciousness of the "I"-narrator. It is the personal identities of the characters Moll and Clarissa that most intrigue us, that give their books a depth absent from earlier fiction, and that allow us to see their worlds with a perspective that is dramatized and hence involving for us.

I said before that the reliance on an "I"-narrator at times removes the reader from the dramatic immediacy of the described scene, of the consciousness of the character in the midst of the dramatized action, and that the novel would develop a third-person technique that would plunge the reader into the character's mind at the time of the central action. *Moll Flanders* and, especially, *Clarissa* create this consciousness during past actions, but not infrequently it is sacrificed to responses at the time of narration. The novel as a dramatic art form eventually follows the most dramatic path, but at this point in its development, emphasis is also given to the train of ideas in the character's mind after the major actions are completed.

Locke uses the term "train" when talking about personal identity to suggest our successive perceptions of past events, which can never be recalled at once: "there being no moment of our lives wherein we have the whole train of all our past actions before our eyes in one view."[30] At another point, he suggests that it is the continuity of the same consciousness, its capacity to absorb a sequence of perceptional experiences throughout a period of time without significantly changing, that creates identity:

> that this *self* has existed in a continued duration more than one instant, and therefore it is possible may exist, as it has done, months and years to come, without any certain bounds to be set to its duration; and may be the same *self* by the same consciousness, continued on for the future.... In all which account of *self*, the same numerical substance is not considered as making the same *self*, but the same continued consciousness....[31]

Tuveson cites Locke's statement that "*Self* is that conscious thinking thing ... which is sensible or conscious of pleasure and pain, capable of happiness or misery, and so is concerned for *itself*, as far as the consciousness extends"[32] to conclude that "the pivot of the self, therefore, is the awareness of easiness or uneasiness, a state of mind rather than a single ego or a self-contained essence."[33] He concludes from this line of reasoning that Locke "in effect transferred the clear identity from the ego to the separate ideas, the simple impressions."[34] The point here is a crucial one, especially in relation to the novel, and I want to make it again, but in a somewhat different way. Consciousness is the organizing mental force which unifies man's disparate perceptions, both past and present, into a unique sense of self—but these disparate perceptions are themselves the building blocks, the very source of identity. Indeed, we can say that self-identity is the individual's attempt to impose a controlling order on experiences and perceptions. Tuveson is actually saying that Locke, in attempting to define this order, also brings attention to the fragmentation and disorder that lie beneath it.

Tuveson might have cited David Hume to show how this implication in Locke's thinking was made explicit during the next century. Hume begins his discussion of personal identity in *A Treatise of Human Nature* by acknowledging that the subject "has become so great a question in philosophy, especially of late years in England," but he immediately places his own stamp on the subject by stating that "The identity, which we ascribe to the mind of man, is only a fictitious one."[35] Hume emphasizes that "every distinct perception, which enters into the composition of the mind, is a distinct existence, and is different and distinguishable, and separable from every other perception, either as temporary or successive." The question is whether identity is "something that really binds our several perceptions together or only associates their ideas in the imagination." Hume, of course, opts for the second explanation. To begin with, the individual "always preserves the memory of a considerable part of past perception," and it is the memory which frequently places together

> resembling perceptions: in the chain of thought, [and] convey[s] the imagination more easily from one link to another, and make[s] the whole seem like the continuance of one object.... the memory not only discovers the identity, but also contributes to its perceptions by producing the relation of resemblance among the perceptions.

But having established for us a "notion of causation" in our perceptions, memory then leaves us free to "extend the same chain of causes and consequently the identity of our persons beyond our memory.... For how few of our past actions are these, of which we have any memory?" Hume is clearly disagreeing with Locke, who limits identity to consciousness. Hume asks if an individual would "affirm because he has entirely forgot the incidents of these days, that the present self is not the same person with the self of that time ...?" For Hume, then, "memory does not so much *produce* as *discover* personal identity, by showing us the relation of cause and effect among our different perceptions...." Identity "depends on the relation of ideas, and these relations produce identity, by means of that easy transition they occasion."

In his discussion of identity, Hume suggests a principal means of characterization in the novel—the description of discrete perceptions both in the present but also in the past through the use of consciousness and memory. Hume denies the reality of identity, or, at least, its verifiability, and claims our notion of identity is the result of seeing a causal relationship in perceptions. What is significant here is that identity is not consciousness or memory itself, though these are necessary for it, nor is it anything complete or even real. It is a notion we have that originates from the flow of perceptions in our mind. *Moll Flanders* and *Clarissa* are each concerned with the struggle of a woman for self-identity, for an awareness of a definable sameness in herself that will give order and meaning to her life. In both novels, however, the attempt for order is dramatized through the character's confrontation with disorder, with her own disparate experiences and perceptions.

I cited before Tuveson's statement that Locke "in effect transferred the clear identity from the ego to the separate ideas, the simple impressions." Tuveson ties this observation in with "the phenomenon of modern thought which Joseph Wood Krutch has termed the 'dissolution of the ego,' wherein a 'fluid' replaces a 'hard core' individual personality."[36] At this point, like Tuveson, I must quote Krutch directly on the older kind of personality:

> The Christian, and to an almost equal extent the classic, conception of the 'persona' or the 'ego' seems to have been of a fully conscious unity, of a soul captain, born with us at birth and perhaps created by God. It is an ultimate continuous reality persisting through time.[37]

What I have been trying to establish through my use of Locke and Hume, and with the assistance of Tuveson and Krutch, are two clearly opposed concepts of personal identity that appeared in the eighteenth-century novel. The first was an older, more formal, less psychological, and, indeed, more moral perspective of personal identity, to which we can link the neoclassic concept of character. This was not a lesser way of depicting character but, rather, a different one that conformed to an older view of human nature. This view did not see individual consciousness as only tentatively definable through the apparent connection of individual perceptions; in other words, it did not emphasize the perceptions themselves, but saw people with relatively fixed egos, with stable, ordered, and definable self-identities that produced fixed and understandable personalities for others to perceive externally. Even with Fielding's knowledge of the complexity of human behavior, even with his refusal to see people as all good or bad, he basically puts forth in *Tom Jones* this view of personal identity. He makes us understand the difficulty in properly perceiving and judging people, and he makes us see that motivations are sometimes difficult to recognize, that people act from conflicting impulses. But he does this with characters who are basically fixed and even typical, who have nonshifting or nonchanging egos and personalities. Fielding sees many of his characters as acting with self-delusion and hypocrisy; he sees them as complicating their sense of themselves and certainly our sense of them in ways typical of both certain groups and human nature in general. To be a type is not necessarily to be simplistic: Fielding's characters are illustrative and typical in so far as they are representative of human confusion and hypocrisy. Fielding writes a novel about perceptions and puts forth a warning about judging hastily and over-righteously. But basically his concept of personal identity conforms to traditional thinking, and he is ready to portray his characters as definable because they have permanent and synchronic identities. The hero is the only character who is supposed to undergo a change—by the end of the novel Tom has matured and achieved prudence and wisdom.[38] But what we really have are two Toms, with little dramatization of a transition from one to the other. There is no single Tom defined for us in time, created through the flow of perceptions. Since his identity is not attached to these, he cannot appear to undergo any kind of significant change, and therefore he becomes, to use again Tuveson's words, two separate "ego[s]...[two] self-contained essence[s]."

Richardson focuses on his characters' sequence of perceptions. The personal identity of his character is established as an emerging pattern from a whole flow of internal reactions. Richardson is an example of a writer who, in his own mind, sums up his characters and morally judges them, but in writing his novels, he is true to his own instincts, and true to the intellectual currents of his time: his characters' identities are more complex, amorphous, difficult, and human than he would allow, since they are created through time and through an endless flow of external and internal experiences.

Fielding's characters are Christian and neoclassic—they are permanent and ultimately definable, and, sooner or later, they must be judged. It is this perspective, this demand to fix personal identity and make the individual morally responsible, that forces Fielding to stay mostly outside his characters and not get caught in the impermanence of the human psyche. Even when he describes their motivations and internal states, he does so in a clear and general way. It is this emphasis on the typical and definable that allows the reader to see and judge the characters as he does people in the world around him: the reader is able to reinforce the fictional characters from his own experience with human nature because he has the same limited access to them that he has to people in his own world, and hence must make the same kind of broad and permanent assessment of their egos and moral qualities that he makes of those individuals he confronts in his everyday life. As characters in fiction become more psychological and internal, as we are given more and more data, they become more difficult to sum up. The coherence and moral order of the older vision is gone.

The way to understand better this concept and depiction of character is to watch Fielding at work, to examine a few specific episodes where he creates and describes the people of his fictional world. Fielding's principal agent for having us see and understand his characters is narrative voice, and to comprehend the workings of this voice and the specific ways in which it creates character, we must begin with its language, the prose style with which it creates the world within the novel.

NARRATIVE VOICE AND CHARACTERIZATION

With all its manipulation of traditional voices and techniques, the narrative voice in *Tom Jones* still maintains a pervasive prose style that encompasses all the other styles. It is this prose which creates for us our sense of the narrator and the world to which he belongs. It also creates for us the world of the novel, while helping to impose upon it an order and meaning. Fielding's basic style is related to the standard literary language of his period, a language shaped by the best writers of the time. Such a language was the stylistic norm because it manifested, in its balance, order, and coherence, the values and self-definition of the period. Fielding's flexibility within this linguistic norm explains much of the work's uniqueness and complexity. The synthesis of personal and standard literary styles is also the foundation of the novel's extraordinary insights into human behavior within a context of traditional eighteenth-century attitudes and values.

Fielding's prose is much closer to that of Richardson than that of Defoe in its formal structure and in the way the various parts work together. It is also closer in that its structure and interplay of parts seem to convey something beyond the mere recording of fact. But within Fielding's prose there is a larger amount of flexibility than within Richardson's, and the narrator is able to convey even more levels of meaning and guide the reader's responses in more subtle and complex ways. Fielding, for the first time in the novel, creates style as a conscious and multipurpose technique. This is not the prose of earlier fiction writers like Lyly and Sidney, where style functions in and of itself, where it is largely divorced from the material it describes and functions mostly for display. Fielding's narrator may at times write in a way that seems mannered or even ostentatious, but the writing is always functional. Fielding is the first fictional stylist in the modern sense, using language consciously for a multitude of effects, some of them scarcely discernible. Jane Austen may be the direct descendant of Richardson in her psychological focus within a domestic and social context, but in matters of style she is the direct descendant of the author of *Tom Jones*.

Within each of Fielding's sentences, discrete units of factual information add to the total meaning while, at the same time, they interact with one another in such a way that their relationships juxtapose with the relationships of the units in other sentences. What is achieved here is a dynamic interplay between the units of each sentence and between the sentences themselves, all giving a larger meaning to the total passage than that acquired from the accumulation of factual information.

He now lived, for the most Part, retired in the Country, with one Sister, for whom he had a very tender Affection. This Lady was now somewhat past the Age of 30, an Era, at which, in the Opinion of the Malicious, the Title of Old Maid may, with no Impropriety, be assumed. She was of that Species of Women whom you commend rather for good Qualities than Beauty, and who are generally called by their own Sex, very good Sort of Women—as good a Sort of Woman, Madam, as you wish to know. Indeed, she was so far from regretting Want of Beauty, that she never mentioned that Perfection (if it can be called one) without Contempt; and would often thank God she was not as handsome as Miss such a one, whom perhaps Beauty had led into Errors, which she might have otherwise avoided.... (P. 28)

The first sentence is structured so that the parts interact in the following way:

He now lived... → with one Sister, ← for whom he had a very tender Affection.

The first part of the sentence tells us that Allworthy lives with someone; the middle part tells us with whom; and the last part tells us about his feelings for the person previously identified in the middle part. The second sentence seems more complex because the interplay of units has been reversed, and because the subject of the sentence is no longer the active agent but is rather the passive recipient of the action described. We can reduce the sentence and its meaning to the following basic structure:

This lady... ← in the Opinion of the Malicious... → [may assume the title] Old Maid....

The reversal of the sentence's movements and the secondary importance of the "Malicious," who are structurally juxtaposed to Allworthy, underscore the moral contrast between the group's "opinion" and Allworthy's "tender Affection" described in the previous sentence. The next sentence is even more complex. Here the lady, as a member of a specific species of women, is acted upon by her "own Sex," a group associated with "the Malicious" of the previous sentence because of their structural juxtaposition and because of the irony with which the narrator describes the group's laudatory sentiments. But the reader is also involved in a way that opens up and compounds the significance of the passage:

She was of that Species of Women ← whom you commend...and
← who are generally called by
their own Sex... →
as good a Sort of Woman, ← Madam, as you wish to know.

The general movement here is similar to that in the previous sentence, except now there are two parallel central clauses acting upon Bridget and her species, one of which involves the reader through its second-person pronoun; and the outward movement at the end of the sentence is suddenly reversed, with "Madam"—meaning both the "Sex" and the reader—acting back upon Bridget and her group. In the last sentence of the passage, the basic order is once more reversed, and instead of Bridget's being acted upon, she herself acts upon someone else, but in such a way that she is clearly linked to her malicious sex:

> [She] would often thank God she was not as handsome → as Miss such a one....

The passage describes Bridget the way others see her, ourselves included, through the way they see the general group to which she belongs, and also describes the way she sees others. We are given not merely a sense of the character but a sense of the world to which she belongs and our own relation to that world. We also receive a sense of human nature in action, that human nature about which the narrator says he is writing his book, conveyed structurally and rhythmically by the writing in the passage. The moral intention of the passage is clear, and clear also is human nature, hardly at its best, in its reactions and interactions.

Allworthy's "tender Affection" for Bridget is from the start of the passage a positive emotion against which the other human responses are measured. The passage moves from his feelings for his sister to the hypocritical and really vindictive "Opinion of the Malicious" concerning the unmarried state of women like Bridget, and then brings together the concepts of tender affection and hypocrisy by stating the apparently benevolent decision of her "own Sex" that Bridget and her type are "good Sort of Women." Such a compliment is, of course, rather suspect, especially since it is given because of the type's want of beauty.

This kind of undercutting which makes suspect the sex's affection for Bridget is one of Fielding's obvious forms of irony. But there is another kind of irony in the very same sentence, one directed outwards towards the reader: it is not merely her "own Sex" that calls females like Bridget "good Sort of Women," but the reader as well. The narrator draws us into the action by his use of second-person pronouns; and when he imitates the voice of a complimenting female, "as good a Sort of Woman, Madam, as you wish to know," he intensifies our involvement by again seeming to address us. We can distinguish these two types of irony throughout the book and ought to call them *inner-directed irony* (toward a character or general group within the novel) and *outer-directed irony* (toward the reader). These types of irony often appear together, as in the above passage, and this concurrence forces the reader into an apparent complicity of values with the subject of attack within the fictional world. This is one of the ways in which Fielding removes the curtain that separates the world of his reader from that of his characters. Fielding's intention is always moral, and the connection between these ironies relates the reader to Fielding's world and forces him to examine the morality of the characters or general groups and compare it with his own. We frequently discover that we possess some of the values of these characters or groups, though not, of course, to such a degree. Sometimes, as we shall later see, Fielding even strips away the stereotypic behavior of his type characters and exposes some basic behavioral patterns that we all share. The complicity of values in both cases fosters some identification for the reader, though not of an extensive or prolonged nature. The involvement we undergo is far more moral and judgmental,[39] and it largely substitutes for the emotional and psychological identification we normally have with the characters of other novels.

The language of this passage gives us further insights into the kind of fictional experience that Fielding creates for the reader. The emphasis is more on a series of general groups or types than on specific characters—"the Malicious," "Species of Woman," "their own Sex," "good Sort of Women," and even "Miss such a one." The movement of the passage takes us from the individuals Allworthy and his sister, to "the Malicious," to Bridget's "Species of Women," to the general reader, and finally to Bridget's "own Sex." Bridget's attitudes are themselves tied in with those of her social world and the reader's world. What is true of characterization in this passage is true throughout the novel: substituted for individual psychology is a more general or universal psychology. Even in the more detailed and visualized scenes that appear later, the truth of characters' behavior is not established by dramatic immediacy. Fielding wants us to see his characters and understand them as we do people in our own world, from the same external and general view, and he wants us then to see ourselves as others must see us, but he wants us finally to recognize how we and the people around us act in common in social and moral ways.

The narrator earlier tells us that his subject will be "HUMAN NATURE" (p. 26). Human nature is general and universal—it is natural to all human beings. The word "NATURE" also suggests a universal order, and within that order certain laws or principles.[40] Yet the world is vast and large, and "in *Human Nature*, 'tho here collected under one general Name, is . . . prodigious variety . . ." (p. 26). The variety, though, is not unlimited and does not allow for idiosyncracy—Fielding means that within human nature are groups of specific types, each group acting according to its own inherent laws. We can distinguish types of human beings and make moral judgments on each group according to social behavior. In the passage we have been analyzing, "the Malicious," a general group, acts immorally within a social context because its members are all motivated by envy and hypocrisy; and since she socially acts in a similar way, we must finally see that Bridget also belongs to this group. Social relationships are primary, since Fielding's novel, written from a Christian and neoclassic point of view, is about man's relationship to man; and social interactions, to an important degree, define the individual character and his group. At the beginning of the passage, Allworthy is presented through his social relationship with his sister, through his "tender Affection" for her. Although he is not made part of a larger group in this passage, he is kept general, and throughout the book his kind of behavior is seen as representative of a definite moral class of people.

Status and situation often influence one's social interactions and hence moral behavior. A particular kind of social behavior characterizes the lower-class characters, especially the servants and innkeepers. Black George is a character forced to act as he does because of his social and economic position. In such cases we find it difficult to make moral judgments, though judgments must still be made. Black George's action when he keeps Tom's £500 is understandable because of his circumstances, and hence it is almost difficult to condemn him. Fielding's portrayal of Black George is masterful because it is complex, and when we judge him, we must do so with the realization of the interaction of status, economics, and moral behavior. In general, the upper-class characters' interaction with others is influenced by their social position and economic situation. Freed from want, their lives empty of meaningful activity, they indulge in satiating their appetites and whims. On the other hand, Allworthy's social interactions are also motivated by his status, but in a positive way. The narrator tells us that Allworthy was "the Favourite of both Nature and Fortune; for both of these seem to have contended which should bless and enrich him most" (p. 27). The point is that Allworthy allows his income to free him from the vices that arise from poverty or aristocratic boredom: his money allows him to act according to a basic, decent, and humane nature within him that is available to everyone. It is this nature which is truly human and truly universal: it exists beneath the general characteristics that typify each group. As Fielding later says, without professional (and, we may add, social and economic) pressures, this basic, benevolent nature would be manifest in all people:

> Habit, it is true, lessens the Horror of those Actions which the Profession makes necessary, and consequently habitual; but in all other Instances, Nature works in Men of all Professions alike.... an Attorney may feel all the Miseries and Distresses of his Fellow Creatures, provided he happens not to be concerned against them. (P. 505)

Fielding measures the moral worth of his characters according to their proximity to or divergence from this basic human nature, which further generalizes his characters and their acts.

The passage we are examining makes clear Allworthy's function throughout much of the book. He functions as a paragon, as an example of human nature acting in a benevolent way, but by feeling an affection that is "tender," that is positive and humane, that orders his relationship with his sister, he also indicates an order in the universe.[41] After Allworthy, we have "the Malicious," the reader, the female sex, and Bridget herself as manifestations of a less benevolent human nature. The interplay back and forth, the somewhat complex and circuitous development of relationships, contrast against the direct and orderly relationship of Allworthy to Bridget—just as throughout the book there exists a sense of order through the presence of Tom, Allworthy, and the narrator, all of whom embody and manifest this excellent human nature, and against whom all the perversions of human nature stand in contrast.

In his dedication, Fielding underscores "that solid inward Comfort of Mind, which is the sure Companion of Innocence and Virtue" (p. 8). In the passage we are studying, as throughout the novel, Allworthy is an example of "Innocence and Virtue"—he does commit errors, but these are errors from misjudgment, not from vice or folly—and of all the characters in the book, he is an example of equanimity of spirit achieved by virtue of intention. Immorality in the book, depicted in terms of social interaction, arises from envy and selfishness, which represent the two greatest threats to Fielding's benevolent and Christian vision of the interrelationship of all men. Compounding the problem is the fact that characters hide their envy and selfishness from others, and even from themselves, through hypocrisy: by pretending to be someone they are not and to act from motives different from those which actually motivate them. It is the hypocrisy which actually makes the book comic. In his preface to *Joseph Andrews*, Fielding states that "the only source of the true Ridiculous...is affection... [which] proceeds from ...vanity or hypocrisy...." He also states that when affectation proceeds from hypocrisy, it is "nearly allied to deceit"—the individual "is the very reverse of what he would *seem* to be."[42] Envy and selfishness are not in themselves comic, but hypocrisy is. The comic element in *Tom Jones* seems largely derived from the facade and affectations which characters assume before others and the delusions with which they fool themselves. At the same time, it is hypocrisy which complicates human nature and explains Fielding's concern with perception. In this passage, Bridget hides her envy for "Miss such a one" and others like her behind her pretense to virtue and her condemnation of such people, a ruse of which Bridget herself is unaware, since she is busy deceiving herself as well as others. We must add at this point that when characters falsely perceive themselves, they are incapable of properly perceiving others; and that when they falsely perceive others, they are incapable of understanding, sympathizing with, and acting for them.[43] This confusion in characters' assessments of themselves and the false facades they put on before others is in part responsible for their complexity— and, indeed, life—but it is a complexity that is fixed, indicative of a class or group, and finally identifiable.

Though Bridget's character is not dramatized in the passage we have been discussing, her hypocrisy and self-delusion are suggested by the language of the narrator's description; in fact, the description itself subtly suggests the voice of Bridget Allworthy exposing her own characteristics: "Indeed, she was so far from regretting Want of Beauty, that she never mentioned that Perfection (if it can be called one) without Contempt; and would often thank God she was not as handsome as Miss such a one. . . . " The following passage continues the development of Bridget's character through the narrator's ironic description, where he first blends his own style with her voice and then enlarges his analysis into a generalization on women:

> Miss *Bridget Allworthy* (for that was the Name of this Lady) very rightly conceived the Charms of Person in a Woman to be no better than Snares for herself, as well as for others; and yet so discreet was she in her Conduct, that her Prudence was as much on the Guard, as if she had all the Snares to apprehend which were ever laid for her whole Sex. Indeed, I have observed (tho' it may seem unaccountable to the Reader) that this Guard of Prudence, like the Trained Bands, is always readiest to go on Duty where there is the least Danger. It often basely and cowardly deserts those Paragons for whom the Men are all wishing, sighing, dying, and spreading every Net in their Power; and constantly attends at the Heels of that Higher Order of Women for whom the other Sex have a more distant and awful Respect, and whom (from Despair, I suppose, of Success) they never venture to attack. (P. 28)

The narrator finally mentions Bridget's name, almost as an afterthought—as if her individuality is not as important as her type of character, as if we should be more interested in what she represents than who she is. Also notice how "very rightly conceived" is a statement by the narrator which not only affirms his own ironic position to what he is describing but which also reaffirms Bridget's self-righteousness. There is, of course, another ironic level here, one that even further emphasizes her hypocrisy, self-deception, and false appearance; it is an ironic level that can be known only when we reach the last part of the book and discover that Tom is the product of her hidden and unsanctified love affair.[44] What the narrator says about Bridget during the first part of the novel seems thematically relevant to the larger context of the work, and we are willing to believe that she is an old-maid figure—jealous, censorious, and condescending to others. In a few pages these qualities are complemented by her religious hypocrisy and overdeveloped sense of decorum in her courtship with Captain Blifil. But, on the other hand, Fielding's world is one of such pretense and false appearance, of such duplicity and double-dealing, that nothing should surprise us, not even the passionate nature and secret love affair of Bridget Allworthy— indeed, Fielding has already laid the groundwork for Bridget's later exposure by emphasizing her hypocrisy and even suggesting her repressed sexual nature. This is Fielding's method of what I call *indirect characterization*, a technique which he uses for a number of characters in the book. *Indirect characterization* develops the vain, selfish, and confused inner world of characters beyond the immediate and direct portrait by employing a number of ironic perspectives: the language and styles of narrative voice,[45] implication and suggestion, and the larger context of plot. We see once more that Fielding achieves a complex perspective of character through a number of strategies, and that, as a result, our responses to his characters, unchanging and typical as these figures may be, are at times as complex as those we have for characters in other novels. But they are responses of a different kind and involve a higher level of awareness and discernment.

Let us complete our examination of the way the narrative voice creates for us an awareness of character in this passage. In the first sentence, "Charms" that are "Snares" are counterbalanced against "discreet" and "Prudence." The entire passage is built around the narrator's judicious juxtaposition of Bridget, and all prudent women, with females possessing "Charms of Person." The passage moves to an essayist's generalization, typing Bridget and further diminishing her immediate presence. It then synthesizes military and courtship similes, generalizing even more the subject of the passage and ridiculing the behavior of all old maids and unattractive women. By this time Bridget is gone from us, and we have, within the narrator's comic perspective, a depiction of a typical social and moral group. What the narrator says about this kind of woman seems true because he seems so intelligent, witty, and hence reliable in his judgment; at the same time, what he says about this type is true according to our own experience: "tho' it may seem unaccountable to the Reader" is an ironic statement and emphasizes that the observation is very accountable to us. In the last part of the passage, the language is kept especially comic and exaggerated with men "wishing, sighing, and dying," and with attractive women seen as "Paragons" and unattractive ones as a "higher Order of Women." The passage is given a comic metaphoric action when Prudence goes on guard and follows at the heels of those who least need her. As in the previous passage, the narrator juxtaposes various groups, and it is the shifting focus of the various relationships that gives the writing a sense of vitality and action. There is a double juxtaposition at first with unattractive women contrasted to attractive ones, and Prudence found similar to Trained Bands; then, further on in the passage, "the other Sex" is contrasted to the Trained Band; and, finally, Prudence is paired with the unattractive group of women, while the male sex is paired with the attractive. The last sentence, which tells us that men stay away from unattractive women "from Despair...of Success," deflates both the pretensions and the false behavior of these females (it is only they who believe that men stay away from them for this reason). Throughout the entire passage, then, it is the narrator's shifting and ironic perspective, manipulation of focus, and flexibility of voice which develop for us a sense of complexity and even drama in the behavior and motivations of characters and the groups to which they belong. So firmly does the narrator have us in his grip that he is free to lead us in any direction that he chooses. The force of the characters does not seem inherent within them, they are not given immediate and dramatic life on the page, nor do they even seem to exist in their own right. And yet it never matters to us. Against every expectation of novel reading, we find ourselves less concerned with being involved *in* the characters than in hearing *about* them from the narrator, in listening to him as he analyzes them and generalizes about them; in watching him peel their outer layers and expose their inner cores; and in feeling ourselves drawn into sharing his perceptions and judgments.

SCENIC TECHNIQUE

Although the type of narration we have been examining in the first part of the book suggests to us much about the narrative technique in the remainder of the work as well, a significant change takes place once we have a sufficient amount of background material, and once Tom grows to manhood and is ready for his adventures: scenes now become more distinct and individually drawn, with a greater amount of description and dramatization. This may be a novel about human nature, about why people act the way they do and how we must perceive them properly— but human nature must ultimately be judged in terms of conduct, the way people act toward one another. To care about the characters, we must see them relating; to care about what happens, we must see it happen; to understand Fielding's world, we must see it portrayed with some specificity. At the same time, Tom and Sophia are basically creatures of action; not internally complex, they display their true nature through what they do, and to perceive them properly we must see them functioning in their world. Allworthy's speech to Captain Blifil (p. 72) outlines a philosophy of good deeds as well as faith, and the novel must show these deeds as they are performed especially by the hero, because for Fielding the ultimate test of a man is in his action, and Tom must be tested in the larger world. Because of this new concern with external action, a larger part of Fielding's humor will now be derived from comic characters of less duplicity, figures whose moral confusions are less internal and dangerous and more external and comic.

What I want to discuss now is how Fielding's scenic technique develops the concept of character, reader involvement, and basic themes I have already discussed in relation to the first part of the work. Again it is the narrative voice, with its developed persona, flexibility in technique, and variation in style, that is responsible for Fielding's achievement. We have more fully dramatized scenes from this point on, but they are still within the context and control of this voice and therefore within the same continuous rhythms of the work. The narrative voice both shows us and guides us: it creates for us a sense of the character's complexity, establishes the comic perspective, controls our involvement, and provokes our moral responses. To see how this works, to see how the book continues the kind of aesthetic experience I have already discussed, I want to outline a series of basic techniques that Fielding uses within these scenes. All of these techniques explain why we never achieve from Fielding's scenes the emotional and psychological involvement we do from Richardson's—but they also explain the comic achievement of Fielding's scenes and our complex reaction to them.

(1) *Asides.* I have already spoken of the interjection of narrative commentary throughout the work. Even in his dramatic scenes where the focus is on character and action, the narrator is always present with

his observations, keeping us somewhat distanced from the material and thinking along certain lines. These asides also function to remind us that it is his own sensibility, his psychology, which is the real focus of the work and the one toward which we ought to be moving. Sometimes we can see the novel's scenes as illustrations of the commentary on human nature developed by the essayist-narrator in these asides and in his introductory chapters. But these asides are never overbearing or even long enough to destroy the dramatic credibility of the action and lessen our interest in Tom and his world. If anything, it is the insight and humor of these asides that often highlight the action, that give it another dimension and increase our interest. For example, when Blifil misdirects his uncle about Sophia's feelings for him without telling an outright lie, the narrator follows with a brief aside on the culpability of those who deceive by "Equivocation and Imposture" (p. 264). The interjection here is not long, nor does it take our eyes off Blifil. We rather see him in a true and more significant moral perspective. Sometimes these asides, while still linking the characters with general human nature, seem to function more as a *jeu d'esprit*, a momentary burst of comic humor that influences our subsequent reading and general attitude towards the narrator and his creations. When the narrator describes Western's violent reactions to Tom upon discovering the hero's relationship with his daughter and then writes a brief discourse on one of the Squire's choice epithets, that the hero "salute that Part [of his anatomy] which is generally introduced into all [such] Controversies" (p. 231), nothing very much has been added to our knowledge of any of the characters, but we are prevented from becoming maudlin about Tom and his difficulties and prepared to continue in a lighthearted way, very much committed to a narrator who can make such humorous and irreverent interjections.

(2) *Irony*. My concern here with this multifaceted and much-discussed technique is only how it contributes to the complex effects of many of the novel's scenes. By seeming to say one thing while meaning another about his characters, and thus undercutting the validity of their assumptions about themselves, the narrator distances us from these figures and forces us into an intellectual act of reinterpretation and judgment. The technique is for both satirization and characterization: it helps establish a context of values, though none expressed directly, within which we judge these figures. Such irony is used in the descriptions of character, as when the narrator tells us about Mrs. Western's accomplishment and learning (pp. 207-8) right before we see her in a scene with her brother. In the scene itself, such verbal refrains by

the woman as "I will disclaim all Knowledge of the World if it is not so; and, I believe, Brother, you will allow I have some" (p. 209) also function ironically and have the character undercut herself in the midst of her own discourse. Ironic descriptions of action permeate the book and make us see what the characters do in a truer light than their own rationalizations would allow. Extreme use of irony in narrating action results in the mock-epic descriptions of Molly's fight after church and the battle at Upton. Even Tom's thinking and behavior receive some ironic treatment, as when he leads the bare-breasted Mrs. Waters to the inn at Upton (p. 378). But here, as throughout the book with Tom, the irony functions in a good-humored and comic way to allow us to see the character's very human failings and to respond to him with forgiveness and even affection. What the irony achieves for us in this case is a feeling *for* the character, not a shared experience *with* him, and a position of intellectual superiority free of moral condemnation.

(3) *Similes.* We could have discussed similes as part of the narrator's use of traditional literary voices, except that they deserve a special prominence because of the consistency with which Fielding uses them and the effect they have within his scenes. Fielding's similes are a mock-epic technique and often bear his own special stamp, though a number of them show his familiarity with their serious prototypes in the epic.[46] Fielding does not so much poke fun at such similes in epic writing as use them to develop his own fictional world. Sometimes he uses the artificiality of this kind of description to contrast with, and hence emphasize the reality of, his own world. He also draws upon other artificial literary sources for his similes, as when he describes the pastoral lovers Strephon and Phyllis, caught in a thunderstorm, to show us Sophia's reaction to her father's tirade (p. 229). Interestingly, this simile is coupled with a realistic one, of two gentlemen at an inn in Salisbury being frightened by the feigned madness of a person named Dowdy.[47] Fielding employs these realistic similes in part as a humorous debunking of such similes in general, but more so to extend the reality of his created world. The hardheartedness of a bailiff to his prisoners makes us realize the unfeeling behavior of Mrs. Western to her niece and the seriousness of Sophia's position in an immediate and brief way (p. 253). The artificiality of the device and its emphasis upon narrative voice also keeps the reader at a distanced perspective, sufficiently removed from the heroine and more concerned with the larger issues of human behavior implied in the scene. Fielding fashioned these realistic similes into a unique and often effective technique for creating his reality in an unrealistic way that was to emphasize the narrator's role as writer and

make the reader aware of the whole problem of perspective. Fielding's similes often evoke a sudden juxtaposition of two discrete and seemingly different situations, one in the book and the other outside, which force us to see unexpected similarities and unity in human experience.

(4) *Generalizations about human nature.* I have already talked about this technique in other contexts and now shall point out only how these generalizations permeate even those scenes which describe the specific acts of individual figures. Most often they are in asides or even brief essays suggested by the behavior of an individual character. Squire Western, for example, takes on another dimension when we are told that he is like many other justices of the peace in not always being attentive to the law, especially when it comes to his own concerns (p. 272). A few pages later, the narrator makes him part of a whole species of parents who love their children and yet manage to torment them (p. 274). We should also note that the universality of such behavior is further developed when, shortly after, Tom meets a Quaker who turns out to be another such father, and when, later on in the book, he confronts Nightingale's tyrannical parent. These generalizations help us to see the characters in a larger context, help us to believe in their credibility, and extend their reality into our own world and our reality into theirs.

(5) *Descriptions of character.* This is another of Fielding's techniques that helps create his fictional world for us while controlling dramatic immediacy and the reader's involvement. The dramatic action of the novel stops dead as we hear the voice of the narrator giving us an in-depth portrait of the person who appears before our eyes, describing his background, past behavior, or general characteristics. Blifil's courtship of Sophia is brought to a sudden halt when the narrator informs us about the character's attitudes towards the heroine and also gives us an extended view of his personality—his "hatred and scorn" of the woman, his appetite for her, his venality, and his hypocrisy (pp. 262-63). Though this kind of study increases our understanding and perception of the character's behavior in the remainder of the scene and in subsequent ones, at such points it reminds us that the focus of the novel is on human nature, and that there is more to understand about people than meets the eye. The long description of the Lieutenant (pp. 282-83), right before the violent dinner the hero shares with the soldiers, prepares us for his future conduct, but, at the same time, it gives us insights into his character beyond what is possible from the scene alone. The Lieutenant is also made representative of a large group of exploited officers in an army run by favoritism, bribery, and corruption: Fielding's novel opens out as the character takes on

significance beyond the immediate scene. Note how smaller character studies, in the midst of a scene, take us away from the immediate action but continue Fielding's panoramic study of human nature. Much of the book's humor and insight into people comes from these sudden bursts of illumination. The Parson, having successfully persuaded Tom to leave the presence of a furious Squire Western, feels pleasure from his role as a peacemaker and eloquently lectures the Squire against anger (pp. 231-32). Western drinks a tankard of beer and ends the Parson's efforts with some vehement language. The narrator then gives us a brief but telling study of the Parson and his dependent relationship with Western. The action in the novel has ceased—indeed, our focus is no longer on the major characters but on a subsidiary figure. Yet the description seems so accurate and amusing that we hardly feel a loss, nor do we feel misdirected. Parson Supple belongs to Fielding's larger gallery of characters: he operates by similar rules and with the same self-deception.

(6) *Illustrative characters and dialogue.* I have already suggested the influence of the drama on Fielding's illustrative characters and their dialogue. Such figures add to the comic vision and verve of the book through their wonderfully funny speech, but they also appeal to a reality beyond that of the scene. A number of scenes are composed mostly of dialogue, with little description of action or even the manner in which characters speak, but Fielding creates his figures through language and idiom as no previous writer of prose fiction, and often in a way that seems immediately to expose their basic nature to us. He is able to depict figures who are hopelessly vain and muddled because of professional pretensions, who lose their humanity to the pose of doctor or lawyer:

> 'In Danger! ay, surely,' cries the Doctor, 'who is there among us, who in the most perfect Health, can be said not to be in Danger? Can a Man, therefore, with so bad a Wound as this be said to be out of Danger? All I can say at present is, that it is well I was called as I was, and perhaps it would have been better if I had been called sooner ... !' (P. 290)

In such instances, there is no problem about perceiving the characters correctly. Through dialogue that seems typical of class, profession, or moral type, characters continuously expose their vanity, selfishness, and hypocrisy; they are always setting themselves up only to pull the rug from beneath their own feet.

But there are other figures in the book who, though distinct and typical in their speech, are treated at greater length and become illustrative of more complex states of mind and motivations. Here we have voices that convey the characteristics of certain kinds of people but at the same time give indications of the complexity of these types and of human nature in general. Squire Western is the Jacobite gentry in all its bumbling ineffectiveness and with all its dedication to country pleasures, but he is also a tyrannical and doting father, a harassed and opportunistic brother, and a warmhearted and selfish friend. Like other characters in the book, Squire Western ultimately transcends the narrow confines of his type to achieve the limitations and contradictions of the species in general, but all this is still accomplished through a distinct Somersetshire dialect and a very specialized kind of speech that immediately places the character in a particular social and moral group.

(7) *Analyses of motives.* We have already established Fielding's great concern with motivation—why his characters behave and interact the way they do—and the burden he frequently places upon the reader to understand and properly judge motives. So intense is his involvement with this problem that at times he halts the movement of his episode for a close analysis of motive, or on occasion even gives over an entire scene to such an investigation. Fielding develops this concern with motives— a concern which was instrumental in creating the new kind of fiction and its realistic techniques—in nonrealistic ways. In presenting such analyses, he is generally more of an essayist than a novelist, giving us point by point the rationalizations of his characters, building up the argument and final conclusion behind their action. To dramatize realistically the character's feelings and inner turmoil, his emotional responses to events and internal groping for meaning, would be to give us a vivid picture and convey to us the myriad thoughts and feelings that make up the inner world, but it would not afford us an insight into human nature and the inevitable way people move themselves to action. Fielding believed that the mind, with all its complexity, could be understood, that it had its own kind of logic and permanence, that we could be made to see why people act the way they do, even when they do not behave in the obvious and recognizable ways of his less complicated illustrative characters. To see clearly, to see the basic working of the character's mind, we must strip away verisimilitude, details, minute movements and vacillations; we must get to the real operating force, the distinct progression of ideas that leads to an action. Tom's process of thought leading to his altruistic departure from Sophia (pp. 238-39) is an example of Fielding describing his character's inner drama in a nonrealistic but analytical way. Emotions are controlled and even reduced to such generalized terms as those in the following passage: "thus Honour at last, backed with Despair, with Gratitude to his Benefactor, and with real Love to his Mistress, got the better of burning Desire, and he resolved rather to quit *Sophia* than pursue her to her Ruin."

In the context of the entire passage, this kind of description is adequate in allowing us to see clearly how and why Tom comes to his decision, though it certainly is neither immediate nor dramatic.

Black George's internal struggle as to whether or not to steal the sixteen guineas Sophia intends for Tom (p. 244) is the best and certainly the most amusing example of this kind of nonmimetic yet realistic analysis of motivation. George takes pride in avoiding the crime, even though he does not reach his decision from honorable motives. Throughout much of the book, self-deception for Fielding is a situation that calls for comic treatment, especially when it is not ultimately dangerous to the fate of the hero. The struggle of base greed to overcome moral compunction is made especially comic by being raised to the level of a dignified courtroom argument, where language and tone are far above the intellectual capacity of the character. There is no question about the validity of such a dilemma for Black George; the reasons for and against the theft are those which he would be likely to feel, though in a more confused and emotional way. Yet the elevation of the argument, the contrasts of its style to the normal speech of the character and its methodical reasoning to his limited power of thought, suggest the speciousness of both his logic and the pride he finally feels from his moral decision. Fielding achieves a brilliant realism from the propriety of the ironic style and comic language for the subject matter at hand, a style and language which allow the narrator to suggest and penetrate through the delusions and self-deceptions of his character. The description of Black George's struggle is not realistic because the character's motivations are finally not real to himself. Yet the narrator finds sufficient stylistic and linguistic correlatives to capture the inner moral qualities of the character and to make his internal world alive: here is a dramatic legal battlefield on which is played out, in a heightened and comic way, the internal process which leads Black George to a specific action. Fielding substitutes his heightened and comic presentation for an accurate dramatization of emotions and inner conflict, but he does so to make us perceive his character clearly and in depth. Black George stands out before our eyes, exposed, vulnerable, confused, and terribly funny. Both his individual characteristics and those qualities which limit him to a specific group are still evident, but the narrator emphasizes those qualities within him that make so much of our species sinful, but comic and forgiveable.

(8) *Authorial ignorance.* Throughout *Tom Jones*, the narrator is fond of suddenly throwing up his hands and confessing ignorance about the motivations of the characters. Such a technique pretends that the

characters are not merely creations of the writer but have a life of their own to which he is only partly privy—he is the historian, and he can record only what he is allowed to see and surmise. Indeed, if we are to understand the characters fully, then we must do so by applying what we know of human nature in the world outside the book, for that is the world to which the characters are supposed to belong:

> Instances of this Behavior in Parents are so common, that the Reader, I doubt not, will be very little astonish'd at the whole Conduct of Mr. *Western*. If he should, I own I am not able to account for it; since that he loved his Daughter most tenderly, is, I think, beyond Dispute. So indeed have many others, who have rendered their Children most completely miserable by the same Conduct; which, tho' it is almost universal in Parents, hath always appeared to me to be the most unaccountable of all the Absurdities, which ever entered into the Brain of *that strange prodigious Creature Man*.[48] (P. 274)

Of course, we realize that the narrator knows why his characters act the way they do—with all his pretense as historian, he is still the novelist who has created them—but a function of these passages is to suggest a complexity to his characters, and to human nature in general, without having to give us a detailed analysis. More than this, he puts the burden of understanding right on the reader's shoulders, asking him to use his own experience and powers of analysis, asking him to get involved in figuring out the characters. When trying to suggest the reason why the landlady enabled Northerton to escape and then allowed the sentinel to be blamed for her action (pp. 299-300), the narrator gives us a series of possibilities: (1) her "Compassion" for Northerton; (2) his gift of £50, "which might possibly have some little Share in this Action"; (3) her lack of "Compassion" for the sentinel; and (4) her failure to be moved by his appearance, though it differed little from that of Northerton. The narrator refuses to "determine" the real reason, though all the possibilities he suggests seem to have had some part in the landlady's behavior. But we easily pick up the hint that the money was the overriding concern: "whatever were the Conditions, certain it is, that she had the Money, and the Ensign his Liberty." We are pleased that we have perceived the character from the material at our disposal. We are also pleased that we have seen through the pretended ignorance of the narrator and picked up his hint; in a sense, we have become partners with him, sharing his superior perspective about the characters while enjoying the game he is playing with us. But this really moves us into another and separate technique which is described in the next section.

(9) *References to the reader.* When claiming ignorance about why the Lieutenant was more concerned with securing Northerton than helping the injured Tom, the narrator concludes by stating that "it is the Part of the learned and sagacious Reader to consult that original Book of Nature, whence every Passage in our Work is transcribed, tho' we quote not always the particular Page for its Authority" (p. 287). But the narrator does not call upon the reader only when he pleads authorial ignorance; throughout the work, he makes explicit references to the reader and calls upon him to become involved, to try to see clearly and make the proper judgment. Fielding, I must state once again, is talking to the actual reader of the novel, not to some implied and fictional creation who functions merely as a rhetorical ploy; and the actual reader responds as he wishes, both to the person who is the narrator and to his characters and their action. The narrator is continually talking to the reader, taking him into his confidence, speaking as a companion whose observations are to be trusted—"That the Reader, therefore, may not conceive the least ill Opinion of such a Person [the sentinel], we shall not delay a Moment in rescuing his Character from the Imputation of this Guilt" (p. 298). But he frequently seems to be playing a game with us, in a good-natured way, so that we are both amused and more involved with what is taking place in the book: "And here I strictly forbid all Male Critics to intermeddle with a Circumstance, which I have recounted only for the sake of the Ladies, and upon which they only are at Liberty to comment" (p. 223). If we can lean upon the narrator, he also can lean upon us: he wins our confidence and goodwill so that he can demand more of us, so that he can insist upon our involvement, both with the characters of the novel and with him as we figure out together their motives and behavior.

(10) *Farcical actions.* There are a number of scenes throughout the novel that emphasize action as well as dialogue—indeed, the entire work finally leaves us with an impression of a world with the constant potential for comic and often explosive actions, but a world where all the violence has somehow been neutralized by the guardian angels of some ministering force. It is a world with the order and movement towards stability that we find in comedy, but one frequently disrupted by the apparently dangerous, yet actually harmless, actions of farce. Fielding probably derived considerable impetus for these farcical actions from the comic romance, but he has integrated them skillfully into his own comic vision. What controls the action and mitigates its danger in our imagination, what keeps it in the central comic rhythms of the work, is

the narrative voice. The scene at the inn in Upton has been much discussed, and I shall not attempt to put forth another examination. I merely want to cite this episode as one of those bursts of spirit which occur frequently to keep the novel lively but which are always related to Fielding's focus on character and his moral perspective: the violence is the result of confused and wrong-headed motivations, when characters' hold on the truth and their own sanity breaks down. We can scarcely bear to witness violence in real life, and we are uncomfortable reading about it in fiction. Fielding, therefore, mutes and controls the violence in his novel, often by preventing the reader from directly seeing it; by making most of his characters appear sufficiently ridiculous so that we never take their actions too seriously or become sorry about what happens to them; by emphasizing that Tom is a hero with sufficient strength to take care of himself; and generally by deflating acts of violence with irony or mock-epic writing. Though these controls are not sufficient to make scenes of violence totally innocent, they are sufficient to blunt the impact Fielding plays down the immediacy and mimetic reality of his scenes to fit the episode into the general context and rhythms of the entire work, to prevent the reader from becoming deeply involved and threatened, and to allow him the use of his intelligence, his moral superiority, and his sense of humour.

(11) *Summary style*. Fielding's basic technique of narrating events is the summary style of most earlier fiction and historical writing. Actions and reactions are generally not given with much detail, and scenes most often are not vividly and dramatically recreated:

> In short, *Sophia* so greatly overacted her Part, that her Aunt was at first staggered, and began to suspect some Affectation in her Niece; but as she was herself a Woman of great Art, so she soon attributed this to extreme Art in Sophia. . . . We cannot here avoid remarking that this Conjecture would have been better founded, had *Sophia* lived ten Years in the Air of *Grosvenor-square*, where young Ladies do learn a wonderful Knack of rallying and playing with that Passion, which is a mighty serious Thing in Woods and Groves an hundred Miles distant from London. (Pp. 212–13)

Throughout the work, characters and actions take on a life of their own, but the emphasis seems more on the man who tells the story and comments on it: everything is within the context of his observations and thoughts. It is, in fact, the narrator's voice, perspective, and commentary which add so much to the summary style of writing, which animate it and give it another dimension, thus making it much more effective than the pedestrian and lifeless style we find so often in earlier narratives. We begin to feel that in the narrator's hands this is not an inferior method to

Richardson's dramatic method but simply a different one, that the narrator knows exactly what he is about:

> To describe every Particular, and to relate the whole Conversation of the ensuing Scene, is not within my Power, unless I had forty Pens, and could, at once, write with them all together, as the Company now spoke....(P. 287)

Of course, we have several passages of lengthy character analysis, scenes of completely recorded dialogue, and a few lengthy episodes of detailed actions, but in general we feel that we are being told only as much as the narrator deems necessary. The summary style of narration gives us only as much information as we need to visualize and respond to the characters; it maintains a sufficient amount of immediacy but prevents us from being swallowed up in the fictional world and losing our capacity for laughter and judgment. If we are told more, if we had the sense that everything was faithfully recorded, the pace of the novel would slow considerably, the narrator would only have opportunity to introduce us to a limited amount of characters and scenes, and the novel would not be able to achieve a broad, panoramic view of Fielding's eighteenth-century world.

(12) *Architectural structure.* All the techniques we have been examining fit within the general structure of each scene and reinforce the overall effect that the novelist strives to achieve from the entire episode. Richardson's scenes basically move chronologically, almost moment by moment, in terms of the character's sequential involvement, and we are often given both the flow of actions and the flow of reactions as they happened in each scene, even though the character writes at a later time. Fielding continually stops the flow of his action and generally remains outside his characters' minds and the fluid movement of their internal responses. When he does go inside his characters in any depth, he gives his analysis as a separate, analytical passage of writing. He seems to conceive of each scene architecturally and thematically rather than temporally and dramatically. Even scenes of dialogue are largely composed of separate blocks of speech, one playing off the other. The same is true of the lengthy scenes of action: Molly's fight and the battle in the Upton inn are made up of separate actions told in a chronological way, but even here we are given a series of discrete pictures, separated by the commentary of the narrator and not described for an immediate or a developing dramatic effect. Whereas Richardson expands the reader's sense of real space within the scene in order to dramatize and usually recreate the behavior of his characters, Fielding

breaks up the scene and spatially juxtaposes its parts for thematic and comic effects. The general structure of Richardson's scenes also reflects his sense of characters living in a continuous movement of time, made up of discrete and individual moments of experience, flowing in an endless succession, whereas Fielding's scenes represent his more spatial and solid concept of human identity, his instinctive belief in identifiable and permanent human characteristics, and his sense of an order to human experience. We can also say that whereas Richardson focuses on individual action and reaction even in the midst of social interchange, Fielding never isolates his characters or sees them as anything less than social animals in the midst of external relationships: his view is always spatial and panoramic, and even plot ultimately functions to reinforce his architectonic view of the universe. Fielding sees his scene as a separate structure, with every element functioning in its overall design; at the same time, each episode is part of the order and spatial structure of the entire work.[49]

The episode in the novel which best illustrates Fielding's compositional artistry is the scene where Square is discovered in a compromising position in Molly's bedroom. Although the scene has been analyzed by numerous critics, its structural features deserve further attention. This is one of Fielding's lengthier and more detailed episodes, but its architectural principles are true of many of the novel's scenes. What we have here is a scene painted with broad and somewhat exaggerated strokes, functioning in terms of its comic effect, yet achieving a realistic context and significance from the narrator's observations and manipulation of its parts. The narrator summarizes sections of the episode, but he does so to highlight and play off one another the more detailed parts of the scene. Tom goes to visit his "Fair-one," and the narrator pretends to explain her hesitation in answering his call:

> The extremes of Grief and Joy have been remarked to produce very similar Effects; and when either of these rushes on us by Surprize, it is apt to create such a total Perturbation and Confusion, that we are often thereby deprived of the Use of all our Faculties. It cannot therefore be wondered at, that the unexpected Sight of Mr. *Jones* should so strongly operate on the Mind of Molly, and should overwhelm her with such Confusion, that for some Minutes she was unable to express the great Raptures, with which the Reader will suppose she was affected on this Occasion. (P. 172)

We shall later discover this explanation to be untrue: the narrator not only avoids dramatic immediacy through narrative summary and commentary but also undercuts the validity of what he has already suggested his characters might be thinking and feeling. The above description functions to evoke from us a later reaction and understanding, not a present involvement; Fielding wants us later to perceive the character's earlier conduct and see through her duplicity. The scene is working through its arrangement of parts and not through any sequential and logical development, nor through the directly narrated experience of any character.

The language describing the meeting between Tom and Molly is general and unnatural: "and after the first Transports of their Meeting were over, he found Means by Degrees to introduce a Discourse on the fatal Consequences which must attend their Amour..." (p. 172). Molly's impassioned speech, especially for one of her class and education, is formal and unreal: "'And this is your Love for me, to forsake me in this manner...'" (pp. 172-73). But though her language is artificial, it succeeds, along with the narrator's previous analysis of her feelings, in misguiding us and hence increasing our surprise when Square suddenly appears. Square's squatting position in Molly's closet is the most unforgettable comic picture of the novel, one that turns out to be appropriate and obscenely symbolic of Square and his philosophic outpouring.[50] A large part of the humor comes from the way in which the narrator keeps pointing up the ludicrousness of the character's position and reminding us of its contrast to his philosophical pretension:

> as Molly pronounced those last Words, which are recorded above, the wicked Rug got loose from its Fastening, and discovered every thing hid behind it; where among other female Utensils appeared—(with Shame I write it, and with Sorrow will it be read)——The philosopher *Square*, in a Posture (for the Place would not near admit his standing upright) as ridiculous as can possibly be conceived.
>
> The Posture, indeed, in which he stood, was not greatly unlike that of a Soldier who is tyed Neck and Heels; or rather resembling the Attitude in which we often see Fellows in the public Streets of *London*, who are not suffering but deserving Punishment by so standing. He had a Night-cap belonging to *Molly* on his Head, and his two large Eyes, the Moment the Rug fell, stared directly at *Jones*; so that when the Idea of Philosophy was added to the Figure now discovered, it would have been very difficult for any Spectator to have refrained from immoderate Laughter. (P. 173)

What we have is not a visual and dramatic description of the life within the novel but a single, funny picture—and even then it is a caricature, rather than a detailed or accurately drawn picture.[51] The comparisons at the beginning of the second paragraph add a considerable amount of ludicrousness and reprehensibility to the figure, but they are hardly a direct method of describing him: these similitudes rather enlarge the figure to cartoon proportions. The effect is comic, but also thematic; again we have a persuasive commentary, through narrative technique, on human pretension and folly. The character's posture is frozen for two pages while the narrator describes the scene, discourses on the appetites of "Philosophers," analyzes Square's motives, and then traces in some detail the events leading up to his present exposure. The analysis of Square seems more significant than the scene itself; like all of us, we are told, he has his passions and appetites, and his philosophic wisdom can hardly suppress or even hide these—indeed, the same wisdom which teaches him how to subdue these also teaches him that it is easier not to. At last we do have a conversation, one between Square and Tom, but it is used to establish further Square's hypocrisy and emphasize the contrast between him and the hero. One of the functions of the scene is to make us even more aware of the openness, natural passion, and good humor of Tom by disclosing the uncontrollable appetite, deception, and self-centeredness of his tutor. The episode also plays a role in the plot's development, allowing Tom to free himself from Molly, especially after he learns about her affair with Will Barnes in the next chapter. The action of the scene, then, is composed of only Molly's speech, one physical occurrence (the fall of the curtain which discloses the philosopher), and one conversation, but the episode itself achieves its comic effect through the arrangement of its parts around the surprising and funny picture of Square in the middle of the chapter, itself developed through two similitudes. The humor of the episode arises from our surprise at Square's exposure and from our realizations concerning his character and that of Molly, but our responses are carefully evoked and arranged by the scene's architectonics.

Having discussed Fielding's scenic techniques from a positive point of view and having explained how they all reinforce the kind of experience he wishes to create for the reader, I also feel compelled, for the sake of accuracy, to take account of the general failure in technique as well as concept during the last part of the novel. There is not a total failure here—we still have some effective scenes, and the resolution of the plot is handled masterfully—but Fielding seems less forgiving of the London upper-class characters that appear in this part of the novel and sees less humor in their affectation and vice,[52] while the middle-class figures that he treats seem shaped by common literary types and weakened by his didactic concerns. Equally significant is the character of sobriety and good sense that Tom acquires, in spite of his affair with Lady Bellaston, a character who also diminishes the book's energy and comic spirit.[53]

That a different kind of sensibility is moving into the novel soon becomes evident in the episode concerning Anderson and his family (pp. 550–53, 556–58). A number of didactic themes are dealt with here: society's responsibility to help the indigent, the individual's responsibility to perform good works, the importance of being prepared for evil, and the necessity of economic stability in marriage. In the context of plot, the episode allows Mrs. Miller to form a favorable opinion of Tom, which later motivates her to help him return to the good graces of Allworthy, and it also functions to show the maturation of the hero's benevolence, thus preparing us for his social elevation. But the entire episode lacks both a complex vision of humanity and any immediate portrayal of character and action. Indeed, Fielding does not present the Anderson family in a direct scene at all, but tells us about them through the sentimentalizing description of Mrs. Miller. What we have here is an indirect presentation of good people suffering under adversity for which they are only partly responsible, and an immediate presentation of good people (Mrs. Miller and her listeners) responding to their plight with pity and benevolence. Again we have Fielding architecturally structuring his scene, but here the architectonics function to direct our attention and emotions to those responding to the difficult situation and not to those actively engaged within it; instead of feeling with those in distress, we are to feel with those feeling for the distressed. In other words, Fielding's didactic intention undercuts the real human dilemma of the episode. For much of the novel, Fielding has had us indirectly responding to his characters through his sagacious and witty narrator, but here we respond through the middle-class and sentimental voice of Mrs. Miller, and here Fielding appeals to our emotions and not our intelligence and understanding. The novel has changed gears, and, instead of trying to correct the vices and follies of the world with ridicule, it tries to rectify them with pity. The comic novel we have been reading appears only sporadically in this part of the book as its author now seems swept along by the rising fashion of his age for tears.

PLOT

We have been considering *Tom Jones* as the first English novel where authenticity and verisimilitude are played down, where author and reader work together to achieve a realistic version of life that transcends the mimetic data of the world within the book. We find this evident not only in the individual sections of the work but in the larger movement and totality as well—in the very development of plot and final assemblage of parts into a single spatial entity. I want to show now that the reader's perceptions are a basic concern in the treatment of plot in *Tom Jones*, that the narrator manipulates and develops our awareness of what takes place in his fictional world as the novel progresses and leads us to an expanded vision that transcends the series of events narrated within the book.

The plot of *Tom Jones* has been universally acclaimed for some time,[54] but a few contemporary critics such as Preston and Goldknopf have offered different appraisals of this aspect of the work. Preston argues that Fielding intentionally made his plot "less an assertion of Augustan rationality than a recognition of the confusion the rationalist can hardly tolerate."[55] The narrator's claim for order and control in the plot are to be taken ironically—indeed, the narrator himself is to be taken ironically: "to pose as a bad writer will help Fielding to avoid slipping into shallow rationalism. If he poses as the invisible Divine presence behind events, it is with a full sense of the kind of error this would be." Preston goes even further than this, arguing for a second reading of the work, where the reader knows more than the narrator and hence the book "gives the impression that in some important ways the novel has written itself."

One performs considerable havoc on the novel by seeing Fielding's narrator as a fool. I doubt if many readers of Fielding's time would have failed to see the narrator in a tradition of literary spokesmen, figures of intelligence and wisdom who used irony as a satiric tool without demeaning their own stature. Of course, Fielding's narrator at times is ironic about his role as author, but, if anything, this is to underscore his control of both the narrative and the reader. Most of the time, however, the narrator does not "pose as a bad writer," and his commentary is to be taken with absolute seriousness. By undercutting the narrator's control over the book's action, by arguing for his ignorance about what happens and the significance of events, Preston also undermines the validity of the narrator's observations on both his characters' behavior and human nature in general; in other words, he undermines the commentary which permeates the entire book, which shapes and animates the characters, and which guides our responses to the fictional world. To deny the narrator's role as the creator of the book, as conscious artist, is also to deny the book's moral power, which rests upon the narrator's ability to develop an intelligent and responsible dialogue with the reader. Preston cites Elanor Hutchens's useful observation that "a curious and subtle means used by Fielding to add irony to a given detail of plotting is to leave the reader to plot a sequence for himself,"[56] but he takes this observation in the wrong direction and finally leaves the book without unity and meaning, without a controlling intelligence and valid perspective. The narrator and reader are partners in this venture, and the novel attempts to bring the latter's perceptions in line with those of the former; hence the plot of *Tom Jones* only makes sense in the context of the narrator's understanding. He is an historian, but he is also portrayed as a novelist who creates the fictional world and therefore must understand it. Our faith in him rests in large part on his role as literary artist.

Goldknopf does not see the narrator ironically, but goes to the other extreme and argues that the novel's "plot falls so far short of doing justice to the author's comprehensive vision that he must repeatedly choose between his narrative and intellectual commitments."[57] Goldknopf claims that Fielding was trying to bring his "picaresque exuberance . . . and the new, aggressive empiricism of his age under a discipline fundamentally unsympathetic to both, the neo-classical canon" which was expressed in the "balance, proportion, and reciprocity" of the work's design. He asks us "to imagine the novel without the introductory chapters, the numerous editorial embellishments and enlightenments, the old-man-of-the-hill episode, the visit with the gypsies, etc., all of which are only tenuously or arbitrarily referenced to the main story, and most of which would probably have been sacrificed in a plot-oriented age. The result would certainly have been a drastically diminished work, a banal, romantic comedy." The argument goes on in this fashion, as we are told that "these interpolations" function to slow down the pace of the story and give the work a more "reflective tone," that the author "compensates for the disengagement of our interest in the narrative by setting up a comrader[y] between himself and us. But the palship is founded on the shared attitude of condescension toward the narrative!"

Most of Goldknopf's analysis, it seems to me, goes against our actual experience of the novel. Goldknopf seems to see *Tom Jones* in parts and not as a functioning whole: he fails to acknowledge the way the parts work together. If we take away the narrator's commentary and interpolations, we are not left with a banal plot—we are left with nothing at all. We have seen that the narrator's values and attitudes are an integral part of almost every characterization and scene, that, indeed, each character and scene is a product of his commentary and interpolations. Perhaps one could lop off the introductory essays and the two or three long digressions without doing much damage to the events of the novel, but the way in which we see the events has been influenced by these lengthy interpolations, and they certainly form an integrated pattern with the smaller interjections which permeate the work.

What Goldknopf may mean is that the novel's story is trivial,[58] but I doubt very much if it is any more trivial than the stories in most fictional and dramatic comedies. Besides, I do not know why anyone would want to isolate and abstract the general action of the novel dealing with Tom and Sophia from the remainder of the work—by itself it tells us little about the novel, and when reading we do not respond to it *in vacuo*. Plot in *Tom Jones* includes more than just the story, and it is dependent upon narrative voice and the reader's responses. Indeed, it is the narrator who guides the reader into putting together the pieces of the novel's plot in their proper causal relationship and finally seeing the work in its totality, a totality which reflects the neoclassic values and moral order of the narrator himself.

R. S. Crane talks about plots "of which the effects derive in a much more immediate way from the particular ethical qualities manifested in their agents' actions and thoughts vis-à-vis the human situations in which they are engaged. When this is the case, we cannot help becoming, in a greater or less degree, emotionally involved; for some of the characters we wish good, for others ill, and, depending on our inferences as to the events, we feel hope or fear, pity or satisfaction, or some modification of these or similar emotions."[59] Crane sees the writer of such a work carefully provoking our responses to his characters and their actions, working along ethical lines to have us feel favorably or unfavorably disposed. He makes a crucial point: "we may be said to have grasped the plot in the full artistic sense only when we have analyzed this interplay of desires and expectations sequentially in relation to the incidents by which it is produced."[60] Crane analyzes *Tom Jones* in this way and outlines Fielding's methods for provoking within the reader the proper emotional and ethical reactions. I want to stress Crane's point that we cannot fully understand Fielding's plot without understanding how we are made to respond to it, but I want to go further and argue that we must also comprehend the ways in which Fielding, through his narrative voice, involves the reader in constructing the plot and improving his perceptions and judgments of the characters and their actions.

Sheridan Baker's following distinction between two concepts of plot in *Tom Jones* is significant in the context of my own discussion:

(1) plot as everything that happens, (2) plot as the story's limited evidence for everything that happens. The first is the story's life, fully understood as to motives, causes, and effects; the second is the disclosure, selection, arrangement, concealment, and revelation. The first is story; the second, storytelling. The first, I would call plot; the second, plotting.[61]

These two concepts of plot are basically the same as the Russian formalists' *sujet* and *fabula*, to which I have already referred: the events and even parts of the novel in the order they are presented, and our reconstruction of what actually happened in the correct sequence.[62] The narrator in *Moll Flanders* cannot possibly describe everything that happened to her and, on occasion, briefly refers to some past event she has already skipped over, but such references generally seem afterthoughts and have little impact on our conception of the heroine and her life. The major events in Moll's life are given in straight order, and there is little distinction in the novel between *sujet* and *fabula*: what we see is what we are to know. Richardson's *Clarissa* is somewhat more complex in the arrangement of its parts—we have letter-writers on occasion narrating different sequences of actions, and we must perceive the interrelationship and proper arrangement of all these actions in our minds; sometimes an earlier event is referred to or described from a second perspective, thus altering our previous conceptions of the episode and the novel's plot—but Richardson's impulse is largely to present most of the events in his novel in straight, chronological sequence, describing each major action in its natural order and leaving little for the reader to reconstruct. Fielding, however, is the first English novelist to suggest throughout much of his work another order of things, to create for us a sense of another reality behind the one we directly view. He describes events in straight, chronological fashion but leaves out crucial episodes and explanations, important actions and motivations, so that we must try to figure things out as we go along and finally reconstruct the plot. Here *sujet* and *fabula* split apart, and Fielding achieves considerable effect by playing one against the other. I would suggest that plot in *Tom Jones* must finally be seen as a combination of the shown and unshown, of the specific and suggested; it is the shifting arrangement of characters and events as the reader comes to perceive them with the help of the narrator. The immediate visible happenings of the novel are only the raw material, the primary data from which we must fashion in our minds what really has happened and is happening. Fielding's novel thus fulfills the intellectual bent of his time as pervasively as the more psychological novels of Richardson and Austen. *Tom Jones* forces the reader to see that both he and the characters of the novel often perceive reality in a subjective and personal way, that what we really know are only our impressions and perceptions of the world outside us, and that such vision, by its very nature, is subject to distortion and inaccuracy. But reality, the way things are, cannot simply be told or taught to us secondhand; it must still be perceived, discovered by our own vision and intelligence, not simply from primary data and the specific details outside us but also from implication and suggestion, from logic and deduction, from our own intelligent assemblage of what we see and don't see. Reality and truth exist and are to be discovered: characters have definable identities and personalities; events work out for the best; the universe is ordered and coherent. We must do more than merely observe the progress of events in the novel: we must also arrange them, along with actions that are disclosed to us only later, into a final arrangement, into a spatial entity that manifests a coherence and logic indicative of Fielding's belief in an ordered and logical universe. Fielding's novel and his techniques of writing are a synthesis of empirical and neoclassic belief, and the narrator in *Tom Jones* is an embodiment—a unique embodiment—of this synthesis, prodding us into perceiving the order in his world through our senses and intelligence and spatial imagination.

Plot, then, is a dynamic and all-inclusive entity for us throughout the work. It manages to gather unto itself many of the novel's characters and actions, and it manages to involve us in its creation. It does all this because of what the narrator chooses to tell us and what he chooses to hide—there is never any doubt that this is his novel, that he has put it all together, and that he has done so with great skill and purpose:

> This Work may, indeed, be considered as a great Creation of our own; and for a little Reptile of a Critic to presume to find Fault with any of its Parts, without knowing the Manner in which the Whole is connected, and before he comes to the final Catastrophe, is a most presumptuous Absurdity. (P. 398)

The tone of this passage may be facetious, but we certainly cannot take its meaning as ironic and refuse to see what the narrator is urging. We are presumptuous to judge precipitately, to judge with only immediate and fragmentary perceptions. The discovery of the novel is to be ours, but only after we have sufficient information, only after we have learned to read properly in the book of human nature and put everything together in our own minds.

I have already discussed Fielding's technique of *indirect characterization* in relation to Bridget Allworthy—that method by which the reader is forced to piece together a complete picture of the character, not only through the straightforward presentation of data but also through narrative style, implication and suggestion, and later information that alters or extends our original concept of the figure.[63] To some extent we perceive most fictional characters in this manner—our understanding of them is in part dependent on our ability to piece together their patterns, to analyze, and to make assessments—but Fielding goes much further in holding back information, in working through implication and suggestion, and in developing a pattern far more complex than the data immediately conveys. Bridget is a fine example of this kind of characterization, since her total person cannot be realized by the reader until the end of the novel, when her role as Tom's mother is disclosed. But there have been hints about her full character, and certainly we have already seen qualities such as her hypocrisy that are in tune with this later information. The reader need not later change his understanding of her so much as deepen his interpretation and place what he already knows in a more complex and fuller context. At the same time, the new information we receive and our developed understanding of her force us to reexamine and reassemble the novel's action, to see more clearly exactly what took place during the first part of the book and the impact of these early events on the subsequent course of the plot.

Bridget is not the only character dependent on the reader's developing perceptions and creative imagination. We must gradually come to understand a number of the characters and their motivations, and we must learn about their specific actions and roles in the novel's plot: we must at times pull together the described and undescribed actions to obtain a full picture of what actually has taken place. We also take great pleasure in putting together the life of Jenny Jones, in seeing how her character and past actions explain so much of what has happened to Tom[64]—indeed, it is she who is chiefly responsible for the discovery of Tom's origins and the shape of his future. At the beginning of the novel, we try to understand what is going on, to perceive the truth about Jenny and Tom's birth, but we are kept in doubt. As Jenny disappears and the novel progresses, these earlier uncertainties influence our perspective of Tom and the work's events. Partridge's announcement later in the work that Mrs. Waters is Jenny suddenly puts us on the alert, makes us view the events of the novel in a more expectant light, and Jenny's confession to Allworthy makes us reconsider and finally understand much of what had gone before.

Another character whose role in the plot is fully ascertained only later in the work is Blifil. Although we learn little that is new about his character, we do at least learn a good deal about his past actions and his effect upon Tom's life. The disclosure of Blifil's machinations explains much about the evil forces that have been attacking the hero but have also been prodding him to moral action and ultimate happiness. Finally, I must mention Dowling, that enigmatic figure who comes in and out of the novel to warn us that what we see, or think we see, is not all we are to know, that he and others are having some effect on the action that we cannot yet perceive.

Throughout the book, the narrator also calls upon us to plot the action in a brief sequence of events, to see for ourselves exactly what has happened. He describes to us the events leading to Bridget's marriage with Captain Blifil (pp. 47-57), yet his description is intentionally obscure, his narration somewhat circumspect about characters' motivations and behavior and about the exact sequence of actions leading from Bridget's earlier relationship with Dr. Blifil to her marriage with his brother. The same kind of reliance upon the reader is obvious in even so minor an occurrence as Northerton's escape, an episode we have already examined.[65] The narrator clearly knows what has taken place and the motivations of the characters involved, but he presents the episode in such a hesitant and teasing way, with such feigned doubt, that we must finally pick up the clues and see the actions of the episode for ourselves. Time and again in *Tom Jones* we are forced to make the discoveries and plot the novel on our own.

All of the characters and actions in the novel are significant in their effect upon the hero and his life. The actions we assemble, the plot we finally perceive, is itself the life of Tom Jones. Conversely, Tom is a touchstone for the people in the book: the way they judge him is an indication of their quality of perception and moral worth. He is also a touchstone for the reader, who is called upon to understand the hero in a fuller and more judicious way than most of the characters throughout the work. The narrator allows us to see Tom's redeeming virtues during the first part of the book and weigh these against his excess of spirit and gullibility. From the very start, we see him as virtuous and openhearted—for Fielding, Tom is the antithesis to the corruption and deception bred by the economic and social pressures of his world. But Fielding was hardly a writer to deny the society and social structure of his time: if Tom has what much of his social world lacks, that world is still the place in which he must live. What we really have in the novel are two countermovements: the adjustment of society to Tom and his virtues, as manifested through the developing awareness of characters like Allworthy and Sophia, and the adjustment of Tom to society, as manifested by his developing prudence and wisdom, his mature and benevolent behavior, especially at the end of the work. Like Defoe and Richardson, Fielding is concerned with his character's role in society, with societal pressures on the individual and individual pressures on society, but unlike them, he is not concerned with the dynamics of personal individualism, nor does his character ever approach a sense of tragic isolation.[66] His novel is always comic and social, and his world always contains the potential for adjustment and unity.

The movements of society's growing awareness of Tom and Tom's growing awareness of society are both developed and synthesized not through the hero's perspective but through our perspective of the hero. By keeping us outside Tom, Fielding tests and develops our powers of perception as he does those of many of the novel's characters. But by doing this, as I have already stated, he also denies us a convincing portrait of the hero's inner growth, of his development from natural instinct and virtue, with their drawbacks, to a state of wise and prudent virtue that leads to social adaptability. Fielding, attempting to utilize the extensive temporal dimension of the novel, worked out a simple equation, one that was to be basic for a type of novel we call the *Bildungsroman*: character + time = maturation.[67] Although Defoe pretends to show a moral development within Moll, and both the heroine and villain of Richardson's *Clarissa* undergo a change in character, the kind of personal development Fielding pointed to, the kind achieved by a host of future writers, is far more extensive and deals with a character's growth from youth to adulthood. But this kind of development is a gradual process that must be shown and dramatized, something which Fielding refused to do: it is not sufficient merely to claim from time to time that it is going on and to demonstrate at the end of the work that the process is complete.

Yet even without the depiction of Tom's inner growth, the plot in *Tom Jones* achieves more than the comic and philosophic structures pointed out by scholars. In being the first of our eighteenth-century novelists to distinguish the *sujet* and *fabula* of his novel, Fielding is also the first writer to involve his reader so actively and extensively in the re-creation of his novel, in the imaginative assemblage of seen and unseen events into an ordered and coherent structure. This relationship with the reader and dependence upon his imaginative powers and intelligence will also play a significant role in *Tristram Shandy*, *Humphry Clinker*, and *Pride and Prejudice*. At the same time, Fielding incorporates in his work, more extensively and explicitly than Richardson, the development and growth of his major character. Though not successful in dramatizing Tom's maturation, Fielding writes his novel so that the reader is aware of this change, and the novel's culmination is dependent upon it. In this respect, Fielding was to have a major influence on the kind of plot created by Jane Austen and followed by a host of writers after her. Austen, however, also made her protagonist fully aware of the change that had taken place within her, so that what we have is a novel of self-discovery. One of our great pleasures in reading *Pride and Prejudice* comes not only from our developing awareness of the heroine's limitations and growth but also from our capacity to share her self-discovery. This particular kind of plot was, indeed, a natural vehicle for Austen, with her continual dramatization of her major character's internal state. But Fielding himself was caught between traditional notions of static identity and man's inherent perfectibility. He was convinced that with intelligent perception and sufficient information, we could see every individual in the fixed context of a particular kind of human behavior. But he was also a moralist and altruist who believed that with proper self-enlightenment, every person could change for the better and free himself from stereotypic conduct. Although he adequately developed his narrative techniques to portray his fixed and universal types, he was not yet ready to recognize or describe the painful uncertainty, the disorienting flux and change, that must come with self-discovery and moral growth.

CHAPTER FOUR

TRISTRAM SHANDY'S
Anatomy of the Mind

THE NOVEL AS AUTOBIOGRAPHY

The voice we hear throughout *Tristram Shandy* (1759-67)[1] is that of a fictional character who claims to be writing his "Life and Opinions," a true autobiographical work and not a novel. In this respect, Tristram is similar to other fictional characters, like Moll and Clarissa, who also seem to be writing true accounts of their own lives. It is with these first-person novels, up to now a dominant form of the new fiction, that Sterne is partly concerned, but he also wishes to confront the problems and possibilities inherent in biographical and historical writing, in any kind of writing that purports to describe reality. Both the outer and inner forms of the work, the novel that Laurence Sterne is actually writing and the autobiography that Tristram Shandy is supposed to be writing, are fictional. Tristram realizes that what he thinks of as reality and attempts to describe as such are fictions of his mind—two different fictions, as a matter of fact—that are transformed into a new fiction by the subjective mind of his reader. For these reasons Tristram, in his autobiography, often talks about himself as a writer of a fictional work and uses the techniques of the novel to depict his conception of reality.

In respect to both Sterne's writing of his novel and Tristram's writing of his "Life and Opinions," *Tristram Shandy* shows a remarkable awareness of the concerns and techniques of the new kind of fiction developed during the earlier part of the century. Sterne takes the possibilities of the form, the potentials inherent in techniques used by Defoe, Richardson, and Fielding, and performs both a tour de force and an analysis of this "new species of writing."[2] Therefore, it is both incorrect and misleading to divorce his work from the fiction of the time, as some scholars have done.[3] Indeed, *Tristram Shandy* tells us more about the novel of the eighteenth century, more about what the first writers of this form were trying to achieve, than any other fictional or nonfictional work of the entire century.[4] Sterne examines this new type of narrative as a product of the human mind, an exploration of the human mind, and an art form meant to appeal to the human mind: for Sterne, the novel is a psychological entity and a perfect form for describing the fictions of the mind. For this reason, autobiography, because of its psychological and subjective nature, is the natural form for his novel.

Tristram Shandy develops to extraordinary lengths the significant realization of earlier novelists: that the new art form is concerned with human psychology, and that psychology is concerned with perception. For the very heart of Sterne's book, the aspect of characterization and the theme that unifies what on the surface seems to be a wildly disorganized and conglomerate work is not associational psychology, the hobbyhorse, or even communication, but rather perceptional psychology: the way the individual perceives himself and reality, and the way these perceptions, at least for Sterne, are themselves fictions. Sterne's novel explores perception and the human mind in the following ways: the work is conceived as (1) a product of Tristram's mind; (2) a work dependent upon the reader's mind; (3) a means of depicting the perceiving mind (through Walter, Toby, and, of course, Tristram himself); (4) a means of depicting the external world as both a projection of characters' minds and an undecipherable entity to those minds; and (5) an exploration of such subjects as reason, imagination, opinion, education, scholasticism, rhetoric, writing, speaking, all of which are seen as attempts of the mind to discover its own reality and that of the world around it. These themes are developed through the narrator's commentary, through his portrayal of character and action, and through his own dramatization, and they depend on the reader's complicity in the creation of the novel's fictional world.

Tristram Shandy is a study of the mind's limitations and triumphs. No sooner were the wonders of the human mind explored during this period, no sooner was man seeking ultimate truths by looking inside himself, than the possibility of any such knowledge was denied. While this was the age of reason, it was also an age of scepticism. While some men advocated the advance of modern knowledge, others denied it.[5] The age which gave rise to Locke also produced David Hume. We must be wary of categorizing both an age and its individuals into a neat system of belief, of finding uniformity where there is only an appearance of similarity. Arthur O. Lovejoy can show the parallelism of deism and neoclassicism, of one set of religious beliefs and one set of cultural beliefs,[6] but this cannot erase the fact that the figures we most associate with neoclassicism—Dryden, Swift, Johnson, and even Pope—would not accept much of what we associate with deism. Sterne, in his own way, can be neoclassic in his satire against all kinds of false learning, in his refusal to grant man any extraordinary capacity for internal and external knowledge, and in his attack against man's presumption, vanity, and pride, but he is also a sentimentalist who believes in the efficacy and truth of man's benevolent feelings.[7] Though Sterne may follow Locke in his treatment of the human mind and involve his characters with social problems inherent in the Lockean psychology, part of his solution to the difficulties in human relationships approximates the following sentiments expressed by Hume:

> no qualities are more entitled to the general good will and approbation of mankind than beneficence and humanity, friendship and gratitude, natural affection and public spirit, or whatever proceeds from a tender sympathy with others and a generous concern for our kind and species. These, wherever they appear, seem to transfuse themselves, in a manner, into each beholder and to call forth, in their own behalf, the same favorable and affectionate sentiments which they exert on all around.[8]

Sterne and Hume are among the sceptics of the period who deny man his new claimed intellectual glory; however, they part company with this group in finding significance in man's emotional communion. But though Sterne and Hume deny man the capacity for much "human understanding," they do not deny him a rich and significant mental life. This mental life is certainly the most considerable and important part of *Tristram Shandy*, even more important than the works' treatment of emotional communion and benevolence.

Every book is concerned with the mental life because every book is the product and bears the imprint of the writer's mind—though every autobiography is to some degree a fiction, all fiction is in this sense an autobiography. Or perhaps we can better say that fiction creates an immediate reality in one respect by conveying the real mind of the author. I am suggesting another connection between the inner and outer forms of *Tristram Shandy*, between Tristram's autobiography and Sterne's novel. The book that Tristram writes is supposed to deal with his perceptions of the real world, but it is also a clear indication of his own psyche; the book that Sterne writes, the one which includes Tristram, may not be based upon his perceptions of an immediate reality, but it conveys his own remarkable and very real mind. Tristram is not Sterne, but he certainly is a projection of Sterne's psyche. In his own life, this was a distinction which Sterne did not always make as he formed for himself a Shandean existence in the image of his own creation. As the novel was a projection of his own mind, so did his personality often become a projection of his own novel. The confusion between fiction and reality is a concern throughout the work much as it became a problem in Sterne's own life.[9]

THE WRITER AND HIS READER

Throughout the novel, Tristram confronts and discusses the problems of writing about real characters and events. The writer can describe only what he perceives to be true, either as a witness or as a reporter of what others have told him. But even when narrating events which he did not personally see, Tristram is writing about characters he knew, and so must still convey his actual perceptions of them, though in an imagined situation. Therefore, the veracity of the book is dependent upon the veracity of Tristram's perceptions of reality, on how well he saw and knew people like Walter and Toby. In a key passage early in the book (pp. 85-86),[10] Tristram cites the sources of mental confusion discussed by Locke in *An Essay Concerning Human Understanding*. Within the passage, he refers to the ways in which we achieve our perceptions: through the impressions on our mind, which arrive there by way of our senses, and through our memory, which recalls past perceptions or creates new ones from earlier sensory experiences. Tristram throughout the work is quick to admit that he is a creature of his senses—indeed, that his ideas are shaped by his highly sensuous nature:

> I love the Pythagorians ... for their ... "*getting out of the body, in order to think well.*" No man thinks right whilst he is in it; blinded as he must be, with his congenial humours, and drawn differently aside ... with too lax or too tense a fibre——REASON is, half of it, SENSE; and the measure of heaven itself is but the measure of our present appetites and concoctions—— (Pp. 493–94)[11]

Because his impressions come through his senses, because of his sensuous nature, Tristram's perceptions and conceptions, his thinking and imagining, are personal and subjective. Our senses are the source of what we know, and to some degree we all share Tristram's sensuousness. If "the measure of heaven itself is but the measure of our present appetites and concoctions," how are we ever to know what heaven really is—or how are we ever to know the reality of anyone or anything, for that matter? We know only our impressions of things, and these may have as much touch with reality as the impressions conveyed to us from any work of fiction. If all that we think we see and know is a fiction, what is real?

Tristram attempts to write a book that describes real people and events, but he frequently acknowledges that these are dependent upon his own mind, which has perceived them subjectively and now attempts to remember them, or what he has heard about them, also subjectively. Indeed, Tristram's memory must now be the chief source of his perceptions as he writes his book, but this source, if anything, seems even more vulnerable to his senses, to his very "appetites and concoctions." Because of this vulnerability, Tristram is frequently swayed by his sensuous nature in the very act of writing:

> I defy, notwithstanding all that has been said upon *straight lines* in sundry pages of my book——I defy the best cabbage planter that ever existed, whether he plants backwards or forwards, it makes little difference in the account (except that he will have more to answer for in the one case than in the other)——I defy him to go on coolly, critically, and canonically, planting his cabbages one by one, in straight lines, and stoical distances, especially if slits in petticoats are unsew'd up——without ever and anon straddling out, or sidling into some bastardly digression—— (P. 539)

Any man's passions will distract him in that way, but Tristram has inherited a sensuous nature stronger than normal from his lascivious Aunt Dinah. Tristram is such a slave to his physical nature when he writes that even his dress influences his book: "when your honours and reverences would know whether I write clean and fit to be read, you will be able to judge full as well by looking into my Laundress's bill, as my book..." (p. 617).

But Tristram's perceptions and his way of thinking can be ascribed to more than his senses and passions; his difficulty in writing in a straight line is a product of more than his Aunt Dinah's lasciviousness. When Tristram explains how hard he works to keep his book together for the reader's sake, he finally admits that he himself is lost. Why? Should his brain be dissected, "you will perceive, without spectacles, that he [his father] has left a large uneven thread...running along the whole length of the web..." (pp. 462-63). Poor Tristram, the inheritor of traits from the diverse and idiosyncratic members of his family,[12] is scarcely in control of the operations of his mind, let alone his book, when he is writing. Indeed, each of his inherited traits frequently runs away with him as he writes. As well as blaming the nature of his book on the sensuous nature he inherited from his Aunt Dinah or his erratic intellect, a legacy of his father, we must also see it in part as a result of his sentimentalism, implanted in him early in life by his Uncle Toby. It is this sentimentalism which leads him into stories like that of Le Fevre and leaves him a prey to his feelings throughout the book: "this I know, that the lesson of universal good-will then taught and imprinted by my uncle *Toby*, has never since been worn out of my mind..." (p. 114).

Tristram's mental processes, his way of perceiving the past and thinking in the present, are vulnerable to his senses and inherited traits, to a host of diverse influences over which he is often not in control. His book is the product of his idiosyncracies and whimsies, of the strange and sometimes inexplicable way in which his mind operates. For this reason, it is almost impossible to expect a coherent and orderly work from such a complex and often uncontrollable source. Indeed, if the writer "is a man of the least spirit, he will have fifty deviations from a straight line to make with this or that party as he goes along, which he can no way avoid. He will have views and prospects to himself perpetually solliciting his eye, which he can no more help standing still to look at than he can fly..." (pp. 36-37). Hence, there are no valid rules to guide the writer, a point Tristram makes over and over. Rules are manmade and arbitrary, and have little to do with any book that is an honest expression of its author:

> And what of this new book the whole world makes such a rout about?——
> Oh! 'tis out of all plumb, my Lord,——quite an irregular thing!——not
> one of the angles at the four corners was a right angle.——I had my rule and
> compasses, &c. my Lord, in my pocket.——Excellent critic! (Pp. 180-81)

A book is the product of a mind, which is itself the product of disorderly and overpowering forces.

Tristram, then, is a writer true to himself and what he is, writing not according to the rule of others but according to his own basic nature. If his work is to be a true "Life and Opinions," a true portrait of himself, it must have the contours of his own mind. Since no one, not even Tristram, knows quite how that mind will work (even hobbyhorses afford no certainty), planning ahead for the book is useless. The art of writing is inspirational—"why do I mention it?——Ask my pen,——it governs me,——I govern not it" (p. 416)—but inspiration clearly is an expression of one's individual nature.

Indeed, all of the book and everything in it, the very way in which it is written, are expressions of Tristram's individual nature. This is the ultimate significance of the way in which he perceives and describes characters and events. Certainly these characters function to inform us about the chief influences on his life and the formation of his mind; certainly they give him the opportunity to express his opinions and hence further develop his character for us; and, of course, they exist on their own as wonderful creations. But their primary significance, it seems to me, is as a projection—indeed, a visual projection—of Tristram's mind and its operations. But with all of the narrator's complaints, with all of his excuses and explanations, and in spite of the collapse of his original hopes for control over the progression of the work, the book does manage to fulfill this major purpose: Tristram's mind is portrayed for us, and though he rarely appears in the events he describes, his presence and personality are felt throughout the book. The way in which the book progresses, the choice of subjects, the way in which each subject is perceived, and the constant commentary of the narrator make of the whole a map of the narrator's mind.[13] Tristram becomes for us the most significant character in the book, even more so that the narrator in *Tom Jones*, because Stern realizes what was implicit in Fielding's approach: any work of art is the product of the mind that creates it, as well as an accurate description of that mind and the way in which it functions. Richardson too had hit upon this truth in having his letters dramatic manifestations of their writer's emotions and personality, but he had not gone as far as Sterne and made the entire structure of his work, the progression of plot and the relationship of the parts, a projection of the narrator's psyche. In his own terms, Tristram writes a valid and authentic autobiography. If other autobiographical authors would only realize the subjective nature of all writing, they would drop their pretense of objectivity and not be limited by artificial rules and forms. If writers of fiction would realize this same truth, Sterne seems to be telling us, if they would use the style and the form of their works to convey the minds of their characters, they would create an illusion of reality more valid than their poor imitations of life.

Sterne's interest in the psychological dimension of both autobiography and the novel even involves him in an examination of the very medium used by writers to create this dimension. Tristram begins chapter XXXVIII of Volume VI with the following request to the reader:

> To conceive this right,——call for pen and ink——here's paper ready to your hand.——Sit down, Sir, paint her [the widow Wadman] to your own

mind——as like your mistress as you can——as unlike your wife as your conscience will let you——'tis all one to me——please put your own fancy in it. (P. 470)

The rest of the page and the entire following one are blank. The reader, then, is asked to supply the character, to fill in the blank pages from his own imagination. There are no words for him, no signs to suggest how he is to do the job: the reader must become novelist. But what is evident from all this is that since the words are missing, the novel, with all its characters and actions, for the moment has ceased to exist. We are forced to realize that the novel is, after all, an artifact and the writer a trickster, a con artist, who manipulates words to create the necessary illusions. The novel, then, can continue only with the return of language—black print on a blank page. The words on the page convey the imagination of the person who puts them there, and they create the narrator and the world of his characters within the reader's mind. Sterne is fascinated by the paradox of the novel's being a physical object and yet the cause of a totally imaginative experience.

Sterne writes a novel about the way in which the writer creates his vision and the way in which the reader recreates that vision in his own mind, how he perceives what he thinks the writer is depicting by reading his language:[14] "——But before the Corporal begins, I must first give you a description of his attitude;——otherwise he will naturally stand represented, by your imagination, in an uneasy posture . . . " (p. 120). But there is another side to the matter, a complex and comic one. Certainly the reader's imagination is at work as he reads the novel. But what if that imagination is on a different track from that of the author? Tristram seems as dismayed at the wayward power of his reader's imagination as we have seen him to be at his own: "I would go fifty miles on foot, for I have not a horse worth riding on, to kiss the hand of that man whose generous heart will give up the reins of his imagination into his author's hands,——be pleased he knows not why, and cares not wherefore" (p. 182). The novel is a result of the author's imagination, and it calls upon the reader to exercise his own imagination in an identical way—but no two imaginations are the same. Sterne's real point here is that individual minds are idiosyncratic, and mutual understanding is very difficult indeed.[15]

We can interject another factor here, one emphasized throughout the work: if the language people use tends to isolate them because it is private and individual,[16] a result of their own hobbyhorses, then there is no reason to believe that the author's language will be any more practical for communicating his vision to the reader. We can understand now Tristram's full dilemma. The people he wishes to write about are real, at least to him, but he knows them only through the impressions he has of them. Therefore, he must describe not the characters but his impressions of them, and to do so he must use language, but a language influenced and shaped by his own mind and personality. When discussing Locke's ideas on the causes of mental confusion, Tristram emphasizes "the unsteady uses of words which have perplexed the clearest and most exalted understandings" (p. 86). This is not only a problem with most of the people that he describes; it is also a chief difficulty for Tristram when he writes his book—a difficulty which he well recognizes. Tristram's personal language must distort his perceptions of reality, which are already subjective in nature. The reader himself is certain to respond to the language in his own subjective way, since words have different connotations and ramifications for different people. Hence, the world which the reader perceives from Tristram's descriptions will not be the exact one the narrator intends to describe and will itself be several times removed from reality. No wonder Tristram at times throws up his hands, refuses to write, and tells the reader to imagine the character or scene for himself.

Tristram is conscious of the medium with which he tries to convey his perceptions of reality, not only the language of his narration but the real physical book he is producing with all its paper, black ink, and the chapter divisions. Tristram, as we shall see, tries throughout the work to create within his reader's mind images of his characters and events through the visual propensity of words, even though he expresses his concern for the subjective and personal nature of language. But sometimes words will not do, and he must ask the reader to paint the picture for himself, or he must substitute for words some type of image on his page. Such devices as the two black pages which appear after "Alas, poor YORICK!" (pp. 33-34), the marble pages which are a "motly emblem" of Tristram's work because of their impenetrable moral (pp. 227-28), the erratic black lines which illustrate the plotting of the novel (pp. 473-74), the strange typography, are all visual devices[17] that underscore the visual nature of the reading experience. But they also remind us of the physical existence of the book itself in our own real world of physical objects. By leaving out an entire chapter of ten pages because its quality was so high "that it could not have remained . . . without depreciating every other scene" (p. 315), Tristram reminds us that the book is made up of pages and chapters, that pages and chapters can be subtracted, added, and rearranged. Chapters XVIII and XIX of Volume IX (pp. 621-22) are left blank because chapter XXV must be written first—the two earlier chapters appear right after XXV. In all of these instances, Tristram is calling attention to his role as creator and manipulator in the very process of writing what is supposed to be an account of real events. Because of the subjective nature of his perceptions, because what he communicates to the reader is as much a creation of his own and the reader's mind as an account of a verifiable reality, Tristram works to call attention to the fictional nature of all writing, and one of the ways he does this is to emphasize the artificial conventions of books—the chapter and volume divisions, the separate pages with their various arrangements of signs, the physical work itself bound in endpapers which start and put an end to the described reality. Tristram often thinks like a novelist and writes like one. He is constantly involving us in the book's illusion of reality, only suddenly to move us onto the stage where we see that what we have imagined as real is only made of cardboard, wood, nails, and paint. The typography itself— dashes, italics, black letters, asterisks, pointing fingers—is used both to achieve special effects and to remind us that what we are looking at is the result of a printing press.[18] *Tristram Shandy* creates a reality that can never accurately convey the real world because it originates in the subjective mind of the writer and is transferred to the subjective mind of the reader through the artificial medium of a book.

Tristram is having a good laugh at man's presumption and vanity, at his false belief in his mental and intellectual superiority. His goal is to have the reader also come to this awareness, but to do so he must manipulate the reader's perceptions, he must guide his mental operations:

> ———Fair and softly, gentle reader!———where is thy fancy carrying thee?——If there is truth in man, by my great grandfather's nose, I mean the external organ of smelling, or that part of man which stands prominent in his face,——and which painters say, in good jolly noses and well-proportioned faces, should comprehend a full third——that is, measuring downwards from the setting on of the hair.——
> ———What a life of it has an author, at this pass! (P. 221)

In spite of all this business about the reader's wayward mind, Tristram knows very well what the reader is thinking, how in this case he is "seeing" the "nose." Tristram is aware because he has been subtly guiding the reader's imagination to that very interpretation. Here he chides the reader for his wandering, salacious imagination, when, in truth, he has been encouraging that imagination to be wandering and salacious. Minds may be idiosyncratic and independent, but to some degree they can be manipulated. In this passage, however, Tristram is not exploiting his partnership with the reader and accusing him of promiscuous thoughts only to get some sexual material and humor into the book. Sterne is the first novelist to deal with the libido in a modern, psychological way. Sex is seen in the novel as a basic internal drive, as part of man's instinctual world, as a major influence on his thought patterns and imagination; sex is part of Sterne's larger treatment of psychology. Certainly this is evident in the treatment of all his characters, Tristram included, where sexuality is often incomplete or ineffective, and where, driven underground, it finds temporary release in various sublimations. Toby overcomes his wounded groin with his military preoccupation, Walter his ineffective marriage with his fantastic theorizing, and Tristram a strongly sensuous and sensual nature with the writing of his book. Indeed, the hobbyhorse in general is seen as a means of sublimation.[19] In Tristram's treatment of the reader is also a recognition of the erotic instincts and the way in which they play on the individual imagination and hamper communication. Tristram explores and exploits the reader's sexuality and points out to him the way in which his thoughts are influenced by his libido, and in doing so he demonstrates the malleable and wayward nature of the reader's mind.

From the very beginning of the book, then, Tristram is almost as concerned with the reader as with the characters in his narration. As in the case of *Tom Jones*, the narrator may create images of several implied readers, but these are only rhetorical ploys, means of getting at the person who is actually reading the book. The actual reader's relationship to the work is of prime importance because Tristram realizes that he is in large part responsible for the way the characters and their world will be seen. As a result, the book is filled with constant comments and conversations addressed to the reader: "As you proceed further with me, the slight acquaintance which is now beginning betwixt us, will grow into familiarity; and that, unless one of us is in fault, will terminate in friendship..." (p. 11). Tristram not only makes of himself and the reader friends; he forms a relationship based upon the reader's confidence in his superior knowledge. Frequently the reader is guided in the direction of what to see: "———How could you, Madam, be so inattentive in reading the last chapter? I told you in it, *That my mother was not a papist*" (p. 56). All this, of course, is to get the reader responding to the narrator's imaginative world, to relax him so that he is following the narrator's leads, and to set him up for the gradual awareness of what is going on in his own mind as he reads the novel. Sterne depends on the reader's imagination, but he uses this imagination to teach the reader how his mind really functions, how similar it is to those which belong to Tristram and the other characters in the book. But Sterne's ultimate purpose, as we shall see, is to demonstrate more than the subjective and wayward operations of the mind: his final goal is to lead the reader to a realization of the potentials of the wonderful machine he carries about in his head.

THE MINDS OF THE CHARACTERS

Authorial psychology and reader psychology interplay on several levels to shape those patterns in *Tristram Shandy* which we call characters. The narrator projects elements of his own personality and psyche into external forms, and the reader reacts and gives life to these forms according to his own nature and experiences. Tristram's mind is developed for us throughout the novel in large part through his portrayals of Walter, Toby, Mrs. Shandy, Obadiah, Trim, Dr. Slop, Yorick, and the widow Wadman, supposedly real people but figures so dependent on Tristram's own personality and imagination that we can refer to them as his creations and characters as if he were a novelist. Tristram frequently challenges us to see how our minds work and what kind of people we are by the ways in which we perceive these characters. Sterne reinforces this last goal by having the reader relate the *outer-directed irony* aimed at him to the *inner-directed irony* aimed at the characters. But the characters themselves, the way in which they function, also tell us a good deal about the human mind in general. Tristram's passage about Momus's glass warns us, though, that his characters are complex, that sometimes they seem chaotic, and that there is no direct way of seeing into them:

> had the said glass been there set up, nothing more would have been wanting, in order to have taken a man's character, but to have taken a chair and gone softly, as you would to a dioptrical bee-hive, and look'd in,—— view'd the soul stark naked;——observ'd all her motions,——her machinations;——traced all her maggots from their first engendering to their crawling forth;——watched her loose in her frisks, her gambols, her capricios; and after some notice of her more solemn deportment, consequent upon such frisks, & c.——then taken your pen and ink and set down nothing but what you had seen, and could have sworn to:——But this is an advantage not to be had by the biographer in this planet.... (P. 74)

But he also tells us that there is an indirect way to see and understand them, that ultimately the human mind and personality are knowable—to some extent: "our minds shine not through the body, but are wrapt up here in a dark covering of uncrystalized flesh and blood; so that if we would come to the specifick characters of them, we must go some other way to work" (p. 75). Sterne is not seeing human nature in some moralistic framework as does Fielding, nor is he presenting human character largely for dramatic and emotional effect as does Richardson. He is concerned with analyzing the very nature and complexity of the human psyche, for to him this is what the new kind of fiction is really about, and this is what its form and techniques can do better than any other literary type.

Sterne's solution to understanding character at first seems quite traditional: "in a word, I will draw my uncle Toby's character from his HOBBY-HORSE" (p. 77). We have here a concept of characterization by humors, of a personality largely developed through a strong commitment to one passion. This emphasis appears in Walter's theorizing and in Toby's militarism. But these passions are very much internalized and developed through Locke's concept of association of ideas.[20] In other words, Sterne's concept of motivation may be traditional, but the machinery through which the individual's motivations work is not. Nor are his characters simplified or limited by these passions—there are also other forces at work within them. Indeed, the hobbyhorse functions in a vast and complex world of internal character:

> But mark, madam, we live amongst riddles and mysteries——the most obvious things, which come in our way, have dark sides, which the quickest sight cannot penetrate into; and even the clearest and most exalted understandings amongst us find ourselves puzzled and at a loss in almost every cranny of nature's works. . . . (P. 293)

The hobbyhorse may explain a good deal and it does offer much fun, but ultimately it too is overwhelmed by the totality of man's complex nature.

Sterne has taken Locke's *An Essay Concerning Human Understanding* and used certain basic concepts to map out the landscape of his characters' minds, but at the same time he finds Locke's suggestions about the complexity and confusion of the psyche more attractive and akin to his own views than Locke's positive paradigms for human understanding and communication.[21] Let us consider more specifically now a passage we have mentioned twice before, Tristram's discussion of Locke's ideas on mental confusion:

> Now if you will venture to go along with me, and look down into the bottom of this matter, it will be found that cause of obscurity and confusion, in the mind of man, is three-fold.

> Dull organs, dear Sir, in the first place. Secondly, slight and transient impressions made by objects when the said organs are not dull. And, thirdly, a memory like unto a sieve, not able to retain what it has received. (Pp. 85–86)

In some way all the characters suffer from one or more of these defects: the novel is filled with instances of misapprehending, misunderstanding, and forgetting. Dr. Slop's and Mrs. Shandy's organs frequently seem very dull indeed; external events are often poorly perceived by all the characters; and Uncle Toby does have a problem remembering a good amount of his brother's ideas. But Tristram also uses Locke to tell us that "the true cause of the confusion in my Uncle *Toby's* discourse" was "the unsteady uses of words" (p. 86). We have already discussed this problem in relation to the writer Tristram and to the reader as well. It is a problem that confronts all the characters within the narration and adds considerably to the comedy of their lives. Locke recognizes the subjectivism of language but ultimately claims that we all have a sufficiently similar notion of individual words to allow for communication. Sterne does not accept this solution: language becomes for him not only a manifestation of his characters' internal hobbyhorses and confusion but a source of further mental confusion as characters find themselves unable to understand one another.

The passage we have just examined makes it clear how close Tristram is to the very characters he writes about, how his mind and passions function in much the same way, and how he projects into them what he knows about himself. Toby, Walter, and the other characters, like Tristram, are creatures of their senses, people trying to respond to reality and one another through the limited means of their impressions and perceptions. Like Tristram, their views of reality are highly subjective, their thought processes individual and idiosyncratic. And like Tristram, they must try to communicate to one another through their own personal use of words. We can even say that the personal qualities Tristram inherited from his father and uncle are projected right back into these characters as he writes about them.

Sterne creates in his characters a tension between order and disorder, the partial or temporary order imposed by the hobbyhorse and association of ideas, and the disorder which frequently overwhelms such patterns of thought and which arises from such problems as poor organs, poor intellect, or a sensuous nature. But we must also see that the hobbyhorse itself is a cause of disorder, isolating characters within their own private universe, making them victims of their ruling passion, forcing them to perceive reality from a biased viewpoint, and destroying the communicability of their language:

> ———My young master in *London* is dead! said *Obadiah.*———
> ———A green sattin night-gown of my mother's, which had been twice scoured, was the first idea which *Obadiah's* exclamation brought into *Susannah's* head.——Well might *Locke* write a chapter upon the imperfections of words.——Then, quoth *Susannah*, we must all go into mourning.——But note a second time: the word *mourning*, notwithstanding *Susannah* made use of it herself——failed also of doing its office; it excited not one single idea, tinged either with grey or black——all was green.——The green sattin night-gown hung there still. (Pp. 359-60)

Sterne's characters are comic portrayals of man's confused internal state, of his psychological absurdity and complexity, of his failure to perceive with either accuracy or good sense the world inside of him and the world outside. They are strange, funny, ignorant, and rarely in control of their thoughts:

> the thought floated only in Dr. *Slop's* mind, without sail or ballast to it, as a simple proposition; millions of which, as your worship knows, are every day swimming quietly in the middle of the thin juice of man's understanding, without being carried backwards or forwards, till some little gusts of passion or interest drive them to one side. (P. 167)

Though the characters within the narration are instrumental in developing Sterne's anatomy of the human mind, we should once again recognize that they never seem to exist with total independence from the mind of Tristram, their supposed creator. They have their own realities and, as we shall see, they often appear in carefully composed dramatic scenes, but we always seem to hear Tristram's voice describing them, analyzing them, commenting upon them. Even when they are dramatized, when they are talking, acting, reacting, Tristram the narrator is right there with them. The connection between Tristram and these characters is continually emphasized, because the characters are presented (1) as similar to Tristram in the workings of their minds; (2) as responsible for what he is through inheritance and environment; and (3) as a projection of Tristram's own mind. Sterne is writing a book that is in part about writing a book; he is creating the world of his book as a map of its narrator's mind. The characters are the central part of that book, and they are also an immediate indication of the narrator's psyche and personality. They are the most immediate and specific way of dramatizing his perceptions of reality. More than that, they are the visual embodiments of his own thoughts and thinking process.

TEMPORAL AND SPATIAL CONSCIOUSNESS

Sterne sees the psyches of his narrator, the characters within the narration, and his reader as functioning much in the same manner. Not only are all their minds both idiosyncratic and wayward, but they are all conceived in a temporal way. We can say that temporality becomes a major concern and a means of developing characters in those novels of the eighteenth century that are dramatic and explicitly psychological, that in the works of Richardson, Sterne, and Austen, a new dimension is used to give validity and immediacy to the created reality. But Sterne goes much further than the other two writers in exploring time-consciousness.[22] In a sense, *Tristram Shandy* is the most concrete literary embodiment of a new sense of time that was developing in both England and Europe.[23] The commercial revolution was bringing considerable attention to the calendar because of a concern with such matters as departure and arrival of ships and lengths of journeys. The industrial revolution was already beginning, bringing with it an increased awareness of clock time: sequence of steps in production, duration of procedures, schedules of production, length of workdays became primary concerns. Though England was still to be an agrarian nation, the development of urbanization and a middle-class culture moved the educated consciousness from seasonal, cyclical, and repetitive time to linear time. City life emphasized time schedules, appointments, scheduled events, hours for shops and employment. In other words, a new way of measuring one's life developed—a new way of defining reality. This was the period when the minute hand became a fixed part of timepieces, when watches came into fashion, and when personal and household clocks were made in large numbers. The books we have been studying were all written during what has been often called "England's Golden Age of Clockmaking." For all of these reasons, the clock can be seen as one of the major symbols of the age, just as the clock which is imposed upon Mr. Shandy's consciousness during Tristram's conception at the very beginning of the novel becomes, in a sense, a chief symbol of what haunts all the characters, Tristram included, during the entire duration of the book.

Philosophy and epistemology also became interested in psychological time, and here Locke's *An Essay Concerning Human Understanding* was of primary importance. The very funny scene in *Tristram Shandy*, where Walter tries to explain Locke's theory of mental time and duration to Toby (pp. 188–191), is an indication of how much Sterne permeates his work with temporality and defines his characters in

the context of this dimension. Walter is not only aware of time passing—
"It is two hours and ten minutes,——and no more——cried my father,
looking at his watch, since Dr. *Slop* and *Obadiah* arrived,——and I
know not how it happens, brother *Toby*,——but to my imagination it
seems almost an age"—but he is very much involved with the
metaphysical implications of the situation: "He was pre-determined in
his mind, to give my Uncle *Toby* a clear account of the matter by a
metaphysical dissertation upon the subject of *duration and its simple
modes.*" Sterne's book is about the human mind, and thus he must deal
with time, since the mind perceives temporally and is concerned with
time. Sterne not only dramatizes his characters' temporal dimension; he
also makes them aware of time the way no fictional characters had
previously been. Also of interest in this scene is the way Walter,
paraphrasing Locke, conceives of time in a spatial way: our sense of
duration is the result of the number, length, and order of one's ideas.

But Sterne is also writing a novel about a man writing his
autobiography, and the temporal reality of the supposed author,
Tristram, who is really the central consciousness of the entire work, is of
major significance. Throughout the book, Tristram not only describes
the temporal reality of the figures within his narration but also conveys
his own temporal reality in the world outside the book, and by doing so
makes his own world part of his novel. His constant reminders of his
own life moving forward in time are meant to create another drama
throughout the work as well as give us an insight into the dynamics of
literary creation.[24] The dramatization of both temporal realities and the
tension between them, as we shall see, is also a means of suggesting an
ultimate atemporality, a triumph over time that can be achieved both in
the novel and in the human mind. But first we must consider the
problems that arise from this dual time scheme:

> I am this month one whole year older than I was this time twelve-month;
> and having got, as you perceive, almost into the middle of my fourth
> volume——and no farther than to my first day's life——'tis demonstrative
> that I have three hundred and sixty-four days more life to write just now,
> than when I first set out; so that instead of advancing, as a common writer,
> in my work with what I have been doing at it——on the contrary, I am just
> thrown so many volumes back——was every day of my life to be as busy a
> day as this——And why not?——and the transactions and opinions of it to
> take up as much description——And for what reason should they be cut
> short? as at this rate I should just live 364 times faster than I should
> write——It must follow, an' please your worships, that the more I write, the
> more I shall have to write.... (Pp. 285-86)

Tristram's personal drama arises from the fact that he is growing older as he writes his novel. To some degree, he can create and even control the temporality of the characters he writes about, but he has no control over his own, at least not in his immediate reality: art is art, and life is life. Early in the work, he lets us know that it is March 9, 1759, when he is writing; 556 pages later we are told, "And here am I sitting, this 12th day of *August*, 1766" (p. 600). Tristram has aged seven years in his writing of the book, while the characters within his narration have not aged at all. As a matter of fact, they have gotten somewhat younger, since we are now engaged in Uncle Toby's affair with the widow Wadman, an event which happened before the events already related. These characters may be time conscious, but they can be brought back and forth in time by the writer, and hence they are temporally free.

But for Tristram there seems to be no respite. As he writes, time moves swiftly until death finally faces him:

> I will not argue the matter: Time wastes too fast: every letter I trace tells me with what rapidity Life follows my pen.... (P. 610)

Tristram's sense of time, his sense of life passing, has reached such a point that it becomes the central concern of the work. Book VII begins with Tristram's urgent flight from death and his journey through Europe. Much of this section is written with a dramatic immediacy, with short, hurried rhythms that give us a sense of Tristram literally writing down his journey while it is in progress and a sense of his impressions and feelings at the very moment he is writing the book. The narrator has succeeded in imposing his own immediate temporal reality upon the work. In *Moll Flanders*, as we have seen, Defoe generally ignores the distinction between the time levels of the narrator and the narrated events; and in *Clarissa*, Richardson often plays one against the other, sometimes at the expense of his narrative's immediacy. In *Tristram Shandy*, however, the story is as much in the telling as in what is told, and the teller and his tale are inseparably related. For this reason, Tristram can play one time scheme against another, even mix them up in a kaleidoscopic fashion and rise above the limitations of any specific level of time. Tristram breaks up the chronology of his characters' lives, rearranges the order of past events until the characters transcend the limitations of time and its erosive powers. But a greater triumph over time occurs in Tristram's own mind—not in his attempt to lose himself in the immediacy of the present, but in his ability to make the past present again.[25] Tristram is now running a mad race with death, but simultaneously, inside his head, is the psychological capacity to relive time past and write about it. Nowhere is this clearer, nowhere do we see time past pushing itself through time present, than in Tristram's narration of his present journey, when a journey of long ago, his grand tour as a youth, forces itself into his mind and his writing:

> ——Now this is the most puzzled skein of all——for in this last chapter, as far at least as it has help'd me through *Auxerre*, I have been getting forwards in two journies together, and with the same dash of the pen——for I have got entirely out of *Auxerre* in this journey which I am writing now, and I am got half way out of *Auxerre* in that which I shall write hereafter—— There is but a certain degree of perfection in every thing; and by pushing at something beyond that, I have brought myself into such a situation, as no traveller ever stood before me; for I am this moment walking across the market-place of *Auxerre* with my father and my uncle *Toby*, in our way back to dinner——and I am this moment also entering *Lyons* with my post-chaise broke into a thousand pieces——and I am moreover this moment in a handsome pavillion built by *Pringello*, upon the banks of the *Garonne*, which Mons. *Sligniac* has lent me, and where I now sit rhapsodizing all these affairs. (Pp. 515–16)

Tristram tries to free himself from time's erosive powers by losing himself in the present, but his success comes from his capacity to have past events push themselves right through the mad desperation of his present journey and into his writing. Hence Tristram as writer can free himself from time by creating a world that follows the timeless direction of his mind. But another triumph over time is suggested in the description of these journeys. By creating two time lines at once, playing one off against the other, and finding what is common to both, Sterne shows how events repeat themselves and hence how life does not really change. Tristram creates for us a Borgesian vision of an atemporal history.[26]

Before drawing our final conclusions, we must consider the third partner in all of this, the reader and his sense of time.

> It is about an hour and a half's tolerable good reading since my uncle *Toby* rung the bell, when *Obadiah* was order'd to saddle a horse and go for Dr. *Slop* the man-midwife;——so that no one can say, with reason, that I have not allowed *Obadiah* time enough, poetically speaking, and considering the emergency too, both to go and come;——tho' morally and truly speaking, the man, perhaps, has scarce had time to get on his boots.
>
> If the hypercritic will go upon this; and is resolved after all to take a pendulum, and measure the true distance betwixt the ringing of the bell, and the rap at the door;——and, after finding it to be no more than two minutes, thirteen seconds, and three fifths,——should take upon him to insult over me for such a breach in the unity, or rather probability, of time;——I would remind him, that the idea of duration and of its simple

modes, is got merely from the train and succession of our ideas,——and is the true scholastic pendulum,——and by which, as a scholar, I will be tried in this matter,——abjuring and detesting the jurisdiction of all other pendulums whatever.

I would, therefore, desire him to consider that it is but poor eight miles from Shandy-Hall to Dr. *Slop*, the man-midwife's house;——and that whilst *Obadiah* has been going those said miles and back, I have brought my uncle *Toby* from *Namur*, quite across all *Flanders*, into *England*:—— That I have had him ill upon my hands near four years;——and have since travelled him and Corporal *Trim*, in a chariot and four, a journey of near two hundred miles down into *Yorkshire*;——all which put together, must have prepared the reader's imagination for the entrance of Dr. *Slop* upon the stage,——as much, at least (I hope) as a dance, a song, or a concerto between the acts. (Pp. 103–04)

The reader has been reading for two and one-half hours, the necessary time for the fetching of Dr. Slop, even though only a few minutes have actually passed within the novel. But since the reader's sense of time is more important for Tristram than the actual time within the novel, Dr. Slop is allowed to arrive. The reader's sense of time is ultimately dependent upon the duration created by the succession of ideas in his own mind—in this case, the succession of ideas is his series of mental perceptions of events described in the novel, whether they belong to the same time sequence or not. But something else is implied here about the reader's role, as it is throughout the book: every time the novel is read, Tristram and the people he writes about are once more re-created into the present, reactivated into the reader's sense of immediacy as he is reading the book. We can understand now a little better Tristram's preoccupation with the reader: another triumph over time is the immortality to be achieved by him and his characters, and this is totally dependent upon the perceiving mind that reads the book.

In our daily existence, we are aware of event following event, of the present starting to slip away from us, and of time passing. But when we have lived through an event, it becomes a complete and permanent part of our memory bank. The event loses its temporality by becoming part of a whole landscape of memories, by fitting spatially into the total vision of our lives, and by being permanently accessible to our immediate consciousness. Sometimes we are even able to see the present event spatially within the context of our total existence. We have the same kind of responses to the events of the novel: when we are in the process of reading, we are aware of individual actions occurring and completing themselves, of one event succeeding another, and, hence, of time passing, but we are also aware of the episodes we have already read and the present one in a spatial arrangement. I am talking again about the visual *gestalt* of the work's totality which we hold in our minds. Few works in English fiction are written so consciously and carefully to appeal to this mental capacity as *Tristram Shandy*.[27] Sterne's most significant triumph over time is achieved by his structuring of the entire novel upon the mind's spatial sense of past and present events and of time itself, a spatial sense achieved by the writer Tristram and communicated to the reader. The normal way to tell a story is in chronological order, which creates for us a sense of time passing, but Sterne takes the plot of the novel, breaks down all of its chronology, and mixes for us various stages of time. In other words, instead of writing a novel that is ordered by a normal, developing plot, he arranged his novel according to structural and spatial principles, the juxtaposition and relationship of episodes that exist in the narrator's mind and suspend time. Tristram writes his novel as ideas spring into his head, as one directs the other, as his mind runs back and forth in time, until there is no destination, no development in the novel—until time is suspended. To call the process of his mind a mere "train of ideas"[28] is to suggest that Tristram's thoughts exist only in a diachronic linear flow, but Tristram's mind does not work like that: the arrangement of his thoughts is associational and synchronic, with one idea suggesting another, with ideas linked together and superimposed upon each other through similarity and repetition. This is my answer to the question of whether Sterne ever completed *Tristram Shandy*.[29] As a novel without a traditional plot, without a diachronic development, the work does not need a specific or even culminating finish. The work rather requires a sufficient number of related episodes to give the reader the sense of the atemporal structure of Tristram's mind, and this it certainly does.

Sterne's achievement, then, is to realize that the novel has a structure that can transcend plot, be it the movement of *sujet* or *fabula*, and that this structure is dependent on the fact that the reader can perceive the novel spatially: "when a man is telling a story in the strange way I do mine, he is obliged continually to be going backwards and forwards to keep all tight together in the reader's fancy..." (p. 462). In a sense, Sterne asks us to see our own lives wholly, to see everything we have experienced and now experience in a total vision; he wants us to see that time can become a delusion if we allow ourselves to accept the atemporality of our minds and the immediacy which the mind grants to past events as well as present. This is the vision of life that the book attempts to create. This is the answer to his fear of time and death that the writer Tristram communicates through his strangely ordered

177

book—strange only because it presents a truer perception of reality than most people can accept. In a comic but very serious way, the novel asks us to see that the true reality is what exists inside of us, that we should see each moment, past and present, in the permanence of that larger context. Existence may be filled with obstacles, confusions, absurdities, but everything fits together, just like the pieces of the novel, if we will only perceive it all as part of our mental lives and unified by the associational procedures of our psyches, as bizarre as these procedures may be. Sterne explores the human mind and finds it a place of confusion and complexity, but at the same time he finds within the mind the capacity to see all of our existence in a complete and ultimately redemptive way.

   We have seen throughout this study a developing spatial awareness in almost all the novels examined, though one relegated mostly to the depiction of individual scenes. The increased spatial dimension was a means by which writers attempted to create for the reader a visual sense of what was happening, especially as it was perceived by the characters of the novel. Sterne conceived the entire structure of his novel, his fictional external world, and individual scenes in a spatial manner. Such a spatial concern was, of course, not restricted to the novel alone. The cosmic geography and very expansiveness of Milton's *Paradise Lost* reflected a new, telescopic vision of the universe. One can argue that the new science that developed during the seventeenth and eighteenth centuries, especially the advancements in astronomy and physics, gradually influenced the way people perceived the world outside of them as well as the universe.[30] Especially significant in this respect was the Newtonian world picture that developed in the eighteenth century and considerably expanded man's spatial awareness. Equally important was Locke's discussion of space in *An Essay Concerning Human Understanding* (II, xiii), which had a strong impact on Berkeley, Hume, and other major thinkers of the period. Space is a consideration in Addison's papers on the imagination and in the aesthetic treatises of writers such as Burke and Alison. This larger spatial imagination is obvious in Thomson's *The Seasons*, a poetic compendium of popular cultural ideas and perceptions, as well as in the "sublime" poems of the mid-century poets. It is within this general context that one can understand the way in which the novel was able to rely upon the reader's newly developed spatial imagination while at the same time expanding it.

WHAT'S OUT THERE?

Sterne, then, goes further than any writer before him in fulfilling the potential of the novel as a psychological literary form. Even in the depiction of external reality, of the world in which the characters live, Sterne extends his psychological drama, for the external dimension is treated as both a continuous challenge to characters' psyches—their minds attempt to understand the reality outside them through their own sense impressions—and as an extension of those psyches—characters attempt to shape external reality from their own subjective point of view. But even in the midst of such interplay with external reality, the physical universe seems to maintain a force of its own: chestnuts move with an independent will, windows are not to be trusted, house-clocks make us creatures of habit, and even a hat can be more eloquent than the greatest rhetorician. No matter what one does, he is confronted with a physical world that seems to make no sense at all:

> ——My father thrust back his chair,——rose up,——put on his hat,—— took four long strides to the door,——jerked it open,——thrust his head half way out,——shut the door again,——took no notice of the bad hinge,——returned to the table,——pluck'd my mother's thread-paper out of *Slawkenbergius's* book,——went hastily to his bureau,——walk'd slowly back, twisting my mother's thread-paper about his thumb,—— unbutton'd his waist-coat,——threw my mother's thread-paper into the fire,——bit her sattin pin-cushion in two, fill'd his mouth with bran,—— confounded it.... (P. 239)

Walter here lays hands on the physical world—on the door, the thread paper, the book, the waistcoat, the pincushion—and tries to incorporate them into his own psychic world, tries to manipulate them into his emotional state, but all he is left with is a mouthful of bran.

What is Diego's nose, after all? And why does it have such a compelling influence on so many people? The tale seems to infuse the nose with some hypnotic power, but, of course, it is the characters within the tale and the readers themselves who make this part of the body into more than a nose. And what are we to do with whiskers? Or buttonholes? Or whiskers and buttonholes in conjunction? Again, it is worthwhile pointing out that Sterne's salaciousness has more of a psychological function than an erotic one. Slawkenbergius's tale is not merely a protracted dirty joke; it is also an elaborate parable about the absurdity and even obscenity of physical reality, about man's inability to understand the physical world outside of him, and about his constant projection of his own drives and fantasies into that world.

179

Because of these concerns, Sterne in his novel takes great pains to present external reality in an immediate and graphic way. In his presentation of the external world, he is again influenced by earlier novels, and again he extends and plays with already established narrative techniques. Or perhaps it would be better to say that Tristram, in writing what he claims to be his autobiography, uses the techniques of the novel to emphasize both his own role as the actual creator of the people and objects that appear in his work, and the fictitious nature of his characters' and his own perceptions of reality. We have seen how earlier novelists developed a scenic presentation of action, where characters perform in a detailed and dramatized way in a physical universe. Note the following description of Walter Shandy's behavior after the unfortunate baptism of his son:

> The moment my father got up into his chamber, he threw himself prostrate across his bed in the wildest disorder imaginable, but at the same time, in the most lamentable attitude of a man borne down with sorrows, that ever the eye of pity dropp'd a tear for.——The palm of his right hand, as he fell upon the bed, receiving his forehead, and covering the greatest part of both his eyes, gently sunk down with his head (his elbow giving way backwards) till his nose touch'd the quilt;——his left arm hung insensible over the side of the bed, his knuckles reclining upon the handle of the chamber pot, which peep'd out beyond the valance,——his right leg (his left being drawn up towards his body) hung half over the side of the bed, the edge of it pressing upon his shinbone.——He felt it not. A fix'd, inflexible sorrow took possession of every line of his face.——He sighed once,—— heaved his breast often,——but utter'd not a word.
>
> An old set-stitch'd chair, valanced and fringed around with party-colour'd worsted bobs, stood at the bed's head, opposite to the side where my father's head reclined.——My uncle *Toby* sat him down in it. (Pp. 215-16)

Here Sterne seems to be developing, and even exploiting for his own purposes, the qualities he found in earlier scenic depictions. Here we have a number of physical objects intruding themselves into the human world—the bed, the quilt, the chamber pot, the valance, the chair. Also interesting is the way in which the parts of Walter's body—the palm of his right hand, his head, his arms, his legs—are given such attention, until they seem disproportionate to the person. Sometimes in the novel, as in the case of Diego's nose, parts of the body are given such significance that they seem to exist by themselves, separated from the individual, as objects of wonder to the perceiving eye. But just as often the parts of the body become an extension of the psychic state of their owner and a means by which we can partly understand what the character is feeling or thinking—position, gesture, motion become a means of communication. In the above scene, Toby sits down and, by perceiving the way in which his brother's body is sprawled across the bed, understands at least in part what he is feeling. But Walter, with such an emphasis on his body and his behavior so detailed, still is a grotesque and pathetic figure.[31] In such scenes, Sterne seems to be making another statement on man's ultimate absurdity, in this case as a physical creature in a physical world.

There is a remarkable visual dimension throughout all of *Tristram Shandy*. Even Tristram's commentaries, his "opinions" on sundry matters, are imagistically conceived: "A Man's body and his mind, with the utmost reverence to both I speak it, are exactly like a jerkin, and a jerkin's lining;——rumple the one——you then rumple the other" (p. 160). Walter Shandy himself uses Locke's comparison of the "train of ideas" and "the images in the inside of a lanthorn turned round by the heat of candle" (p. 191).[32] But Tristram's thoughts are mostly developed through a series of strongly visual images of characters and actions. Sterne's novel develops a host of scenes where attention is given to the details of physical behavior in a physically real world. Like Richardson, he does not describe in detail the appearance of his settings but rather integrates into descriptions of his characters' movements an ever-present reality. Characters are constantly running into and trying to manipulate the objects that surround them; and both characters and objects are played against each other in a spatially conceived scene. At the same time, like Richardson, his emphasis in his depiction of characters is always on gesture and movement, not on physical characteristics.[33]

As well as seeing the mind spatially and structuring his entire novel from a spatial perspective, Sterne depicts his characters as part of a surrounding spatial reality that helps develop his vision of the human predicament. Sterne does more than create for us a visual sense of the immediate world, of the arrangement of the various rooms and the relationship between the brothers' homes and Toby's bowling green; he does more than spatially arrange such scenes as the brothers coming down the stairs or Walter sprawled across the bed. He dramatizes a physical universe which surrounds the characters, one filled with objects and parts of bodies, with falling windows, flying hats, rolling chestnuts, incredible noses, gesticulating hands, and wounded sex organs. All the details of Walter's external behavior as he lies sprawled across the bed, of his spatial definition and relation to the various objects around him— all manifest his internal state, but also his grand frustration and isolation. This is a picture of the limitations of the human mind, of its befuddlement and separation in an absurd and undecipherable world.

In our examination of *Tristram Shandy*, we have gradually moved inward, from the reader-narrator relationship to that between the narrator and the characters about whom he writes, to that between the characters and the real world which confronts them. From one perspective, the novel is a series of frames or Chinese boxes, with the reader moving ever inwards to find the core of reality, the inmost box from which all the perceptions in the novel originate. But it would be more accurate to say that the novel develops in us the sense of being several times removed from this core, that subjective perspectives multiply one upon the other until we feel the full imponderability of reality that Sterne wishes to communicate to us. We must see through Tristram's mind, which sees through the minds of the characters in his narration, which try to see into the reality that surrounds them. Perhaps we might even add another frame or box to this sequence, and say that we must see through Sterne's perceptions of Tristram's perceptions of the character's perceptions of reality. Whatever the case, such perspectives within perspectives disorient and distance us, until we finally find order and harmony in Tristram's psychological triumph over the fragments of existence and the erosive powers of time.

All the efforts of this novel, all its themes and subthemes, relate to this movement toward order and harmony. The book looks with amused irony at the misguided attempts of man to find a path through the labyrinth of his own perceptions, at his vain pursuits for understanding. *Tristram Shandy* has an encyclopedic nature to it that reminds one of such earlier satiric works of the period as *Tale of a Tub* and *Memoirs of Martinus Scriblerus*.[34] Like these works, the novel uses erudition, learning, the paraphernalia of learned names, quotations, and footnotes to mock man's pretense of knowledge.[35] But *Tristram Shandy* is more concerned with the human brain in general, and it presents in realistic and novelistic fashion its psychological narrator and characters. Its satire is directed against the misguided efforts of men toward self-understanding, toward some comprehension of the human mind, and against an art form that too facely orders and explains the mind. The countless authors whom Tristram is always quoting or referring to— some obsolete and funny because of their ludicrous failure at knowledge, others comic fictions of Sterne's mind—all relate to the major concerns of the work. Walter's opinions, his learned discourses, and his never-completed *Tristra-poedia* for the development of his son's mind are attempts on his part to come to grips with human understanding and are manifestations of his own lack of knowledge. The meeting of the learned men about the changing of Tristram's name, their own comprehension of reality and their learned discourse—all shattered by the hot reality of the chestnut—illustrate human confusion and vanity. Everything seems to point out our ignorance. Even Tristram's writing, which manifests the wayward progress of his thinking and his love for pedantry, shows that he himself is a victim of the same kinds of mental limitations and confusions that he consciously depicts in others. *Tristram Shandy* is an attack not so much against what man doesn't know as what he thinks he knows. Even the sage Locke, who has written the greatest history of the mind, must receive his share of ridicule.

Sterne denies us the ability to understand ourselves or others or even the world outside us in any meaningful way. He does so because of that strange and uncontrollable machine we carry around inside our heads. Man's confusion and intellectual failure, however, is presented not with sadness and pessimism but with a wonderful zaniness and healthy humor. Sterne can afford to be funny because for him the universe is hardly a bleak place. In *Humphry Clinker*, which we shall examine in the next chapter, Smollett investigates similar issues about perception and reality, but sees the universe as ultimately a dark and hostile place. In *Tristram Shandy*, people have the capacity to feel for one another, to express their feelings, and to act upon them: Sterne's characters are sentimental and benevolent, qualities that are not often enough found in Smollett's general depiction of mankind. But more significantly, and this is the major point I have tried to make in this chapter, Sterne finally sees the mind—hobbyhorses, complexity, and all—as a rather wonderful machine with the capacity to offer us a full and varied mental life, a mental life achieved by Tristram in the writing of his book and one sufficient for us to overcome the imponderable universe outside of us. For Sterne, the mind can put at our disposal the whole range and totality of our experience, and even open up to our imagination the lives of others. Each of us has the capacity to relive and ultimately transcend time, to become artists and immortals in the richness of our mental lives.

CHAPTER FIVE

HUMPHRY CLINKER
and Parallactic Narration

THE TRAVELOGUE AS NOVEL

On first examination, Smollett's *Humphry Clinker* (1771) seems less a novel than any of the books we have already analyzed. Recent discussions of the work have tried to establish its credentials as a novel by finding within it some obvious qualities we normally associate with the genre—but always, it seems to me, these discussions are beside the point. To try to assert, for example, that the work has a unity and order in tracing the physical and psychological development of Matt Bramble,[1] or that it tells the story of how people pull together under the pressures of a journey,[2] is only to isolate a strand in the context of a more complicated book. Here again, as with the works we have already studied, it is the narrative techniques and, through them, the kind of experience created in the reader that explain why *Humphry Clinker*, even with its de-emphasis on plot, dramatic conflict, and psychological exploration, is a novel, and why, more than any of Smollett's other works of fiction, it seems central to the development of the genre. Individual perceptions and point of view are the foundations of this work.[3] What we have are five characters seeing and responding to the world around them in their own particular ways and forcing the reader to take a stance with each of them, to view reality through their eyes and understand it with their minds. What Smollett has done is to take the travel book and subjectify it with elements from the epistolary novel: he has synthesized a nonfictional and fictional form.[4] The focus and general structure of the travel book give *Humphry Clinker* verisimilitude and authenticity—this is an account of real places in England and Scotland—and the multiple first-person points of view of the epistolary novel bring the world alive by infusing it with a reality and immediacy that can come only from the perceiving mind.

Smollett draws upon the travelogue, both fictional and nonfictional,[5] and his own earlier writings about his travels.[6] Of course, he was not the first writer to use epistles for a travel book[7]—letters were a natural vehicle to reinforce the travel book's authenticity, to authenticate further its mode of composition and observations—but the extent of this influence was not great. The single work of this type, which had a direct impact on Smollett, was Christopher Anstey's popular *The New Bath Guide* (1766),[8] a book which describes the visit to Bath of Mr. B-n-r-d, his sister Prudence, their cousin Jenny, and the servant Tabby Runt. Here is Smollett's small family unit, and, to some extent, here are the prototypes for four of his letter-writers. Most of Anstey's letters, however, are written by only Mr. B-n-r-d and Jenny. Mr. B-n-r-d, like Matt, suffers from ill health and writes some caustic commentary on Bath; Jenny plays the same ingénue role as Lydia and reacts to her surroundings with a similar romantic and wide-eyed awe. We find out little about Prudence in Anstey's work, but her conversion to Methodism gives her some similarity to Smollett's Tabitha, who actually takes the name of Anstey's servant. Tabby Runt is also kept in the background, but the fact that she is made pregnant by a Moravian priest gives her at least some approximation to Smollett's Winifred Jenkins, who is also a sexual creature, though one more proper in her deportment and fortunate in her conclusions. Some of Mr. B-n-r-d's commentary on the bathing and gambling, and on a public breakfast at Bath, reminds us of Matt's more bitter and condemning discourses on life in this city; and certainly the episode where Mr. B-n-r-d's musicians are the cause of an altercation with Lord Ringbone is the source of a similar event in *Humphry Clinker*, where Matt is disturbed by the French-horn players of Colonel Rigworm. If Smollett, however, received the idea for his work and some of his characters from Anstey, the development and amplification were all his own. Not only do the travels of his family group range far beyond Bath, but he adds a host of characters and events, which he ties together by a number of his own significant themes. At the same time, Anstey's two major correspondents are scarcely developed as individuals, and the pedestrian verse with which they write their letters works against any significant characterization. One of the most pleasing aspects of Smollett's work is the five distinct personalities through whom we view the events of the novel.

Actually, we can find in several epistolary travelogues which appeared before *Humphry Clinker* letters written by different people, but the personal element is never sufficiently developed to individualize the letters or to allow the outside world to appear through the prism of distinct and unique perspectives, nor are these works structured to allow much interplay between the epistles. All this was Smollett's achievement when he developed the subjective element of the letters, focused on the characters' perceptions, and made his chief structural force and unity the relationship of the epistles, thus creating a novel and not a travelogue or a fictitious travel book. The elements of plot that we find in the novel, as well as the interplay of fictitious characters, add to the novelistic quality of the work, but by themselves they would not suffice to tie in *Humphry Clinker* with the major fictional developments of his century.

The subjective element that brings these descriptions of places and people alive came from the epistolary novel, especially from the works of Richardson. Smollett was influenced by Richardson in writing epistles that both create the particular voice and personality of the correspondent, and also convey the way the individual sees reality. But the distinction between these writers' accomplishments, between the personal and subjective natures of their individual characters, must be underscored. Iser suggests that the difference arises from the earlier writer's emphasis on his characters' self-analysis,[9] but I think we can make a broader and more pervasive distinction than that. Richardson's characters spend much time dramatizing their inner states as well as analyzing them; Smollett's characters mostly describe and respond to the external world in an immediate way and do not create within themselves a sustained or developed inner drama. Richardson's characters describe external events in great detail, but mostly to heighten their internal conflicts and to serve as a starting point for their internal reactions. Smollett's characters use internal reactions in order to heighten and develop the world outside them, in order to make us see it and sense it through their responses. The external world is Smollett's major concern; what is happening to that world is his major theme; and the various voices exist not so much to establish their own characters as to give us a view of the physical world from various perspectives and through various perceptions. Like *Clarissa*, *Humphry Clinker* creates a series of distinct characters through their own epistolary voices. But unlike *Clarissa*, Smollett's work features no characters who experience a large assortment of emotional and psychological responses, who are portrayed with a great deal of complexity, or who undergo any significant change or development. Matt's movement towards physical health and mental equanimity functions more to underscore the change in external location than to demonstrate any psychological drama.[10] Matt Bramble is a successful character, but what we most admire about him is not the person he is or what happens to him inside; we enjoy him because of his responses to the external world, because of his perspective, because he sees things from a personal viewpoint we find entertaining and often truthful.

Smollett's work, then, is concerned with credible human beings and their relationship to the outside world; the aesthetic experience he creates is dependent upon a stance the reader takes with certain characters as they perceive that outside world. But Smollett's emphasis is neither upon the individual's situation in that world, as is Defoe's, nor on the character's internal drama in his interaction with that world, as is Richardson's—it is upon physical reality itself, the external world which surrounds and confronts the characters, and the way in which it receives its immediacy and significance from the minds that see it.

PARALLACTIC VISION

In Sterne's *Tristram Shandy*, we saw a conscious attempt to explore problems about human perception and about the relation between mind and matter that were discussed in the major philosophical treatises of the time and implicitly considered in the other novels we had studied. *Humphry Clinker* is a novel where such matters are not confronted from any extensive philosophical or even psychological position, but where the very nature of the narrative techniques adopted and their relation to the work's social themes force Smollett to some practical considerations and realizations about the individual's relationship to the world outside him. Smollett explores some of the same issues as Sterne, but his investigation is rooted in a cosmos far less inexplicable and absurd, far more concerned with the realities of everyday life, and his locations are for more extensive, immediate, and socially significant. At the same time, the minds which perceive this world are less comic, complex, and confused, and more natural and even pertinent to our own habits of thought. Smollett's novel confronts immediate and real social problems in a vast and varying social scene; his characters must struggle through the limitations of their own personalities and psychic responses to learn to live and survive in this world with equanimity and grace.

The novel is structured as a collection of letters written by five correspondents of the same family group. The correspondents, with the exception of Tabitha, describe the places and people they see on their journey and also their own adventures; however, they do so not to one another but to various people in different locations. Hence, there is little plot development from the interaction of letters, from correspondent writing to correspondent, as in the case of *Clarissa*. We can go further than this and say that there is little plot development even from the relationship of the correspondents during their journey. Certainly they talk about one another, undergo some of their adventures together, and sometimes respond to one another in a particular situation, but, in general, at least until the final part of the work, their letters basically function to give us discrete perceptions of the world through which they travel. The real unity of the book comes from the interaction of the letters that we, the readers, perceive. There is no way for the correspondents to know what the others are writing and hence no way for any single mind within the work to perceive the relationship among the letters. Hence, the meaning and significance of the work that comes from the interplay of letters is dependent on the reader's perceptions and capacity to interrelate the various epistles. He must do so on his own, with no help from an interjecting narrative voice. The reader must see the letters as related through the ways in which the characters respond to the same locations or people, and through the common concerns which they express in their writing.[11] Indeed, we can say that both of these unifying elements are themselves related, since the characters' perceptions of reality and the relationship of these perceptions result in some of the work's major thematic concerns. Because the reader is led into perceiving the world of England and Scotland with these characters, the variety of perceptions belonging to different figures which pass through his mind leads him to discover some of these themes through his own involvement with the novel and his own aesthetic experience.

Had Smollett been consistent with this kind of structure throughout his book, he would have written a marvel among works of fiction during this period. But though he apparently intended to unify his work in the ways I have suggested, he sometimes neglected his less perceptive characters, and, in the second half of his novel, he was frequently overcome by the number of places and people he wished to describe and had not time to present all of these through multiple perspectives; on such occasions the novel gives way to the travelogue. Whatever failure the reader may feel in the work, then, does not arise from a poor plot or undeveloped characters; it is the result of Smollett's inability to carry through the basic structure and narrative techniques with which he conceived his book.

But let us consider the many parts of the work that do achieve the kind of multiple perspectives and composite structure I have been describing. In a work dependent upon the interplay between individual letters, the distinct qualities of each writer must be established immediately. Part of the delight we feel from the way these letters play off one another comes not from watching the development of characters but from observing in how many varied locations and situations characters can behave as uniquely themselves. The distinctiveness of the voices has several effects upon us. To begin with, the specificity of voice, the discernible traits of character and habits of language, allow us to perceive the character and form a mental image of him. I have already argued that the data we receive to formulate a character in our mind need not be visual, that we associate visual images or characteristics with kinds of speech as well as personal traits. Smollett's voices are specific and concrete. The characters are not especially complicated, and their patterns of traits are quickly established for us. The pictures we form of these figures tend to be subjective, since there are no detailed physical descriptions to guide us, and the visual associations we make from characters' speech and traits are as much dependent on the workings of our own mind as on any universal responses to the novelists' language. Tabitha is the only correspondent to be described with specificity, but this comes later in the book (p. 90)[12]—detailed physical descriptions, as we shall see, are mostly reserved for the characters the correspondents meet on their journey.

The distinctions and particularity of the first-person narrative voice at first tends to solidify and distance the character for us; the visual image we receive from such specificity of voice keeps the character outside of us. But if the character is not too comic, if the language is not too broad or foreign to us, another process begins. The act of reading these first-person epistles is really an act of reciting all the lines in our minds, of slowly beginning to feel that the first-person pronouns belong to us, and that we, to some extent, are the letter-writers: the statements that pass through our minds become our statements, the observations and perspectives belong to us. There is no way we can identify with characters like Tabby and Winifred, since we cannot introject their idiosyncratic language and comic personalities, but at least in the case of Winifred, we are allowed to perceive with the character her responses to the external world. Matt's voice is no less distinct, but his intelligence and attitudes are closer to what ours would be, his language is more literate, and so we tend to be more involved in the workings of his mind and emotions. Lydia's language is at times romantic and juvenile, but the idiosyncratic and comic is minimal in her letters; as a result, the flow of her thoughts and responses allows us some empathy and even identification with her. Nor does Jery's youthful arrogance and superiority prevent us from involving ourselves with his often shrewd and intelligent observations on the world outside him. In all the characters, however, there is not enough psychological development, not enough depth, to get us strongly involved with them. Our identification is controlled, and we are always aware of each character's bias and limitations. This is essential, because the major effect of Smollett's novel comes not from any individual psychological exploration or development but from the way in which the letters of these distinct people play off one another, and to enjoy this we cannot be over-involved with any single voice and person. Smollett's novel is partly concerned with the relationship between mind and matter, and because matter is perceived by the subjective mind, it becomes a relative quantity. Smollett's multiple voices emphasize the relativity of reality, a perspective we can only achieve by comprehending all the singular visions at once.

Once this period began to see reality as dependent on the perceiving mind, the whole question of subjectivity and relativity had to arise, as well as doubts about our capacity to see things the way they are: this is the important philosophical and psychological shift we have been discussing throughout this study. For Sterne, as we have seen, man can bumble through with his isolated and individual perceptions and achieve some basic kinds of understanding and communication. This is also true for Smollett, though in a different way. The subjectivity of perception is a fact of life, but it need not hide reality and the truth from us: "I am...mortified to reflect what flagrant injustice we every day commit, and what absurd judgment we form, in viewing objects through the falsifying mediums of prejudice and passion" (p. 374). Jery's words well describe one of the book's major concerns and contribute to our understanding of its epistolary technique. The letters allow us to see eighteenth-century England and Scotland through a number of perspectives that are, to varying degrees, clouded by "prejudice and passion": Matt's ill health and preoccupation with personal comfort cause him to focus on the physical nature of his surroundings while influencing his perceptions and making of him a partial misanthrope; Jery's youth and education, his concern with people and culture, his sense of his own superiority, guide his interests and commentary;[13] Lydia's youth and limited experience, her romantic reading and inclinations, shape the way she sees the world; and certainly Winifred's lower-class sensibility affects her view of reality, while Tabby's provincialism, avariciousness, and desperate desire for a husband influence her perceptions. What plot we have in the novel is concerned with righting the wrongs caused by misinterpretations and false appearances: the true identities of Wilson and Humphry must be discovered before they can be properly accepted by the other characters and before we can have the necessary marriages and happy ending. More significantly, we, as readers, must recognize the letter-writers' myopia before we can compensate for their vision and get a more rounded and less limited view of reality. We are significantly aided in this effort by the multiple perspectives which, to some degree, correct or simply add to one another.

We might take as an example the way London appears to the eyes of the different characters. For Matt, it is a place crowded "with streets and squares, and palaces, and churches," though it must be admitted "that London and Westminster are much better paved and lighted than they were formerly. The new streets are spacious, regular, and airy; and the houses generally convenient" (pp. 117-18). But even Matt's responses to the positive aspects of the city cannot overcome his disgust for it as a "grand source of luxury and corruption" (p. 118-19). For Lydia, however, London is a source of excitement and color, a place where "there is such an infinity of gay equipages, coaches, chariots, chaises, and other carriages, continually rolling and shifting before your eyes, that one's head grows giddy looking at them; and the imagination is quite confounded with splendour and variety"; a place where "the prospect by water [is no] less grand and astonishing than that by land . . ." (p. 123). Jery's perspective on London emphasizes the strange and perverse ways of its inhabitants, the social and political life at locations like St. James's, where appear "a great assemblage of distinguished characters" (p. 128), and at events like the duke of N——'s levee. Winifred's view of the great city, on the other hand, is summed up in her awed responses to Sadler's-wells, "where I saw such a tumbling and dancing upon ropes and wires, that I was frightened and ready to go into a fit—I tho't it was all inchantment . . ." (p. 140).

The same kind of multiple vision is used to portray the characters for us. Not only do we get separate views of the letter-writers' behavior and actions from their own epistles and the letters of their fellow correspondents, but other characters are described from the different perceptions of the various correspondents. Note, for example, the composite view of Lismahago we initially receive. Jery first gives us an extraordinarily detailed description of his physical appearance and behavior—I quote only a small part of this portrait:

> He wore a coat, the cloth of which had once been scarlet, trimmed with Brandenburgs, now totally deprived of their metal, and he had holster-caps and housing of the same stuff and the same antiquity.... the saddle turned, down came the cavalier to the ground, and his hat and perriwig falling off, displayed a head-piece of various colours, patched and plaistered in a woeful condition.... He would have measured above six feet in height had he stood upright.... (Pp. 222-23)

Matt sees Lismahago as "one of the most singular personages I ever encountered" and gives a lengthy description of his conversation and opinions: "The spirit of contradiction is naturally so strong in Lismahago, that I believe in my conscience he has rummaged, and read, and studied with indefatigable attention, in order to qualify himself to refute established maxims, and thus raise trophies for the gratification of polemical pride" (pp. 238-39). After Matt tells us about Lismahago's views on the present state of Scotland and England, he finally admits "I believe...that I shall for some time continue to chew the cud of reflection upon many observations which this original discharged" (p. 242). To round out the picture, we have Winifred's view of Lismahago as a suitor to her mistress: "There has been a deal of huggling and flurtation betwixt mistress and an ould Scotch officer, called Kismycago. He looks for all the orld [sic] like the scare-crow that our gardener had set up to frite away the sparrows ... " (p. 257). Even after their initial characterizations, figures like Lismahago, Humphry, and the correspondents themselves receive the same kind of multiple descriptions, as their various exploits and behavior are described to us from the distinct perceptions of different letter-writers.

I do not mean to minimize the validity of each individual perspective, since reality has no meaning without the mind that sees it, and each perception is real enough to the perceiver. Nor do I mean to suggest that we must see the characters' perceptions as totally subjective and distorted. The difference here from Sterne's outlook about reality is crucial: while *Tristram Shandy* points out the impossibility of ever knowing the physical universe, *Humphry Clinker* shows us that what we see is limited by our own partial vision—but that our partial vision is still valid. With the exception of Tabby, characters' "prejudices and passions" are neither extreme nor reprehensible; they rather add the necessary personal and subjective qualities to individualize the characters. Matt, Jery, and even Lydia are intelligent and perceptive enough to make us feel that what they describe is a fairly accurate presentation of the real world. The subjective element does not so much distort or change reality as choose which aspects to describe, aspects which are of most significance to the individual writer. The technique of description in Smollett's epistles is impressionistic in that it re-creates the external world in the way that it impresses the individual mind and sensibility of each writer, but the general structure of the work is parallactic in that it assembles a number of perspectives, each different but each in its own way valid. As we continue to read much of the work, this larger perspective develops in our mind, one that assembles the individual points of view; and by the time we have finished the novel, we have assembled in our mind a large and multifaceted view of England and Scotland during the eighteenth century. Smollett's triumph is to write a travel book like none ever written before. By using certain techniques basic to the new novel form, he has avoided the dull, methodical descriptions of the travel book and brought to life the world he describes; he has given us a more realistic and wider view of reality.

What we have, then, for large parts of the work, are separate characters responding to the world through which they travel in distinct ways, conveying separate sets of images which we must hold in our mind and match one against the other. The purpose of this procedure is not only to allow the reader to see and understand the different personalities through their different perceptions, but also to permit him a composite vision of places and people by fitting together the different descriptions. We can go further than this and say that the letters create distinctive personalities and perspectives in order to convey to us a multifaceted and extensive picture of eighteenth-century England and Scotland as it appeared to Tobias Smollett. For this reason it is unwise to connect any single perspective to that of the author, even though Matt's personality and physical health may approximate those of Smollett. The author's vision is the total vision that the book creates; and the total vision for him is largely a parallactic one—the world the way it is seen from different perspectives. The point I must emphasize again is that any individual view of reality though personal and relative is legitimate and real. It is not that individuals distort the reality outside them so much as they select only those elements of the world which they wish to see, which most relate to their own personalities. Therefore, in order to see the world with some fullness and accuracy, we must view it from a number of individual perceptions—we must see it with parallactic vision.

By defining parallactic narration as the description of the same places, characters, or events from the perspectives of several different characters, we can see that elements of this technique appeared in earlier fictional forms, in Longus's Greek romance *Daphnis and Chloe*, and in Chaucer's *Troilus and Creseyde*, for example, where in each work the same events are responded to by the hero and heroine individually. But because of the novel's capacity to convey psychological states and dramatize individual perspectives, the technique can be found more readily in this form. To some extent parallax is implicit in all first-person novels. Moll Flanders, at least in the first part of Defoe's work, gives us a double perspective of events by narrating both her responses when she participated in the action and her present responses at the time of writing. Epistolary fiction seems an even more natural vehicle for this kind of narration, with the correspondents not only describing their own past and present responses to the same action but simultaneously writing about one another and their adventures together. In *Clarissa*, Richardson experimented with this type of writing, though only to a limited degree. Both the heroine and Lovelace partly describe, or at least refer to, the same scene on occasion from their own distinct perspectives. More often, the reader supplies his own parallactic vision, reading the scene from the correspondent's perspective and almost simultaneously imagining it from the other major character's point of view. In addition to *Humphry Clinker*, we might mention a French epistolary novel of the eighteenth century which uses parallactic narration to a considerable degree, Laclos's *Les Liaisons dangereuses*, published in 1782.

But parallactic vision, though more available in the form of first-person and especially epistolary novels, is to some degree possible in all types of novels. In works like *Tom Jones*, where there is a developed third-person narrative voice, we have the double perspective in each scene of the central character and the omniscient narrator. One of the pleasures in reading *Pride and Prejudice* comes from our seeing the action through both Elizabeth's and the narrator's eyes. Works using frameworks—that is, narrations within narrations—can multiply this effect. *Wuthering Heights*, for example, allows us to see the same action not only through the perspectives of both Heathcliff and Cathy but also through the eyes of Nelly Dean, who narrates events to Lockwood, and through his eyes as well as he narrates events to us.[14] One of the most striking examples of this last kind of narration appears in Faulkner's *Absalom, Absalom!*, which seeks to bring us the truth about Sutpen and his descendants through a series of frames, of character narrating to character and each trying to piece together his own perception of the same events while adding to our own total vision.

In the case of *Humphry Clinker*, however, we are talking about a work largely structured according to the multiple perspectives of characters within the central narration, a work that achieves its effect through the dramatization of various individuals' perceptions of the same places, people, and events and that allows us to bring together these perceptions into a total picture. Smollett extends in this direction the possibilities inherent within the novel form, within the basic novelistic techniques of exploring human psychology and dramatizing individual perspectives. What he has done is to exploit the reader's capacity to hold simultaneously within his own spatial imagination the various perspectives and to unify them into a total vision. For several reasons this will not be a dominant form of fiction, though we can, of course, see the technique used in parts of future works, where specific effects are achieved through narrating the simultaneous responses of characters within the action to the same material. Mary Shelley's *Frankenstein* achieves a striking effect when we hear the monster relate the first moments of his life, which we have already heard described by his creator. There is the splendid doubloon scene in *Moby Dick*, where Ahab, Starbuck, Stubb, and other characters describe and react to the gold coin nailed to the mainmast. Sometimes we can find an expansion of this technique: in such works as *Middlemarch* and *War and Peace*, for example, there is room both to narrate the psychological development of several characters and, occasionally, to interplay their simultaneous responses to the same events.

Of course there are works with structures similar to that of *Humphry Clinker*. One thinks immediately of Faulkner's *As I Lay Dying* and, to some extent, *The Sound and the Fury*, of Conrad's *Nostromo*, and Durrell's *Alexandria Quartet*. But this kind of narrative structure has not been used often, since writers have not wanted to dilute our involvement with one or two major characters, or to stay the movement of plot by restating events, even from new perspectives. In the case of *Humphry Clinker*, however, where the emphasis is on the external world, and where a too-close involvement with any single character would get in the way of the composite picture of reality we are to achieve, parallactic narration is the natural technique, at least for much of the work. We can say of Smollett that he was the first novelist to realize an inherent capacity in the novel form, a capacity to enrich and extend the created reality through multiple perspectives; and that after him, the technique was generally used, with some obvious exceptions, in a more limited way, as one of the many narrative techniques with which the writer could enrich his total vision.

THE WORLD OUTSIDE

There is no novel up to this point, and none for some time after, that gives us such a wide and detailed sense of the external world, such a specific and visual sense of setting, of actual physical places.[15] Defoe at times, and Richardson far more consistently, create scenes that are visual and dramatic and convey to us a sense of place, but they generally do so without detailed descriptions of setting.[16] The point here, and one that we have already made in our discussions of both these writers, is that detailed descriptions of setting are not necessary prerequisites for visualizing the scenes of a novel. As for Smollett, he is the first novelist to use detailed descriptions of physical setting as a means of satisfying the reader's visual imagination, a technique which appears far more developed in this work than in his other fiction because of his intention to make *Humphry Clinker* a travelogue as well as a novel. Not all future novelists would make so much of setting, but certainly Smollett had added another possible dimension to the new kind of fiction, another possible visual technique. Much of what I have said also applies to Smollett's physical descriptions of characters, though we can find this technique already in his other fiction. The novelists we have already studied give full descriptions of their characters' appearances only on occasion, but in *Humphry Clinker*, we are given a full description of a number of characters so that we may see them clearly and specifically as part of Smollett's comic and often grotesque world. If we wish to single out at least one writer who was directly influenced in his descriptions of both setting and character by Smollett, the logical choice would be Charles Dickens, whose locations have much of the same specific and animated quality, and whose figures appear with much the same detailed grotesquery.[17] Since Matt's descriptions of settings are the most protracted, successful, and thematically significant in the work, and since the same can be said of Jery's descriptions of characters, both in their appearance and behavior, we must now examine the descriptive techniques of these letter-writers in further detail.

Matt's descriptions are successful in giving us a detailed picture of place and an understanding of the way he sees and what concerns him most: both the place is made vivid, and its method of description makes the describer vivid. Because Matt is a character we like, because to a large degree we trust his observations, the significance he infuses in the external world and the social and moral commentary he draws from it become for us primary thematic concerns of the work. I want to emphasize this point as strongly as I can to refute Professor Karl's argument, in his study of eighteenth-century fiction, that "Smollett lacks...a 'philosophy' of people, things, and life that is more than the sum of realistic detail." Karl states that "despite his intense observations of visual objects, Smollett lacks the view of them that would turn them from detail to meaning."[18] Matt's physical descriptions of the external world are reinforced by the judgments of other characters, and these descriptions are shaped not merely by his subjective personality but also by an attitude towards reality, a social, cultural, and moral perspective that is coherent and meaningful in terms of eighteenth-century life. We can go further than this and say that not only do the characters' individual descriptions have "meaning," but the way these descriptions fit together throughout the book forms a definite thematic pattern, one that starts to take shape, as we shall now see, from Matt's descriptions of Bath at the beginning of the work.

Matt describes the Circus at Bath in some detail, finding it a "pretty bauble, contrived for shew, and look[ing] like Vespasian's amphitheatre turned outside in" (p. 63). All his descriptions have a moral basis and praise the usefulness as well as the common sense of a place, while condemning all show and ostentation. Matt is fond of using striking analogies to make his scene graphic. He continues with his description of the Circus, emphasizing its architectural absurdity and suggesting the physical difficulties in living there, and he concludes by conveying an atmospheric sense of the place that communicates his own preoccupation with comfort: "the clouds, formed by the constant evaporation from the baths and rivers in the bottom, will, in their ascent this way, be first attracted and detained by the hill that rises close behind the Circus, and load the air with a perpetual succession of vapours..." (pp. 64-65). Through such descriptions, not only do we learn what Bath looked like from one point of view, but at the same time we learn about Matt's values of simplicity and order, his way of seeing everything in terms of human orientation and function; we are given a vivid sense of the place's unpleasant and unwholesome atmosphere, while also realizing Matt's preoccupation with physical comfort and health.

Matt's descriptions of Bath and London underscore the artificiality, disorderliness, and corruption of these places. Bath, according to Matt, is a result of England's new affluence, of the great commercial age that has destroyed any semblance of social and aesthetic order (pp. 65-67). It is this new wealth in England that has led to art and artifice, to opulence and ostentation, to a world that is in direct contrast with the world of nature and naturalness that we will see in Scotland. In Smollett's vision, such artificiality inevitably leads to decadence—to corruption and disease. One of Matt's most striking descriptions in the book is his Dantesque vision of the waters of Bath; the technique is impressionistic, the function thematic:

> The first object that saluted my eye, was a child full of scrophulous ulcers, carried in the arms of one of the guides, under the very noses of the bathers.... To purify myself from all such contamination, I went to the duke of Kingston's private Bath, and there I was almost suffocated for want of free air; the place was so small, and the steam so stifling. (P. 75)

There is a physical corruption brought about by a mental one— common sense has been subverted and nature distorted. Matt's prose is at times as metaphoric, impressionistic, vivid, and evocative as the language of Charles Dickens will be: London "is become an overgrown monster; which, like a dropsical head, will in time leave the body and extremities without nourishment and support" (p. 118). Like Dickens's physical settings, those in *Humphry Clinker* are infused with social and thematic meaning: "There are many causes that contribute to the daily increase of this enormous mass; but they may all be resolved into the grand source of luxury and corruption . . ." (pp. 118–19). Matt and his entourage must leave this part of England and travel to Scotland to see a better, more natural, and healthier world. Throughout the remainder of the work, Matt continues to give us descriptions of places, demonstrating at the same time his own particular interests and psychological bent:

> On this side they [the banks] display a sweet variety of woodland, cornfield, and pasture, with several agreeable villas emerging as it were out of the lake, till, at some distance, the prospect terminates in huge mountains covered with heath, which being in the bloom affords a very rich covering of purple. Every thing here is romantic beyond imagination. This country is justly stiled the Arcadia of Scotland; and I don't doubt but it may vie with Arcadia in every thing but climate. (P. 286)

This particular perspective in the book can only belong to Matt Bramble, with his obsession with order and propriety. Here the landscape is nicely arranged between beauty and husbandry: everything has its place and fits together. The mountains are a delight to see, and yet their presence contrasts with and hence reinforces our sense of man's control of nature along the banks. The lake, the cultivated banks with villas interspersed, and the mountains in the distance form a harmonious picture, an aesthetic delight: man has not invaded or destroyed nature but become integrated into it. Yet Matt finds the climate unsuitable to his health and his civilized tastes. At the same time, one senses that there is too much nature here and perhaps too little civilization.[19] Matt is still an educated man, concerned with his comfort and concerned with progress—though a controlled progress. Such a place, where nature becomes advanced by progress, where simplicity and civilization blend, will be discovered by Matt and described by his pen at the end of the novel, when he arrives at the Dennison estate back in England.[20]

Jery describes a number of the book's locations from his special point of view, but it is his lot to describe for us most of the strange and comic characters who pass through the landscape. These characters are treated as if they were part of the landscape—they receive the same kind of emphasis on physical appearance, and their actions seem to have the same kind of largeness and turbulence as the world around them. In various ways, these characters embody the same social and moral themes as the novel's physical world, and they also serve to develop the work's concern with perception, since we see them through the different perspectives of the other-letter writers as well as through Jery's eyes. There are a whole series of these character sketches that permeate the work—indeed, we can say that the travel-book format serves to describe human oddities as much as locations. That the two fit together so well, that character and setting seem to develop and reinforce each other, is the result of the totality and completeness of Smollett's vision, a vision skillfully constructed from the separate perspectives of the letter-writers.

I am talking now about the grotesques in the novel, those broad, funny, unrealistic creatures who are painted with the kind of exaggeration that makes them more physical objects than living and breathing people.[21] Many of these characters have the same kind of physical distortions: they are long, thin, bent, and rawboned, and possess long jaws or distorted mouths—this description also fits Tabitha, the only grotesque among the letter writers. Though the descriptions of these grotesques are not very different, they are highly comic in diverse ways. Jery uses the term "originals" for most of the characters he describes in his letters, including such non-grotesque figures as Quin and even Matt. Jery has two meanings behind the term: the first refers to "the original of a character, which you and I have often laughed at in descriptions" (p. 48), and the second clearly refers to singular, different, and distinct kinds of characters, such as H——t, who is described as "one of the most original characters upon earth" (p. 216), or Lismahago, who is called "one of the most singular personages I ever encountered" (p. 238). It is the second definition which best suits most of Smollett's grotesques.[22]

To see these characters basically as types, as generally typical of human nature, is to miss what is unusual and comic in them. Certainly, as in the case of all people, they are to some degree generic—i.e., Tabby is an old-maid figure and Lismahago an impoverished Scot—but that aspect of characterization is Fielding's emphasis and not Smollett's. The individual, very specific, and ludicrous qualities of these characters belong to them alone, as Jery many times reminds us. Characters like Tabitha and Miclewhimmen are part of a disordered external world; they are unlike normal humans in being objects, machines that in their distortions bear only mock resemblance to their mortal brothers: they are physical and not psychological creatures. The emphasis in their portrayals is on the idiosyncratic, strange, and comic. Fielding's comic caricatures are emblematic of certain kinds of moral, social, and group behavior; Smollett's characters are ultimately representative of nothing but themselves. The force, then, in Smollett's novel is outward, centrifugal, to the separate and disparate. His characters are peculiar and different, representing nothing but themselves; they seem to be going their own ways, occasionally running into one another, colliding, and moving apart.[23] The characters seem to explode into violent actions much as the new commercialized and chaotic world of modern England seems to be exploding apart for Smollett. Both Fielding's and Smollett's caricatures are presented as distortions from some norm, but the caricaturable behavior of Fielding's figures is both typical and meant to hide and yet emphasize what is natural to all men, to remind us of what is hidden somewhere inside the characters themselves. The purpose of Fielding's novel is to strip away affectation, hypocrisy, and overintellectualization and to show the potential for benevolence, true feeling, and brotherhood in all men. Therefore, the force in *Tom Jones* is inward, toward a core of fundamental and universal benevolence, toward that which ties people together, toward their common humanity. Fielding's vision, then, is ultimately comic and optimistic.[24] Smollett presents benevolence as an alternative to selfish and acquisitive behavior, but such altruism is not seen as part of general human nature and hardly makes us feel better about the hostility in his fictional world. Of course, the caricatures in *Humphry Clinker* often seem comically absurd and perform actions that are farcical and funny, but the ultimate sense of them that we derive is neither comic nor funny; they are rather part of a view of society and human nature that is basically somber.

It is Matt, then, who gives us more of the physical descriptions of Bath and London at the beginning of the book, and Jery more of the characters and their behavior.[25] The interplay between their two voices and their different, though not contradictory, perspectives establishes a counterpoint and rhythm throughout this part of the work. But in the second part of the book, rather than continually playing one against the other, Smollett frequently has their letters supplement each other; rather than presenting the same event or location from two points of view, he has each of the writers continue where the other has left off. The closer proximity of the letter-writers' viewpoints is underscored by the closer proximity of their language. Smollett loses some of the earlier vitality of the work and sacrifices the dramatic interaction between their letters on those occasions when he uses the two voices of Matt and Jery as continuous narrators in order to get into his novel a vast amount of descriptive material.

The world of the first half of *Humphry Clinker* is a strange, disordered place, filled with strange, disordered characters. It is a place where people act like selfish and aggressive machines:

> The tea-drinking passed as usual, and the company having risen from the tables, were sauntering in groupes, in expectation of the signal for attack, when the bell beginning to ring, they flew with eagerness to the dessert, and the whole place was instantly in commotion. There was nothing but justling, scrambling, pulling, snatching, struggling, scolding, and screaming. The nosegays were torn from one another's hands and bosoms; the glasses and china went to wreck; the tables and floors were strewed with comfits. Some cried; some swore; and the tropes and figures of Billingsgate were used without reserve in all their native zest and flavour; nor were those flowers of rhetoric unattended with significant gesticulation. Some snapped their fingers; some forked them out; some clapped their hands, and some their back-sides; at length, they fairly proceeded to pulling caps, and every thing seemed to presage a general battle.... (Pp. 81–82)

Jery's description has something of arrogance and even cynicism in it, but we are to take it at face value—it certainly is corroborated by Matt's perceptions of the physical settings at Bath. Like the settings, people lack taste and propriety. Here confusion and insubordination reign—this is a world gone mad with money and affectation. But even when the novel changes to the less turbulent background of northern England and Scotland, when the physical world becomes healthier and saner, when nature and natural living are stressed, Smollett's strange caricatures still pass across the landscape, and violence and disorder, the sudden and chaotic actions we associate with Bath and London, explode before our eyes. The universe is basically for Smollett a potentially dangerous place. Matt and his family, even outside of Bath and London, find themselves victims of threatening external forces: three severe accidents with the carriage, the last of which almost drowns Matt; the fire at

Harrigate; Matt's painful and unnecessary rescue from the sea by Humphry; Winifred's experience at the theater; the altercation with Lord Oxmington; the practical jokes at Sir Bullford's estate—all create for us a world where the unexpected is likely to happen, where everyone is a potential victim for sudden violence, whether from other people or seemingly random natural forces. Fielding's *Tom Jones* certainly has its share of violence, but in most cases much of the threat is taken out of such experiences, and, in general, the work's good spirits and optimism keep us from ever feeling disturbed.[26] Smollett's world seems constantly filled with threatening actions that transcend the level of farce and against which there is no mitigating benevolent order. We may be entertained by the comic behavior of numerous characters, charmed by the goodness of the crusty old Matt, encouraged by such people as Mr. Smollett and Dennison, but by no means is this the total effect of the book. The vision of the world—of setting, character, and action— though distinctly marked by Smollett's own violent and paranoiac nature, has much in it that is akin to the dark and absurdist visions of the great Augustan satirists, of Pope's *Dunciad* and Swift's *Gulliver's Travels*, where in spite of some wonderfully comic moments, man's perverse ways are reflected by a universe that seems hostile and threatening.

MIND AND MATTER

Although each character's response to the physical world is to be seen as valid, this does not negate the fact that problems concerning perception and one's relationship to the external world still exist. There is always the possibility of being too biased and prejudiced, too overcome by one's subjective nature, or simply of failing to recognize the legitimacy of other points of view. This is the significance of Jery's statement about "prejudice and passion," which we have already examined. We have discussed how such individual problems in perception are corrected by the different perspectives of other characters, but this does not negate the fact that the individual must still confront reality with only his partial and personal vision.

In one important respect, Matt faces the same difficulty as the characters in *Tristram Shandy*: how to rectify the distortions in his impressions and perceptions caused by his own physical nature. Matt's ill health and preoccupation with his own body very much influence his outlook on the world about him and shape his perceptions.[27] Not only is he frequently concerned with the physical aspects of reality that affect his own well-being, but also he is forced to confront the relationship between his soul and body, and between his spiritual being and physical reality in general. In his very first letter in the novel, Matt's diction shows an immediate concern for health, disease, and physical functions: "The pills are good for nothing—I might as well swallow snowballs to cool my reins . . . " (p. 33).[28] Even when talking about other people, he uses the metaphors of health and disease: "those children of my sister are left me for a perpetual source of vexation—what business have people to get children to plague their neighbors" (p. 33). In this case, it is the spirit that is assaulted and not the body, but from the start, Matt is quick to relate physical and mental health, one to the other: "I am as lame and as much tortured in all my limbs as if I was broke upon the wheel: indeed, I am equally distressed in mind and body . . . " (p. 33). The basic problems for Matt are to react to the world outside him without having his perceptions distorted by his physical being, and to bring into some kind of balance both his spirit and physical matter. We already sense one possible solution to these problems in this his first letter, as Matt demonstrates that somewhere within him is an already developed sensibility, a kindly and humane spirit that can control his responses to the world in general.[29] The conflict, then, between mind and matter promises to be resolved by a balance between feeling and fact, between sentiment and condemning reason. The solution is already suggested in the structure of the letter, where the first part, in which he discourses on his body and the plague of his relatives, is balanced by the last part, where he shows his concern for the spiritual state of his neighbor Griffin, the well-being of Morgan's widow and children, and the trouble he must be causing "Dear" Dr. Lewis.

The problem of seeing clearly, of balancing mind and body, and spirit and matter, confronts all the correspondents in the novel. Matt's sister Tabitha, who writes the second letter in the collection, not only immediately establishes her mean-spirited, vulgar, avaricious, and ridiculous personality but also shows herself to be an individual totally preoccupied with matter and almost devoid of a spiritual dimension. Her letter is brief, as indeed are all her epistles throughout the work— Tabitha does not have the mind or soul to be much concerned with the world through which she passes; she does not have the education or intelligence to write at length about anything; nor does she have the sociability or openness of heart to communicate her feelings or experiences to another. In her letters, she is mostly concerned with the running of Bramble Hall and its farm, and especially with ruling servants and making money. While the other characters are busy describing the world around them, Tabitha's single description of any length, which appears in her first letter, is limited to those personal possessions which she wishes sent to her:

> [Send] my rose collar neglejay, with green robins, my yellow damask, and my black velvet suit, with the short hoop; my bloo quilted petticot, my green manteel, my laced apron, my French commode, Macklin head and lappets, and the litel box with my jowls. Williams may bring over my bum-daffee, and the viol with the easings of Dr. Hill's dockwater, and Chowder's lacksitif. The poor creature has been terribly constuprated ever since we left huom. (P. 34)

The list, in its specificity, its banality, and its misspellings, gives us both the sound of Tabitha's voice and the shallowness of her personality. She is a character obsessed by the physical world, but by matter devoid of spiritual meaning. The world of matter that concerns her is that of physical possessions, of clothes and agricultural products used to purchase such items—though Tabby is also parsimonious and hoards much of her money. She is stingy with the servants, treating them like possessions and denying them pleasure. The only indication she gives of any affection and soul is in her relationship to her ugly and mean-spirited dog, Chowder. But Chowder, we are now told, is "constu-prated," the way Tabitha is constipated in her relation to the world around her—in the way she holds back her feelings as well as her money.

Winifred's letter, which follows directly after, develops a voice that is even more illiterate—the misspellings and mispronunciations have become downright malapropisms (p. 35)—but the letter also develops a personality more vivacious and alert, more open to experience and excitement. Winifred is a somewhat scatterbrained, talkative, and uneducated girl who responds to the world around her with awe and gullibility. In her later description of Sadler's-wells, which we have already mentioned, we find an indication of the vulgar and topsy-turvy world being shaped by the rising lower classes:

> I saw such tumbling and dancing upon ropes and wires, that I was frightened and ready to go into a fit—I tho't it was all inchantment.... here was flying without any broom-stick ... and firing of pistols in the air, and blowing of trumpets, and swinging, and rolling of wheel-barrows upon a wire (God bless us!) no thicker than a sewing thread; that, to be sure, they must deal with the devil!" (P. 140)

Winifred never seems to get hold of the world she finds around her: both her senses and her mind are overcome. She is vulnerable to impressions and appearances and never writes with much detail or specificity: the world is the way it immediately strikes her lower-class and untrained sensibilities. Winifred's perspective fits well into the novel's multileveled view: we see the world not only from the perspectives of age and personality but also from that of class. As the novel progresses, Winifred shows a hardening of spirit because of her exposure to the external world: she develops an interest in clothing and appearance and a related concern with status and position. Poor Winifred, with all her charms of person, becomes sullied by and obsessed with the corruptible world of matter that surrounds her.

The next letter-writer who appears is Jery, and here we find a character far more intelligent, controlled, and cognizant of the world outside him. Certainly we sense some snobbishness and self-importance in his letters—but Jery is, after all, a young man recently out of college, one feeling his own superiority and newfound freedom. The world appears before him ready to be tasted and enjoyed, ready to be savored with his newly developed mind and sensibilities. His letters, however, are not stiff or difficult to read: there is a good deal of flexibility and sprightliness in his sentences, and his language, though showing a keen observer and penetrating critic, is at times colloquial and even colorful. Paulson has stated that while Matt's satire is Juvenalian, Jerry's is Horatian: "While his uncle scourges, Jery lets folly speak for itself and condemn itself.... with his objectivity he lacks his uncle's moral purpose and the personal involvement occasioned by his ill health...."[30] The observation is valid, though we must also acknowledge that Jery often paints human stupidity and vice with the same harsh and condemning strokes as his uncle, even if he does seem less emotionally involved. Perhaps we can also make the following distinction: while Matt is always struggling with physical reality and trying to find decent spiritual values in the world of matter, Jery is not quite so overcome by matter and focuses more on intellectual concerns: while he is quick to respond to physical reality, he has the ready capacity to find within that world redeeming spiritual values. In Jery's descriptions is a proper balance between matter and mind, between the physical reality that surrounds him and the values he seeks to find there, a vision which Matt more easily achieves in the rural landscape.

Lydia, who is the last of the correspondents to make her entry in the work, immediately seems to us a person caught up in appearances, in the way things seem on the surface. This superficial vision often leaves her in a state of confusion and even suffering. Lydia is a young girl of only seventeen, making her first entry into the world. She is, of course, more educated, intelligent, and refined than Tabitha and Winifred, but she lacks her brother's maturity and understanding. Lydia's view of

London, as we have already seen, focuses on what is exciting and dazzling. She fails to see the social upheaval or breakdown of order implicit in the scene—her perspective is only partial. Lydia can never penetrate the surface of things; she can only judge by appearance, which, as we know, can be very incomplete or even deceiving. Lydia seems to have been nourished on romantic novels, a literature which directly influences her diction and the way in which she sees reality.[31] She is the poor, suffering heroine, alone in the world: "Having no mother of my own, I hope you will give me leave to disburden my poor heart to you..." (p. 37). Her language is that of a virtuous and suffering innocent who constantly turns her own experiences into those of a romance: "He behaved so modest and respectful, and seemed to be so melancholy and timorous, that I could not find in my heart to do anything that should make him miserable and desperate" (p. 37). Her lover, the strange Mr. Wilson, is actually in disguise, and this hardly helps her to get a grip on reality—he is as busy playing a game of make-believe and romance as is she. This love affair appears perfunctorily throughout the book and is one of the threads which gives a certain amount of plot to the work, but it serves a greater function in underscoring the book's general concern with physical appearances, with the way things seem to the perceiving eye.

Lydia's relationship with Wilson, then, is thematically related to the work's larger concerns as well as its techniques. *Humphry Clinker* allows us to see the way a number of characters view reality and conveys to us the problems in seeing clearly. Physical appearances can be deceptive either because we perceive partially or because things are simply not what they seem. To some extent, Lydia does see Wilson accurately, by recognizing his superior qualities and the fact that he is more than what he pretends to be. But he remains an enigma throughout the book, an indication that the complete truth is not immediately discernible, that appearance and reality can at times be two separate matters.

The same kind of issue is involved in the portrayal of Humphry Clinker, the amusing and yet tender character after whom the book is named. Humphry's portrait must be partly understood in terms of Smollett's preoccupation with order and stratification. Humphry is a bastard, pure and simple—the Bramble blood in his veins will not free him from this birth or his uneducated ways. Humphry's initial grotesque description (p. 112), his continually comic presentation, even when we are to admire his behavior, and his marriage at the end of the novel to the servant Winifred are Smollett's answer to the fictional tradition of such social upstarts as Pamela and Tom Jones, characters who by either upbringing or birth do not deserve the social rewards that come with either a fortunate marriage or newly discovered lineage. In Smollett's presentation of Humphry, we see perhaps his most subtle argument in the novel for class distinction and propriety.[32]

But Humphry also raises the question about appearance, about things being only partly what they seem or being at times not what they seem at all. Most of the correspondents agree in assessing Humphry's salient points, though, of course, they emphasize different aspects of his appearance and behavior. But the parallactic vision still fails to tell us all we ought to know about him. We must come to the conclusion that it is not always possible to know everything from appearances, that though several viewpoints are better than one, even all of these do not always put together the truth. Let me emphasize that in one light Humphry is what he seems: a poor, uneducated, well-meaning, enthusiastic, and somewhat bumptious individual. There are no hidden qualities or attributes to his character. In this respect, physical appearance does not lie. But there are other matters to know, facts about identity and human relationships that physical appearance can not communicate. Clinker links up with Matt by sheer chance, and the discovery of his birth, when he hears his master's former name uttered later in the book, also seems a fortuitous accident. The man who utters that name, who has come to aid Matt and his entourage because of an accident with their carriage, also turns out to be Wilson's father.

These happy circumstances are no indication of any providence in the universe or design in the scheme of things—we are not in Fielding's fictional world. Things resolve themselves by sheer accident because Smollett is writing a work of fiction and must bring all his major characters to a happy conclusion, even in a world that is hardly the best of all possible places. The novel, with all its emphasis on physical reality, with its creation of a parallactic vision that brings us close to a full assessment of the external world, still leaves us with a sense of man's vulnerability, with a sense of his spiritual and intellectual limitations, with a realization that we are not gods and cannot know everything. We are creatures limited in external time and space.

SOLUTIONS TO THE PROBLEMS OF CIVILIZATION

Humphry Clinker turns out, then, to be more than a simple fictitious travelogue. Smollett is sufficiently honest and complex in dramatizing the way individuals respond to the world around them to involve us in problems of perception and understanding, and he is sufficiently skillful and detailed in presenting the way he sees his own world to raise some crucial problems not only about the development of civilization but also about the individual's relationship to a changing physical reality and to other humans also involved in that changing world. But though the novel is often negative in its implications, though its humor and comic robustness are often overtaken by a somber vision of men and manners, the work still manages to explore and put forth a number of solutions to the ills that beset the eighteenth-century world. The picture that Smollett tries to present is one that balances good and evil, one in which hope struggles valiantly against despair.

We have already referred to Matt's sentimentalism, to the benevolence and tenderness that lie beneath his angry facade, and we must now go further with the subject. Jery makes the following significant observation about his uncle: "I think his peevishness arises partly from bodily pain, and partly from a natural excess of mental sensibility; for, I suppose, the mind as well as the body, is in some cases endued with a morbid excess of sensation" (p. 45). It is a nice touch, a lovely bit of psychology to explain Matt's satiric thrusts and sentimental excesses. He is a man of feeling, both physically and mentally, and the same sensitivity which forces him to react angrily to the vice and stupidity he sees around him allows him to shed tears for the plight of others. The same man who can paint Bath in such bold strokes can also fall victim to the plight of "a decent sort of woman, not disagreeable in her person, that comes to the Well, with a poor emaciated child, far gone in a consumption" (p. 49). Jery continues, "I had caught my uncle's eyes several times directed to this person, with a very suspicious expression in them, and every time he saw himself observed, he hastily withdrew them, with evident marks of confusion . . ." (p. 49). The woman is called to Matt's chambers, given £20 by him, and overcome with gratitude. What is also interesting about the scene is the way in which the sentimentalism is immediately suppressed by the intrusion of Tabby and her violent behavior:

> she bounded into the parlour in a violent rage, that dyed the tip of her nose of a purple hue,—'Fy upon you, Matt! (cried she) what doings are these, to disgrace your own character, and disparage your family?'— Then, snatching the bank-note out of the stranger's hand, she went on—'How, now, twenty pounds!—here is temptation with a witness!—Good-woman, go about your business—Brother, brother, I know now which most to admire; your concupissins, or your extravagance!—' (P. 50)

This kind of counterpoint between human brutality and moments of compassion and feeling is frequent throughout the book and occurs even within Matt. There is a constant tension in the book between the strong sense of physical reality—the violent settings and crowds, the unexpected behavior of the characters, the explosive actions that seem to take place almost gratuitously—and the inner feeling—the sentiment, tenderness, and compassion. From a slightly different perspective, we can see this as a tension between the vision of the satirist,[33] with his view of the world as a somber place and man as a hostile creature, and the vision of the sentimentalist, with his belief in man's benevolence and moral feelings. Smolletts's novel embodies the tension between two major literary and cultural forces of his century, which we have already discussed in relation to Sterne, between the satiric vision of writers like Pope, Swift, and Churchill, and the sentimental and optimistic vision of men like Steele and Thomson. Both the satiric and sentimental visions were in part different responses to the same ills that seemed to beset civilization.

We have mentioned several times Matt's preoccupation with his physical health and his related concern with the world around him, especially as it affects his own well-being. At least for the first part of the book, Matt knows that he has a corrupted and dying body. One of the most striking scenes in the work takes place at a coffeehouse in Bath, where Matt is one "of thirteen individuals; seven lamed by the gout, rheumatism, or palsy; three maimed by accident; and the rest either deaf or blind" (p. 84). Finding there some friends, Matt considers the meeting "a renovation of youth; a kind of resuscitation of the dead" (p. 85), and enjoys "a strain of melancholy, produced by the remembrance of past scenes, that conjured up the ideas of some endearing connexions, which the hand of Death had actually dissolved" (pp. 85–86). Matt's awareness of decay and death, his own especially, projects itself into the surrounding physical world: he is concerned with physical reality not only because it affects his health but because he sees it, particularly in London and Bath, as corrupt and dying also. We can relate Matt's satiric vision to his ill health, but we can also see his sentiment, his developed world of inner feeling, as an answer to the breakdown of physical reality—Matt compensates for the impoverishment of both his own physical life and physical reality around him with a developed sensibility. In a similar way, the new cult of sensibility in the eighteenth century, like the satiric vision, was a response to a changing world, a world of reason and science, of knowledge and fact, of commercialism and incipient industrialization, of material prosperity but confusing alteration. Unlike satire, however, sentimentalism was a flight from the reality outside to the world inside, from a direct confrontation with the problems that beset mankind to a preoccupation with emotional responses, from a realization of man's limitations to an exaggerated glorification of his virtues.

In *Humphry Clinker*, the satiric and sentimental visions achieve only a tentative balance, and though the novel ends well and goodness seems to triumph, the victory is precarious. Smollett's novel has much the same kind of tentative balance that Dickens was to achieve in his work during the next century. In the novels of both writers, we find a satiric and basically dark vision of the world, an emphasis upon physical detail to create a striking picture of setting and character, the use of grotesque and often wildly funny caricatures, and a countering force of sentimentalism. Perhaps most striking is the similar drama that both writers create: that of the feeling individual in a hostile, sometimes nightmarish world. In this sense both men were deeply responsive to a major trauma taking place in modern England, a trauma that had already begun by the time of Smollett and that was to become even more obvious in the nineteenth century. A significant theme in *Humphry Clinker* that we have already discussed is the economic revolution and its bad effects upon English life. One of the reasons why this novel is better than any Smollett had written before is because in it he bases his angry view of the world on an actual economic and sociologic foundation; here the vision is not merely personal but is provoked by a larger awareness and more universal concerns. Bath is described by Matt as a modern vanity fair, a place "where a very inconsiderable proportion of genteel people are lost in a mob of impudent plebians" (p. 66), where all kinds of absurdities exist as a result of "the general tide of luxury, which hath overspread the nation" (p. 65). He finds that in London "luxury and corruption" result in "no distinction or subordination," that "the different departments of life are jumbled together—" (p. 119). The duke of N——'s levee, described in great detail by Jery (pp. 141-47), makes flattery, favoritism, and corruption seem the dominant ways among the great and pseudogreat. Matt asks "whether the world was always as contemptible as it appears to me at present?" (p. 138). This is not merely the question of a quarrelsome old man, but the moral response of a person who knows the answer to be no.

Smollett attacks Methodism with much vehemence throughout the book; he does so partly because it is another example of the presumption of the lower classes, but his major purpose is to show how our inner reality can needlessly become misguided and corrupted:

> 'What you imagine to be the new light of grace . . . I take to be a deceitful vapour, glimmering through a crack in your upper story—In a word, Mr. Clinker, I will have no light in my family but what pays the king's taxes,

unless it be the light of reason, which you don't pretend to follow.' (Pp. 170-71)

Smollett's sentiments bring to mind those of the Augustan satirists—in a few seconds, Matt is accusing Humphry of being "either an hypocritical knave, or a wrong-headed enthusiast" (p. 171). Instead of prejudice, passion, or some inner light, there should be reason in our "upper story"; but this is something man does not always achieve. Matt himself believes in reason, but he is not always reasonable.

There is, then, as there always has been, a solution to the problems of man's existence, one not dependent on something as personal and ephemeral as sentiment and benevolence. The problems that beset civilization could be solved if reason were allowed to rule—as it has in the past. By reason Smollett means common sense; and common sense should guide us to lives of moderation and compromise:

> Woe be to that nation, where the multitude is at liberty to follow their own inclinations! Commerce is undoubtedly a blessing, while restrained within its proper channels; but a glut of wealth brings along with it a glut of evils: it brings false taste, false appetite, false wants, profusion, venality, contempt of order, engendering a spirit of licentiousness, insolence, and faction, that keeps the community in continual ferment, and in time destroys all the distinctions of civil society; so that universal anarchy and uproar must ensue. (P. 319)

The words are Lismahago's, but the sentiments clearly belong to Smollett. Matt adds, "I am one of those who think, that, by proper regulations, commerce may produce every national benefit, without the allay of such concomitant evils" (p. 319). Smollett's attack against his society points in a somewhat different direction from that of Dickens, even though the sensibilities of both writers are similar and they present analogous visions of the evils of the new capitalism. Smollett's position in the eighteenth century was the "intelligent" one, the one we associate with the best writers and thinkers of the period, but by Dickens's time, the tables had considerably turned, and the nineteenth-century writer's greater sympathy for the poor and his more democratic sensibility had become the enlightened and attractive response.

Smollett attempted to respond to the evils he saw in his world in ways that were typical of his own century. His impulse is always to move toward balance, to a reasonable middle way that shares the best of seemingly conflicting forces. The world achieved at Dennison's estate is one of civilization and nature, of progress and tradition, of the useful and simple. The state of mind often achieved by both Matt and Jery is one of thought and feeling, of judgment and compassion. The continuous concern with the physical reality throughout the book—with bodily health and appearance, with locations and settings—is matched by a dramatization of characters' minds and souls. Physical health must go with mental health; a concern for the physical reality must be balanced by a concern with cultural and spiritual values. Throughout the novel, the world inside the characters responds to the world outside. Reality ultimately takes significance from the minds that perceive it, and no individual need be lost in the subjectivity and relativity of his own perceptions, since there are always available to him other minds with which he can discover the truth. These are the possibilities within Smollett's fictional world—decidedly eighteenth-century possibilities. But the truth of Smollett's vision, the harsh reality he confronts and depicts through his parallactic technique, seems too much for such hope, for such balance and common sense. Smollett's realism often seems to smother the work's moral pattern; the travelogue often overcomes the novel. Not even the saving grace of the author's humor and comic spirit is enough to suppress the book's worry and incipient despair.

But in spite of their differences, Smollett and Dickens are strongly linked by their ability to bring larger economic and social concerns into the novel, to objectify them through character, action, and setting, and to seek solutions to these major issues of the real world through fictional explication and techniques. Smollett's achievement in the novel is significant, and if he did not have the psychological insight of Richardson or the wisdom of Fielding, he did know how to bring another dimension into the novel. The world of *Humphry Clinker* represents the world in which men live and to which they mentally and spiritually respond. It is a world that embodies those man-made forces which are of immediate significance to the general quality of life and the destiny of the individual.

CHAPTER SIX

PRIDE AND PREJUDICE:
The Paradigmatic Novel

JANE AUSTEN AND THE EIGHTEENTH CENTURY

The final figure in my study, Jane Austen, demonstrates most clearly what the novel was up to; she successfully dramatizes the concerns and satisfies the functions of the new fiction, while she synthesizes and brings to fruition the various techniques developed in the genre during the eighteenth century. Without belittling the writers we have studied, it is fair to say that the eighteenth-century novel seems to progress toward and culminate in the works of Austen. Though *Sense and Sensibility* was published in 1811 and *Pride and Prejudice* in 1813, Austen was at work on an earlier version of the former in 1796 and the latter in 1796 and 1797.[1] Twenty-five years, then, separate her actual writing from the last of the books we have already studied, *Humphry Clinker*, a period devoid of any major fictional talent with the exception, perhaps, of Fanny Burney. It was as if the first stage were over, as if the new literary form had exploded upon the scene and it was time for the dust to settle, for the imitators and second-rate talents to have their day. A more practical consideration is that no writer existed with sufficient genius or awareness to take stock of what had happened in fiction, to synthesize the past achievements and advance the form—that is, until Austen began to write. Jane Austen undoubtedly read a number of the works written during the preceding twenty-five years,[2] but, with the exception of Burney's first two novels, *Evelina* (1778) and *Cecilia* (1782), I doubt if any significantly influenced her own writing[3]—her attitude toward much of the fiction written during the period is evident in her parodying of both its material and its narrative techniques in her own works.[4] Jane Austen had to receive much of her schooling from the earlier novelists, especially from Richardson and Fielding. Even Fanny Burney's *Evelina* and *Cecilia* are more connected with the works of Richardson, Fielding, and Smollett than with the works of Burney's own contemporaries.

Jane Austen's appeal to her readers was one of shared human experience, the same kind of shared human experience that had been achieved with the characters of the earlier novelists we have studied. The eighteenth century had seen the triumph of the empirical world over the spiritual; dogmatic and eschatological religious faith had given way to a dominating concern with man's life in this world. A morality and system of behavior to achieve security and happiness no longer was derived from the church but had to be derived from society, from man-made institutions and human relationships. This is the world we see reflected in the major novelists of the period. The world of the romantic historical novels, of the gothic romance, even of many of the domestic novels of manners, is a world of dream and fantasy, of release and relief from the serious and more everyday concerns of the major novels and the real world.

The provincial world in which Jane Austen lived and about which she wrote belonged more to the mainstream of eighteenth-century life and thought than to the final decades of the period and the coming century. Austen's fictional world is the eighteenth-century world at its best—as it liked to see itself. In her works we see that civilization has achieved a balance, an order, a healthy optimism. Money may play a crucial role, economic class may be asserting pressure against economic class,[5] and social values may at times seem distorted or even conflicting, but the structure of society is basically strong and flexible. Here is a civilization in which the individual can take his place, where security can be achieved, but not at the expense of personal happiness or one's individuality. Clarissa need no longer be raped, nor must she leave this world to find happiness. Civilization has become civilized; the individual can fit into society even with its limitations, and not compromise his values. Characters like Mr. Collins and Lady Catherine de Bourgh, who represent extremes of social values and behavior, cannot destroy the fundamental equanimity and sanity of the social world, nor do they really pose much of a threat to the intelligent individual. For this is a world in which the individual and society are ultimately in harmony, in which they both share the same decent values, and in which the needs and desires of one are satisfied by the other. This is the direction in which all of Austen's novels move, and this is the strength and stability which they finally depict at their conclusions.[6] A belief in individual capacity and in a stable, civilized society, a belief in a knowable, practical system of morality and conduct, and a strong belief in this world as it is lived from day to day mark all her books.

Having committed herself to a subject matter already established in the novel (men and women living their lives in a world like our own), Austen imposes upon her fictional reality a type of plot especially developed by Fielding and Burney.[7] *Tom Jones* is in part held together by the hero's maturation: admittedly, this internal growth is not sufficiently dramatized, and we see it largely through Tom's external actions and dialogue, but much of the novel's ordering and final impact still depend on it. The heroine of Fanny Burney's *Evelina* also goes through such a process: the novel is basically concerned with a young girl's maturation in the social world. Jane Austen goes further than Fielding and Burney, tracing the growth of her protagonist but also highlighting the character's self-discovery and arranging the novel's events around this realization. Her works, especially *Pride and Prejudice*, are significantly concerned with the growth of intelligence and sensibility—much still happens in the external world, but what happens there is mostly seen as it affects or results from this internal movement. *Pride and Prejudice* is not merely a novel about two characters who overcome external obstacles and marry; it is a book about two people who learn to understand themselves and hence learn to see and understand the world better, and who, because of this process of internal change, are finally able to marry. We have seen from the start how the novel was concerned with the problem of personal identity; in its focus upon character, in its exploration and dramatization of human thought and behavior, and, finally, in its depiction of character in a world of demanding social values, the novel became the literary form which confronted human identity from psychological and social perspectives. Much of the eighteenth century was on the surface a relatively stable time, and such stability allowed the freedom to confront the instability, the growing uncertainty beneath the surface, an instability caused by the decline of traditional institutions and modes of thought. Implicit in the characters of Moll Flanders and Clarissa is the concept of identity as composed of discrete moments of experience;[8] in these figures, the human drama is an ongoing process, and each character must struggle to achieve a stable sense of self, a stability of personal identity which came handily to Fielding's characters because of his more traditional sense of human personality. For Elizabeth Bennet, existence is an inner and ongoing process, but more honestly than Moll and more easily and explicitly than Clarissa, she achieves a final sense of self. Personal identity is a struggle, but a struggle won neither by self-delusion nor by death. Unlike Fielding's characters, Elizabeth's reality is internal and changing. But unlike the heroines of Defoe's and Richardson's novels, her psychological drama is given direction and stability both by a greater intelligence and self-awareness and by acceptable moral values implicit, though sometimes ignored or even contradicted, in her stable social world.

All of the heroines we have studied must play out their inner drama in a social context—they must struggle with both internal and external limits of freedom. How does one assert individuality while still fulfilling a necessary and proper social role?[9] Clarissa may rise above her social world and appeal to a higher judge, but that never negates the significance of that society; indeed, it only underscores the failure of her social world to fulfill its responsibilities to her as an individual. We can say of the novel in the eighteenth century that it was able to combine tragedy's emphasis on individuality with comedy's emphasis on society. *Clarissa* is perhaps the only novel that leans quite so much toward tragedy. *Pride and Prejudice* shows a concern for internal states similar to that of *Clarissa*, but it resembles Richardson's final novel, *Sir Charles Grandison* (1753–1754), in its exploration of character within a fully created social, everyday world and in its use of a plot that relates internal states to social manners. There is less internal complexity and growth in Richardson's final novel, and for that reason it is much less successful than *Clarissa*, but the social reality is successful, and it was a dimension of the novel which Miss Austen admired greatly.[10]

In her synthesis of psychology and society, individual and social morality, Austen's way had also been prepared by Fanny Burney's early novels. The heroine of *Evelina* begins the novel as an inexperienced juvenile and develops into a more mature and worldly-wise individual. Society has its aberrations, but it also has its moral values, and it is the place in which the heroine must learn to live. Evelina develops by learning about society, about how she should behave in society and how she should expect others to behave to her. The narrow range of the heroine's responses and her limited intelligence ultimately place the novel on a lower rung of achievement than the books we are examining, but the work does create a rich social texture and successfully explores the impact of social relationships upon the girl's expanding consciousness.

Fanny Burney's *Cecelia* may have even more relevance to a discussion of the background to *Pride and Prejudice*. The narrator in *Northanger Abbey* (pub. 1818) mentions the novel in the following positive way: " 'It is only *Cecilia*, or *Camilla*, or *Belinda*'; or, in short, some work in which the greatest powers of the mind are displayed, in which the most thorough knowledge of human nature, the happiest delineation of its varieties, the liveliest effusions of wit and humors, are conveyed to the world in the best chosen language."[11] The title of *Pride and Prejudice* was probably taken from the conclusion of Burney's novel,[12] but beyond this there seems to be no critical agreement on the amount of influence that the earlier work had on the later.[13] There are remarkable parallels between the two novels, parallels that cannot be made easily with other works of the period. Both *Cecilia* and *Pride and Prejudice* focus on the relationship between individual and social values, and both do so in terms of "pride" and "prejudice";[14] both explore these concerns by developing the consciousness of a leading character in a richly drawn social world and by involving her in a plot that deals with marriage and the alliance of families. I do not wish to push the relationship of the books too far, but there are also some strikingly similar scenes in both novels that argue for Burney's influence on Jane Austen. For example, the scene in which Delvile explains to Cecilia his feelings for her and why he cannot marry her reminds one of Darcy's actual proposal to Elizabeth. In fact, Cecelia's responses, though in a scene right after, are much the same as Elizabeth's:

> "Yet my family," he says,—unexpected condescension! my family and every other circumstance is unexceptionable; how feeble, then, is that regard which yields to one only objection! how potent that haughtiness which to nothing will give way! Well, let him keep his name! since so wondrous its properties, so all-sufficient its preservation; what vanity, what presumption in me, to suppose myself an equivalent for its loss![15]

Delvile's reluctance to marry Cecilia stems from his unwillingness to give up his family name for hers, a sacrifice necessary if the heroine is to receive her inheritance, but the thematic and personal conflicts, even in the very language of the characters, bring to mind the parallel situation between the hero and heroine of Jane Austen's novel. In both works we see the conflict between private inclination and social consciousness, between personal dignity and public opinion, between individual worth and snobbery; in both works we see the characters behaving and thinking in similar ways and the plot developing along similar lines. These parallels are maintained when Delvile proposes to Cecilia and then sends her a letter explaining his past actions and change of heart. The heroine's responses to the letter again remind us of Elizabeth's in a similar situation:

> Cecilia read and re-read this letter, but with a perturbation of mind that made her little able to weigh its contents. Paragraph by paragraph her

sentiments varied, and her determination was changed: the earnestness of his supplication now softened her into compliance, the acknowledged pride of his family now irritated her into resentment, and the confession of his own regret now sickened her into despondence.[16]

Elizabeth's thinking when reading Darcy's letter is more controlled, her understanding of the situation more balanced, and her contrition greater, but there can be no doubt that we have two very similar dramatic scenes here, with both heroines facing similar personal conflicts and reacting in analogous ways to the confessional letters of the heroes.

I am not arguing for a strong reliance on these earlier works by Austen—her novel is ultimately a different and far better work. I am rather trying to establish the context in which she wrote her book, the novels which she had read and to which, in her mind, she adjoined her own narrative. Like any writer, Jane Austen was influenced in varying degrees by her literary predecessors, but it was her role in the history of fiction to bring to fruition so much of what had gone before. Like *Sir Charles Grandison* and the early novels of Fanny Burney, *Pride and Prejudice* is equally concerned with the inner world and the outer social world; like them, it is a novel in which the former cannot be understood without reference to the latter. But *Pride and Prejudice* creates a social setting—an everyday world of balls and parties, of conversations and social interaction, of courtship and marriage, of manners and morals— richer, more subtle, and more credible than any that had been achieved before. At the same time, the world of *Pride and Prejudice* achieves significance only as Elizabeth perceives it and learns to understand it and her relationship to it. In this respect especially, *Pride and Prejudice* is related to all the major novels of the eighteenth century that we have been studying, and to *Sir Charles Grandison*, *Evelina*, and *Cecilia* as well. Like all these works, it achieves its primary effect by focusing on a character's perceptions of reality and by involving the reader in the very act of perceiving. But here again Austen outstrips her predecessors by creating a more convincing, interesting, and intelligent perceiving mind, and by dramatizing it in such a way that the reader achieves both a more compelling involvement and a more immediate understanding of what is happening within the character.

FALSE IMPRESSIONS

If we examine the external events of *Pride and Prejudice*, we discover the traditional comic plot line that brings the hero and heroine through adversity to the state of marriage; the movement is from separation to unity, from instability to stability.[17] Like traditional comedy, the novel traces as well the movement toward unity of a subsidiary couple whose fate is tied in with that of the hero and heroine. In the development of this general plot line, *Pride and Prejudice* is also traditional in its use of certain kinds of figures who stand in the way of the hero and heroine's marriage, figures responsible, in varying degrees, for some of the plot's complications and whose influence must ultimately be neutralized. The parent or guardian, a figure who involves the protagonists in a conflict between age and youth, is represented by both Mrs. Bennet and Darcy's aunt, Lady Catherine; and Mr. Collins is the unwanted suitor, the man of vain pretensions whose values are generally antithetical to those necessary for a good marriage. But in *Pride and Prejudice*, these figures pose only a small threat to Elizabeth and Darcy. Wickham is another kind of unwanted suitor, but one whose mercenary and libidinous impulses are more dangerous than the foolish behavior and actions of Collins. In the first part of the novel, Wickham is a serious complication for Elizabeth and Darcy, but even he is only a temporary and not ultimately serious problem. In the context of English literature, Wickham is a watered-down version of the villainous Restoration rake, a figure who by this time had been considerably emasculated in his literary characterization by the morality of eighteenth-century drama and fiction. Wickham at first adds to the misunderstanding between heroine and hero, but Darcy's letter easily exposes him to Elizabeth. If anything, Wickham's elopement with Lydia later in the book serves more to bring heroine and hero together than to threaten their happiness.

The initial title of the novel, "First Impressions," tells us as much about the larger issues of the work as its final title, *Pride and Prejudice*. Our knowledge of the world outside us is a result of our impressions, and these, as we so well know by now, can easily be distorted by our subjective or false perspectives, by our pride or prejudice, for example. A test of character is the capacity to overcome initial impressions that are generally distorted, to correct improper vision and see clearly.

The real obstacles in the novel, the complications that threaten the union of hero and heroine, are not so much external characters as their own misconceptions, their failures to perceive correctly and to understand themselves. Union is not so much dependent upon exposing external machinations and circumventing threatening figures as it is upon following the arduous path to enlightenment and awareness. This is the real plot of *Pride and Prejudice*, this is the significance of all the novel's events, and this is what links Jane Austen's works to the Age of

Reason and not to the Age of Sensibility. One of Austen's accomplishments was to incorporate external events into her heroine's point of view and internal growth, to incorporate all the actions of the novel into one major development and achieve an admirable unity and wholeness in the work.

By developing so consistently her heroine's internal drama, by having us see all the external events in light of this development and through Elizabeth's eyes, Austen brought to fruition the perceptional dimension of the new kind of fiction. Her basic narrative techniques function to create a rich perceptional experience by having the reader consistently and clearly see the world of the novel with Elizabeth; her basic plot is primarily concerned with developing the heroine's capacity for accurate perception;[18] and the novel's values are all tied in with the subject—even pride and prejudice are part of the larger concern of perceiving others correctly through self-understanding.

But we must qualify our statements here, since to allow the reader to perceive as only Elizabeth perceives would be to limit severely the possibilities of the form and the larger perceptions it can offer. In *Humphry Clinker*, to a greater extent than in *Clarissa*, we have the various letter-writers complementing, but also qualifying and setting in a larger perspective, the epistles of the other characters. Jane Austen manages to create something of the same effect, having us perceive with Elizabeth while also perceiving her in a larger drama through insights and understanding that belong to other characters and the narrator as well. But she accomplishes this without sacrificing the unity and flow of the entire work, without having to play letter against letter, voice against voice, as did the epistolary novelists; though she may occasionally create a parallactic vision, the structure of her novel is not parallactic but remains singularly linear, fluid, and rhythmic. One of the achievements of the various novelists we have examined is the way they involve us with their characters and control that involvement, the way they achieve for us the excitement of experiencing as another person and the satisfaction of simultaneously transcending that experience. No writer up to this point, it seems to me, accomplishes this with more flexibility and skill than Austen. Much of the time we are unaware that we are being manipulated and controlled, that our degree of involvement with Elizabeth is being altered, or that we are being given information and perspectives that allow us to understand her better than she does herself. Although Austen develops our perceptional ties with her protagonist so fully and skillfully, she also creates for the reader, almost simultaneously, a comprehensive vision and intellectual experience as satisfying as the one achieved from *Tom Jones.*

The turning point of the novel is, of course, the scene where Elizabeth reads and comprehends Darcy's letter after she has refused his proposal of marriage (pp. 153–58). It is here that she comes to realizations about her false perceptions, about her inadequate "discernment" (p. 156); it is here that she must "see" all the events and characters of the novel over again. But before we look at the scene, we must briefly examine the way Jane Austen leads up to the event, the way the plot develops inevitably to Elizabeth's self-examination and enlightenment, and the way we are prepared, through our involvement with the heroine and through our greater awareness of her personality and situation, for this crisis. I want to examine one of Austen's scenic techniques in the first half of the work, but I also want to relate this technique to the human values she explores. I hope to do this by looking at only three scenes in this part of the work, but scenes crucial to our understanding of what is going on and exemplary of Austen's writing at its best.

SCENES OF DIALOGUE

The episodes I shall discuss take place in Bingley's home when Elizabeth is looking after Jane during her illness. These scenes are largely in dialogue, a technique Austen relies on extensively and employs with a subtlety and sophistication unmatched in any novel up to this time.[19] Whereas Fielding emphasizes the individual and often illustrative speeches of his characters,[20] Austen develops the dramatic interplay of dialogue, the way individual lines and intentions play off one another. She can employ extensive scenes of dialogue at this point in the work because we are already impelled to see matters from Elizabeth's perspective without the necessity of frequent internal passages. But Austen has also developed within us by this time a more comprehensive knowledge of events than that possessed by the heroine—indeed, a more comprehensive knowledge of Elizabeth's character even than that possessed by the heroine herself. Because we are sufficiently enlightened by now, the narrative voice need not explain much and can remain unobtrusive throughout these scenes. Of course, there are brief passages that directly narrate Elizabeth's thoughts or convey the narrator's attitude towards the characters, but these are played down and subtly woven into the fabric of the scene; they function largely to maintain and control our responses to the work. At this point, the dialogue can take on a richness and suggestiveness from the novel's context, from what we already know about the characters and their relationships.

Jane Austen's dialogue functions in numerous ways throughout these scenes. It allows us to maintain a wider perspective than that allowed by a too-dogged attachment to the heroine's thoughts because we are able to see her as a single participant in the world outside her, and to hear and analyze the other characters ourselves without having their words filtered through her mind. Austen is extremely skillful at disclosing personality and thought, conscious and unconscious, through a character's speech. At the same time, these dialogues move the plot forward and develop thematic concerns in a subtle and unobtrusive way: characters change attitudes and alter relationships in response to what they say to one another, while the reader, from a somewhat detached position, is able to see the progressing thematic patterns and ultimate moral significance of their interchanges. The focus of the novel is certainly the internal consciousness of Elizabeth Bennet, but personal psychology is intimately related to societal relationships, and these also are primarily defined and developed through verbal communication. *Pride and Prejudice* is concerned with its heroine's internal development, but the self-understanding she achieves allows her to act in a free but socially responsible way. Finally, it is Jane Austen's dialogue that dramatically creates for us a picture of her social world, the external reality that exists outside of Elizabeth.

Austen disliked detailed description, whether of setting, character, or action. Throughout these scenes, there is a minimal but necessary amount of stage directions: we are told the general movements of the characters and have some spatial sense of the scene—"she [Elizabeth] drew near the card-table, and stationed herself between Mr. Bingley and his eldest sister, to observe the game" (p. 28). We know who is present, who enters, what the characters are doing, their general change of position—but none of this is described graphically or in detail. Yet such general stage directions are sufficient to give us the outlines within which we may supply our own notions of the appearance of things from the singular and characteristic language of the figures. As I have already discussed, the reader's mind is always transmitting a novelist's words into visual images, and the writer controls this visualization through a variety of techniques. Smollett's detailed description of setting, character, and action is not the only way to evoke and control visual images. Indeed, once having established for us the characters and general situation of a work, the novelist can suggest a good deal about behavior and actions with only minimal signs. Relying upon the reader's instinct to imagine the way people look from what they say, and on the propensity of human nature to associate certain physical characteristics with certain types of personality, the novelist can also satisfy the reader's visual needs through individualized speech—indeed, the more vivid and real the dialogue, the more vivid and real the images of the characters who are speaking. Jane Austen, then, creates a dramatic and convincing picture of her social world, of her characters' behavior and appearance, through the most polished and lively dialogue yet to appear in fiction.[21]

Each of the scenes we shall discuss is a small drama with a structure and development of its own. I spoke earlier about Fielding's architecturally designed scenes, where section plays against section, technique against technique.[22] A number of Austen's larger scenes have a structure based upon juxtaposition of both characters and sections of dialogue. This is especially true of the episodes we are now examining, where she plays off Elizabeth against both Darcy and Miss Bingley, and Darcy against Bingley, while establishing certain thematic points through the contrasts of their personalities and the relationship of parts of their moral discourse. But Austen's scenes are less static than Fielding's, more fluid and dramatic. While we are continuously relating characters and ideas, the episode moves forward through the continuous flow of dialogue and the dramatic development of the characters' relationships.

To remind us that though we are more committed to Elizabeth than the other characters, and that though we must finally assess matters in relation to her we are also to see her as only one of several participants in the scene, Austen at times employs indirect discourse for the heroine's speech and gives only brief descriptions of her thinking. In the first of these scenes, which takes place the night of Elizabeth's arrival, the heroine's initial speech is several times summarized rather than completely recorded. We thus become somewhat detached from her, not forced to concentrate in great detail on her words, and we are allowed to focus more on the other characters, to see and hear them more directly than we do Elizabeth. Indeed, we tend to see them as would the heroine— obviously, we neither see ourselves when we participate in conversation, nor register our own words in our minds as distinctly as those of others. But even when Austen moves us inside of Elizabeth, she does not portray her responses in depth or with much detail but only reinforces our sense of the perspective through which we should be viewing the action—the emphasis of the drama is still on the outside, on the interplay of characters, and we are allowed the satisfaction of interpreting these figures for ourselves, unswayed by the heroine's prejudice, though we generally can surmise what is going on inside of her.

Sometimes these brief and unspecific trips inside of Elizabeth reinforce her perspective while also indicating that not very much is going on there at all, that she reacts to the conversation with interest but no personal involvement. I make this last point to emphasize that we must not read more into these scenes than the novel will allow, that when Austen wants us to know something about her heroine, she either gives us ample clues or simply tells us. For example, early in this first scene, when the subject of Pemberley arises, we move briefly inside of Elizabeth and are told that she "was so much caught by what passed, as to leave her very little attention for her book; and soon laying it wholly aside, she drew near the card-table, and stationed herself between Miss Bingley and his elder sister, to observe the game" (p. 28). The narrator neither tells us why Elizabeth is interested in the subject nor describes for us her specific reactions to the conversation; we listen rather with the heroine in an interested, though neutral, way. It would be a mistake to see Elizabeth's interest in the discussion of Pemberley as indicative of some hidden love for Darcy or of mercenary inclinations. It has already been made clear that Elizabeth does not like Darcy, a fact which is further emphasized during these scenes;[23] and certainly we have already been shown that the heroine is not a mercenary or self-seeking person. My point is that Austen is one of the least confusing or conspiratorial of authors. What we must do is read the novel carefully: the burden is upon the reader to put the pieces together, to see the novel in his own mind, but at the same time not to overextend himself and write the novel for the author. The discussion of Pemberley interests Elizabeth because, as we have already seen in the novel, property, estates, and inheritances are of prime importance to her society—the social structure in *Pride and Prejudice* is dependent upon marriage, settlements, and the alliance of families. It is also significant that large estates, in economically supporting many people, in looking after their needs, and in giving them a social context, are one of the bulwarks of society at large. Throughout the book, we hear much about estates: Longbourn, Netherfield Park, Rosings, and Pemberley.[24] Elizabeth, sharing the values of her society, has an interest in estates, and what this episode indicates is not a hidden or half-conscious intention but a level of correspondence, a mutual attitude she shares with Darcy and others in the book. Elizabeth's interest in the subject also prepares us for her visit to Pemberley later in the novel, when the estate itself allows her to understand Darcy in the context of his greater social role.

All the information we need is conveyed to us from our past reading and what the characters now say to one another. The pleasure we derive from these scenes is from watching the drama take place and listening to the characters, understanding the significance and interplay of their words at times better than they do, since we know more about what is going on, and our own perspective is not subjectively distorted. While Fielding plays with our expectations and hopes, keeping information hidden or disguised and then surprising us with a sudden turn in events, forcing us continually to reassess character, plot, and our own perceptions, Austen builds her novel along clearer and more logical lines, relying upon the reader's accurate perceptions from the start. Her book maintains within the reader a confidence in his understanding, while bringing the heroine and hero to a point where they lose confidence in theirs. Although we can see these early scenes as battles of wit,[25] it seems more useful to me to read them as conflicts dependent upon misunderstanding, as scenes showing pride, prejudice, and other forms of subjective distortion that prevent accurate perception. Ironically, while all this misunderstanding is going on, the characters are busy in their discourse trying to define the "accomplished" woman and to establish the proper behavior for a true man. In their arguments about how others should behave, Elizabeth and Darcy exhibit some ignorance about themselves and a related failure to see each other fairly and with accuracy—but of the two, Elizabeth is clearly the more culpable.

In the scene we are examining, Bingley defines what is commonly referred to as "an accomplished woman"—one who "paint[s] tables, cover[s] skreens and net purses" (p. 28). Darcy challenges this definition, and against it is placed a demanding and unrealistic one, ironically contributed to by both Miss Bingley, who is not very accomplished, and Darcy himself, who is not much admired by the only accomplished lady in the scene, Elizabeth. The contrast between Miss Bingley and Elizabeth is brought home to us by Darcy, who, after Miss Bingley comments on the skills and deportment necessary for a woman to be accomplished, states that such a person must also "add something more substantial, in the improvement of her mind by extensive reading" (p. 29). The point obviously is directed at Elizabeth, who at the beginning of the scene has chosen to read rather than play cards. "Reading" is a major motif throughout these episodes and a measure of a character's intelligence. In the present scene, we are to commend Elizabeth because she chooses to read rather than play loo, and Darcy because he considers reading a prime activity for an accomplished woman. We are to condemn Mr.

Hurst because of his surprise that Elizabeth prefers reading to playing cards, and Miss Bingley because she clumsily uses the library at Pemberley as a means of complimenting Darcy. Bingley is to be praised for wishing that he had more books to offer Elizabeth and for admitting that he does not read enough, and censured for the reading deficiency he confesses.[26]

Elizabeth is blind to Darcy's indirect compliment about her reading because she still believes that he dislikes her. Her own dislike for him is underscored by her reaction to his definition of "an accomplished woman," a reaction which contrasts with that of both the Bingley sisters:

> "*I* never saw such a woman, *I* never saw such capacity, and taste, and application, and elegance, as you describe, united."
> Mrs. Hurst and Miss Bingley both cried out against the injustice of her implied doubt, and were both protesting that they knew many women who answered this description.... (P. 29)

But the more significant interplay in this discussion is between Elizabeth and Darcy, who have been arguing at cross-purposes. Clearly they are ignorant of each other's feelings and intentions (as we are not), and so manage continuously to misinterpret one another. Darcy is really complimenting Elizabeth, but since she is ignorant of his growing interest in her and still sees him in light of his insult at the ball, she interprets his high standards as further evidence of his conceit and pride, while suspecting that he is also deprecating her. He is ignorant of her dislike for him, and so rather interprets her remarks as evidence of her own high standards and superiority. The misunderstanding extends to Miss Bingley, who claims, after Elizabeth has left the room, that the heroine's remarks were meant to recommend herself above the rest of her sex. Darcy's reply is intended to put Miss Bingley in her place, but it also serves to remind us of his feelings for Elizabeth: "Undoubtedly ... there is meanness in *all* the arts which ladies sometimes condescend to employ for captivation. Whatever bears affinity to cunning is despicable" (p. 29). A drama is taking place of which all the characters are ignorant. At no point need Austen tell us exactly what is going on, since we have enough information to understand matters on our own. We are involved, then, in the scene through our association with Elizabeth; and we also feel pleasure from an awareness greater than that which belongs to her or any of the characters. We are perceiving with Elizabeth and perceiving her as part of a drama about human perception. But we have also become somewhat involved with Darcy: we are starting to understand him better than does Elizabeth, because we listen to him more objectively, and because now we have heard him speak admirably while she has been out of the room.[27] Certainly Darcy is a snob, and his arrogance at times leads him to some very distorted views about others and about himself—but he is much more than this.[28] To say the least, he is an intelligent and sensitive individual, and both these qualities become clearly manifested in his growing admiration for Elizabeth. This perception of Darcy, which becomes more distinct as these scenes continue and as he becomes more familiar to us and clearer as a character in his own right, is one of the reasons why we are prevented from over-committing ourselves to Elizabeth and her judgments.

A similar scene occurs the next evening, again with the same interplay of characters and again primarily from the vantage point of the heroine: "Elizabeth took up some needlework, and was sufficiently amused in attending to what passed between Darcy and his companion" (p. 34). We are reminded of Elizabeth's predisposition toward people when we are told that Miss Bingley's flattery and Darcy's unconcern were "exactly in unison with her opinion of each" (p. 34). The discourse is again moral in nature, as the characters once more attempt to define proper and intelligent behavior, but, as in the previous night, opinion is distorted by conflicts between characters and individual myopia. In the earlier scene, the major subject discussed was the definition of an "accomplished woman"; here the subject can be seen as the behavior of a true man. The two antithetical definitions presented are the person who sacrifices his plans for the desire of a friend, something Bingley would do, and the person who does not; the second person is seen by Darcy as a man of strength and responsibility, someone, he undoubtedly thinks, like himself. In the earlier scene, Darcy's comments about an "accomplished woman" were refuted by Elizabeth, even though they had been intended to describe her. Here again she refutes Darcy's opinion, this time because she recognizes that it describes the way he would act. Elizabeth, Darcy, and Bingley become involved in this subject, each arguing from different preconceptions and from different personal involvements. Elizabeth argues *against* Darcy, willfully misrepresenting what he says because she is continuously misunderstanding his character and censuring him. Even good-natured Bingley sees this: " 'I am exceedingly gratified,' said Bingley, 'by your converting what my friend says into a compliment on the sweetness of my temper. But I am afraid you are giving it a turn which that gentleman did by no means intend...' " (p. 36).

Darcy argues from principle and not according to the temper of his opponent. He is an uncompromising person at this point in the novel and would not sacrifice a belief even to free himself from an uncomfortable situation. Elizabeth forces him into a rigid moral position from which he will not back down: " 'You expect me to account for opinions which you chuse to call mine, but which I have never acknowledged. [Allow]... the case, however, to stand according to your representation...' " (p. 36). Bingley, who is not a fool, understands what Elizabeth and Darcy are doing in their argument, but he has no idea why they are doing it. His good-natured description of Darcy— " 'I do not know a more aweful object than Darcy, on particular occasions, and in particular places; at his own house especially, and of a Sunday evening when he has nothing to do' " (p. 37)—is meant to lighten the argument, and should make Elizabeth see that Darcy is not such a bad fellow if Bingley can joke about him in this manner. Elizabeth does realize that Darcy is somewhat offended and "therefore checked her laugh," yet she perceives Darcy no more clearly from the incident and continues in her obdurate way.

We are still participating in the scene with Elizabeth, feeling her superiority to the hopeless Miss Bingley, triumphing through her wit and intelligence in the conversation; yet, at the same time, we are also detached, seeing her prejudice bring her more into error in regard to Darcy. There should be no doubt in our mind that her dislike for him leads to faulty perceptions and errors in judgment, and both of these lead to arrogance in attitude and behavior—prejudice is clearly leading to pride.[29] Darcy, on the other hand, may be proud and even a little pompous, but Austen, through a number of techniques, makes us see that there are many redeeming aspects to him, not least of all his admiration for Elizabeth. This conversation also prepares us for later attitudes and behavior. Elizabeth and Darcy argue about friendship, defining for themselves the attitude of the other on this subject. Elizabeth's willful misunderstanding of Darcy's position prepares her to condemn him later in the novel, with some injustice, for persuading his friend Bingley to leave Netherfield Park and Jane; hence, the present argument is ultimately connected to her attack against him when he proposes to her.

Right after this discussion when Bingley's sisters are musically performing, Elizabeth notices that Darcy is staring at her, but she can imagine only "that she drew his notice because there was a something about her more wrong and reprehensible, according to his ideas of right, than in any other person present. The supposition did not pain her. She liked him too little to care for his approbation" (p. 38). This is the second time in the book that Elizabeth has noticed Darcy's attention and the second time she has misinterpreted it, so strong is her feeling against him. But even Elizabeth must take notice that Darcy is not always the pompous snob she would like him to be. When responding to his question whether the music does not make her want to dance a reel (p. 38), she tells him she will answer "no" rather than "yes" in order to avoid his contempt. She then challenges him to "despise" her if he dare, but when Darcy answers " 'Indeed I do not dare,' " Elizabeth is "amazed at his gallantry," especially since she has tried to affront him. But Elizabeth goes no further than being amazed—she is still ignorant of what is going on inside of Darcy. To make absolutely sure that we are not, Austen briefly moves us into Darcy's consciousness, to show us what he is thinking, and then to an outside observer, Miss Bingley, to demonstrate that even she understands Darcy better than Elizabeth. The scene moves quickly from Elizabeth to Darcy and then to Miss Bingley:

> Elizabeth, having rather expected to affront him, was amazed at his gallantry; but there was a mixture of sweetness and archness in her manner which made it difficult for her to affront anybody; and Darcy had never been so bewitched by any woman as he was by her. He really believed, that were it not for the inferiority of her connections, he should be in some danger.
> Miss Bingley saw, or suspected enough to be jealous; and her great anxiety for the recovery of her dear friend Jane, received some assistance from her desire of getting rid of Elizabeth. (P. 38)

We are only briefly with Darcy and Miss Bingley, but our stay with them is sufficient for us to receive the multiple perspectives, the parallactic vision, necessary to round out the drama and increase our insights into the various characters. We are able to make these sudden, though unobtrusive, transitions from character to character because we have not been totally committed to the heroine's point of view, and because the narrator has been subtly present throughout the scene, guiding us whenever necessary, giving us on occasion information and insights denied the heroine. Of course, we see that Darcy is still a snob, sensitive to the "inferiority of her [Elizabeth's] connections," but we also see that he has the capacity to overcome his limitations. In any case, we must admire him for appreciating the heroine, as we must admire Elizabeth for handling herself so well, even when she is so flagrantly wrong.

The third of these scenes takes place the next evening, when Jane is well enough to join the company downstairs. Once more books become a subject of discourse and are again employed by Austen to make the distinction between good and bad minds. While Darcy reads, Miss Bingley pretends to read, again functioning as a contrast to Elizabeth, not only in her foolishness and snobbishness but also in her banal flattery of Darcy: the book she pretends to read is the second volume to the one he is reading. A few moments later, she tries to impress Darcy by stating that balls would be better if one conversed at such events instead of danced. Bingley intelligently responds, " 'Much more rational, my dear Caroline, I dare say, but it would not be near so much like a ball' " (p. 41). Unable to succeed with her mind, Miss Bingley decides to walk about and show off her figure to Darcy.[30] Elizabeth accepts her invitation to walk about the room also, and Darcy, "as much awake to the novelty of attention in that quarter as Elizabeth herself could be" (p. 41), closes his book and watches. His blunt assertion that they are either walking together to tell secrets or display their figures shows his usual intelligence and also demonstrates a lack of tact that often breaks forth in his social intercourse—with all his gallantry and propriety, Darcy must still be educated in his social behavior. But Elizabeth's attacks against Darcy are clearly overstated: her retorts, though witty and clever, are motivated and hence somewhat misdirected by her ill feelings towards him. Without knowing it, she consistently comes off the loser in these interchanges, and Darcy, because of her behavior, looks better and better in our eyes:

> "Mr. Darcy is not to be laughed at!" cried Elizabeth. "That is an uncommon advantage, and uncommon I hope it will continue, for it would be a great loss to *me* to have many such acquaintance. I dearly love a laugh."
> "Miss Bingley," said he, "has given me credit for more than can be. The wisest and the best of men, nay, the wisest and best of their actions, may be rendered ridiculous by a person whose first object in life is a joke." (P. 42)

There is, of course, some truth in what each is saying. Darcy is proud enough to consider himself above being laughed at, and Elizabeth is quick to make a joke, especially in a situation where she is emotionally involved, but neither is nearly as bad as the other defensively suggests. Both characters expose themselves more than they do the other.

As Darcy feels himself more attracted to Elizabeth, her resentment against him seems to grow. Though he exhibits certain flaws, we tend to sympathize with him as the victim of her attacks. Austen is clearly establishing our support for Darcy, even though we are still admiring and associating with the heroine. We are becoming more aware of Elizabeth's shortcomings, and we are being prepared for her later change of heart about Darcy. Right now, however, Elizabeth's animosity keeps getting confused with her moral fervor:

"Certainly," replied Elizabeth—"there are such people, but I hope I am not one of *them*. I hope I never ridicule what is wise or good. Follies and nonsense, whims and inconsistencies *do* divert me, I own, and I laugh at them whenever I can.—But these, I suppose, are precisely what you are without." (P. 42)

Elizabeth's attacks succeed in putting Darcy on the defensive and forcing him to reveal himself:

"Perhaps this is not possible for any one. But it has been the study of my life to avoid those weaknesses which often expose a strong understanding to ridicule."
"Such as vanity and pride."
"Yes, vanity is a weakness indeed. But pride—where there is a real superiority of mind, pride will be always under good regulation."
Elizabeth turned away to hide a smile. (P. 43)

The smile is deserved, though not from Elizabeth at this point. Her statement about "vanity and pride" is a direct attack against Darcy, who defends his position and himself as best he can. What he says is right, but it is his saying it about himself that is wrong. The issues he deals with are some of the major issues of the book, and the answers he presents are acceptable within the context of the book, but in his mouth and about himself these sentiments become boastful and proud. Besides, at this point in the novel Darcy has not quite attained the superiority of mind he thinks he has—certainly no more than Elizabeth. The novel itself makes the same distinction between vanity and pride that Darcy suggests: vanity is self-glorification for mean or empty accomplishments, a quality possessed by people like Mr. Collins and Lady Catherine; true pride is related to "a real superiority of mind," which is the highest human achievement that the work advocates.[31] It is such an intelligence that Elizabeth and Darcy almost possess at this point and finally acquire later in the book; it is their capacity to achieve this superiority that distinguishes them from the other characters.

When Miss Bingley asks, " 'Your examination of Mr. Darcy is over, I presume . . . and pray what is the result?' " (p. 43), she expresses exactly what the characters are doing: examining one another. The very topics of their discourse throughout these scenes, the analyses of behavior and intelligence, are directly related to their views of one another. We can go further and say that the characters' own behavior and intelligence dramatize the very subjects they discuss. Elizabeth's examination, though, is predetermined. She will not like Darcy and is ready to misinterpret and misjudge him: " 'I am perfectly convinced by it that

Mr. Darcy has no defect. He owns it himself without disguise' " (p. 43). That is exactly what Darcy has not owned: " 'No'—said Darcy, 'I have made no such pretension' " (p. 43). He tries to maintain his previous point, that whatever his faults they are not of "understanding." But throughout these scenes, we have been aware that, like Elizabeth, Darcy is deficient in some aspects of his understanding. Both characters insufficiently understand themselves and hence misunderstand others; both are victims of pride and prejudice and hence distort the world outside them. Darcy admits to the flaw of having a temper that is "too little yielding"; he admits to being "resentful": " 'My good opinion once lost is lost forever' " (p. 43). What he is saying here is that once having made up his mind about someone, he is blind to any new information or ideas, that he will see only what he wants to see. Darcy concedes to Elizabeth that he does have a flaw, but he presents his flaw in a boastful manner—his vanity and egotism also show forth here. Elizabeth is quite taken back—she had no idea she would succeed so well. Darcy has exposed himself. But she cannot help exposing herself also in reply to Darcy's boastful concession:

> "There is, I believe, in every disposition a tendency to some particular evil, a natural defect, which not even the best education can overcome."
> "And *your* defect is a propensity to hate every body."
> "And yours," he replied with a smile, "is willfully to misunderstand them." (P. 43)

Understand him she has, but she has also very much misunderstood him. Elizabeth's description of Darcy's defect is grossly overstated and shows more of her own weakness than his. She will understand him no more than he will understand those who have lost his favor. Darcy is much on the defensive during this last scene, but once Elizabeth makes her final, painfully incorrect statement, he is able to reply with equanimity and a smile. Like Elizabeth, in most ways he also is an intelligent person, intelligent enough to see that at least for the moment the advantage is his.

Pride and Prejudice is a book about moral and social intelligence: the way we see ourselves in relation to others, and the way we see others in relation to one another and ourselves. This concern explains not only the narrative focus on Elizabeth's inner world, her perceiving mind, but also the focus on scenes of dialogue that give us an accurate picture of the world which she perceives at times with some distortion. Throughout these scenes of lively and entertaining dialogue, we achieve the simultaneous visions of Elizabeth's world as she sees it, and that world with Elizabeth as a single participant in its ongoing interaction and drama. *Pride and Prejudice*, better than any novel we have discussed so far, dramatizes the dual realities that haunted the eighteenth century—the subjective and objective realities. That it does so in such a comic, witty, and intelligent way in these early scenes indicates its optimism and healthy spirit and foreshadows the ultimate integration of these realities later in the novel when Elizabeth learns to perceive the world outside her with accuracy and understanding.

ENLIGHTENMENT

Perhaps no chapter in the book expresses so well what Jane Austen is about as that in which Elizabeth reads Darcy's letter and comes to her realizations about herself, about him, and about the other characters in the work. It is the chapter to which all previous events move, and it is the chapter which sets the course of action for the remainder of the book. It is also in many ways the chapter to which my own study has been progressing, for within it we see the resolution of conflicts about the nature of man that had been embodied in the major novels of the period, and the culmination of narrative techniques that had been developing for almost three-quarters of a century. This is the moment when the heroine looks inside herself and, with an act of will and intelligence, pulls her disparate memories and responses together, when she overcomes the limitations and distortions of her mind and emotions to achieve a marvelous cohesion and clarity of self. What is achieved here is not the universal permanence and uniformity of Fielding's characters, many of whom remain in a perpetual state of confusion and unreason, but an awareness that leads to a self-imposed order, a conscious, sustained, and successful effort to overcome the flux and change of the inner world. Elizabeth is still alive to the sequence of impressions, thoughts, and emotions that pass perennially through her psyche. Her inner world does not become dormant; her personal sense of self, her identity, does not become fixed and simplistic. Elizabeth is still vulnerable to the limitations of being human, the limitations that Sterne so comically treated, but she confronts the problems of the self far more knowingly than did Moll and far more reasonably than did Clarissa. What we witness is the power of the mind to confront unreason and emotion, of human intelligence to overcome pride, prejudice, and all the subjective sins that distort the individual's view of himself and prevent him from seeing and hence relating to others in a proper and humane way. Elizabeth examines herself and her responses to the world outside her; she breaks through a distorted and false sense of herself and others to achieve a valid and functional personal identity—functional because she can now survive in her world honestly and openly, without sacrificing any part of her individuality. For ultimately this is the true meaning of "know thy self," at least in the eighteenth century: to know thyself is to be thyself and survive with independence, integrity, and responsibility; it means removing the self-delusions and personal weaknesses which distort our vision of the world outside, and understanding ourselves by recognizing the human limitations and aspirations we share with others. Personal identity can be found and asserted only through interpersonal relationships. Moll's self-discovery in Newgate is not merely false: it leads nowhere, because the heroine must finally flee the real world of England and live an exile with her Lancashire husband in the colonies. Clarissa's self-discovery is far more convincing, but it is finally unsupportable in this life and can only be fulfilled in the next. Elizabeth makes her discovery and stays in the here and now; as a result of her new awareness, she marries Darcy and lives as a socially responsible human being happily ever after.

This episode is also impressive because of the way in which it is written, because of the narrative techniques with which Jane Austen presents Elizabeth's internal drama. Austen was the first novelist to employ a third-person narrative voice for creating in a sustained, convincing, and dramatic way the psychic dimension of character. *Pride and Prejudice* is the first of her novels in which this technique is fully developed and consistently employed. Throughout this study, we have seen that the major eighteenth-century novelists used first-person narrative voices to create the subjective dimension of character. Influenced primarily by Richardson, Jane Austen seems to have begun her first two published works as epistolary novels[32] in order to create the subjective drama, but then transposed them into third-person narrations to achieve as well a greater perspective and control of narrative elements. In *Pride and Prejudice*, she skillfully integrates both the subjective dimension of first-person narration and the omniscient vision of third-person. The potential for this technique was actually in Richardson's *Clarissa*, in the heroine's letters where we have the double perspective of the character during the narrated event and at the time of her writing. The next step in the development of narrative technique was to give the perspective at the time of writing to a third-person narrator, while still maintaining the point of view of the character at the time of the recorded event. The narrative voice could then be widened to incorporate the comprehensive vision and, to some degree, commentary of Fielding's narrator, while the full dramatic emphasis would still fall on the event itself and the heroine's point of view at the time. We can see attempts to evoke the psychic dimension through third-person narration in other works of the period—in Fanny Burney's *Cecilia*, for example—but no one accomplishes this, no one makes third-person narrative voice into a flexible, controlling, and also psychological and subjective technique, until Jane Austen.

It is for this reason that her development of this technique seems influenced by both Richardson and her own efforts in writing first-person epistolary fiction, where the double perspective already existed and the possibility for third-person subjective narration was inherent. Objectifying the narrative voice into third-person narration and infusing it with wit, irony, and a greater intelligence would follow naturally. The advantages of this technique over first-person narration for the kind of novel she wished to write are obvious: third-person narration allowed her to insert her narrator's commentary, in a relatively unobtrusive way, so that the reader gives ear to a more knowing intelligence; it allowed her to transcend the heroine's perspective in order to give a wider and more objective portrait of the social world; it allowed her to portray, and have her narrator comment upon, the heroine at times from a distance in order to have the reader see Elizabeth as she could not see herself; and, finally, it allowed her occasionally to move to other points of view, thus giving the reader a fuller awareness of the drama's complexity while also developing her themes about perception and understanding.

In the scene we shall examine, in the five pages which record for us Elizabeth's internal crisis and triumph, we seem to stay largely within the inner space of the heroine's mind, though we are still aware of the larger perspective. The double perspective is sometimes owing to an overt use of narrative voice, but the major cause is more complex and subtle: it is Jane Austen's language—the words, sentence structure, and general expository development with which she creates Elizabeth's internal drama—that allows us this effect.[33] Austen describes Elizabeth's internal drama in such a way that to some degree we see and feel as she does, but the language which describes the internal drama controls our involvement, prevents a too-intensive identification with the character. Elizabeth's experience must be made real to us, but, on the other hand, we also have to see her at this moment as part of the novel's larger context, as an element in its larger thematic concerns and general development.

Since we have already examined Darcy's letter before the scene's commencement, we are free to concentrate on the heroine's reactions as she reads the letter twice. The first sentence—"IF ELIZABETH, when Mr. Darcy gave her the letter, did not expect it to contain a renewal of his offers, she had formed no expectation at all of its contents" (p. 153)—is more dramatic in structure than reportorial: it does not tell us exactly what Elizabeth thinks, but its delayed meaning and the hesitant movement of its two-part structure, with the first part broken by a parenthetical clause, convey to us a sense of her uncertainty and surprise. Throughout this scene, Austen does not give us great detail or specificity, yet she dramatically creates Elizabeth's inner conflicts and ultimate resolution through the structure of her sentences and paragraphs as well as the interplay of her language. In the next two sentences—"But such as they were, it may be well supposed how eagerly she went through them, and what a contrariety of emotion they excited. Her feelings as she read were scarcely to be defined" (p. 153)—the narrator tells us three times that she is not describing what the heroine actually felt: Elizabeth's expectations are referred to as "such as they were," her eagerness is left for the reader to "suppose," and her feelings as she reads can "scarcely be described." Austen does not chain herself to the exact sequence of thoughts and emotions in Elizabeth. What she conveys in the first of these sentences is a dramatic sense of the "contrariety of emotions" the heroine feels through the rather elongated and fragmented structure, and, in the second sentence, the intensity of "her feelings" through the brief and sudden structure.

Throughout this scene, the narrator describes Elizabeth's emotions with a general vocabulary that keeps the heroine within a universal eighteenth-century social and moral context but still manages to convey to us what she is feeling.[34] This communication is achieved because the language is sufficiently suggestive and the general linguistic context dramatic enough to evoke from the reader's own experience a feeling parallel to that of the heroine, though, of course, one more subdued and controlled. I am describing here a narrative technique especially developed by Austen, a technique by which the narrator is in complete control of the passage, describing an internal state in her own language, language which places the character in the larger social and moral concerns developed throughout the work, yet re-creating for the reader an immediate sense of that state through evocative language in an evocative linguistic context:

> With amazement did she first understand that he believed any apology to be in his power; and stedfastly was she persuaded that he could have no explanation to give, which a just sense of shame would not conceal. With a

strong prejudice against every thing he might say, she began his account of
what had happened at Netherfield. She read, with an eagerness which
hardly left her power of comprehension, and from impatience of knowing
what the next sentence might bring, was incapable of attending to the sense
of the one before her eyes. (P. 153)

"Amazement," "eagerness," and "impatience" play against
"stedfastly," "persuaded," and "strong prejudice"—her feelings of
surprise and curiosity threaten to undermine preconceptions and set
attitudes. Through the linguistic drama of conflicting words, the reader
is allowed to sense the emotional conflict that goes on inside the heroine.
Equally significant is the rhythm of the prose, which also adds to our
sense of Elizabeth's internal drama. "With amazement" begins the
passage abruptly and emphatically, but the phrase is balanced and
Elizabeth's emotional state made to seem checked by "stedfastly was she
persuaded," which appears at the start of the second half of the sentence.
The sentence breaks in two, with the additional clause at the end of the
second part also seeming to bring under control the emotion expressed
in the first part. But at the same time, all of the linguistic components we
are discussing and the sense of the heroine's emotional state which they
create within us contribute to the two visual levels of the scene—to the
drama of Elizabeth as she confronts Darcy's letter, and to the brief and
passing images of the past which the epistle evokes in her brain. An
amazed but resolute Elizabeth stands apart in our mind's eye, letter in
hand, while at the same time we are inside her, identifying with her as
her thoughts pass through our own minds, as we perceive with her an
image of Darcy and, soon after, images of the events at Netherfield.

Structure and rhythm contribute to our emotional sense of the scene
in the following sentence:

> But when this subject was succeeded by his account of Mr. Wickham, when
> she read with somewhat clearer attention, a relation of events, which, if
> true, must overthrow every cherished opinion of his worth, and which bore
> so alarming an affinity to his own history of himself, her feelings were yet
> more acutely painful and more difficult of definition. (P. 153)

We have here a series of subordinate clauses suspending the continuum
of Elizabeth's thoughts, creating a sense of her uncertainty, and building
up to her acute state of pain and confusion, which is emphasized by the
finality of the major clause at the end. Also striking about this sentence is
its overall structure, its eighteenth-century balanced and ordered prose,
which serves the dramatic needs of the scene. The two "when" clauses
and the following two "which" clauses give the balance and symmetry
to the sentence we are used to in the more formal writing of the period,

while also developing Elizabeth's emotional drama. These four clauses, while adding information, intensify a sense of doubt and uncertainty; yet the build-up from the linguistic repetitions increases our readiness for the emotional state discussed at the end of the sentence. At the same time, these structural repetitions and the bipartite predicate of the final clause suggest a sense of order to Elizabeth's responses and prepare us for the control she later imposes upon her feelings as she achieves her state of self-understanding.

We can say of Jane Austen's prose, in general, that though influenced in its formal aspects by the writings of the great eighteenth-century essayists, a more immediate influence came from the novelists themselves, and from Fielding and Burney in particular.[35] Austen incorporates the formal language of social and moral judgment written by the essayists, but she learned from the novelists how to use the ordered and well-structured prose of third-person narrative voice to tell her story. But while it was from Fielding that she learned to write this prose, especially in her narrative commentary, with flexibility, wit, and irony,[36] it was her own unique achievement to employ it in dramatically conveying her characters' inner lives, in creating the subjective element she found in Richardson's works. The fact that she employs the same kind of formalistic sentence structure, relying upon balance, antithesis, repetition, and sudden finality for the description of both her narrator's brief commentaries and her main character's inner state, contributes to the continuity of the work and creates a wholeness of tone; it is for this reason that we can move so easily and imperceptibly in and out of Elizabeth's mind, from the depiction of her internal drama to the narrator's viewpoint and occasional commentary.

In the next sentence in the passage, "Astonishment, apprehension, and even horror, oppressed her" (p. 153), three abstract nouns individually generalize and distance Elizabeth's emotions, but together they convey to us the intensity of her feelings by their accumulative effect. These three nouns and the verb "oppressed," which repeats the hard "p" sound of "apprehension," bury the heroine's monosyllabic pronoun at the end of the sentence. Elizabeth's sudden statements— "'This must be false! This cannot be! This must be the grossest falsehood!'"—like the nouns of the previous sentence, also follow in triplet form,[37] a repetition which here conveys the heroine trying to order and control her emotions but which also dramatizes and emphasizes her sudden and strong sense of panic that she has been wrong. In the last part of the paragraph, we find the same combination of formal and dramatic structure:

and when she had gone through the whole letter, though scarcely knowing any thing of the last page or two, put it hastily away, protesting that she would not regard it, that she would never look in it again. (P. 153)

The "when" clause, with "she" as subject, is followed by a modifying eliptical clause which contains a participle, and the clause "put it hastily away," with "she" understood, is followed by a participial phrase which introduces two parallel noun clauses. The suggestions of balance and structural repetition dramatize Elizabeth's internal struggle to maintain her initial impressions, but the succession of clauses, the rapid movement from one to another, suggests the flow of thoughts and inevitable change taking place in her mind.

All the while, Austen keeps her heroine rooted in the physical world, allowing us the constant visual sense of her appearance and actions: we must have some concrete image in our mind into which we can channel Elizabeth's emotions and responses, and into which we can also channel the fleeting images of her thoughts:

In this perturbed state of mind, with thoughts that could rest on nothing, she walked on; but it would not do; in half a minute the letter was unfolded again, and collecting herself as well as she could, she again began the mortifying perusal of all that related to Wickham, and commanded herself so far as to examine the meaning of every sentence. (Pp. 153-54)

But this passage also rhythmically helps to create Elizabeth's inner conflict: her perturbed state is suggested by the division of the first part of the sentence into three segments, and "but it would not do" comes as a jolt in the middle of the sentence to suggest the heroine's sudden resolution.

It is not merely in individual sentences that we find a balanced structure and dramatic development at the same time, but within the entire episode as well. One can find throughout these paragraphs a series of key sentences that establish the major dramatic points of Elizabeth's internal action. Each of these sentences pinpoints an internal stage in her thoughts which then is developed or explained until the next key sentence, which pinpoints another stage. What is created here, then, is both a sense of linear development, of idea working its way to idea, and an architectural structure of the whole internal drama, a sense of order and balance that emphasizes the reasonable and intelligent way in which the character is thinking. Let us examine some of the key statements from a few of these paragraphs:

So far each recital confirmed the other: but when she came to the will, the difference was great. (P. 154)

239

But every line proved more clearly that the affair ... was capable of a turn which must make him [Darcy] entirely blameless throughout the whole. (P. 154)

The extravagance and general profligacy which he scrupled not to lay to Mr. Wickham's charge, exceedingly shocked her.... (P. 154)

She tried to recollect some instance of goodness.... But no such recollection befriended her. (P. 154)

She was *now* struck with the impropriety of such communications to a stranger.... (P. 155)

How differently did every thing now appear in which he was concerned! (P. 155)

Our sense of the order and control in Elizabeth's thinking created by these key statements is reinforced by parallel sentence structures within the chapter's paragraphs. Sometimes the key sentences themselves are part of their paragraph's parallelism: for example, the second half of the first quotation—"but when she came to the will, the difference was great"—is soon echoed by "But when she read, and re-read with the closest attention...." This last sentence finishes with "again was she forced to hesitate," which is echoed a few lines later with "Again she read on...."

Elizabeth's realization about the two men, led up to point by point, is followed by clarification and amplification. The past situation becomes fully clear to her and suddenly, as a result, she has a realization about herself: "She grew absolutely ashamed of herself.—Of neither Darcy nor Wickham could she think, without feeling that she had been blind, partial, prejudiced, absurd" (p. 156). The self here scrutinizes the self and finds itself wanting. Self-analysis leads to self-condemnation. Shame is felt not from what others think but from what the individual thinks of herself. The individual has become cognizant of her own identity, of who and what she is and how she ought to behave. Her past thoughts, emotions, and conduct are measured according to her own definition of self—she has not been true to others because she has not been true to herself. Elizabeth's realization is made more immediate and dramatic by being described and set off in a single brief and emphatic paragraph. The suddenness and directness of the first sentence help convey to us the intensity of her feelings. The listing off of "blind, partial, prejudiced, absurd" in the second sentence hammers home and compounds our sense of her self-castigation. This is not a direct transcription of an interior monologue—the thinking process is itself visual, as Elizabeth remembers her past behavior to Darcy and Wickham, and the realization which follows is both emotional and intellectual, transcending verbal thought. The narrator describes Elizabeth's realization in rational and moral terms that in their selection and ordering dramatically convey what is going on inside of her, while emphasizing the intelligent and responsible nature of her entire internal development.

Elizabeth's own words are recorded in the monologue which immediately follows. Without sacrificing the necessary personal and emotional elements, Austen gives her heroine a language which has the same formal structures and kind of diction as her third-person narrative voice:

> "How despicably have I acted!" she cried—"I, who have prided myself on my discernment!—I, who have valued myself on my abilities! who have often disdained the generous candour of my sister, and gratified my vanity, in useless or blameable distrust.—How humiliating is this discovery!—Yet, how just a humiliation!—Had I been in love, I could not have been more wretchedly blind. But vanity, not love, has been my folly.—Pleased with the preference of one, and offended by the neglect of the other, on the very beginning of our acquaintance, I have courted prepossession and ignorance, and driven reason away, where either were concerned. Till this moment, I never knew myself." (P. 156)

Elizabeth speaks aloud to herself in a credible and dramatic way, yet the writing is formal with some alliteration (note the repetition of words beginning with "d" in the first part of the paragraph and with "p" in the last), repetition (in the middle of the paragraph, for example, "vanity" is repeated twice and "humiliation" plays off "humility"), and balance (at the very beginning of the passage, three statements of guilt are spoken in parallel linguistic structures, the first two beginning with "I who have" and the third with "who have," and later on there is the double parallelism in the sentence beginning "Pleased with the preference of one"). The formal elements within Elizabeth's dramatic monologue keep her speech in harmony with the cadences of the narrator's voice. At the same time, she repeats the same moral and social language we have heard throughout the work in the narrator's commentary and descriptions of Elizabeth's thoughts, and even in the scenes of dialogue. Here again it is the dramatic patterning of these words that adds significantly to the writing's impact. The subject of Elizabeth's verbal examination of herself is "discernment," and such words as "prided," "valued myself," and "gratified my vanity" synthesize with "blind," "prepossession," and "ignorance" to lead to the final sentence: "till this moment, I never knew myself." Elizabeth now employs this language in a cognizant and accurate way—she is at last aware of the moral and social issues involved in her relationships with Darcy and Wickham, issues which we have been aware of all along. Her proper use of this language now marks the close proximity of her intelligence and awareness to those of the narrator. At this point in the novel, Elizabeth's moral consciousness is sufficiently developed for her to perceive and articulate the values which Austen wishes to communicate through her work. The narrative voice need no longer be so concerned with enlightening the reader through commentary and irony since the heroine has become a dramatic embodiment and spokesman for all the correct values. But Elizabeth will still be dramatized within the controlling rhythms of the narrative voice, so that even in the midst of our involvement with her, we can also see her with sufficient detachment to enjoy her confusions and uncertainty as she moves towards marriage with Darcy. Narrative voice must also be dominant so that the novel's pace can be accelerated when necessary, and the rhythmic unity of the book be maintained.

But before we allow the heroine to make use of her self-knowledge and improved perception, there is one more point I wish to make about the way Jane Austen portrays Elizabeth's mind. The brief monologue is over and we return to her interior world: "From herself to Jane—from Jane to Bingley, her thoughts were in a line which soon brought to her recollection that Mr. Darcy's explanation *there*, had appeared very insufficient . . ." (p. 156). The statement about the linear progression of her thoughts, noted obviously by the narrator and not Elizabeth herself, well describes the continual forward movement of the heroine's thinking throughout the book. Even with her learning process, her realization of past errors and the significance of past actions, Elizabeth's mind rarely dwells on the past. Much of this episode deals with past events, and yet they are not remembered with much specificity nor lingered upon for long; they become general and fleeting images in the mind's confrontation with present reality:

> When she came to that part of the letter in which her family were mentioned, in terms of such mortifying, yet merited reproach, her sense of shame was severe. The justice of the charge struck her too forcibly for denial, and the circumstances to which he particularly alluded, as having passed at the Netherfield ball, and as confirming all his first disapprobation, could not have made a stronger impression on his mind than on hers. (Pp. 156-57)

Described here is Elizabeth's present shame and her realization of the validity of Darcy's charges. Past events, alluded to as no more than "circumstances... having passed at the Netherfield ball," are not sufficiently conjured up in Elizabeth's mind to shatter her hold on the present. The references to past events function largely to validate Darcy's opinions in the letter and to support the heroine's present mental growth. The "mortifying" reproach, her "severe" sense of shame, the justice of his charge striking her "too forcibly for denial," and the fact that "circumstances" at the Netherfield ball are merely alluded to and now serve primarily to provoke an immediate response within her, keep the focus of the passage on Elizabeth's mental action in time present. As we follow her thoughts, our minds receive the same brief and passing images with which she remembers past events, but the predominant images we receive are those of the heroine herself as she undergoes her psychic drama.

THE INTEGRATION OF NARRATIVE TECHNIQUES

Though the scenes of dialogue we have studied possess a unity and development, they are woven into the general fabric of the novel and become an inherent and unobtrusive element in the work's movement. The scene of Elizabeth's self-discovery, because of its importance, is unique in its length and its separation from the remainder of the novel— her passages of introspection are normally integrated with other types of narration. *Pride and Prejudice* has an artistry in its composition, movement, and totality that did not exist before in any novel. The epistolary novel by its very nature is a work of individual pieces that achieves its unity through the ordering force of plot and the interplay of letters, but the reader must always be aware of the distinct and separate epistles and their voices. Fielding in *Tom Jones* succeeds in imposing order upon disorder, in creating a work that turns out to be wonderfully cohesive in the relationship of its actions; he also gives a unifying rhythm and tone to the entire work by his dominating narrative voice. But his narrator removes us from the novel's dramatic action by constantly asserting his presence, and breaks the continuity of the work's movement by separating the narrative into books, divided by his own extended essays, and the books into chapters. Sterne, more than Fielding, breaks the novel into fragments, destroying all hopes of continuity and development to assert the synchronic unifying power of his narrator's mind. Even the relatively uncomplex third-person narratives of writers like Fanny Burney, Charlotte Smith, and Maria Edgeworth stumble along, with fragmented movements and without any sense of continuity and rhythm. More than any other writer before her and than most after, Jane Austen saw the novel as a compositional whole, not merely as a series of scenes and episodes leading to a particular denouement. She was the first to have at her disposal a full array of narrative techniques with which to achieve a multitude of effects, and the first to know how to modulate and integrate these into a single harmonious unit. In this respect, Austen created a kind of novel that was to become classic in its technique and structure, a work which went beyond its predecessors and became a model against which to measure future novels. I am not discounting the enormous range in future fiction, not the large and varied structures of the Victorian novel, for example; I am claiming that Austen created a paradigm of what the novel could be, a basic form and structure which was still written amidst periods of great fictional diversity or innovation. The kind of work Austen wrote remains even today the basic form and structure of numerous novels.

As in the case of *Tom Jones*, narrative voice in *Pride and Prejudice* both manipulates our responses and pulls together the work's elements, though in a far less obvious way. We have seen the narrator's subtle and pervasive control even in those passages concerned largely with Elizabeth's perspective and reactions. When we are outside of Elizabeth and the voice clearly speaks to us—giving a quick characterization, a summary of action, a transition in time, some information unknown to the heroine—it does so in a brief and unobtrusive way, without breaking the work's dramatic immediacy. Ironic observations are quick and subtle, almost slipping past our awareness. The narrator does not refer to herself with first-person pronouns, nor does she speak to us with a strongly developed personality. The results are a simultaneity of vision—the dominating perspective of the heroine and the wider perspective and intelligence of the narrator with which we see Elizabeth and her world—and also a continuous movement and unifying rhythm. The narrator is always in control, moving in and out of the heroine, giving some internal passages with more specificity than others, summarizing her reactions, or simply describing external events and allowing us to surmise her responses for ourselves. The description of external actions varies according to the intensity of Elizabeth's perspective and the dramatic requirements of the scene. The narrator breaks up a major action or episode into a sequence of scenes, semi-scenes, and passages of exposition of various lengths, employing a variety of techniques to achieve a larger unified effect that fits into the novel's general development.

For example, the ball at Netherfield (pp. 67-78) is composed of a series of fourteen distinct segments which describe a number of interactions and reactions with varying degrees of detail and summary; yet most of these parts are seen from Elizabeth's point of view, itself created with different amounts of specificity, and all of them work perfectly together to describe a single event. The first three segments are foreshortened and modulated to build up to the important conversation between Elizabeth and Darcy when they dance. Elizabeth enters the drawing room and looks for Wickham. After she overhears that he will not be there because of Darcy's presence, her reactions to this information are described. This first segment takes only one page, but immediacy is created by a line of dialogue, spoken by Mr. Denny, and by the paragraph which describes the heroine's feelings in relative detail—Elizabeth's reactions to Wickham's absence are important at this point because her interest in him has a direct bearing on her relationship with Darcy and will affect her conversation with him. In the first sentence of the next section, we are told that Elizabeth discloses her grief to Charlotte and then changes her mood as she begins to talk to Mr. Collins. The remainder of the paragraph briefly describes her reactions as she dances with her cousin. Collins is not given detailed consideration here because he is not yet of any significance in Elizabeth's life. The "shame" and "misery" he causes her are described merely as that "which a disagreeable partner for a couple of dances can give" (p. 68). The next section takes only one brief paragraph: after rapidly telling us that Elizabeth dances with an officer and returns to Charlotte, it concludes with Darcy's invitation for a dance and puts us right on the threshold of their important talk. The scene describing Elizabeth's dance with Darcy, largely in dialogue and lasting for three-and-a-half pages, is immediate and detailed, contrasting with the rapid pace and frequent summary descriptions of the previous page and a half. The dialogue is given at length because it advances the relationship between the two characters and allows them to develop further the moral concepts they discussed in the scenes we have earlier analyzed, concepts which are directly related in their minds to their own relationship. After some ineffective clashing of their egos at the start of the scene, Elizabeth brings up the subject of Wickham. Sir William Lucas intrudes upon them and clumsily alludes to the hoped-for marriage of Jane and Bingley. Darcy is struck by these words, and it is obvious that Elizabeth notices. When Sir William departs, the two talk about prejudice, judgment, and proper behavior. These subjects are nicely tied in with perception when Elizabeth tells Darcy, " 'I hear such different accounts of you as puzzle me exceedingly,' " and a moment later says, " 'But if I do not take your likeness now, I may never have another opportunity' " (p. 71). Ironically, Elizabeth directs this discussion in order to accuse Darcy of prejudice, actually in relation to Wickham, whom she does not name—she cannot work her way free of her own biased viewpoint concerning her partner. To emphasize this and keep us informed of Darcy's true feelings for Elizabeth, the narrator briefly tells us, staying with him once the two have parted, that in his breast "was a tolerable powerful feeling towards her."

The next two sections of the chapter are related to this interchange and make us reflect upon it. Elizabeth has conversations first with Miss Bingley, then with Jane on the subject of Wickham and Darcy. Both scenes are kept short, subsidiary to the previous one, yet the dialogue is given in full, since it reports important information. Both Miss Bingley and Jane tell Elizabeth the same thing, that Darcy is not culpable in his relationship with Wickham, but on both occasions she finds reason to ignore their words. Elizabeth responds to Miss Bingley's speech with a single statement, and her reactions to the conversation are described in only one sentence to suggest that she dismisses the woman and her opinions a little too readily from her mind. Since she is more willing to listen to her sister, their conversation is more protracted, but even here she will not accept what goes against her preconceptions and dismisses the source of Jane's opinions, Bingley, as biased by friendship and uninformed about Darcy's behavior towards Wickham.

Later in the novel, Elizabeth will remember Jane's words as she reads through Darcy's letter. Indeed, all of the remaining eight parts of the chapter are also significant in relation to the earlier conversation between Elizabeth and Darcy and in relation to the novel's future action. What we have from this point on is largely an embarrassing display of Elizabeth's family—most of the scenes are short vignettes that portray the various members at their worst and develop Elizabeth's alarm about Darcy's negative attitudes towards Bingley and Jane's relationship, something first suggested to her by his reactions to Sir William's words on the subject. Elizabeth is also embarrassed because of the superior position she had tried to assume during their conversation—now she feels herself brought low by the antics of her family. All of her family's behavior does affect Darcy and is instrumental later in his persuading Bingley to flee from Netherfield, and all of it is remembered by Elizabeth when she reads Darcy's letter and acknowledges the validity of his accusations (p. 157).

The first of these short scenes begins when Collins discusses with Elizabeth his plan to introduce himself to Darcy—his foolish character is emphasized here through his directly narrated pompous speech, and through the underplayed, indirectly narrated argument of the heroine. The scene continues when the actual meeting is observed from a distance by Elizabeth and described from her point of view. Next we are given a brief, transitional semi-scene, in which Elizabeth happily observes Bingley and Jane and reflects on their future but notices her mother doing the same. She resolves to stay away from her mother, but the narrator, using this moment as a springboard across time, next describes Elizabeth one seat away from the woman at supper later that night. The entire supper is recorded in only one page and is mostly taken up by Mrs. Bennet's monologue to Lady Lucas about a match between Jane and Bingley. The speech is summarized, but the narrator's indirect reporting has the breathlessness and, at times, the sound of Mrs. Bennet's actual discourse. We are told that Elizabeth tries to stop her mother, and two lines of the interchange are directly recorded. Then we are briefly told of the heroine's vexation and, through her eyes, of Darcy's reactions. The brief scene after supper is divided between an amusing summary of Mary's singing from Elizabeth's point of view, and Collins's directly narrated and ridiculous speech on the duties of a clergyman.

All these scenes have been brief, and they have been described through summary and a deft use of detailed description or direct discourse—a general description of behavior and conversation is suddenly punctuated and given immediacy with a specific action or directly narrated speech or interchange; a passage moving across time is given a sudden solidity with an extended observation on the part of the heroine or a conversation. At the same time, we are made to view these scenes from the heroine's perspective and to react to them much as she does. These four separate segments dealing with Elizabeth's family seem to form a montage, a general impression in her mind that is related to Jane and Bingley. They all lead to the segment, actually a short paragraph, which summarizes Elizabeth's general feelings about the night—"To Elizabeth it appeared that her family made an agreement to expose themselves as much as they could during the evening..." (p. 77).

Before the present chapter ends, Austen is already preparing us for the next. The following paragraph quickly sums up the remainder of the ball from Elizabeth's point of view—"The rest of the evening brought her little amusement" (p. 77)—and tells us about Collins's continuous attention to her, thus foreshadowing his proposal, which comes at the start of the very next chapter. The entire ball episode, however, concludes with an ironic coda, two brief segments which bring to a head the disastrous behavior of her family and cap off the evening for Elizabeth. The narrative voice disengages from Elizabeth during these parts, allowing a wider coverage of characters but also allowing for the brief description of Mrs. Bennet's thoughts at the end of the chapter and Collins's thoughts at the start of the next. In the penultimate section of the chapter, Mrs. Bennet has arranged for her family to be the last to leave; as they await their coach with Bingley and his group, a thumbnail sketch is given of the behavior and attitude of each character. Elizabeth's silence is mentioned toward the end of the paragraph. The final semi-scene of the chapter describes the actual departure of the Bennets by summarizing in one paragraph Mrs. Bennet's earnest invitation to Bingley and his party to come for dinner and the young man's equally earnest reply, and in another paragraph the mother's happy expectations, as she quits the house, of Jane's marriage to Bingley and Elizabeth's marriage to Collins. The chapter thus ends with an ironic distancing, a comic summary of all the characters, and a final plunge into the confused mind of Mrs. Bennet.

In *Pride and Prejudice*, every chapter works into the next, and often within each, individual pieces fit together in a linear and progressive way, while still interacting and frequently achieving a total and spatial effect. The ball at Netherfield is narrated through fourteen interlacing segments, most dealing with Elizabeth's interactions with or responses to another character, and the final two bringing all the characters together. The segments smoothly run by, suggesting the rapid movement of the night in Elizabeth's mind. But at the same time, because of the immediate effect of these individual scenes and semi-scenes—with a face suddenly appearing and speaking, a character's behavior briefly but succinctly portrayed—all these moments and images finally create a single spatial effect of the entire ball as it assaults the heroine's senses almost at once. Time melts together, the separation between segments dissolves, and we are left with Elizabeth's impression of the entire night as she sits silently waiting for the coach.

The first half of the novel develops personality and situation, dwelling on a number of lively episodes amidst a pattern of interlacing and interacting segments of various lengths and kinds. Individual chapters are more frequently devoted to single events or even scenes than in the second part of the novel. But once Elizabeth's feelings for Darcy change, and her hopes for an alliance with him seem disappointed by Lydia's elopement with Wickham, the complications must be resolved and the tension that has been building in the novel released. Events now have the primary function of bringing Elizabeth rapidly and expeditiously to her goal and satisfying the hope and expectation that have been developed in the reader—the novel's design moves to completion. Because of the heroine's change of mind and heart, there are no more confrontations between her and Darcy and hence no protracted scenes of witty dialogue.[38] Because of the exigencies of plot, the necessity of dealing with Lydia and Wickham's relationship and bringing the heroine and hero together, the novel describes in more rapid fashion a continuum of separate, though related, events, many brief but all closely knit and progressing with a greater sense of direction than those in the first part of the work. At the same time, there is a greater amount of narrative exposition, summarizing situations, carrying us across time, and linking individual scenes.[39]

Chapter 11 of Volume III is a good illustration of how Austen can pull together in a single chapter a series of discrete scenes, separated in time and variously described, while accelerating the novel forward. We have here the same kind of development and interaction between parts as we saw in the single event, the Netherfield ball, but now the narrator must extend herself more to bridge the temporal gaps between the individual scenes. Chapter 10 has concluded with Elizabeth and Wickham's conversation, and chapter 11 begins with their reactions to this discussion. Here the irony of language and telescoping of both characters' point of view assert the presence of the narrator:

> MR. WICKHAM was so perfectly satisfied with this conversation, that he never again distressed himself, or provoked his dear sister Elizabeth, by introducing the subject of it; and she was pleased to find that she had said enough to keep him quiet. (Pp. 245–46)

The next sentence continues to discuss Wickham, but also sends us forward in time: "The day of his and Lydia's departure soon came. . . ." The entire departure scene is collapsed into a third of a page. It is given immediacy by the speeches of Mrs. Bennet, Lydia, and Mr. Bennet, and the actions of Wickham, and given both irony and humor by the way these are highlighted and the way they play off one another:

> The day of his and Lydia's departure soon came, and Mrs. Bennet was forced to submit to a separation, which, as her husband by no means entered into her scheme of their all going to Newcastle, was likely to continue at least a twelvemonth.
>
> "Oh! my dear Lydia," she cried, "when shall we meet again?"
>
> "Oh, lord! I don't know. Not these two or three years perhaps."
>
> "Write to me very often, my dear."

"As often as I can. But you know married women have never much time for writing. My sisters may write to *me*. They will have nothing else to do."

Mr. Wickham's adieus were much more affectionate than his wife's. He smiled, looked handsome, and said many pretty things.

"He is as fine a fellow," said Mr. Bennet, as soon as they were out of the house, "as ever I saw. He simpers, and smirks, and makes love to us all. I am prodigiously proud of him. I defy even Sir William Lucas himself, to produce a more valuable son-in-law." (P. 46)

This brief episode allows us to articulate something true of many of Austen's scenes, including those at the Netherfield ball, something which explains a good deal about Austen's narrative art. The episode is played against our expectation of the full dramatic scene: the fragments we receive therefore take on more prominence and the speeches more impact, even though Wickham is made to seem personally insignificant by the rapidity with which his departure is treated. The scene works because it is also played against a background of information that we already have. Character patterns have been well established for these figures, and their small speeches or limited actions present the essences of their personalities. Economy and succinctness are the secrets to the passage's effect and, indeed, to most of the scenes and semi-scenes in the book—the narrator, controlling the spatial perimeters of her scenes, selects and thus focuses, reduces and thus intensifies, but at the same time moves the novel forward with rapidity and precision.[40] Examine again the two lines concerning Wickham to see how economy and succinctness have become in Austen's hands the ultimate tools of irony and characterization: "Mr. Wickham's adieus were much more affectionate than his wife's. He smiled, looked handsome, and said many pretty things." This scene is a prime example of how far narrative technique has advanced in the novel and the degree to which the public had been trained to read these books. Scenes are now expanded and reduced to work together in the novel's plot development and rhythmic movement; they are to be seen by the reader not as isolated and self-contained units but as related images in the work's total structure.

A series of brief scenes next takes place: a short conversation between Mrs. Bennet and Elizabeth on the loss of Lydia; a speech by Mrs. Bennet and one by Mrs. Phillips from their conversation on the expected return of Mr. Bingley; and Jane's speech to Elizabeth on the same subject. By reducing and concentrating these scenes, Austen also highlights and increases the immediacy of the passage describing Elizabeth's introspection which follows. The passage keeps Elizabeth as the central personage and consciousness in all of this action, even though the subject under consideration is the relationship of Jane and Bingley. The dialogue which follows between Mr. and Mrs. Bennet functions mostly to set up the subject of the next exchange between Jane and Elizabeth, which starts with Jane saying: " 'I begin to be sorry that he [Bingley] comes at all.... I can hardly bear to hear it thus perpetually talked of' " (p. 248). Here we see not only the way these small scenes develop the action, but the way in which the general situation is created and intensified by their interaction. All of these brief scenes increase our awareness of Jane's feelings and her difficult situation, and all of them prepare us for the longer scene with which the chapter ends, the visit of Bingley and Darcy to the Bennets (pp. 248-52). We are becoming involved with Jane's situation, but we are doing so from Elizabeth's point of view, and we are moving inevitably to some significant stage in her relationship with Darcy.

Though the visit is described in more detail than the other scenes in the chapter, and though it is the culminating event, we see it not frontally, but from an oblique angle. The point of view belongs to Elizabeth, and we are given those details and impressions that suggest her state of mind during the visit. The episode is foreshortened into only four pages, but so precise and telling are the narrated elements and their arrangement that the entire effect is again a montage of impressions and an immediately created state of mind. Here we see once more that the impulse behind Jane Austen's technique is dramatic: though she does not strive for verisimilitude, for the fully and dramatically created external scene, she seeks to create the psychic drama, the mind in the act of perceiving the scene.

The only speaking voice that we directly hear throughout the scene is that of Mrs. Bennet, which, indeed, is the only one that Elizabeth would notice, since Darcy is largely silent and since his is the voice that weighs most heavily on her mind. In Elizabeth's thoughts, Mrs. Bennet is still a threat to any relationship the heroine might have with Darcy. The speeches of both Elizabeth and Bingley are summarized and underplayed, buried beneath the weight of the mother's verbiage and colossal stupidity. Darcy is depicted only as Elizabeth sees him and imagines him to be responding to the present scene. Throughout the scene, Elizabeth's feelings are described, and on several occasions her verbal thoughts are directly narrated so that her mind is kept immediate and central to the scene. But other points of view are interspersed to permit us a wider vision that that of the heroine and to increase our sense of the event's complexity and irony. The scene begins with Jane looking at Elizabeth "with surprise and concern," and toward the end, Bingley's and Jane's reactions to one another are briefly described. This last departure from Elizabeth's consciousness allows the chapter, like the one describing the Netherfield ball, to end ironically and comically, with another of Mrs. Bennet's invitations to Bingley and with a final paragraph describing her monolithic thinking.

In this scene, as throughout the chapter, the selection and ordering of the various elements make us aware of the narrator who is actually describing the scene. Signs of this presence are at times overt, as when we are given two points of view at once—"He [Bingley] was received by Mrs. Bennet with a degree of civility, which made her two daughters ashamed . . ." (p. 250)—or when the heroine is quickly brought from one emotional state to another—for Elizabeth, "the misery, for which years of happiness were to offer no compensation, received soon afterwards material relief . . ." (p. 251). The narrator's presence, though more assertive in this part of the novel, is still carefully modulated and integrated into the dramatic immediacy of the narration in order not to weaken our involvement with the heroine. We are still very much identifying with Elizabeth, seeing the world largely through her eyes and hoping along with her for a happy conclusion to events. But narrative voice again functions to control our identification, to allow us a wider, more knowing, and enjoyable perspective at the same time. Narrative voice also functions in more subtle and subliminal ways in this scene and throughout the entire chapter: by describing the heroine's psychic responses in a carefully selective and controlled manner, it reinforces our sense of her rational and logical mind; and by skillfully assembling the various elements of the narrative, it creates for us a sense of order in the heroine's cosmos—this is a reasonable universe, where confusion can be resolved through individual intelligence and will. Art and meaning continuously come together in *Pride and Prejudice*: Jane Austen's narrative skills are an embodiment of her thematic concerns with understanding, control, and order.

THIRD-PERSON NARRATION

First-person and third-person narratives have continued to be written since the time of Jane Austen. It would be foolish to argue for the preference of one over the other, since each form has its particular strengths, and since the writer's choice ultimately depends on the kind of fictional world he wishes to create and the nature of the fictional experience he wishes to evoke within the reader—different perspectives create different kinds of novels. One of the developments I have traced in this study has been the emergence of a particular type of third-person narration from a century in which most of the great novels were written in the first person. I have done this to show not only that this third-person narration emerged to solve problems inherent in first-person narration, but that its seeds were already apparent in the earlier type of fiction. The other kind of third-person narrative, which employs a more traditional storyteller, the kind found in fiction before the advent of the novel—in Aphra Behn's works, for example—was to be developed along a different line by Fielding, made richer, more complex, and even more omniscient. Fielding's third-person style would be used, in varying degrees, by those writers who sought the more distanced and less dramatic approach to their characters, who sought a comic or philosophic perspective to their fictional worlds, and Jane Austen's by those who sought to get close to their characters and intensify the reader's involvement in their lives while also allowing a wider view of the fictional world. In certain novels, of course, like those by George Eliot, both styles would be employed together to achieve a variety of effects.

Jane Austen's third-person narration incorporates the subjective dimension of Richardson's novels, while at the same time her detached narrative voice allows her to create a more objective and wider external reality through her manipulation of narrative techniques and controlled commentary. What she achieves, then, is both the personal drama of her characters and the interpersonal tensions and conflicts of the social world. *Pride and Prejudice* embodies both the psychic problems of the individual in an age which had set loose the mind to define its own identity, and the cosmic and cultural problems of a civilization which had to adjust itself to this new kind of individualism. All of the works we have studied embody these problems to some degree and with varying amounts of success, but Austen's novel most successfully confronts and resolves them—both the heroine and her social world are strong enough to make the adjustments.

The English novel of the eighteenth century, from Defoe to Austen, was concerned with the major cultural issues of its time; the fictional methods of its writers and the development of its narrative technique were a direct outgrowth of these issues. These are two positions I have tried to maintain throughout this study to counteract what has generally been in scholarship a rather piecemeal approach to the fiction of the period and a fragmentary consideration of narrative art. Jane Austen's particular development of third-person narration verifies my arguments: not only does it allow us the inner and outer dimensions I have explored throughout this study, but it also is an affirmation of that reason and order which the writer sees and feels as controlling her best of all possible worlds, a reason and order looked for and tested by the major novelists of the period. In the works of Defoe, Richardson, and Smollett, we have indications of an editor, but this presence is scarcely defined or emphasized—the novels take place in the consciousness of first-person narrators. The ultimate dangers of this subjective world are explored in Sterne's *Tristram Shandy*; but even before this Fielding argued against the subjective freedom of fictional characters in his creation of a narrator whose wisdom and power shaped the novel instead of his characters' uncertainty, struggles, and choices, instead of the flux and change of their psyches. Fielding's plot is ultimately controlled by his narrator and not by the people who inhabit his fictional world. On the other hand, Jane Austen's plot is dependent upon her major character; thus there is no inevitability, no superimposed order—events in her novel are the result of her heroine's reactions and interactions. Since events in *Tom Jones* are caused by external forces—the narrator and his agent, Fortune—we never know what will happen next; since events in *Pride and Prejudice* are caused by internal forces, which can be unpredictable, we are also in a state of uncertainty about what will take place. But matters will conclude as fortunately in one cosmos as in the other—of that we are sure. We are sure in Fielding's novel because of the presence of our guide and teacher, the omniscient narrator. We are sure in Austen's novel because of the intelligence that we feel throughout the work—the intelligence, for example, that is narrating events with such skill and control, that is leading us with such cunning to interpret characters and events perceptively and accurately. This is not the developed personality of Fielding's narrator—such a presence would intrude upon and suppress the subjective dimension of character that is the center of Austen's novel—but it is an intelligence which guides our thoughts and manipulates our responses through the way in which it creates that subjective dimension as well as the world in which the characters function. It is this intelligence which encourages us to see the heroine with reason and understanding while seeing through her eyes. The fact that Elizabeth's own intelligence and language are so close to those of the narrative voice also gives us hope for her reformation and happiness, for a satisfying conclusion to all the novel's events. Her intelligence is the force within her against psychological disorder. The narrator's intelligence is the force outside the heroine against social and universal disorder. No one is manipulating events here; it is our faith in the force of human reason, manifested in heroine and narrator, that gives us our happy expectations for the future.

Austen's novel, then, incorporates a number of cultural problems embodied in the works of the eighteenth century that we have studied, combines them, and leaves us with a last positive stance before the onslaught of the nineteenth and twentieth centuries. The confusion in personal identity we saw as a result of a struggle between religious and empirical modes of thought in the character Moll Flanders or between the individual and society in Clarissa Harlowe is here resolved through reason and common sense. The conflict explored in *Tom Jones* between egoism and altruism, between vanity, affectation, and hypocrisy on the one hand and decent human nature on the other, here becomes resolved by the powers of the human mind. For Sterne, reason is no match for the unconscious and wayward imagination, and man must find redemption in the richness of his mental life. Jane Austen simply dismisses the unconscious and wayward imagination, and refuses to place her faith in the subjective and uncontrollable forces of the mind. Sterne also finds solace in the holiness of the heart's affections. Elizabeth and Darcy are in love, and this basic fact places them miles apart from the unhappily married couples in *Pride and Prejudice*. But for Austen, true love arises only where there is a meeting of the minds—reasonable people can find happiness because they can love reasonably. Her novels, therefore, present a resolution to the previous century's conflict between reason and feeling by accepting both, but she still, unequivocably, places her emphasis and her hope on reason.[41]

Both Sterne and Smollett frontally face the basic conflict between subjectivity and objectivity, between the mind and matter. Their novels raise the basic issue of perception, whether the mind can ever see clearly and correctly. *Pride and Prejudice* is a novel about seeing, about moral vision. It is a novel about learning how to see. It is also the work which most develops and controls the perceptional dimension of the novel form, a dimension which had been there from the beginning, since all the novels we have studied, in one way or another, are concerned with the problem of seeing honestly and seek to engage the reader by offering him a perceptional experience with the characters or, in the case of *Tom Jones*, with the narrator. The technique of *Pride and Prejudice* entices the reader into such an experience with the heroine, while also allowing him from the start the wisdom which she must acquire and which makes accurate and honest perception possible.

Jane Austen's novel shows an awareness of the reader's experience that we find present in all the novels of this period: in Defoe's claim for authenticity and moral value, in Richardson's concern with dramatic immediacy, in the narrator's dialogue with the reader in Fielding's *Tom Jones*, in Sterne's involvement of the reader in the writing of the novel, in Smollett's multiple perspectives and detailed settings. What is most exciting about the novel is its demand upon the reader for participation and involvement through imaginative perception—the reader's private vision, the images created within him from the text, removes him from the outside world into a created reality that exists entirely within his own mind. This is the aesthetic achievement of the form that Jane Austen inherited from her predecessors and that she developed and enriched.

There was no significant body of critical material concerning the novel when she began to write, nor did there have to be—great art has rarely arisen from the concepts and precepts of critics. With the exception of her general and comic attack against the gothic romance in *Northanger Abbey,* she writes infrequently on fiction and makes no telling statements of purpose nor explanations of methods in her books and letters, nor in her novels does she refer to the reader or try to educate him to the fictional experience she is creating for him. All this was unnecessary, since a group of novels already existed that had established the way, and since there was in her own mind a sophisticated reader with a trained imagination and cultivated sensibility—one who, in fact, had been awaiting her for more than a quarter of a century.

Conclusion

A number of the narratives written during this period fail to satisfy the definition of the novel I have been establishing in this study—the worlds of the romantic histories and gothic tales, for example, are far removed from the more everyday reality and lack the dramatic narrative techniques and developed perceptional dimension of the major novels of the century.[1] We must simply acknowledge that although the novel was to become the major fictional tradition in England, works were still written that are more easily related to earlier narrative types, especially the romance. This is not to deny the considerable advances in verisimilitude and narration in some of these works that were the result of the novel's influence, but it makes more sense to understand such works as developments of an earlier tradition rather than as central to the new fictional movement. I must make this claim for the gothic romances of Clara Reeve and Ann Radcliffe as well, though here we find ourselves in an in-between world, one that synthesizes the fantastic elements of the old fiction with the greater care for credibility and immediacy of the new. In such works, we also at times seem drawn into a perceptional experience with some of the characters, though one limited by their incomplete characterizations. More often, however, the aesthetic experience that Reeve and Radcliffe evoke is one of vicarious association, of projection rather than introjection and identity: there is not enough dramatic and realistic internalization to replace or synthesize with our own thoughts and responses, and we see the characters as separate and apart from us, though they are given shape within our own imaginations. Perhaps such works can be called novels, but it is more accurate simply to allow that in one way or another the new fiction had an impact on narrative in general—even those works which are more directly related to the fantasy and "marvelous" narrations of the past. In the future, the novel would absorb romantic and gothic elements in order to expand its dimension of reality and bring the reader into the world of fantasy and dream, of nightmare and hallucination, of neurosis and psychosis. I have in mind, of course, works by such writers as Dickens, Hawthorne, Melville, Dostoevsky, and Kafka.

But we must also consider the host of secondary narratives written during the period about apparently credible people in a world that approximates the real one of the time. Such works vary widely in purpose, focus, and competence, but all of them are united in their attempt to create some sort of verisimilitude, and a number even seem to be trying to evoke in the reader a perceptional experience with their major characters. Unquestionably these books were influenced in one way or another by the novels we have been studying, and it would not be difficult to trace their concerns and narrative techniques, as clumsy as these generally are, to specific works by the earlier novelists. But though we must recognize such books as distinct from contemporary historical and gothic romances, we must also see that most of them are rudimentary in their portrayal of character and fall short in their attempts to create the kind of perceptional experience for the reader created by the major novels; this is also true of the more convincing and cohesive narratives of writers like Jane West, Charlotte Smith, and Maria Edgeworth.

Clara Reeve's definition of the novel formulated in 1785—"The Novel is a picture of real life and manners, and of the times in which it is written"[2]—is meant to include both the works we have studied and the minor fiction we are now discussing. But the major novels and this secondary fiction differ in the skill with which the "picture of real life and manners" is depicted, and also in the intensity of the perceptional experience allowed. Still, we must recognize that a large number of writers attempted to follow in the footsteps of the major novelists and wrote works influenced in varying degrees by their achievements, and we must consider these secondary works as minor novels at least. The argument I am making is that a genre must be defined by its major works, and its minor products judged by the degree to which they approximate these significant texts.

In the major fiction from the eighteenth century on we can see the concerns and techniques we have studied explored and developed, sometimes to a new and exciting degree. Since I have discussed these concerns and techniques in separate chapters on individual authors, it seems appropriate in concluding to recapitulate and bring together the various advances made in fiction from Defoe to Austen, advances that caused major mutations in prose narrative and brought about what we call "the modern novel." Fiction does not begin in the eighteenth century, but we can recognize the birth of a particular kind of narrative that would both dominate and influence fiction in general until and beyond the present time.

On the most basic level, all the works we have studied attempt to create a world related to the everyday reality of the reader. Defoe did not write *Moll Flanders* for prostitutes and criminals, but prostitutes and criminals very much existed in the reader's world. The fictional world is always one of possibility, and it involves us because the events we read about could conceivably happen to us—not that they are likely to happen to us, for the pleasure we derive from fiction comes from the extension of our experience, the enjoyment, on an imaginative level, in safety and security, of actions and feelings inaccessible to us in real life. Our experience with the novel, then, is very different from our experience with the earlier romance, which is primarily one of escape— of fantasy, not of sensibility, of projection, not of introjection. But even in the novel, the amount of identification we feel with the major characters is always controlled. To some degree we are always in our own senses, making distinctions and discriminations. Indeed, the involvement we feel in the novel is moral and judgmental as well as emotional: there is always something we learn from reading these works—about others, but also about ourselves and our own potentials. There is little that elicits our moral concern in the earlier romance, since the world is too remote, the actions too impossible. I think that this demand for moral concern and judgment in the early novel explains what is often superficially seen as these works' didactic bias.[3] Defoe, in *Moll Flanders*, and Richardson, in *Clarissa*, reacted to the unreal worlds and concerns of earlier fiction and involved themselves, in part consciously and in part instinctively, with deeper moral issues about the individual and society, about personal identity. Judgment outweighs feeling for the reader when he responds to *Tom Jones*, but the involvement is no less pertinent and no less real. Sterne, like Fielding, has us judge, and, by doing so, also forces us into acts of complicity and involvement with his characters in *Tristram Shandy*.

Lesser works of the period presented a world more everyday and natural than that in the earlier romance, but the major novelists to a greater degree, a degree that in all cases greatly affected technique, were concerned with perception. Sometimes in *Moll Flanders*, and frequently in *Clarissa*, *Humphry Clinker*, and *Pride and Prejudice*, a character's perceptions take over point of view and entice the reader to see and respond with the character, hence deepening the reader's involvement and bringing both the internal and external worlds of the novel dramatically alive. If we often do not perceive with the characters of *Tom Jones*, we frequently do so with the narrator; and Fielding, like Sterne after him, provokes us to assess our own perceptions of the figures within the novel and also to compare our perceptions with those of the characters. In all cases, it is the concern with perception which dominates the major novels of the period and intensifies the reader's involvement.

The subject of perception was itself part of a whole complex of concerns which begin to push their way into Restoration and eighteenth-century thought. With the exception of Sterne, I have not argued for a conscious awareness and adaptation on the part of these authors, but rather for a shared climate of ideas, for a fictional movement parallel to certain currents in contemporary thought. In many respects, the novels we have studied are fictional embodiments of certain cultural and intellectual trends, trends manifested not only in the novel's content but also in its development of fictional technique. The emphasis in my study has been on narrative technique and the phenomenology of reading, but I have also sought to understand these subjects in light of the larger movements to which they belong. As twentieth-century critics, we cannot neglect to understand the relationship between the text and its time, for the very techniques and reading responses we seek to understand from our contemporary perspectives can be further understood in light of the cultural and intellectual context of the period.

Important in the cultural and intellectual trends we have studied, and very much related to perception, are the subjects of individuality and personal identity, subjects met head-on in the novels of Defoe, Richardson, and Austen. Perception became a means within the novel of exploring individual consciousness and self-awareness, of relating the struggle for a true sense of self to the character's vision of the social world outside. By focusing on the individual's perceptions of self and by developing the character's perceptions of external reality, novelists also explored, either implicitly or explicitly, another philosophic issue of the time, the conflict between subjectivity and objectivity, the question of whether we can ever know with accuracy the world outside us. In the novels of Defoe, Richardson, Sterne, Smollett, and Austen, perceptional point of view allows us to see with the characters and judge their subjective responses to external reality. Through Fielding's and Sterne's dialogue with the reader, we are forced to match our own subjective perceptions against those of the characters and test our vision of the world within the novel against theirs.

Related to this exploration of inner and outer reality, to this conflict between subjectivity and objectivity, is the development of psychological and external space—both the landscape of the mind and the landscape of the world outside had to be expanded and created with greater detail, and these details had to be seen in spatial relationships. Internal consciousness is at times expanded in *Moll Flanders*, and portrayed with fullness in *Clarissa, Tristram Shandy*, and *Pride and Prejudice*. Against the flow and change of characters' thoughts, especially in the works of the last three authors, psychic patterns cohere, levels of response play off one another, and the mind is conceived spatially. Defoe, on occasion, spatially defines the external scene, depicting the relationships between objects and the relationships between character and objects, but space is further developed by Richardson in his scenes of dramatic interplay between characters, extended by Smollett to re-create the physical worlds of England and Scotland, manipulated by Sterne to develop his absurdist comedy about inner and outer reality, and condensed and controlled by Austen in the general rhythm of her work. Fielding spatially constructs his scenes, architecturally arranging element against element to convey his comic and moral vision, but he also forces the reader to restructure the events of his novel, to see the work finally as a spatially conceived entity. The novel, then, expanded space, increased the perimeters of the reader's visual and spatial imagination: the mind, the external scene, the very structure of the work, were given a care and specificity, were arranged and ordered in ways new to fiction.

Also new to narrative, and very much related to the expansion of fictional space, was the development and manipulation of fictional time—the dramatization of the character's temporal awareness in works by Richardson, Sterne, and Austen, and the control of the reader's sense of time in works by Richardson, Fielding, Sterne, and Austen. Once Richardson centered *Clarissa* in the consciousness of his characters and created with detail their inner and outer realities, once he dramatically and spatially depicted psychological and external action, the pace of fiction slowed down considerably and its temporality began to approximate, or at least to suggest, the measure of real time. Narration changed from summation to presentation;[4] thoughts and actions seemed fully presented, moving in a sequence of natural temporality. Fielding was not concerned with dramatizing psychological time, though he did plot *Tom Jones* against the calendar and the historical events of 1745. Fielding also showed an awareness of the reader's sense of time and was influenced by that awareness in writing his book. Sterne, even more consciously and consistently than Richardson, created a fictional sense of time while also spatializing temporality in *Tristram Shandy*. He played various time levels, including the supposed writer's and reader's, one against the other, and also achieved in Tristram's mind a triumph over time through the character's creative reconstruction of the past. Austen's *Pride and Prejudice* is a masterwork of temporal control, creating and fusing psychological and external time, lengthening and foreshortening both temporalities in a modulated and singular rhythmic flow. In all of these novels, space and time create and define character and action; in all of these novels, character and action are created through the reader's own spatial and temporal awareness. The modern novel, in this respect, is an exploration of the ontology of space and time. It is an exploration of epistemology in relation to this ontology.

All of these concerns are made meaningful to the reader only through narrative technique, for only through narrative technique are we made to experience and finally to realize the nature of individuality, the problem of identity, the conflict between subjectivity and objectivity, the extent of mental and external space, the reality and unreality of time. Only through narrative technique can we perceive the world of the novel, can we make it, to some degree, our own, and can we fuse our own subjectivity with the subjectivity within the text. All of the techniques we have studied are in some way related to perception; all of them provoke and control our visualization of the characters, their actions, and their setting. The reader, relying upon what is given in the text, fills in the gaps, draws to some degree upon his own experience, and imaginatively re-creates the world within the novel. The authors we have studied are linked together not only by common human concerns but by their conscious attempt to make narrative technique into a means of developing reader involvement. Narrative technique must be understood in the way it fosters both an emotional and an intellectual involvement within the reader by provoking specific mental acts of perception, cognition, and judgment.

The relative brevity of the period we have studied and the suddenness of the novel's emergence argue for the coalescing of certain cultural forces necessary for the establishment of this new literary form. We have seen how the development of certain concepts about man, about his inner world and his relation to external reality, established a context for the transformation of traditional, and the creation of innovative narrative techniques, techniques which gave rise to a new fictional experience for the reader. With all the divergence in their works, the authors we have studied are linked together by certain basic fictional aims and methods. One of the goals of this study has been to dispel a pervasive scholarly attitude which sees these writers as different and unrelated, even while considering them as part of a single literary movement. I have not ignored the uniqueness of these authors and their individual accomplishments, but at the same time I have tried to demonstrate their common literary achievements.

Notes

INTRODUCTION

1. I am distinguishing the novel as a separate category of fiction that begins in the eighteenth century. My definition of the novel will become clear as the introduction continues.

2. Ian Watt, in *The Rise of the Novel* (Berkeley: Univ. of California Press, 1957), shows that Fielding's ideas about the new fiction moved closer to those of Richardson with the writing of *Amelia* (pp. 255-57).

3. From a transcript of a letter dated "21 or 22 March 1742," in the Forster Collection, Victoria and Albert Museum, London.

4. II, 308 (rpt. Carbondale: Southern Illinois Univ. Press, 1965).

5. See especially Wayne C. Booth, *The Rhetoric of Fiction* (Chicago: Univ. of Chicago Press, 1961), pp. 53-60. W. J. Harvey, in *Character and the Novel* (London: Chatto & Windus, 1965), claims that "The texture of the created fictional world—the society portrayed, the values assumed, the emotions rendered—may be alien, but the shape of that world will be familiar" (p. 22).

6. Alice R. Kaminsky briefly surveys the changing nature of philosophic and cultural notions of reality in "On Literary Realism," *The Theory of the Novel: New Essays*, ed. John Halperin (New York: Oxford Univ. Press, 1974), pp. 213-32. Reference must also be made to Erich Auerbach's seminal work, *Mimesis: The Representation of Reality in Western Literature*, trans. Willard R. Tusk (Princeton: Princeton Univ. Press, 1953), which examines "the interpretation of reality through literary representation or 'imitation' " (p. 554) from antiquity to Virginia Woolf.

7. *The Rise of the Novel*, p. 32.

8. John Preston's *The Created Self: The Reader's Role in Eighteenth-Century Fiction* (London: Heinemann, 1970) attempts to discuss the reader as a major component in several eighteenth-century texts, but it seems to me that his interpretations are sometimes forced, and he never treats with any precision or persuasion the reading experience itself or the author's strategies to provoke that experience. Robert W. Uphaus's *The Impossible Observer: Reason and the Reader in Eighteenth-Century Prose* (Lexington, Ky.: Univ. Press of Kentucky, 1979), regardless of its title, is not actually concerned with the reader's relationship to the texts of the period. A significant study of the reader and the novel in general is Wolfgang Iser's *The Implied Reader: Patterns of Communication from Bunyan to Beckett* (Baltimore: The Johns Hopkins Univ. Press, 1974). The only novelists that Iser and I both discuss are Fielding and Smollett, and only with the latter do we confront some of the same issues. Iser

amplifies the theoretical ideas in his final chapter of *The Implied Reader*, "The Reading Process: A Phenomenological Approach," in *The Act of Reading: A Theory of Aesthetic Response* (Baltimore: The Johns Hopkins Univ. Press, 1979). Iser's phenomenological approach to reading is considerably influenced by Roman Ingarden's work (see below, n. 44). Both Iser and Hans Robert Jauss are major figures in the Konstanz school of literary studies at the University of Konstanz in Germany, a group of scholars known for their work in reader-response criticism. An important essay by Jauss on this subject is "Literary History as a Challenge to Literary Theory," in *Toward an Aesthetic of Reception*, trans. Timothy Bahti (Minneapolis: Univ. of Minnesota Press, 1982). Two recent collections of essays which discuss the reader and the text are *Reader-Response Criticism: From Formalism to Post-Structuralism*, ed. Jane P. Tompkins (Baltimore: The Johns Hopkins Univ. Press, 1980); and *The Reader in the Text: Essays on Audience and Interpretation*, ed. Susan R. Suleiman and Inge Crosman (Princeton: Princeton Univ. Press, 1980).

9. *The Dynamics of Literary Response* (New York: Oxford Univ. Press, 1968), p. 278.

10. See especially p. 96 of his study. Holland has gone further with his psychoanalytical investigation of literary response in *Five Readers Reading* (New Haven: Yale Univ. Press, 1975), where he analyzes the reactions of five graduate students of English literature to several short stories. A problem with his method is that he does not examine his students in the active process of reading, but talks with them on several occasions after they have read the story, each succeeding occasion taking the individual further away from his or her direct confrontation with the text. What he really examines are students' recollections about texts they have read sometime before, and the re-creation on their part of the reading experience they think they have undergone. The presence of Holland, asking questions, recording on tape, and taking notes in a closed room with each student, must also inhibit and affect the recollection of that experience, a fact which he himself acknowledges.

11. *The Ego and the Mechanisms of Defense*, trans. Cecil Baines (New York: International Univ. Press, 1946), p. 140.

12. Iser, in *The Implied Reader*, denies the possibility of identifying with a character because "someone else's thoughts can only take a form in our consciousness if, in the process, our unformulated faculty for deciphering those thoughts is brought into play—a faculty which, in the act of deciphering, also formulates itself" (p. 294). I agree about our self-awareness, but this does not deny a partial identification with the character—it is not an either/or situation. I shall be further discussing the nature of the reader's identification with fictional characters and the controls on that state throughout the introduction and also at times in my chapters on the individual novels.

13. For a more appreciative assessment of some of this fiction, see John J. Richetti, *Popular Fiction Before Richardson: Narrative Patterns, 1700–1739* (Oxford: Clarendon Press, 1969).

14. D. W. Harding, in "Psychological Processes in the Reading of Fiction," *British Journal of Aesthetics*, 2, (1962), 133–47, makes the point that the reader is never completely involved with the characters of fiction but also plays the role of an evaluating spectator. Georges Poulet describes this as a "schizoid distinction between what I feel and the other feels; a confused awareness of delay..." ("Phenomenology of Reading," *New Literary History*, 1 [October 1969], 59).

15. "Preface to Shakespeare," in *Johnson on Shakespeare*, ed. Arthur Sherbo, Vol. VII of *The Yale Edition of the Works of Samuel Johnson* (New Haven: Yale Univ. Press, 1969), p. 12.

16. Essay No. 4 in *The Rambler*, ed. W. J. Bate and Albrecht B. Strauss, Vol. III of *The Yale Edition of the Works of Samuel Johnson* (New Haven: Yale Univ. Press, 1969), p. 12.

17. Ibid.

18. See below, pp. 119-21.

19. "Preface," p. 78.

20. Robert Scholes and Robert Kellogg, *The Nature of Narrative* (New York: Oxford Univ. Press, 1966), p. 157. A brief but standard discussion of point of view is Norman Friedman's "Point of View in Fiction: The Development of a Critical Concept," *PMLA*, 70 (December 1955), 1160-84.

21. *The Rise of the Novel*, p. 31.

22. "Locke's picture of the mind came to be, in the eighteenth century, the normal possession of the educated and enlightened of Europe" (Basil Willey, *The Seventeenth Century Background* [1935; rpt. New York: Doubleday, 1953], p. 264). A succinct discussion of psychology and epistemology in Europe during this period appears in Ernst Cassirer's *The Philosophy of the Enlightenment* (Princeton: Princeton Univ. Press, 1951), pp. 93-133.

23. Cassirer, p. 95.

24. *An Essay Concerning Human Understanding*, ed. John W. Yolton, Everyman's Library, 332 and 984 (London: Dent, 1961), I, 111-12.

25. Ibid., I, 117.

26. Ibid., I, 330.

27. Ibid., I, 261.

28. Cassirer, pp. 110 and 117.

29. *A Treatise ...* , ed. Colin M. Turboyne (Indianapolis: Liberal Arts Press, 1957), pp. 25-26.

30. *A Treatise of Human Nature*, ed. L. A. Selby-Bigge (Oxford: Clarendon Press, 1888), pp. 67-68. The passage is also cited in Willey, p. 114.

31. See Hume's *A Treatise of Human Nature*, p. 180.

32. See C. L. Lewis's "Addison," in *Essays on the Eighteenth Century, Presented to David Nichol Smith in Honor of his Seventieth Birthday* (Oxford: Clarendon Press, 1945), pp. 1-14.

33. See Samuel H. Monk, *The Sublime: A Study of Critical Theory in XVIII-Century England* (1935; rpt. Ann Arbor: Univ. of Michigan Press, 1960).

34. Also note Iser's quotation, in his discussion of Smollett's *Humphry Clinker*, from Lord Kames's *Elements of Criticism* (1761): "A third rule or observation is, That where the subject is intended for entertainment solely, not for instruction, a thing ought to be described as it appears, not as it is in reality" (*The Implied Reader*, p. 74).

35. Poulet states that the thoughts which pass through our mind when we read and the consciousness which seems to be ours belong to the author of the work ("Phenomenology of Reading," p. 56). Poulet's comments are the basis of Iser's discussion of identity in *The Implied Reader* (pp. 292-94; also see my n. 12).

36. The size of the reading public did not grow significantly during this period. Richard D. Altick, in *The English Common Reader: A Social History of the Mass Reading Public, 1800-1900* (Chicago: Univ. of Chicago Press, 1957),

points out that "single editions of the novels of Richardson, Fielding, and Smollett seldom exceeded 4,000 copies, and four or five editions, totaling less than 9,000 copies, were all the market could absorb . . . in a single year" (p. 50). A good discussion of the changing nature of the reading public is in Watt's *The Rise of the Novel*, pp. 35–39.

37. *The Imagination as a Means of Grace: Locke and the Aesthetics of Romanticism* (Berkeley: Univ. of California Press, 1960), p. 73.

38. *Essay*, I, 78.

39. *The Imagination as a Means of Grace*, p. 18. The Locke quotation is from *Essay*, I, 80.

40. *Observations on Man, His Frame, His Duty, His Expectations* (1749; rpt. Hildesheim: George Olms, 1967), I, 276.

41. *The Ego and the Id*, trans. James Strachey (New York: Norton, 1962), p. 21.

42. *Visual Thinking* (Berkeley: Univ. of California Press, 1969). The quotations in the remainder of the paragraph are from pp. 232–42 of Arnheim's book.

43. Sterne does seem to be using Locke's statement about the mind's actions passing "like floated visions" (cited above) to describe one of Dr. Slop's thoughts: "the thought floated only in Dr. Slop's mind, without sail or ballast to it, as a simple proposition " (*The Life and Opinions of Tristram Shandy, Gentleman*, ed. James Aiken Work [New York: Odyssey Press, 1940], p. 167). The argument for this direct influence is more persuasive if I point out that Locke's image appears in a paragraph where he discusses the thinking of children (*Essay*, I, 80).

44. Roman Ingarden, who sees the reader's response to the literary text as finally a visual experience, states that "one must often go far beyond what is actually contained in the objective stratum of the work in the process of objectifying the portrayed activities." Ingarden sees the text as filled with "places of indeterminacy" which the reader, through the peculiar nature of the work and his or her own inclinations, "fills out." For Ingarden, "it is a question of experienced, not objectified, concrete aspects of things and people, which exercise the function of bringing things to appearance only when the sense of the words and sentences direct the reader's attention to the portrayed things and people and when the mere naming of certain perceptible attributes or sides of things has the result that the appropriate aspects are forced upon the reader at once" (*The Cognition of the Literary Work of Art*, trans. Ruth Ann Crowley and Kenneth R. Olson [Evanston: Northwestern Univ. Press, 1973], pp. 50–63). See Iser's discussion of Ingarden's concept of "indeterminacy," in *The Act of Reading*, pp. 170–79.

45. New York: Doubleday, 1935, p. xiv.

46. "Novel and Camera," in Halperin, *Theory of the Novel*, p. 181. As James himself says, "the analogy between the art of the painter and the art of the novelist is, so far as I am able to see, complete. Their inspiration is the same, their process (allowing for the different quality of the vehicle) is the same, their success is the same" ("The Art of Fiction," in Henry James, *The Future of the Novel*, ed. Leon Edel [New York: Vintage Books, 1956], p. 5).

47. A related point about Smollett's *Humphry Clinker* is made by Iser, *The Implied Reader*, pp. 78–80.

48. The Russian formalist Victor Shklovsky, in his essay "Art as Technique" (1917), claims that because life habitualizes us to the surrounding world, we lose the sensation of things. Art functions to defamiliarize objects, "to increase the difficulty and length of perception because the process of perception is an aesthetic end in itself and must be prolonged. *Art is a way of experiencing the artfulness of an object; the object is not important*" (in *Russian Formalist Criticism: Four Essays*, trans. Lee T. Lemon and Marion J. Reis [Lincoln: Univ. of Nebraska Press, 1965], p. 12). Robert Scholes translates this last line to read: "*In art, it is our experience of the process of construction that counts, not the finished product* (*Structuralism in Literature: An Introduction* [New Haven: Yale Univ. Press, 1974], p. 84). The point is that art teaches us to see anew.

49. Roland Barthes sees this collaboration between reader and text as more fixed and typed. In his application of Saussure's theory of signs to writing in *Elements of Semiology*, he first states that the verbal sign is composed of both the signifier (the word's sound) and the signified (the concept or mental image), and then claims that the link between the two, the signification, is largely "contractual" in nature, a result of collective training (*Writing Degree Zero and Elements of Semiology*, trans. Annette Lavers and Colin Smith [Boston: Beacon Press, 1970], pp. 38-51). In a later study, he distinguishes between "the writerly texts," works that we ourselves write when we read, and the "readerly texts," works that have largely become "plasticized by some singular system (Ideology, Genus, Criticism) which reduces the plurality of entrances." The second type makes up most of our literature. In both cases, however, the reader's subjectivity, with its "deceptive plenitude," is nothing more than "the wake of all the codes which constitute me, so that my subjectivity has ultimately the generality of stereotypes" (*S/Z*, trans. Richard Miller [New York: Hill & Wang, 1970], pp. 5 and 10). Stanly Fish argues, in a related manner, that "selves are constituted by the ways of thinking and seeing that inhere in social organizations...and these constituted selves in turn constitute texts according to these same ways" ("How to Recognize a Poem When You See One," in *Is There a Text in This Class* [Cambridge, Mass.: Harvard Univ. Press, 1980], p. 336).

50. *Art and Illusion: A Study in the Psychology of Pictorial Representation*, 2nd ed. (1961; rpt. Princeton: Princeton Univ. Press, 1969). See especially p. 49.

51. We actually perceive the novel's action in two ways: both in the order that events first appear in the work, and in the order that we rearrange them to follow a true chronological order. The Russian Formalists refer to the first order as *sujet* and to the second as *fabula*. See especially Boris Tomashevsky's "Thematics," pp. 67-68, and Victor Shklovsky's essay, "Sterne's *Tristram Shandy*: Stylistic Commentary," in *Russian Formalist Criticism*. Also see Meir Sternberg, *Expositional Modes and Temporal Ordering in Fiction* (Baltimore: The Johns Hopkins Univ. Press, 1978), pp. 8-14.

52. Eric S. Rabkin, in *Narrative Suspense: "When Slim Turned Sideways"* (Ann Arbor: Univ. of Michigan Press, 1973), discusses this interest in future events as "*subliminal suspense*: that engagement with structure which involves us in waiting for formal completion but of which we are not consciously aware" (p. 186).

53. See Ingarden, pp. 102-4; and Iser, *The Implied Reader*, pp. 278-80.

54. *Gestalt Psychology*, 1947; rpt. New York: Liveright, 1970.

55. Ibid., p. 289.

56. Watt's excellent study primarily discusses Defoe, Richardson, and Fielding and does not concentrate on technique. Alan Dugald McKillop's *The Early Masters of English Fiction* (Lawrence: Univ. of Kansas Press, 1956) offers useful introductory essays on the works of the five major eighteenth century novelists. Sheldon Sacks, in *Fiction and the Shape of Belief* (Berkeley: Univ. of California Press, 1964), analyzes the fiction of the period as three separate categories: satire, which ridicules the external world; the apologue, which deals with exemplified truth; and "represented action," which is a "complicated reconciliation of the two" (p. 15). Arthur Sherbo's *Studies in the Eighteenth-Century English Novel* (East Lansing: Michigan State Univ. Press, 1969) is partly a diatribe against other critics' work and partly a random discussion of some major texts. Frederick R. Karl's *A Reader's Guide to the Eighteenth-Century English Novel* (New York: Noonday Press, 1974) is sometimes extravagant in its analysis and often limited by seeing the novel largely in an adversary role to contemporary culture and as significantly influenced by picaresque fiction. W. Austin Flanders, in *Structures of Experience: History, Society, and Personal Life in the Eighteenth-Century British Novel* (Columbia: Univ. of South Carolina Press, 1984), energetically discusses the fiction of the period as dealing with the conflict between the individual and society, but his treatment of the subject seems somewhat reductive and unoriginal at this point in time.

CHAPTER ONE: *MOLL FLANDERS*

1. See Ian Watt, *"Robinson Crusoe* as a Myth," *Essays in Criticism,* I (1951), 95-119. Karl, however, argues for a complex reading of Robinson's religious development and claims that this dimension is more significant than the mythic one (*A Reader's Guide*, pp. 68-86).

2. One hundred and one separate works of fiction from this period can be studied in a photo-facsimile edition of seventy-one volumes, *Foundations of the Novel: Representative Early Eighteenth-Century Fiction, 1700-1739*, ed. Michael F. Shugrue (New York: Garland, 1972-73).

3. See Q. D. Leavis, *Fiction and the Reading Public* (1932; rpt. London: Chatto & Windus, 1965), p. 102.

4. See the early samples of "criticism" in *Novel and Romance, 1700-1800: A Documentary Record*, ed. Ioan M. Williams (London: Routledge, 1970).

5. All citations to *Moll Flanders* are to the Riverside edition, ed. James Sutherland (Boston: Houghton Mifflin, 1959). Page references follow quotations in the body of my text. I have chosen editions of all the novels I discuss in this study that are both dependable and easily available.

6. David Blewett, in *Defoe's Art of Fiction* (Toronto: Univ. of Toronto Press, 1979), pp. 15-16, points out that there is a "shift in emphasis from the authenticity of the tale," in the preface to the first part of *Robinson Crusoe* (1719), to "dressing up the story," in the preface to *Roxana* (1724). The preface to *Moll Flanders*, which was written between these two statements of narrative intention, indicates the conflict more clearly, it seems to me. Maximillian E.

Novak makes an interesting attempt to get a cohesive theory of fiction out of Defoe's writings in "Defoe's Theory of Fiction," *Studies in Philology*, 61 (1964), 650-68.

7. See John Robert Moore, *Daniel Defoe, Citizen of the Modern World* (Chicago: Univ. of Chicago Press, 1958), p. 268.

8. For a general discussion of morality and entertainment in Defoe's writing, see Peter Earle, *The World of Defoe* (New York: Atheneum, 1977), pp. 30-36.

9. See Ernest Bernbaum, *The Mary Carleton Narratives, 1663-1673* (Cambridge, Mass.: Harvard Univ. Press, 1914). The similarities between *Moll Flanders* and Francis Kirkman's *The Counterfeit Lady Unveiled* demonstrate this point convincingly.

10. See above, pp. 7-10. John J. Richetti, in *Defoe's Narratives: Situations and Structures* (Oxford: Clarendon Press, 1975), states that Defoe's importance as a writer is a result of his "promoting the self by establishing its primacy as the perceiver and guarantor of reality" (p. 19).

11. David Goldknopf's point about "the confessional increment"—that "everything an I-narrator tells us has a certain characterizing significance over and above its data value, by virtue of the fact that he is telling it to us" (*The Life of the Novel* [Chicago: Univ. of Chicago Press, 1973], pp. 38-39)—has to be used with great care, especially when his own theory leads him to conclude that "*Moll Flanders* is really Moll's way of reliving her illicit pleasures and triumphs, in the mellowness of her waning years" (p. 79). First-person narration is a convention which the reader accepts with its limitations. Matters "confessed" to us in our own world that seem significant from the fact of their being "confessed" do not always seem so in fiction. "The confessional increment" seems applicable when the writer either intends the effect or simply creates his narrator badly.

12. In *History of the Royal Society*, 4th ed. (London, 1734), p. 113.

13. See Watt's discussion of Defoe's prose in *The Rise of the Novel*, pp. 100-104; and Bonamy Dobrée's "Some Aspects of Defoe's Prose," in *Pope and His Contemporaries, Essays Presented to George Sherburn*, ed. James L. Clifford and Louis A. Landa (Oxford: Clarendon Press, 1949), pp. 171-84.

14. Michael Shinagel, in *Daniel Defoe and Middle-Class Gentility* (Cambridge, Mass.: Harvard Univ. Press, 1968), sees all of Defoe's characters sharing, "as a result of what befalls them early in life," an "ambition to better themselves and their fortunes and so move to a more preferred position in the social hierarchy." "In this common attitude," he claims, "they are all middle class" (p. 123). For a discussion of economics in *Moll Flanders*, see Maximillian E. Novak, *Economics and the Fiction of Daniel Defoe* (Berkeley: Univ. of California Press, 1962), especially pp. 83-88 and 93-102. Nancy K. Miller, in *The Heroine's Text: Readings in the French and English Novel, 1722-1782* (New York: Columbia Univ. Press, 1980), warns that Moll's life must be seen as "a literary inscription of a woman's life" and not merely as a "form of eighteenth-century economic man" (p. 4). I think, however, that Lois A. Chaber, in her recent Marxist and feminist reading of the novel, "Matriarchal Mirror: Women and Capital in *Moll Flanders*," *PMLA*, 97 (1982), 212-26, goes too far in this direction when she argues that since Moll rejects a patriarchal capitalist society and turns to "female role models," the "book's real structure is matriarchal" (p. 214).

15. G. A. Starr, in *Defoe and Spiritual Autobiography* (Princeton: Princeton Univ. Press, 1965), argues that *"Robinson Crusoe,* and to a lesser extent *Moll Flanders* and *Roxana"* (p. vii), are related to the spiritual autobiography in their development of the first-person narrator's inner state. In *Defoe and Casuistry* (Princeton: Princeton Univ. Press, 1971), Starr also relates the scenes of conscience in Defoe's novels to the casuistic tradition.

16. Roland Barthes states that "when identical semes [the unit of the signifier] traverse the same proper name several times and appear to settle upon it, a character is created. Thus the character is the product of combinations: the combination is relatively stable (denoted by the recurrence of the semes) and more or less complex (involving more or less congruent, more or less contradictory figures); this complexity determines the character's 'personality'..." (*S/Z,* p. 67).

17. See Dorothy Van Ghent, *The English Novel: Form and Function* (New York: Rinehart, 1953), pp. 37–39; and Robert Alter, *Rogue's Progress: Studies in the Picaresque Novel* (Cambridge, Mass.: Harvard Univ. Press, 1964), pp. 49–50.

18. Chief among those who argue for such irony is Van Ghent, in her essay on the work in *The English Novel.* But also see Howard L. Koonce, "Moll's Muddle: Defoe's Use of Irony in *Moll Flanders," ELH,* 30 (1963), 377–94; Robert R. Columbus, "Conscious Artistry in *Moll Flanders," Studies in English Literature, 1500-1900,* 3 (1963), 415–32; Maximillian E. Novak, "Conscious Irony in *Moll Flanders," College English,* 25 (1964), 198–204; and Robert Alan Donovan's analysis of the novel in *The Shaping Vision: Imagination in the Novel from Defoe to Dickens* (Ithaca: Cornell Univ. Press, 1966). Everett Zimmerman, in *Defoe and the Novel* (Berkeley: Univ. of Calif. Press, 1975), argues that "a carefully defined ironic perspective" in *Moll Flanders* "succumbs to the formlessness" of the heroine's mind, since "in some sense Defoe shared Moll's confusion" (p. 106). Laura A. Curtis has recently taken an extreme position when claiming that Defoe's novel is "a hoax, or, near cousin to a hoax, a put on," in *The Elusive Daniel Defoe* (New York: Barnes & Noble, 1984), p. 148. For a strong argument against irony in *Moll Flanders,* see Watt, *The Rise of the Novel,* pp. 118–30. The issue has been much discussed, but I must raise it again to sort out Defoe's achievements and failures as a narrative writer and creator of character.

19. I am referring here to serious narrative, not to satires such as *A Tale of a Tub* where such a technique is used.

20. Columbus, in "Conscious Artistry in *Moll Flanders,"* points out that Moll is left £1,200 after the death of her husband, a "sum which could make her secure and independent," but "her greed for security" drives her to search for a good marriage (p. 423). She might live on that money for a lifetime should she retire, at her young age, to some secluded and quiet existence, but she certainly would not live well. In any case, Moll soon spends enough of the money to be really concerned about poverty. One might also add that a single life was neither the best nor the most secure kind for a woman at that time. In "Moll's Muddle: Defoe's Use of Irony in *Moll Flanders,"* Koonce also argues against Moll's dire economic situation and claims that never once in the novel does she "descend to anything like missing a meal, let alone starvation" (p. 338). We may never see Moll miss a meal, but she certainly tells us enough times that she was on the edge

of poverty (pp. 58–59 and 165 are good examples). One must often see Moll as an outright liar in order to argue for an ironic interpretation of the book.

21. The subject of time in Defoe's novels is discussed by Paul K. Alkon in *Defoe and Fictional Time* (Athens: Univ. of Georgia Press, 1979). Alkon sees far more skill and consciousness in Defoe's manipulation of fictional time than I do (see especially pp. 110–32).

22. Maximillian E. Novak, in *Defoe and the Nature of Man* (New York: Oxford Univ. Press, 1963), sees "necessity" for Defoe and his contemporaries as "a state of desperation, usually associated with starvation and destitution, in which the victim is forced to choose between certain death or a life prolonged only by violating the laws of society, religion, or personal honor" (p. 66). Whereas most contemporary thinkers would not excuse the individual for violating such laws, Professor Novak points out that Defoe clearly did. He also states that Defoe was the first to extend the doctrine of necessity to prostitution (p. 81).

23. A similar point is made by Karl, *A Reader's Guide*, p. 87; and Zimmerman, *Defoe and the Novel*, p. 100. See Blewett's interesting discussion of the name "Moll Flanders" as it relates to the theme of "appearance and disguise" in the novel, in *Defoe's Art of Fiction*, pp. 56–60.

24. Richetti, in *Defoe's Narratives*, states that "Moll pretends to be a novelistic character who is subject to compulsions of development within the conditions of her environment, so that her story may deliver the pattern of an indestructible and elastic self which reduces apparently formless incidents to a pattern of survival" (p. 119). I think that Blewett's general argument for the thematic and structural unity of *Moll Flanders*, in *Defoe's Art of Fiction*, is too selective and forced to be convincing (see especially pp. 81–83).

25. Rudolf G. Stamm, "Daniel Defoe: An Artist in the Puritan Tradition," *Philological Quarterly*, 15 (1936), 227.

26. Starr, however, finds that the "genuineness" of Moll's final repentance "is emphasized not only by its contrast with all the insincere and incomplete versions that have preceded it, but also by its conformity to the classic pattern of spiritual rebirth" (in *Defoe and Spiritual Autobiography*, p. 157).

27. Watt discusses this aspect of Calvinism in relation to *Robinson Crusoe* (*The Rise of the Novel*, pp. 73–74).

28. See especially R. H. Tawney, *Religion and the Rise of Capitalism* (London: J. Murray, 1926).

29. In 1921, Percy Lubbock stated in *The Craft of Fiction* that "the art of fiction does not begin until the novelist thinks of his story as a matter to be *shown*, to be so exhibited that it will tell itself" (London: Cape, 1921, p. 62). Booth's *Rhetoric of Fiction* is in part an argument against the modern preference for "showing" over "telling."

30. I discuss this point in the last chapter of *Samuel Richardson and the Dramatic Novel* (Lexington: Univ. of Kentucky Press, 1968).

31. See above, pp. 37–38.

32. Van Ghent demonstrates that Moll's description of objects are evaluative and not sensuous (*The English Novel*, pp. 34–35).

33. This is done by Elizabeth A. Drew in *The Novel: A Modern Guide to Fifteen English Masterpieces* (New York: Dell, 1963), pp. 35–36.

CHAPTER TWO: *CLARISSA*

1. Unless otherwise stated, citations to *Clarissa* are to the Everyman's Library (London: Dent, 1932). Page references follow quotations in the body of my text.

2. *Tom Jones* may at first seem to challenge this statement, but it certainly offers a narrator who is sufficiently developed as a character to serve this purpose. See below, pp. 109-10.

3. A trend in Richardson criticism is to emphasize the isolation of character in the act of writing letters and hence to negate the social dimension of the novel. See Anthony M. Kearney, "*Clarissa* and the Epistolary Form," *Essays in Criticism*, 16 (1966), 45; and Preston, *The Created Self*, p. 41. An argument against this position is offered by Mark Kinkead-Weekes in *Samuel Richardson: Dramatic Novelist* (Ithaca: Cornell Univ. Press, 1973), pp. 459-61.

4. See Arnold Kettle, *An Introduction to the English Novel* (1951; rpt. London: Hutchinson, 1973), I, 23.

5. William Beatty Warner, in *Reading* Clarissa: *The Struggles of Interpretation* (New Haven: Yale Univ. Press, 1979), states that Clarissa's comparative judging of herself and others is a means of inventing a "self" (p. 17).

6. Preface, *Clarissa*, Shakespeare Head Edition (Oxford: Basil Blackwell, 1930), I, xiii-xiv.

7. It seems that Richardson originally intended Clarissa to love Lovelace, but changed his mind after the publication of part of the work, when he discovered that some of his audience were responding too favorably to the villain. In completing the work and in subsequent rewriting, he tried to deny Clarissa's earlier feelings for Lovelace, a point made in an article by Gerard A. Barker, "Clarissa's 'Command of her Passions': Self-Censorship in the Third Edition," *Studies in English Literature, 1500-1900*, 10 (1970), 525-32.

8. Morris Golden, in *Richardson's Characters* (Ann Arbor: Univ. of Michigan Press, 1963), states "the central issue of life [for Richardson] is the conflict ... of reason and the passions" (p. 182), but he goes on to relate these passions to "the cult of feeling becoming popular in religion, philosophy, and literature." Professor Golden admits the contemporary respect for these feelings but sees in Richardson a fear of their "social effects." He makes this point without defining what he means by those "emotions" popular at the time and without relating them in a specific way to the novel. It is impossible, I believe, to make a convincing argument that *Clarissa* shows any kind of fear about the cult of sensibility developing in the age, a cult to which the novel itself makes such a major contribution. Richardson is quite clear about those "passions" which he fears. R. F. Brissenden, in *Virtue in Distress: Studies in the Novel of Sentiment from Richardson to Sade* (London: Macmillan, 1974), presents a good rebuttal to this position when he shows that during this period, "the role of feelings, especially in the formation of moral judgments, was especially emphasized" (p. 24). For him, Clarissa's "story is a comment on the facile assumption that man is naturally a rational and benevolent creature," while Lovelace "demonstrates the value and importance of the sentimental ideal, of the hope that man can release his potentialities for altruism, generosity, and honesty ... " (p. 186).

9. See Christopher Hill, "Clarissa Harlowe and Her Times," *Essays in Criticism*, 5 (1955), 315-40; and Terry Eagleton's recent Marxist and feminist

reading of the novel, *The Rape of Clarissa* (Oxford: Basil Blackwell, 1982). Eagleton makes the point that the heroine's "spiritual individualism is the acceptable face of the very system which kills Clarissa" (p. 87).

10. From a letter to Sarah Chapone, dated 2 March 1752 (*Selected Letters of Samuel Richardson*, ed. John Carroll [Oxford: Clarendon Press, 1974], p. 201).

11. V. S. Pritchett, however, argues that "Like Lovelace, her [Clarissa's] sexuality is really violent, insatiable in its wish for destruction" (*The Living Novel* [London: Chatto & Windus, 1946], p. 13). This approach is further developed by Van Ghent in *The English Novel*, pp. 50-51 and 61. For discussions of Clarissa's denial of her sexuality, see Norman Rabkin, "*Clarissa:* A Study in the Nature of Convention," *ELH*, 23 (1956), 204-17; and Allan Wendt, "Clarissa's Coffin," *Philological Quarterly*, 39 (1960), 481-95. Miller, in *The Heroine's Text*, makes the interesting point that Clarissa is trapped by "a loathing for female sexuality as it has been inscribed for her by Lovelace and her father," and that "the rape itself is a hyperbole" of this loathing (p. 95).

12. In his portrayal of Clarissa as a tragic heroine with a flawed character, Richardson seems to have been influenced by dramatic theory and practice (see my *Samuel Richardson and the Dramatic Novel*, pp. 74-94).

13. A similar point is made by T. Duncan Eaves and Ben D. Kimpel, in *Samuel Richardson: A Biography* (Oxford: Clarendon Press, 1971): "She [Clarissa] ... comes to recognize that it is towards God she should be humble, and to a certain extent that makes her more independent of the world, since she is no longer so dependent on its opinion" (p. 270).

14. John A. Dussinger goes too far, however, when he sees the entire novel as a "parable illustrating the fundamental doctrine of the cross," in "Conscience and the Pattern of Christian Perfection in *Clarissa*," *PMLA*, 81 (1966), 236-45.

15. See Cynthia Griffin Wolff, *Samuel Richardson and the Eighteenth-Century Puritan Character* (Hamden, Conn.: Archon, 1972). I discuss this subject further on pp. 69-70.

16. See Watt, *The Rise of the Novel*, pp. 75-78.

17. From a letter to William Warburton, dated 19 April 1748 (*Selected Letters*, p. 85).

18. Kinkead-Weekes describes Clarissa's style in the following way: "Hers is primarily an analytic mode in which words are taken seriously, weighed against one another, assayed by repeated examination. The structure of her sentences has a constant tendency to balance and antithesis, moving words into meaningful collocation or distinction. (Her first two sentences in the book weigh 'politeness' and 'sincerity,' 'partiality' and 'judgment.') There is a large conceptual vocabulary, aiming at precision. The movement has the steady progression of a mind thinking" (*Samuel Richardson: Dramatic Novelist*, pp. 433-34).

19. Preface, *Clarissa*, Shakespeare Head Edition, I, xiv.

20. Richardson had already written a guidebook for epistolary correspondence, *Letters Written to and For Particular Friends, On the Most Important Occasions* ... (1741; republished as *Familiar Letters on Important Occasions*, ed. Brian W. Downs [London: G. Routledge, 1928]).

21. Margaret Anne Doody, in *A Natural Passion: A Study of the Novels of Samuel Richardson* (Oxford: Clarendon Press, 1974), also argues for the influence of the "novels of love and seduction" on Clarissa and Lovelace (pp. 128-50).

22. The recently available works of the Russian critic, M. M. Bakhtin are making scholars and students more aware of the various languages and styles that comprise a single novel. Bakhtin argues that "The novel can be defined as a diversity of social speech types (sometimes even diversity of languages) and a diversity of individual voices, artistically organized," in "Discourse in the Novel," *The Dialogic Imagination*, ed. Michael Holquist, trans. Caryl Emerson and Michael Holquist (Austin: Univ. of Texas Press, 1981), p. 262.

23. See Alan Dugald McKillop, "Samuel Richardson's Advice to an Apprentice," *Journal of English and Germanic Philology*, 42 (1943), 40-54; and "Richardson's Early Writings—Another Pamphlet," *Journal of English and Germanic Philology*, 53 (1954), 72-75.

24. The influence of the conduct books on the subject matter of Richardson's novels receives some attention in Katharine Hornbeak's "Richardson's Familiar Letters and the Domestic Conduct Books," *Smith College Studies in Modern Languages*, 19 (1938), 1-29.

25. A good study of this literature is Owen C. Watkins's *The Puritan Experience* (London: Routledge, 1972). See also Wolff, *Samuel Richardson and the Eighteenth-Century Puritan Character*, pp. 18-40; and Jerry C. Beasley, *Novels of the 1740s* (Athens: Univ. of Georgia Press, 1982), pp. 128-34.

26. See Eaves and Kimpel, *Samuel Richardson: A Biography*, pp. 582-83.

27. See especially Belford's comparison of the characters of the novel with those in Rowe's *The Fair Penitent* (IV, 117-20).

28. Alan Dugald McKillop's claim is significant here: "If we think of heroic drama and Restoration comedy as representing an aristocratic code, however spurious, and the later sentimental tragedy as representing a movement toward middle-class levels, then Richardson, in representing a conflict between the censurably aristocratic code of Lovelace and the sober, pure, and dignified ideals of Clarissa, draws on both types of drama to point the opposition" (*Samuel Richardson: Printer and Novelist* [1936; rpt. Chapel Hill: Univ. of North Carolina Press, 1960], p. 147). Sentimental tragedies, however, do not offer many heroines like Clarissa, unless one uses the term "sentimental" very broadly. Clarissa's prototypes can be found in heroic tragedy and the she-tragedy (a term coined by Rowe, in his preface to *The Tragedy of Jane Shore* [1742], for those plays with suffering heroines as their protagonists). See my *Samuel Richardson and the Dramatic Novel*, pp. 33-48.

29. From Nathaniel Lee's *Rival Queens* (V.i.62-67), in *The Works of Nathaniel Lee*, ed. Thomas B. Stroup and Arthur L. Cooke (New Brunswick, N.J.: Scarecrow Press, 1954), I, 273.

30. See below, pp. 74-78. Warner, however, makes the argument, in *Reading* Clarissa, that the heroine seeks "to plot a significant life story" as a "paragon" of virtue (p. 23) and uses her narrative art as a means of doing so. After her rape, she uses her remaining time on earth arranging for her own epistles and those of others to be brought together as a "book called 'The History of Clarissa Harlowe' " (p. 93).

31. For related discussions of Lovelace's role playing see Kinkead-Weekes, *Samuel Richardson: Dramatic Novelist*, pp. 157 and 439; Doody, *A Natural Passion*, pp. 110-14; and Terry Castle, *Clarissa's Ciphers: Meaning and Disruption in Clarissa* (Ithaca: Cornell Univ. Press, 1982), pp. 84-85.

32. See my *Samuel Richardson and the Dramatic Novel*, pp. 36-38.

33. *The Works of Nathaniel Lee*, I, 312.

34. Concerning the influence of the courtly letter on Lovelace's epistles, see William J. Farrell, "The Style and the Action in *Clarissa*," *Studies in English Literature, 1500-1900*, 3 (1963), 365-75; and especially Katherine Hornbeak, "The Complete Letter-Writer in English, 1500-1800," *Smith College Studies in Modern Languages*, 15 (1934), 50-76.

35. See, for example, IV, 376-77.

36. Doody discusses the imagistic and emblematic nature of Lovelace's writing in *A Natural Passion*, pp. 221-40.

37. See Godfrey Frank Singer, *The Epistolary Novel* (Philadelphia: Univ. of Pennsylvania Press, 1933); and Robert Adams Day, *Told in Letters: Epistolary Fiction before Richardson* (Ann Arbor: Univ. of Michigan Press, 1966). A recent collection of earlier epistolary fiction is *The Novel in Letters: Epistolary Fiction in the Early English Novel, 1678-1740*, ed. Natascha Würzbach (London: Routledge, 1969).

38. Day (in *Told in Letters*, especially p. 147) argues otherwise, but the works he discusses scarcely support his claim. Two books which purport to study the novelist's narrative theory and achievements are Donald L. Ball's *Samuel Richardson's Theory of Fiction* (The Hague: Mouton, 1971), and Elizabeth Bergen Brophy's *Samuel Richardson: The Triumph of Craft* (Knoxville: Univ. of Tennessee Press, 1974), but the first work is strangely dated in its critical approach, and the second treats the subject in only a superficial way. Many of the techniques that Fred Kaplan claims to be "innovative" in "'Our Short Story': The Narrative Devices of *Clarissa*," *Studies in English Literature, 1500-1900*, 11 (1971), 549-62, can be found in earlier fiction, and most hardly make a contribution to the development of the novel.

39. Frank G. Black, in "The Epistolary Novel in the Late Eighteenth Century," *Studies in Literature and Philology*, No. 2 (Eugene: Univ. of Oregon, 1940), discusses Richardson's epistolary descendants.

40. See above, pp. 163-64.

41. This aspect of the novel is discussed by Alan Dugald McKillop in "Epistolary Technique in Richardson's Novels," *Rice Institute Pamphlets*, 38 (1951), 36-54.

42. There are exceptions, of course, such as the physical description of Mrs. Sinclair when she is dying (II, 382), but here the portrait is more emblematic and surrealistic than natural or credible.

43. The reader might examine some of the guides to acting published during the period to see the relationship between many of Richardson's descriptions of behavior and the typed and stylized behavior on the stage. An interesting text would be *The Art of Acting*, written by Richardson's close friend Aaron Hill and published by the novelist's printing firm in 1746.

44. On the last point, see Leo Hughes, "Theatrical Convention in Richardson: Some Observations on a Novelist's Technique," in *Restoration and Eighteenth-Century Literature: Essays in Honor of Alan Dugald McKillop*, ed. Carrol Camden (Chicago: Univ. of Chicago Press, 1963), pp. 239-50.

45. Watt points out the greater awareness of space and time in the development of "narrative realism" (*The Rise of the Novel*, pp. 21-27). An important discussion of space in literature is still Joseph Frank's "Spatial Form in Modern Literature," *Sewanee Review*, 53 (Spring Summer Autumn 1945),

221–40, 433–56, 643–53. An interesting discussion of the temporal dimension in fiction is A. A. Mendilow's *Time in the Novel* (London: P. Nevill, 1952).

46. Doody discusses houses and rooms in *Clarissa* and finds them suggesting the psychological state of the heroine. She sees the novel as developing an increasing sense of imprisonment and claustrophobia (*A Natural Passion*, pp. 188–215).

47. See my *Samuel Richardson and the Dramatic Novel*, pp. 87–88. Congreve, in his preface to *Incognita* (1692), claims that he is striving for the unity of plot found in the drama by making his narrative take place within three days. In this respect his work was also unusual.

48. Day argues that this inherent quality in the letter form was already developed by earlier writers of epistolary fiction (*Told in Letters*, p. 8), but it is evident from the examples he cites that "subjective" states in earlier epistolary works were limited in scope and terribly artificial.

49. See A. R. Humphreys, "Richardson's Novels: Words and the 'Movements Within,'" *Essays and Studies by Members of the English Association*, 23 (1970), 34–50, for a discussion of Richardson's "power of conveying sensations immediately, by devices of style and syntax..." (p. 41).

50. A point also made by Kinkead-Weekes in *Samuel Richardson: Dramatic Novelist*, p. 396.

51. Richardson refers to his "New Manner of Writing—to the Moment" in a letter to Lady Bradshaigh, dated 9 October 1756 (in *Selected Letters*, p. 329). See George Sherburn, "'Writing to the Moment': One Aspect," in *Restoration and Eighteenth-Century Literature*, pp. 201–10.

52. Preface, *Clarissa*, Shakespeare Head Edition, I, xiv.

53. See below, p. 295 n. 32.

54. Percy Lubbock, in *The Craft of Fiction*, saw the complete dramatization and integration into the narrative of third-person point of view as Henry James's major contribution to the novel.

55. Eaves and Kimpel make a similar point in *Samuel Richardson: A Biography*, p. 617.

56. *Virtue in Distress*, especially pp. 50–54.

57. Ibid., p. 100.

58. Anthony Ashley Cooper, third earl of Shaftesbury, *Characteristics*, 2nd ed. (London: 1714), II, 99.

59. From a letter to Lady Bradshaigh, dated 14 February 1754 (*Selected Letters*, p. 286).

60. Van Ghent makes the following related argument concerning Clarissa and Lovelace: "Their passion symbolizes gratification, not of sensual life, but of a submerged portion of the emotional life whose tendency actually opposes gratification of the senses—the death wish, the desire for destruction" (*The English Novel*, p. 62).

61. Frederick W. Hilles's argument, in "The Plan of *Clarissa*," *Philological Quarterly*, 45 (1966), 236–48, that Richardson "wrote out what must have been a very full sketch of the book" (p. 236) and worked accordingly does not answer this objection, nor is his argument for the work's "symmetry" convincing. Terry Castle, in her sometimes extravagant reading of the novel, argues that "*Clarissa*'s remarkable form—the intricate, clumsy, strangely beautiful 'Epistolary Manner of Writing'... simultaneously alludes to hundreds

of fictional acts of interpretation within the text and demands still another—our own" (in *Clarissa's Ciphers*, pp. 16–17).

62. Both of these concerns are discussed by Richardson in his postscript to *Clarissa* (see Vol. VIII of the Shakespeare Head Edition).

63. *The Rise of the Novel*, p. 135.

64. The novel first appeared in seven volumes but was later published also as eight. See below, p. 279 n. 1.

CHAPTER THREE: *TOM JONES*

1. Richardson wrote a preface and postscript for the first edition and revised them for the third edition of eight volumes and the fourth of seven volumes, both published in 1751. William Warburton's preface to Volume IV, which had appeared with the first two editions, was dropped with the third and fourth. See above, pp. 63–64.

2. Watt, for example, finds Fielding's neoclassicism working against the realistic requirements of the novel form. For this reason he seems to find Fielding less significant as a novelist than both Defoe and Richardson. See especially pp. 271–76 of *The Rise of the Novel*.

3. Martin C. Battestin suggests that the "allusive ridicule of Richardson (in *Joseph Andrews*) is intended as a kind of foil, setting off to advantage Fielding's own ambitious attempt at reconstruction, at presenting in 'the manner of Cervantes,' a fresh conception of the art of the novel" (*The Moral Basis of Fielding's Art: A Study of* Joseph Andrews[Middletown, Conn.: Wesleyan Univ. Press, 1959], p. 9).

4. There has been some argument that Fielding was aware of Richardson's work on *Clarissa* when writing *Tom Jones* and fashioned elements in his own novel in response to what he imagined to be the plot and general approach in his rival's work. See especially Howard Anderson, "Answers to the Author of *Clarissa*: Theme and Narrative Technique in *Tom Jones* and *Tristram Shandy*," *Philological Quarterly*, 51 (1972), 859–73.

5. In *Joseph Andrews and Shamela*, ed. Martin C. Battestin, Riverside Edition (Boston: Houghton Mifflin, 1961), pp. 313 and 327.

6. See especially Henry Knight Miller, "Some Functions of Rhetoric in *Tom Jones*," *Philological Quarterly*, 45 (1966), 224–27; and Sherbo, *Studies in the Eighteenth-Century English Novel*, pp. 36 and 48. Iser uses the term "implied reader" in a more encompassing and flexible way: "this term incorporates both the prestructuring of the potential meaning by the text, and the reader's actualization of this potential through the reading process" (*The Implied Reader*, p. xii). The term "implied reader" is, of course, derived from Booth's "implied author" in *The Rhetoric of Fiction* (especially pp. 70–75). Without using the term "implied reader," Booth discusses the "image of his reader" created by the author, and states that "the most successful reading is one in which the created selves, author and reader, can find complete agreement" (ibid., p. 138).

7. See Ronald Paulson's discussion of *Tom Jones* in *Satire and the Novel in Eighteenth-Century England* (New Haven: Yale Univ. Press, 1967), pp. 141–50,

in which he states that "the search for the meaning of actions, and in particular of motive in relation to action, is one of the central concerns of the novel" (p. 142). Leo Braudy, in his chapter on *Tom Jones*, in *Narrative Form in History and Fiction: Hume, Fielding and Gibbon* (Princeton: Princeton Univ. Press, 1970), sees the novel in a similar way and claims that "When characters try to fathom the motives of others, they usually project their personal natures, instead of trying to understand someone else's individuality" (p. 171). Preston's following observation, in *The Created Self*, p. 117, is also relevant: "The reader has his responsibility also: he must try to judge well. To encourage him to do so is itself a part of the subject of the book. That is, the book is *about* judgment."

8. By "History," Fielding clearly means a writer of a particular kind of fiction. Beasley, in *Novels of the 1740s*, points out that in the early part of the century "the story of a life, whether real or feigned, was considered an exercise in historical writing . . . for [it] gave expression to important ideals or anxieties of the culture" (p. 44). Sheridan Baker, in "Henry Fielding's Comic Romances," *Papers of the Michigan Academy of Science, Arts, and Letters*, 45 (1960), 412, points out that Cervantes in *Don Quixote* and Scarron in *Roman comique* refer to their works on several occasions as histories. The relationship between *Tom Jones* and actual histories of the period, especially those written by Hume and Gibbon, is discussed by Braudy in *Narrative Form in History and Fiction*.

9. All citations to *Tom Jones* are to the Norton Critical Edition, ed. Sheridan Baker (New York: Norton, 1973). Page references follow quotations in the body of my text. For this edition, Baker uses "the fourth and last printing of *Tom Jones* during Fielding's life, dated 1750, but published 11 December 1749" (p. viii). Baker claims that this printing is "the best text, not only in its correction of many small errors, but in representing Fielding's fullest and final attention" (p. viii).

10. Later in the work, Fielding adds another level of chronological historicity by paralleling the adventures on the road with the Jacobite Rebellion of 1745.

11. Fielding's technique of contrast is discussed by Dorothy Van Ghent in *The English Novel*, pp. 73–75; and by J. Paul Hunter in Chapter 8 of his *Occasional Form: Henry Fielding and the Chain of Circumstance* (Baltimore: The Johns Hopkins Univ. Press, 1975).

12. In *The Chapter in Fiction: Theories of Narrative Division* (Syracuse: Syracuse Univ. Press, 1970), Philip Stevick emphasizes that Fielding ends his chapters to accommodate the reader's attention span (p. 25).

13. Wilber Cross claims that Fielding was influenced in his chapter divisions and titles by Cervantes (*The History of Henry Fielding* [New Haven: Yale Univ. Press, 1918], I, 322); and Baker argues that he was also influenced in this respect by Scarron ("Henry Fielding's Comic Romances," p. 413). But a comparison between chapter divisions and titles in these earlier works and *Tom Jones* easily demonstrates that Fielding uses these aspects of his work to a far greater extent than either Cervantes or Scarron.

14. See his essays from *The Champion, The True-Patriot,* and *The Jacobite's Journal* in the William Ernest Henley edition of Fielding's *Works* (New York: Croscus and Sterling, 1902); and Gerard E. Jensen's edition of *The Convent-Garden Journal* (New Haven: Yale Univ. Press, 1915).

15. A similar point is made by Henry Knight Miller, in "The Voices of Henry Fielding: Style in *Tom Jones*," *The Augustan Milieu: Essays Presented to*

Louis Landa, ed. Henry Knight Miller, Eric Rothstein, and G. S. Rousseau (Oxford: Clarendon Press, 1970), p. 268.

16. Fielding's satiric techniques and irony have been frequently discussed. See especially Paulson's discussion of *Tom Jones* in *Satire and the Novel*; Eleanor Newman Hutchens's *Irony in* Tom Jones (University: Univ. of Alabama Press, 1965); and William Empson's discussion of Fielding's "double irony" in "Tom Jones," *The Kenyon Review,* 20 (Spring 1958), 217-49.

17. Paulson also relates the narrator's satiric point of view to Lucian, in ibid., pp. 134-41.

18. For discussions of epic influence on Fielding's novels, see Ethel Margaret Thornbury, *Henry Fielding's Theory of the Comic Prose Epic* (1931; rpt. New York: Russell and Russell, 1966); and Thomas E. Maresca, *Epic to Novel* (Columbus: Ohio State Univ. Press, 1974). Watt denies any significant epic influence on *Tom Jones* in *The Rise of the Novel,* pp. 251-53, as does E.M.W. Tillyard in his chapter on the novel in *The Epic Strain in the English Novel* (London: Chatto & Windus, 1958). My own remarks for epic influence take a different direction from Thornbury's and Maresca's discussions.

19. Baker, who points this out in his edition of the novel, suggests that perhaps Fielding, "with a touch of irony, thus casts Tom Jones as something of a young and modern Odysseus, discovering the ways of the world as he wanders to find his proper home" (p. 4). Hunter, in *Occasional Form,* discusses the relationship between *Tom Jones* and the *Odyssey* (pp. 130-32), but argues for the greater influence of Fénelon's *Télémaque* (1699) on Fielding's work (pp. 133-35). Also see Maresca, *Epic to Novel,* p. 203.

20. Martin C. Battestin describes "Fortune ... [as] no more than a figure of speech, a convenient vulgarism, enabling one to talk of Providence while avoiding the note of pious sobriety ... " (*The Providence of Wit: Aspects of Form in Augustan Literature and the Arts* [Oxford: Clarendon Press, 1974], p. 157). Also see Aubrey Williams, "Interpositions of Providence and the Design of Fielding's Novels," *The South Atlantic Quarterly,* 70 (1971), 265-86.

21. Hunter claims that during the period "the tradition of the work-behind-the-work usually justified itself thematically rather than structurally, and the 'model' especially expressed a concern related to the concern of the new work and asserted a control that was first of all a guide towards meaning" (*Occasional Form,* p. 135). Also see Ralph Cohen, "The Augustan Mode in English Poetry," *Eighteenth-Century Studies,* 1 (1967), 3-32.

22. "Henry Fielding's Comic Romances."

23. *The Art of* Joseph Andrews (Chicago: Univ. of Chicago Press, 1969). Also see Paulson, *Satire and the Novel,* pp. 110-21. My discussion of comic romance elements in *Tom Jones* is developed from ideas in Chapter 2 of Goldberg's book.

24. Henry Knight Miller, in "Henry Fielding's *Tom Jones* and The Romantic Tradition," *English Literary Studies Monograph Series,* No. 6 (Victoria: Univ. of Victoria, 1976), argues that *Tom Jones* "in all major essentials [is] a romance" (p. 9). Miller, it seems to me, seriously overstates this influence, as an examination of his analogies demonstrates, and fails to recognize the complexity of the relationship between *Tom Jones* and literary precedent. He also weakens his argument by a general confusion of epic and romance. Beasley, in *Novels of the 1740s,* points out that though Richardson,

Fielding, and Smollett may have borrowed "devices and strategies" from the romance, they clearly stood "in opposition" to such works (p. 42).

25. Fielding may have also obtained his initial idea for the intrusive narrator in *Joseph Andrews* and *Tom Jones* from Cervantes and Scarron. For example, both these writers hint at the discussions of authorial problems which form such a significant pattern in the commentary of the narrator in *Tom Jones*. Fielding's narrator is, of course, far more developed and functions with greater purpose and skill, and his voice is related more specifically to the various contemporary literary sources that I have already identified; yet the special relationship in his work between narrator and narrative was already hinted at in the works of these earlier writers. Of related interest is Wayne Booth's "The Self-Conscious Narrator in Comic Fiction before *Tristram Shandy*," *PMLA*, 67 (1952), 163-85. In "Fielding's Familiar Style," *ELH*, 34 (1967), 65-77, William J. Farrell attempts to link Fielding's intrusive narrators in *Joseph Andrews* and *Tom Jones* with narrative voice in earlier historical and biographical writing.

26. See Reuben Brower, *Alexander Pope: The Poetry of Allusion* (Oxford: Clarendon Press, 1957).

27. Patricia Meyer Spacks, in *Imagining a Self: Autobiography and Novel in Eighteenth-Century England* (Cambridge, Mass.: Harvard Univ. Press, 1976), discusses the subject of identity as it was explored in some autobiographies and novels in the eighteenth century. Professor Spacks discusses some of the same philosophical texts that I do, but the only novel we both examine at length is *Tristram Shandy*, and here our approaches differ.

28. *An Essay Concerning Human Understanding*, I, 281.

29. Ibid.

30. Ibid.

31. Ibid., I, 290.

32. Ibid., I, 286.

33. *The Imagination as a Means of Grace*, p. 27.

34. Ibid., p. 29.

35. Quotations in this discussion are from pp. 259-62 of Hume's *Treatise*.

36. P. 29. The reference is to Joseph Wood Krutch, *"Modernism" in the Modern Drama* (Ithaca: Cornell Univ. Press, 1953), p. 83.

37. Ibid., p. 84.

38. For discussions of the theme of "prudence" in *Tom Jones*, see Hutchens, *Irony in* Tom Jones, pp. 101-18; and Glenn W. Hatfield, *Henry Fielding and the Language of Irony* (Chicago: Univ. of Chicago Press, 1968), pp. 179-96. Also see Battestin's chapter "Fielding: The Definition of Wisdom," in *The Providence of Wit*, pp. 164-92.

39. Robert Alter, in *Fielding and the Nature of the Novel* (Cambridge, Mass.: Harvard Univ. Press, 1968), states that "Fielding shifts the onus of crucial decision from the characters to the reader, who is called upon to play the role of judge..." (p. 21).

40. The "aesthetic uses" of the term "nature" during this period are discussed by Arthur O. Lovejoy, in *Essays in the History of Ideas* (1949; rpt. New York: Putnam's, 1960), pp. 69-77.

41. The world vision here is Shaftesburian and benevolent, but Shaftesbury's vision has much of the order, harmony, and universality of deistic and neoclassic belief in it. See "The Parallel of Deism and Classicism," in

Lovejoy's *Essays in the History of Ideas,* pp. 78-79, and also the previously cited essays of Battestin and Williams. In *Henry Fielding and the Augustan Ideal under Stress* (London: Routledge, 1972), C. J. Rawson argues that by the time of *Tom Jones,* one can see doubts on Fielding's part concerning "Nature's ordering role" (p. 55). I feel strongly, however, that Rawson's comments on *Tom Jones* are not sufficient to overthrow the more accepted emphasis on Fielding's benevolent order in that novel by such critics as Battestin and Williams in their previously cited essays.

42. In *Joseph Andrews and Shamela,* pp. 10-11.

43. Morris Golden, in *Fielding's Moral Psychology* (Amherst: Univ. of Massachusetts Press, 1966), states that in *Tom Jones,* the individual's vanity and hypocrisy cause distortions in his assessment of others (p. 68) and hence prevent him from sympathizing with them (p. 64). Also relevant is Michael Bliss's observation, in "Fielding's Bill of Fare in *Tom Jones,*" *ELH,* 30 (1963), 236-43, that "mutuality depends on perception and perception depends on mutuality" (p. 243).

44. Sheridan Baker analyzes Bridget's characterization and its relationship to Fielding's plot from this perspective in "Bridget Allworthy: The Creative Pressures of Fielding's Plot," *Papers of the Michigan Academy of Science, Arts, and Letters,* 52 (1967), 345-56.

45. Frank Kermode makes the following relevant point, in "Richardson and Fielding," *Cambridge Journal,* 4 (1950-51), 106-14: "The complexity of Fielding inheres in his texture—it is a matter of verbal suggestiveness; but of Richardson in his structure—a matter of the suggestiveness of *event,* and this last quality is essential to the major form as we now understand it" (p. 111). Kermode states that Fielding approaches stock or traditional types with irony, especially "the mock-heroic point of view," to create a dualistic sense of character (p. 113). Also see Alter, *Fielding and the Nature of the Novel,* p. 71; and Karl, *A Reader's Guide,* p. 174.

46. This point is made by Goldberg in relation to the similes in *Joseph Andrews (The Art of Joseph Andrews,* pp. 234-35).

47. See Baker's edition of *Tom Jones,* 92n and 229n.

48. The italicized words are from the opening of Rochester's *Satyr Against Mankind.*

49. Irvin Ehrenpreis describes Fielding's scenic technique in the following way: "He can create an elaborate comic scene playing one elemental humour against a second; he can endow the scene with so much internal coherence that its power seems independent of the history which gives rise to it; he can relate the scene in language that minutely enriches it with the generalized ironies of human nature; and then, when you suppose his work is done, he can root the scene back in the plot again so that every gesture and speech emanates some particular irony alluding to the main action of the whole work" (in *Fielding:* Tom Jones [London: Edward Arnold, 1964], p. 73).

50. Alter suggests that in the passage describing Square, quoted below in my text, "The Fellows in the Public Streets" are defecating (*Fielding and the Nature of the Novel,* pp. 33 and 206n).

51. Paulson, commenting on Fielding's analogy in *Joseph Andrews* between his novel and Hogarth's prints, states that the novelist wishes to "replace the fantasy of traditional, emblematic, and Augustan satire with a more

restrained delineation, closer to experience, and reliant on 'character' rather than 'caricature,' on the variety rather than the exaggeration of expression" (*Satire and the Novel*, p. 108). There is some truth to this, and Fielding certainly wishes to evoke the same realistic social context we find in Hogarth's prints. But in both *Joseph Andrews* and *Tom Jones*, where he also cites Hogarth on occasion (see, for example, p. 51), we get exaggeration in his pictorial representations and not much "variety." The problem arises from trying to compare a spatial and external art form with a verbal and mental one. Fielding achieves a Hogarthian satiric realism, but largely through his choice of subject matter and analytic commentary, not through his method of delineation. In his book, *Emblem and Expression: Meaning in English Art of the Eighteenth Century* (Cambridge, Mass.: Harvard Univ. Press, 1975), especially pp. 130-36, Paulson further develops some of his ideas on the relationship between fiction and painting during this period.

52. See George Sherburn, "Fielding's Social Outlook," *Philological Quarterly*, 35 (1956), 7.

53. Tom now resembles the man of sense, who was becoming a significant character type in both drama and fiction. The hero of Richardson's final novel, *Sir Charles Grandison*, also bears a significant resemblance to this dramatic character type. For a discussion of the man of sense in the drama see John Harrington Smith's *The Gay Couple in Restoration Comedy* (Cambridge, Mass.: Harvard Univ. Press, 1948), pp. 211-14.

54. Coleridge's statement is well known: "What a master of composition Fielding was! Upon my word, I think the *Oedipus Tyrannus*, the *Alchemist*, and *Tom Jones*, the three most perfect plots ever planned" (*Table Talk*, July 5, 1834, in *The Table Talk and Omniana* [London: Oxford Univ. Press, 1917], p. 312).

55. In this paragraph, the first two quotations are from p. 101 and the third from p. 111 of *The Created Self*.

56. *Ibid*, p. 97. Hutchens's statement is from p. 41 of *Irony in* Tom Jones.

57. The citations in the following paragraph are to pp. 126-39 of *The Life of the Novel*.

58. By "story" I mean the general movement of the novel's action, the reduction of all its individual events to a simple narrative pattern. Like E. M. Forster, in *Aspects of the Novel* (New York: Harcourt, Brace, 1927), p. 131, I mean "plot," at this point, to convey the specific actions of the novel and their causal relationship, but I go on to use the term in a more inclusive way which will become clear as my discussion continues.

59. "The Concept of Plot and the Plot of *Tom Jones*," in *Critics and Criticism: Ancient and Modern*, ed. R. S. Crane (Chicago: Univ. of Chicago Press, 1952), pp. 621-22.

60. Ibid., p. 622.

61. "Bridget Allworthy: The Creative Pressures of Fielding's Plot," p. 345.

62. See above, p. 269 n. 51. Also see Sternberg's discussion of "informational distribution" in *Tom Jones* (in *Expositional Modes and Temporal Ordering in Fiction*, pp. 263-68).

63. See above, p. 131.

64. See Alter's interesting analysis of Jenny Jones in *Fielding and the Nature of the Novel*, pp. 66-68.

65. See above, p. 140.

66. Fielding finally confronts these problems in *Amelia*.

67. Karl also makes this point in *A Reader's Guide*, p. 164. Hunter, in *Occasional Form*, pp. 143-48, discusses the journey as a process of education in eighteenth-century fiction.

CHAPTER FOUR: *TRISTRAM SHANDY*

1. The first two volumes of *The Life and Opinions of Tristram Shandy, Gentleman* were published in December 1759, in York, and in January 1761, in London. Volumes III and IV were published in January 1761; V and VI in December 1761; VII and VIII in January 1765; and IX in January 1767.

2. Sterne's indebtedness to earlier fiction has been claimed by E. A. Baker, *The History of the English Novel* (London: Wetherby, 1929), IV, 197. Also see H. K. Russell, "*Tristram Shandy* and the Technique of the Novel," *Studies in Philology*, 42 (1945), 581-93.

3. Henri Fluchère, for example, argues this position in *Laurence Sterne: From Tristram to Yorick: An Interpretation of* Tristram Shandy, trans. and abr. Barbara Bray (London: Oxford Univ. Press, 1965), pp. 9 and 17. B. H. Lehman, in his seminal article "Of Time, Personality, and Author, A Study of *Tristram Shandy*: Comedy," *University of California Publications in English*, 8 (1941), 233-50, makes a similar point in a different context when he claims that "the perfect naturalness of Sterne's psyche" reacted against "the unreality of even the great novels of Richardson and Fielding" (p. 233).

4. Sterne also used techniques from older, more traditional, literary forms and imposed them upon the novel. John M. Stedmond, in *The Comic Art of Laurence Sterne* (Toronto: Univ. of Toronto Press, 1967), makes this point in relation to such earlier works as Cervantes's *Don Quixote*, Rabelais's *Gargantua and Pantagruel*, Burton's *Anatomy of Melancholy*, and Swift's *Tale of a Tub*. Richard A. Lanham, in *Tristram Shandy: The Games of Pleasure* (Berkeley: Univ. of California Press, 1973), overstates the case, however, when he argues that Sterne "did not extend the domain of the novel. Much rather, he appropriated its subject for an elaborate game with classical narrative patterns..." (pp. 27-28). Lanham claims that it was "through Rabelais" that Sterne learned to play with the "forms of classical historical narrative" (p. 22).

5. Stedmond makes a similar point in *The Comic Art of Laurence Sterne*, pp. 53-54. Mark Loveridge, in *Laurence Sterne and the Argument about Design* (London: Macmillan, 1982), claims that Sterne, in *Tristram Shandy*, "is trying to take patterns other people have made during the previous decades of the eighteenth century, and to show that what, there, appears to be an harmonious and viable set of ideas and beliefs is in truth based on a conjunction or arrangement of ideas which is perverse or which has comic or quixotic overtones" (p. 93).

6. "The Parallel of Deism and Classicism," in *Essays in the History of Ideas*, pp. 78-98.

7. This last point has been discussed by a number of scholars. See, for example, John Traugott's *Tristram Shandy's World: Sterne's Philosophical*

Rhetoric (Berkeley: Univ. of California Press, 1954), pp. 73–75; and Battestin, *The Providence of Wit*, pp. 253–54.

8. *An Inquiry Concerning The Principles of Morals* (1751), ed. Charles H. Hendel, The Library of Liberal Arts (Indianapolis: Bobbs-Merill, 1957), pp. 10–11. Traugott also links Sterne's sentimentalism to Hume's doctrine of sympathy in *Tristram Shandy's World*, pp. 73–74.

9. This point is to some degree the basis of Ernest Nevin Dilworth's uncomplimentary study of Sterne, *The Unsentimental Journey of Laurence Sterne* (New York: King's Crown Press, 1948).

10. All citations in my work to *The Life and Opinions of Tristram Shandy, Gentleman* are to James Aiken Work, ed. (New York: Odyssey Press, 1940). Page references follow quotations in the body of my text.

11. Locke's influence on Sterne has been discussed extensively by Traugott in *Tristram Shandy's World* and, more recently, by Helene Moglen in *The Philosophical Irony of Laurence Sterne* (Gainesville: Univ. Presses of Florida, 1975). My own discussion emphasizes different aspects of this influence and places the relationship between the two writers in a different critical context. James E. Swearinger, in his phenomenological study of the novel, *Reflexivity in Tristram Shandy* (New Haven: Yale Univ. Press, 1977), claims that Sterne went further than Locke in his treatment of "Transcendental subjectivity," but overstates his case when he argues that "in contrast with Locke's elemental psychology Tristram makes the whole of consciousness primary.... where Locke neglects to account for the existence of reflection, beyond deriving its contents from sensation, Tristram shows relatively little interest in the empirical thesis" (p. 10).

12. Eric Rothstein carries the relationship between Tristram and his "elders" further than most critics in *Systems of Order and Inquiry in Later Eighteenth-Century Fiction* (Berkeley: Univ. of California Press, 1975), pp. 62–79.

13. Moglen makes the interesting observation that "Tristram is an autobiographer who remembers in order to understand himself. Demonstrating the Lockean relation of identity with memory, he proceeds unconsciously as artist and eccentric, haphazardly piecing together those fragments of his life which are inextricably bound up with the lives closest to his own" (*The Philosophical Irony of Laurence Sterne*, p. 55). Robert Alter, in *Partial Magic: The Novel as Self-Conscious Genre* (Berkeley: Univ. of California Press, 1975), states that the novel's many mirrors "catch its own operations . . . [and] give us back the image of the mind in action." In this way, "the work's literary self-consciousness paradoxically proves to be a technique of realism as well" (p. 56). Rothstein, however, in his chapter on *Tristram Shandy* in *Systems of Order and Inquiry*, argues that beneath this surface, Sterne "keep[s] formal control, developing episodes with internal structures and rhythms, working with incremental repetition and fulcrums . . . and in contriving emblems that embody a complex of values. The chief procedures for these . . . are analogy and modification . . . " (p. 108). Also see Van Ghent, *The English Novel*, pp. 83 and 87.

14. Preston states that "since Tristram is always asking for the collaboration of his readers, and thus is creating partly through the imaginations of his readers, Sterne is in effect projecting an image of the creative

act of reading" (*The Created Self*, p. 134). Preston goes on to say that "the novel is a conversation [with the reader] about the failure of conversations" (p. 146).

15. Howard Anderson, in "*Tristram Shandy* and the Reader's Imagination," *PMLA*, 86 (1971), 966–73, claims that "Tristram has set out to educate and train our imaginations, rather than allow us the simpler pleasures of giving free rein to our own conceptions or passively relying on his" (p. 967).

16. See especially pp. 51–61 of Traugott's *Tristram Shandy's World*. Donovan's chapter on the novel, "Sterne and the Logos," in *The Shaping Vision*, also discusses the work's concern with language.

17. Battestin makes the same point in *The Providence of Wit*, p. 268.

18. Ian Watt makes the following point in "The Comic Syntax of *Tristram Shandy*," *Studies in Criticism and Aesthetics, 1660–1800: Essays in Honor of S. H. Monk*, ed. Howard Anderson and John S. Shea (Minneapolis: Univ. of Minnesota Press, 1967, pp. 315–31): "The typographical tricks . . . at least serve to remind us that the image reflected in the mirror is less real than the mirror itself . . ." (p. 323). William V. Holtz, in "Typography, *Tristram Shandy*, Aposiopesis, etc.," in *The Winged Skull: Papers from the Laurence Sterne Bicentenary Conference*, ed. Arthur H. Cash and John M. Stedmond (London: Methuen, 1971), makes a similar point (p. 254).

19. This point has been made by several scholars. See A. R. Towers, "Sterne's Cock and Bull Story," *ELH*, 24 (1957), 12–29; and Robert Alter, "*Tristram Shandy* and the Game of Love," *American Scholar*, 37 (1968), 316–32.

20. Kenneth MacLean, in *John Locke and English Literature of the Eighteenth Century* (New Haven: Yale Univ. Press, 1936), states that Locke saw the association of ideas as leading to mental confusion and chaos and that this is the way Sterne used the concept (p. 134). Traugott, in *Tristram Shandy's World*, claims that Tristram's digressions are a result of a more traditional and literary kind of association of ideas, but Locke's associational psychology, which is related to madness, "is the very being of Toby's characterization" (pp. 45–47). In "The Lockean Psychology of *Tristram Shandy*," *ELH*, 22 (1955), 125–35, Arthur H. Cash argues that Locke's concept of the "train of ideas," rather than his notion of "association of ideas," which was only an afterthought, influenced Sterne in his creation of his characters (p. 129). Fluchère, in *Laurence Sterne*, claims that Sterne used Locke's associational psychology, which explains irrationality, for the monolithic characters of Tristram's narration, and the more orthodox associational psychology of later philosophers for Tristram himself (pp. 68–72). Finally, Moglen, in *The Philosophical Irony of Laurence Sterne*, states that "in the theory of association, Sterne found the greatest possibilities for suggesting the uniqueness of individual development within a context of universal conditioning" (p. 16). My own reading of Tristram and the other characters sees them all working partly along the lines of Locke's associational concept, with its emphasis on singularity and irrationality. The predicament which faces Sterne's characters is their inability to relate their idiosyncratic internal worlds to the world that surrounds them.

21. See Traugott, *Tristram Shandy's World*, p. 57; and Ernest Tuveson, "Locke and Sterne," in *Reason and the Imagination: Studies in the History of Ideas, 1600–1800*, ed. J. A. Mazzeo (New York: Columbia Univ. Press, 1962), p. 262.

22. Theodore Baird, in "The Time-Scheme of *Tristram Shandy* and a Source," *PMLA*, 51 (1936), 803–29, has demonstrated that "there is a carefully planned and executed framework of calendar time" within the novel (p. 804). Mendilow, in *Time and the Novel*, chapter XII, presents an interesting and relevant discussion of the time shifts in *Tristram Shandy*.

23. The subject is discussed, although superficially, in section II of *Probability, Time, and Space in Eighteenth-Century Literature*, ed. Paula R. Backscheider (New York: AMS Press, 1979).

24. Stedmond makes a somewhat related point: "As another structural pattern, time in *Tristram Shandy* is a continuous present. The focus is on the act of creation, though the 'events' recorded all have their being in the past" (*The Comic Art of Laurence Sterne*, p. 100). Also see Moglen, *The Philosophical Irony of Laurence Sterne*, p. 56.

25. For related discussions see Battestin, *The Providence of Wit*, pp. 263–65; and Preston, *The Created Self*, pp. 136–37.

26. See Jorge Luis Borges's essay "A New Refutation of Time," in *Labyrinths: Selected Stories and Other Writings*, ed. Donald A. Yates and James E. Irby, 2nd ed. (New York: New Directions, 1964), pp. 217-34.

27. William V. Holtz, in discussing the effect of pictorial art on Sterne in *Image and Immortality: A Study of* Tristram Shandy (Providence: Brown Univ. Press, 1970), sees the novel working beyond any temporal order to create "Tristram's own awareness in himself as the complex result of a history still totally present in his mind" (p. 105). Swearingen, in *Reflexivity in* Tristram Shandy, pp. 119-20, responds to Holtz by arguing that the novel as "phenomenological reflection" creates a more complex temporality in Tristram's mind than mere "sequential presentation," and that "space does not enter the novel as an independent time...[since it] is the domain of the empirical and Tristram's mind is not empirical."

28. See Cash, "The Lockean Psychology of *Tristram Shandy*, p. 129; and my n. 20. Sterne's comic treatment of Locke's notion of "train of ideas" on pp. 190–91 of the novel should also be noted.

29. The question has been discussed by various critics. See, for example, Wayne Booth's "Did Sterne Complete *Tristram Shandy?*" *Modern Philology*, 47 (1951), 172-83.

30. The subject is touched upon throughout section III of *Probability, Time, and Space*, ed. Backsheider.

31. McKillop states that Sterne's use of gesture is an elaboration of "a technique already developed by Defoe and Richardson, and at the same time reminds us, in a variation of the manner of Swift, that man is grotesquely involved with a body" (*The Early Masters of English Fiction*, p. 187).

32. Locke's comparison appears in *An Essay Concerning Human Understanding*, I, 149.

33. Holtz, in *Image and Immortality*, attempts to link "Sterne's ability...to capture the nuances of gesture and attitude" (p. 53) with painting, and he relates Sterne's presentation of gesture to the "theory of comic forms" that Hogarth presents in *The Analysis of Beauty* (p. 29). Also see Martin Price's discussion of Sterne's depiction of gesture, in *To the Palace of Wisdom: Studies in Order and Energy from Dryden to Blake* (Carbondale: Southern Illinois Univ. Press, 1964), pp. 333-36.

34. In *Laurence Sterne as Satirist: A Reading of* Tristram Shandy (Gainesville: Univ. Presses of Florida, 1969), Melvyn New argues that the work should be read as a satire and not a novel.

35. These are some of the features which make the work for Northrop Frye as much an anatomy or Menippean satire as a novel (in *Anatomy of Criticism* [Princeton: Princeton Univ. Press, 1957], pp. 311-12). D. W. Jefferson, in "*Tristram Shandy* and the Tradition of Learned Wit," *Essays in Criticism*, 1 (1951), 225-48, argues that Sterne, like Pope and Swift before him, attacks "intellectual habits belonging to the pre-Enlightenment world of thought" (p. 227).

CHAPTER FIVE: *HUMPHRY CLINKER*

1. See William A. West, "Matt Bramble's Journey to Health," *Texas Studies in Language and Literature*, 2 (1969), 1197-1208.

2. See Robert Folkenflik, "Self and Society: Comic Union in *Humphry Clinker*," *Philological Quarterly*, 53 (1974), 195-204.

3. This aspect of the work is also discussed by Iser in *The Implied Reader*, pp. 57-80. Although Iser and I make a few similar points, our discussions are generally dissimilar, and the context of my entire study puts a very different emphasis on my observations.

4. Iser sees the travel book, epistolary novel, and picaresque novel as the chief literary sources from which *Humphry Clinker* is drawn, (*ibid.*, pp. 69-70).

5. See George M. Kahrl, *Tobias Smollett: Traveler-Novelist* (Chicago: Univ. of Chicago Press, 1945), pp. 36-50.

6. See Louis L. Martz, *The Later Career of Tobias Smollett* (New Haven: Yale Univ. Press, 1942), pp. 146-80.

7. See Kahrl, *Tobias Smollett*, pp. 129-30.

8. The full title of Anstey's work is *The New Bath Guide: or, Memoirs of the B-R-D Family in a Series of Poetical Epistles*. Martz, pp. 133-34, and Paulson, *Satire and the Novel*, pp. 200-21, briefly discuss Anstey's work.

9. *The Implied Reader*, p. 69.

10. A similar point about Matt's character is made by Donovan, in *The Shaping Vision*, pp. 121-24.

11. For this reason I prefer not to argue for the relation between the novel's structure and that in picaresque fiction, as does, for example, Robert Donald Spector, in *Tobias George Smollett* (New York: Twayne, 1968), pp. 128-30, and, to some extent, Iser, in *The Implied Reader*, 67-68. The structure of *Humphry Clinker* is often quite sophisticated in the ways the separate letters work together and the characters are thematically related and developed.

12. All citations in my work to *The Expedition of Humphry Clinker* are to Angus Ross, ed. (Harmondsworth, Eng.: Penguin, 1961). Page references follow quotations in the body of my text.

13. As the novel progresses, there is some development in Matt's physical and mental health, and, as a result, his descriptions become somewhat less impassioned and prejudicial. Jery too seems to adjust to the world, and his snobbishness and arrogance become less apparent. But the alterations in these

characters are as much due to the change in location as any internal growth. Were the characters to return to the earlier locations, it is likely that their previous responses would be repeated. Both Matt and Jery never completely lose their earlier "prejudice and passion"; rather, these aspects of their personalities are brought under control by their better feelings, which themselves are brought forth by the improved landscape.

14. Such novels are not first-person narratives in the sense that I have used the term above, since the narrators were not principal agents in the actions they describe.

15. Lewis Mansfield Knapp, in *Tobias Smollett: Doctor of Men and Manners* (Princeton: Princeton Univ. Press, 1949), mentions the novel's "eagle-eyed etchings of eighteenth-century scenes and manners, upon which social historians draw so heavily..." (p. 324).

16. The major exception to this statement in relation to *Clarissa* is the description of the room in which the heroine is confined during her arrest (III, 444–45). We are not given many specific details about the physical appearance of the Harlowe home, Mrs. Sinclair's house, or the room where Clarissa dies, though we are well aware of the spatial arrangements of these places. The same observations can be made about the locations for the more developed scenes in *Moll Flanders*. For further comments on this subject see above, pp. 48–49 and 84–87.

17. That Dickens appreciated Smollett's works is made evident in *David Copperfield*, chapter IV, and in *The Uncommercial Traveller*, chapter XII. McKillop, in *The Early Masters of English Fiction*, also refers to these two eulogies of Smollett's novels by Dickens (p. 180n.).

18. *A Reader's Guide*, pp. 186–87.

19. M. A. Goldberg makes a similar point about Scotland in general, in *Smollett and the Scottish School* (Albuquerque: Univ. of New Mexico Press, 1959), p. 163.

20. Goldberg describes this compromise as one where "ideas of primitivism are reconciled with ideas of progress" (p. 18). In "'Humphry Clinker': Smollett's Tempered Augustanism," *Criticism*, 9 (1967), 257–74, David L. Evans claims that "Dennison provides a living example of the successful fusion of Augustan order and business-like industry" (p. 269). Also see Paulson, *Satire and the Novel*, pp. 207–8.

21. Two essays on Smollett's grotesques are Robert Hopkins's "The Function of the Grotesque in *Humphry Clinker*," *Huntington Library Quarterly*, 32 (1969), 163–77; and George M. Kahrl's "Smollett as a Caricaturist," in *Tobias Smollett: Bicentennial Essays Presented to Lewis M. Knapp*, ed. G. S. Rousseau and P. G. Boucé (New York: Oxford Univ. Press, 1971), pp. 169–200.

22. This point is also made by Paulson, *Satire and the Novel*, pp. 205–6; and Iser, *The Implied Reader*, pp. 72–74.

23. An observation made by Van Ghent about Dicken's characters in *The English Novel*, p. 127.

24. See above, p. 282 n. 41, for reference to Rawson's more cautious view of Fielding's optimism in *Tom Jones*.

25. Matt himself says, "I have done with the science of men, and must now endeavour to amuse myself with the novelty of things" (p. 139).

26. See Crane, "The Concept of Plot and the Plot of *Tom Jones*, pp. 633–37; and above, pp. 141–42.

27. Matt's concern with health and disease is also discussed by West, in "Matt Bramble's Journey to Health," and by Folkenflik, in "Self and Society." Rothstein, in *Systems of Order and Inquiry*, states that "society's and Bramble's disorders have . . . the same symptoms, and the same reciprocity between body and spirit—so that in interacting, the man and the world reflect one another . . ." (p. 119). A similar point is made about Smollett's novels by Francis Russell Hart in his brief discussion of the writer in *The Scottish Novel: From Smollett to Spark* (Cambridge, Mass.: Harvard Univ. Press, 1978), pp. 15-17.

28. According to the Oxford English Dictionary, "reins" is now an archaic word for the kidneys; and in Biblical usage, the "reins" were seen as the seat of the feelings or affections.

29. See Thomas R. Preston, "Smollett and the Benevolent Misanthrope Type," *PMLA*, 79 (March 1964), 51-57; and Robert W. Uphaus, "Sentiment and Spleen: Travels with Sterne and Smollett," *Centennial Review of Arts and Sciences*, 15 (1971), 406-21.

30. *Satire and the Novel*, p. 202.

31. For a discussion of Romance elements in the work, see Sheridan Baker, "*Humphry Clinker* as Comic Romance," in *Papers of the Michigan Academy of Science, Arts, and Letters*, 46 (1961), 645-54.

32. For these reasons I think Karl goes too far in seeing Humphry as a representative of the "new kind of society in which the traditional family is losing or has lost its functions," and in arguing that "in virtually every phase of his activities, Humphry threatens Bramble's world." This kind of assumption, which is made not from the work itself but from later social history, leads Karl to make the highly dubious statement that after the "near-mythical-ritual process" in which Humphry saves Matt from "death by water," he is "reborn as legitimate . . . [and] usurps the father and the father's role" (*A Reader's Guide*, pp. 202-3).

33. See Paulson's discussion of Matt as a satiric observer in *Satire and the Novel*, pp. 194-98.

CHAPTER SIX: *PRIDE AND PREJUDICE*

1. See F. B. Pinion, *A Jane Austen Companion* (London: Macmillan, 1973), pp. 85 and 92.

2. Jane Austen's reading is briefly discussed by R. W. Chapman, in *Jane Austen: Facts and Problems* (Oxford: Clarendon Press, 1948), pp. 37-38; and also by Pinion, pp. 158-79.

3. The literary background to Austen's novels still has not been explored sufficiently. Henrietta ten Harmsel's *Jane Austen: A Study in Fictional Conventions* (The Hague: Mouton, 1964) and Frank W. Bradbrook's *Jane Austen and Her Predecessors* (Cambridge, Eng.: Cambridge Univ. Press, 1966) tend to be vague and general. Marilyn Butler, in *Jane Austen and the War of Ideas* (Oxford: Clarendon Press, 1975), marshals little convincing evidence that Austen was directly influenced by the fiction of the "conservative Christian moralists" of the 1790s.

4. See especially Mary Lascelles, *Jane Austen and her Art* (1939; rpt. London: Oxford Univ. Press, 1963), chapter 2. A more elaborate, but frequently

unconvincing, discussion about Jane Austen's allusions to traditional fictional elements is Kenneth L. Moler's *Jane Austen's Art of Allusion* (Lincoln: Univ. of Nebraska Press, 1968).

5. This is the thrust of Mark Schorer's interpretation in the introduction to the Riverside Edition of the work (Boston: Houghton Mifflin, 1956), pp. v–xxi. Citations in my work to *Pride and Prejudice* are to this edition, and page references follow quotations in the body of my text. The Riverside Edition, like most paperback publications of the novel, uses the text edited by R. W. Chapman for Oxford Univ. Press (3rd ed., 1932).

6. I think that D. W. Harding, in "Regulated Hatred: An Aspect of the Works of Jane Austen," *Scrutiny* 8 (1940), 346–62, and Marvin Mudrick, in *Jane Austen: Irony as Defense and Discovery* (Princeton: Princeton Univ. Press, 1952), seriously overemphasize the negative aspects of Austen's attitudes toward her society. Of the numerous critics who have countered this argument see, for example, Alistair M. Duckworth, *The Improvement of the Estate: A Study of Jane Austen's Novels* (Baltimore: The Johns Hopkins Univ. Press, 1971); and David Monaghan, *Jane Austen, Structure and Social Vision* (London: Macmillan, 1980).

7. Studies of Austen's narrative technique generally have to do with language, but two books that cover a wider range are Karl Kroeber's *Styles in Fictional Structure: The Art of Jane Austen, Charlotte Brontë, and George Eliot* (Princeton: Princeton Univ. Press, 1971); and Lloyd W. Brown's *Bits of Ivory: Narrative Techniques in Jane Austen's Fiction* (Baton Rouge: Louisiana State Univ. Press, 1973). It is difficult to accept Kroeber's claim that he is writing a new kind of criticism, but his method of comparatively discussing three writers is interesting and allows him to make a number of useful statements about the form of Jane Austen's fiction.

8. See above, pp. 118–23.

9. Karl Kroeber properly asserts the novel's social dimension, but goes too far when he claims that since "a personality exists only interactively (for Austen)...we notice that our 'identity crisis' never occurs in her fiction" (in "*Pride and Prejudice*: Fiction's Lasting Novelty," *Jane Austen Bicentenary Essays*, ed. John Halperin [Cambridge, Eng.: Cambridge Univ. Press, 1975], p. 150). On the other hand, E. Rubinstein's argument that Austen's novels reflect "the ascendancy of Romanticism, with its new emphasis upon the cultivation of the individual," shows a failure to understand concepts of individualism in the eighteenth century and the nature of the individualism of Austen's characters (in "Jane Austen's Novels: The Metaphor of Rank," *Literary Monographs*, Vol. 2, ed. Eric Rothstein and Richard N. Ringler [Madison: Univ. of Wisconsin Press, 1969], p. 103). Monaghan argues more reasonably that the social and personal are "closely bound together in the relationship between Elizabeth and Darcy" (in *Jane Austen, Structure and Social Vision*, p. 67).

10. "Every circumstance narrated in Sir Charles Grandison, all that was ever said or done in the cedar parlour, was familiar to her; and the wedding days of Lady L. and Lady G. were as well remembered as if they had been living friends" (J. E. Austen-Leigh, *Memoirs of Jane Austen*, ed. R. W. Chapman [Oxford: Clarendon Press, 1926], p. 89).

11. In *Northanger Abbey and Persuasion*, ed. John Davie (London: Oxford Univ. Press, 1971), p. 33. The other references are to Fanny Burney's *Camilla: or, A Picture of Youth* (1796) and Maria Edgeworth's *Belinda* (1801).

12. See *Cecilia of Memoirs of an Heiress*, ed. Annie Raine Ellis (London: G. Bell and Sons, 1914), II, 462.

13. Q. D. Lewis, in "A Critical Theory of Jane Austen's Writings," *Scrutiny*, 10 (1941), 61–87, claims that the initial version of *Pride and Prejudice*, "First Impressions," was conceived as a rewriting of "the story of Cecilia in realistic terms" (p. 71). A. Walton Litz, however, claims that Leavis "exaggerates this debt in her statement" (in *Jane Austen: A Study of her Artistic Development* [New York: Oxford Univ. Press, 1965], p. 100). Also see Pinion, pp. 168–71, for an argument against any significant debt. My own argument for influence does not cover the same ground nor go quite so far as that of Leavis.

14. See especially pp. 71, 90, 232, and 240 of Vol. II of *Cecilia*.

15. Ibid., II, 59.

16. Ibid., II, 107.

17. See Frye, *Anatomy of Criticism*, pp. 163–64.

18. Susan Morgan, in *In the Meantime: Character and Perception in Jane Austen's Fiction* (Chicago: Univ. of Chicago Press, 1980), argues that the subject of all Austen's novels "is the problem of perception" (p. 3), but she links the novelist's treatment of the subject with that of the Romantic poets and claims, with insufficient discussion, that Austin "reject[s] the inheritance of Locke" (p. 4). Although I agree with Morgan's general argument about *Pride and Prejudice*, I must point out that she does little with linking the subject of perception to the novel's technique, and her essay largely functions to prove her point that in the book Elizabeth moves from a position where she attempts to perceive without personal involvement to one where she "has come to value the connections and partialities which inform truth" (p. 104).

19. For other discussions of Jane Austen's dialogue, see Howard S. Babb, *Jane Austen's Novels: The Fabric of Dialogue* (Columbus: Ohio State Univ. Press, 1962); and Norman Page, *The Language of Jane Austen* (Oxford: Basil Blackwell, 1972). Relevant to my own analyses is Reuben A. Brower's essay "Light and Bright and Sparkling: Irony and Fiction in *Pride and Prejudice*," in *The Fields of Light: An Experiment in Critical Reading* (New York: Oxford Univ. Press, 1951), pp. 164–81.

20. See above, pp. 137–38.

21. Lascelles suggests that Austen's dialogue in *Pride and Prejudice* was influenced by both the comic dramatists and essayists of her time (*Jane Austen and her Art*, p. 107). Brower relates her dialogue to the Augustan "poetry of wit" ("Light and Bright and Sparkling," pp. 165–66).

22. See above, pp. 143–46.

23. That Elizabeth loves Darcy all along but is ignorant of the fact is claimed, for example, by Andrew H. Wright, in *Jane Austen's Novels: A Study in Structure* (London: Chatto & Windus, 1957), pp. 113–14; and E. M. Halliday, in "Narrative Perspective in *Pride and Prejudice*," *Nineteenth-Century Fiction*, 15 (1960), 67–69. However, the text clearly shows that Elizabeth dislikes the man she thinks Darcy is. It is not until she comes to see the real man and understands his past actions that she finds the person she can love. This process starts with his letter and is aided by Darcy's own self-awareness and development of character that result from her refusal of his proposal. Elizabeth realizes the extent of her feelings for Darcy when she learns of Lydia's elopement and fears that she can never marry him.

24. Charles J. McCann, in "Setting and Character in *Pride and Prejudice*," *Nineteenth-Century Fiction*, 19 (1964), 65–75, claims that each country house in the novel "is a recognizable emblem for a complex of social, economic, and intellectual realities" (p. 65). Also see Monaghan, *Jane Austen, Structure and Social Vision*, for a discussion of the contrasting behavior of the characters at the Rosings and Pemberley estates which indicates to Elizabeth "the essential qualities . . . of the aristocracy" (p. 81).

25. As does Brower, in "Light and Bright and Sparkling."

26. Of course, too much reading and too little experience in the world of reality can be detrimental to common sense, as in the case of Mary, and debilitating in daily affairs, as in the case of Mr. Bennet.

27. I disagree with Babb's claim that "when the author describes Darcy's growing attachment, she narrates it in such a way that we are less aware of his affection than his pride . . ." (*Jane Austen's Novels*, p. 116). It also seems to me that Brown overstates the degree to which the reader "participate[s] in . . . incidents of misjudgment . . ." in the novel (*Bits of Ivory*, p. 38). Part of our pleasure in this work comes from seeing our suspicions and tentative judgments confirmed. Austen, as I am trying to demonstrate, employs her narrative techniques to have us respond to the events of the novel with more awareness than Elizabeth, even though we are emotionally committed to the heroine. Brower's following comments seem relevant here: "Though we are always being led to make double interpretations, we are never in confusion about what the alternatives are. It is also important that in these ironic dialogues no comment is included that makes us take Darcy's behavior in only an unpleasant sense. . . . Since more kindly views of Darcy have been introduced through the flow of witty talk, Darcy does not at that point have to be remade but merely reread" ("Light and Bright and Sparkling," pp. 175–76). Halliday's following comment on a scene between Elizabeth and Wickham is also relevant to my discussion of the way in which we perceive Darcy in these scenes: "yet in spite of many insights into her mental reaction to Wickham, the reader can maintain a certain detachment of judgment because the bulk of the chapter is fully recorded conversation—and what Wickham says constitutes his impropriety" ("Narrative Perspectives in *Pride and Prejudice*," p. 70). In the scene I am examining, what Darcy says suggests a better man than the one Elizabeth thinks she hears.

28. Wright suggests that Darcy's "austerity of manner . . . stems partly from an inordinate shyness" (*Jane Austen's Novels*, p. 118).

29. Wright describes the general theme of pride and prejudice in the book in the following way: "To say that Darcy is proud and Elizabeth prejudiced is to tell but half the story. Pride and prejudice are faults; but they are also the necessary defects of desirable merits: self-respect and intelligence. Moreover, the novel makes clear the fact that Darcy's pride leads to prejudice and Elizabeth's prejudice stems from a pride in her own perceptions. So the ironic theme of the book might be said to center on the dangers of intellectual complexity" (ibid., p. 106). Also see Robert B. Heilman, "E Pluribus Unum: Parts and Whole in *Pride and Prejudice*," in *Jane Austen Bicentenary Essays*, especially p. 131, for a similar commentary.

30. Kroeber points out, with the help of a computer, that "Jane Austen uses fewer substantives referring to parts of the body than do Eliot, Dickens, or

Charlotte Brontë" (*Styles in Fictional Structure*, p. 11). In *Pride and Prejudice*, physical attraction is treated with suspicion. Mr. Bennet had married Mrs. Bennet because of her physical appearance, and, as a result, is forced to carry on his life in the seclusion of his study. The one sexual affair that takes place in the book, the elopement of Lydia and Wickham, is treated at a distance and severely condemned. Even the treatment of bodies in this present scene is antiseptic and witty.

31. Mary's distinction between these terms is worth noting: "Pride relates more to our opinion of ourselves, vanity to what we would have others think of us" (p. 14). Though Mary's character is ridiculed in the book, her statement comes from some worthwhile reading (a similar definition from Blair's *Lectures* appears in *The Oxford English Dictionary*) and has relevance to Darcy's comments: we are likely to need the approbation of others for the lesser accomplishments, which evoke vanity, but "a real superiority of mind," which produces pride, hardly needs the admiration of others.

32. It has generally been thought that *Sense and Sensibility* and *Pride and Prejudice* were first written in epistolary form, though there is some argument about the latter (see Pinion, pp. 94–95). Robert Liddell, in *The Novels of Jane Austen* (London: Longmans, 1963), relates the significance of letters in *Pride and Prejudice* to the novel's original epistolary form (pp. 34–36). For a discussion of the importance of letters in Jane Austen's works see Ian Jack, "The Epistolary Element in Jane Austen," *English Studies Today, Second Series*, ed. G. A. Bonnard (Bern: A. Francke, 1961), pp. 173–86.

33. Austen's language when describing Elizabeth's thoughts in this episode, and for the most part throughout the work, is too general and formal to be "free indirect speech." For a discussion of "free indirect speech" in Jane Austen's novels, see Page, *The Language of Jane Austen*, pp. 123–37. Litz describes the effect Austen achieves with the language that generally portrays Elizabeth's point of view in the following way: "Such a method is really a compromise: it combines in a limited form the omniscience of traditional third-person narration with the immediacy of first-person narrative, giving the reader a sense of involvement and identification while simultaneously providing the perspective necessary for moral judgment" (*Jane Austen: A Study of her Artistic Development*, pp. 110–11).

34. In addition to the studies of Jane Austen's language already cited, K. C. Phillipp's rather specialized study, *Jane Austen's English* (London: Deutsch, 1970), should be noted. Also of interest is Stuart Tave's *Some Words of Jane Austen* (Chicago: Univ. of Chicago Press, 1973). Tave's discussion of *Pride and Prejudice* focuses largely on the words "amiable," "affection," and "mortification," through which he presents a general interpretation of the novel (pp. 116–57). John Odmark, in the last chapter of his *An Understanding of Jane Austen's Novels* (Oxford: Basil Blackwell, 1981), discusses the "semantic fields" of Austen's language.

35. Though Fielding himself was influenced by the earlier essayists of the period, and we can find within his and Austen's writing a basic eighteenth-century prose style, her writing is somewhat more formal because of the influence of Dr. Johnson. In relation to Dr. Johnson's influence on Austen, see Lascelles, *Jane Austen and Her Art*, p. 109; and C. S. Lewis, "A Note on Jane Austen," in *Selected Literary Essays by C. S. Lewis*, ed. Walter Hooper

NOTES

(Cambridge, Eng.: Cambridge Univ. Press, 1969), p. 178. Since Burney's writing in *Cecilia* was strongly influenced by Johnson's prose, it is likely that some of the Johnsonian elements in Austen's writing came from, or at least were reinforced by, this source.

36. Though Austen did not appreciate Fielding's novels because of their "grossness," she had read his works and knew them well (see Pinion, pp. 164–65). Watt's statement concerning Jane Austen's relation to Richardson and Fielding is worth quoting at this point: Miss Austen's novels "must be seen as the most successful solutions of the two general narrative problems for which Richardson and Fielding had provided only partial answers. She was able to combine into a harmonious unity the advantages both of realism of presentation and realism of assessment, of the internal and of the external approaches to character..." (*The Rise of the Novel*, p. 297).

37. Page mentions that Austen employs three-part structure for patterning and variation (*The Language of Jane Austen*, pp. 104 and 109). For a discussion of two-part structure in Austen's sentences, see Babb, *Jane Austen's Novels*, pp. 25–27.

38. Brower comments on the absence of complexity and irony in the second half of the novel ("Light and Bright and Sparkling," p. 180). Morgan claims, however, that "The second half of *Pride and Prejudice* may be less sparkling than the first, but the quieter pleasure it offers is an extended view of Elizabeth's fate entwined with the lives of those around her" (*In the Meantime*, pp. 103–4).

39. A similar point is made by Litz, in *Jane Austen: A Study of her Artistic Development*, p. 110; and by Everett Zimmerman, in "Pride and Prejudice *in* Pride and Prejudice," *Nineteenth-Century Fiction*, 23 (1968), 71.

40. Page makes a relevant point when comparing Austen's scenic technique to that of the drama: "the novelist is at liberty to present as fully or as briefly as she wishes the various phases of a scene or episode, making possible a flexibility of pace and...a speed and economy that would hardly be in the theatre..." (*The Language of Jane Austen*, 28n).

41. Litz sees Austen more "on the side of benevolence and feeling" in this conflict (*Jane Austen: A Study of her Artistic Development*, p. 8).

CONCLUSION

1. The standard discussion of fiction during the last part of the eighteenth century is J.M.S. Tompkin's *The Popular Novel in England, 1770–1800* (1932; rpt. Lincoln: Univ. of Nebraska Press, 1961).

2. *The Progress of Romance through Times, Countries, and Manners* (1785; facsimile rpt. New York: Facsimile Text Soc., 1930), p. 111. This definition is also quoted by Scholes and Kellogg in *The Nature of Narrative*, p. 7.

3. See, for example, Irma Z. Sherwood, "The Novelist as Commentators," in *The Age of Johnson; Essays Presented to Chauncey Brewster Tinker* (New Haven: Yale, Univ. Press, 1949), pp. 113–25.

4. José Ortega y Gasset, in "Notes on the Novel," *The Dehumanization of Art and other Writings on Art and Culture* (New York: Doubleday, 1956), claims that the modern novel has become "presentative": "from being pure narration which but alludes, the novel has advanced to strict presentation" (p. 57).

Works Cited

Alkon, Paul K. *Defoe and Fictional Time*. Athens: Univ. of Georgia Press, 1979.

Alter, Robert. *Partial Magic: The Novel as Self-Conscious Genre*. Berkeley: Univ. of California Press, 1975.

———. *Fielding and the Nature of the Novel*. Cambridge, Mass.: Harvard Univ. Press, 1968.

———. "*Tristram Shandy* and the Game of Love." *American Scholar*, 37 (1968), 316–32.

———. *Rogue's Progress: Studies in the Picaresque Novel*. Cambridge, Mass.: Harvard Univ. Press, 1964.

Altick, Richard D. *The English Common Reader: A Social History of the Mass Reading Public, 1800–1900*. Chicago: Univ. of Chicago Press, 1957.

Anderson, Howard. "Answers to the Author of *Clarissa*: Theme and Narrative Technique in *Tom Jones* and *Tristram Shandy*." *Philological Quarterly*, 51 (1972), 859–73.

———. "*Tristram Shandy* and the Reader's Imagination." *PMLA*, 86 (1971), 966–73.

Anstey, Christopher. *The New Bath Guide: or, Memoirs of the B–R–D Family in a Series of Poetical Epistles*. 3rd ed. London: 1766.

Arnheim, Rudolf. *Visual Thinking*. Berkeley: Univ. of California Press, 1969.

Auerbach, Erich. *Mimesis: The Representation of Reality in Western Literature*. Trans. Willard R. Tusk. Princeton: Princeton Univ. Press, 1953.

Austen, Jane. *Northanger Abbey and Persuasion*. Ed. John Davie. London: Oxford Univ. Press, 1971.

———. *Sense and Sensibility*. Ed. Claire Lamont. London: Oxford Univ. Press, 1970.

———. *Pride and Prejudice*. Ed. Mark Schorer. Riverside Edition. Boston: Houghton Mifflin, 1956.

Austen-Leigh, J. E. *Memoirs of Jane Austen*. Ed. R. W. Chapman. Oxford: Clarendon Press, 1926.

Babb, Howard S. *Jane Austen's Novels: The Fabric of Dialogue*. Columbus: Ohio State Univ. Press, 1962.

Backscheider, Paula R., ed. *Probability, Time, and Space in Eighteenth-Century Literature*. New York: AMS Press, 1979.

Baird, Theodore. "The Time-Scheme of *Tristram Shandy* and a Source." *PMLA*, 51 (1936), 803–20.

Baker, E. A. *The History of the English Novel*. Vol. 3. London: Wetherby, 1929.

Baker, Sheridan. "Bridget Allworthy: The Creative Pressures of Fielding's Plot." *Papers of the Michigan Academy of Science, Arts, and Letters*, 52 (1967), 345–56.

————. "*Humphry Clinker* as Comic Romance." *Papers of the Michigan Academy of Science, Arts, and Letters,* 46 (1961), 645-54.

————. "Henry Fielding's Comic Romances." *Papers of the Michigan Academy of Science, Arts, and Letters,* 45 (1960), 411-19.

Bakhtin, M. M. *The Dialogic Imagination.* Ed. Michael Holquist. Trans. Caryl Emerson and Michael Holquist. Austin: Univ. of Texas Press, 1981.

Ball, Donald L. *Samuel Richardson's Theory of Fiction.* The Hague: Mouton, 1971.

Barker, Gerard A. "Clarissa's 'Command of her Passions': Self-Censorship in the Third Edition." *Studies in English Literature, 1500-1900,* 10 (1970), 525-32.

Barthes, Roland. *S/Z.* Trans. Richard Miller. New York: Hill & Wang, 1970.

————. *Writing Degree Zero and Elements of Semiology.* Trans. Annette Lavers and Colin Smith. Boston: Beacon Press, 1970.

Battestin, Martin C. *The Providence of Wit: Aspects of Form in Augustan Literature and the Arts.* Oxford: Clarendon Press, 1974.

————. *The Moral Basis of Fielding's Art: A Study of* Joseph Andrews. Middletown, Conn.: Wesleyan Univ. Press, 1959.

Beasley, Jerry C. *Novels of the 1740s.* Athens: Univ. of Georgia Press, 1982.

Berkeley, George. *A Treatise Concerning the Principles of Human Knowledge.* Ed. Colin M. Turboyne. Indianapolis: Liberal Arts Press, 1957.

————. *The Theory of Vision, or Visual Language, Shewing the Immediate Presence and Providence of a Deity, Vindicated and Explained.* London: 1733.

————. *An Essay Towards a New Theory of Vision.* London: 1709.

Bernbaum, Ernest. *The Mary Carleton Narratives, 1663-1673.* Cambridge, Mass.: Harvard Univ. Press, 1914.

Black, Frank G. "The Epistolary Novel in the Late Eighteenth Century." *Studies in Literature and Philology,* No. 2. Eugene: Univ. of Oregon, 1940.

Blair, Hugh. *Lectures on Rhetoric and Belles Lettres.* 2 vols. Rpt. Carbondale: Southern Illinois Univ. Press, 1965.

Blewett, David. *Defoe's Art of Fiction.* Toronto: Univ. of Toronto Press, 1979.

Bliss, Michael. "Fielding's Bill of Fare in *Tom Jones.*" *ELH,* 30 (1963), 236-43.

Boethius. *The Consolation of Philosophy.* Trans. Richard Green. Indianapolis: Bobbs-Merrill, 1962.

Booth, Wayne C. *The Rhetoric of Fiction.* Chicago: Univ. of Chicago Press, 1961.

————. "The Self-Conscious Narrator in Comic Fiction before *Tristram Shandy.*" *PMLA,* 67 (1952), 163-85.

————. "Did Sterne Complete *Tristram Shandy?*" *Modern Philology,* 47 (1951), 172-83.

Borges, Jorge Luis. *Labyrinths: Selected Stories and Other Writings.* Ed. Donald A. Yates and James E. Irby. 2nd ed. New York: New Directions, 1964..

Bradbrook, Frank W. *Jane Austen and Her Predecessors.* Cambridge, Eng.: Cambridge Univ. Press, 1966.

Braudy, Leo. *Narrative Form in History and Fiction: Hume, Fielding, and Gibbon.* Princeton: Princeton Univ. Press, 1970.

Brissenden, R. F. *Virtue in Distress: Studies in the Novel of Sentiment from Richardson to Sade.* London: Macmillan, 1974.

Brontë, Emily. *Wuthering Heights.* Ed. Hilda Marsden and Ian Jack. Oxford: Clarendon Press, 1976.

Brophy, Elizabeth Bergen. *Samuel Richardson: The Triumph of Craft.* Knoxville: Univ. of Tennessee Press, 1974.

Brower, Reuben. *Alexander Pope: The Poetry of Allusion.* Oxford: Clarendon Press, 1957.

———. "Light and Bright and Sparkling: Irony and Fiction in *Pride and Prejudice.*" In *The Fields of Light: An Experiment in Critical Reading.* New York: Oxford Univ. Press, 1951, pp. 164-81.

Brown, Lloyd W. *Bits of Ivory: Narrative Techniques in Jane Austen's Fiction.* Baton Rouge: Louisiana State Univ. Press, 1973.

Brown, Thomas. *The Adventures of Lindamira.* Ed. Benjamin Boyce. Minneapolis: Univ. of Minnesota Press, 1949.

Burney, Fanny. *Camilla: or, a Picture of Youth.* Ed. Edward A. Bloom and Lillian D. Bloom. London: Oxford Univ. Press, 1972.

———. *Evelina, or A Young Lady's Entrance Into the World.* Everyman's Library 352. London: Dent, 1958.

———. *Cecilia or Memoirs of an Heiress.* Ed. Annie Raine Ellis. 2 vols. London: G. Bell and Sons, 1914.

Butler, Marilyn. *Jane Austen and the War of Ideas.* Oxford: Clarendon Press, 1975.

Cash, Arthur H. "The Lockean Psychology of *Tristram Shandy.*" *ELH*, 22 (1955), 125-35.

Cassirer, Ernst. *The Philosophy of the Enlightenment.* Princeton: Princeton Univ. Press, 1951.

Castle, Terry. *Clarissa's Ciphers: Meaning and Disruption in* Clarissa. Ithaca: Cornell Univ. Press, 1982.

Cervantes, Miguel de. *Don Quixote.* Trans. Samuel Putnam. 2 vols. New York: Viking Press, 1949.

Chaber, Lois A. "Matriarchal Mirror: Women and Capital in *Moll Flanders.*" *PMLA*, 97 (1982), 212-26.

Chapman, R. W. *Jane Austen: Facts and Problems.* Oxford: Clarendon Press, 1948.

Chaucer, Geoffrey. *The Book of Troilus and Creseyde.* Ed. Robert Kilburn Root. Princeton: Princeton Univ. Press, 1926.

Cohen, Ralph. "The Augustan Mode in English Poetry." *Eighteenth-Century Studies*, 1 (1967), 3-32.

Coleridge, Samuel Taylor. *The Table Talk and Omniana.* London: Oxford Univ. Press, 1917.

Columbus, Robert R. "Conscious Artistry in *Moll Flanders.*" *Studies in English Literature, 1500-1900*, 3 (1963), 415-32.

Congreve, William. *Incognita: or Love and Duty Reconcil'd.* Ed. H.F.B. Brett-Smith. Boston: Houghton Mifflin, 1922.

Conrad, Joseph. *Nostromo.* New York: New American Library, 1960.

———. *The Nigger of the Narcissus.* New York: Doubleday, 1935.

Cooper, Anthony Ashley, third earl of Shaftesbury. *Characteristics.* 2nd ed. London: 1714.

Cowper, William. *Poetical Works.* Ed. H. S. Milford. 4th ed. London: Oxford Univ. Press, 1967.

Crane, R. S. "The Concept of Plot and the Plot of *Tom Jones.*" In *Critics and Criticism: Ancient and Modern.* Ed. R. S. Crane. Chicago: Univ. of Chicago Press, 1952, pp. 621-33.

Cross, Wilber. *The History of Henry Fielding.* 3 vols. New Haven: Yale Univ. Press, 1918.

Curtis, Laura A. *The Elusive Daniel Defoe.* New York: Barnes & Noble, 1984.

Day, Robert Adams. *Told in Letters: Epistolary Fiction before Richardson.* Ann Arbor: Univ. of Michigan Press, 1966.

Defoe, Daniel. *Memoirs of a Cavalier.* Ed. James T. Boulton. London: Oxford Univ. Press, 1972.

————. *Robinson Crusoe and Other Writings.* Ed. James Sutherland. Riverside Edition. Boston: Houghton Mifflin, 1968.

————. *Roxana, The Fortunate Mistress.* Ed. Jane Jack. London: Oxford Univ. Press, 1964.

————. *Moll Flanders.* Ed. James Sutherland. Riverside Edition. Boston: Houghton Mifflin, 1959.

————. *The Life of Captain Singleton.* Everyman's Library 74. London: Dent, 1951.

————. *Religious Courtship.* Vol. 14. *The Novels and Miscellaneous Works of Daniel Defoe.* London: 1840-41.

————. *The Family Instructor.* Vols. 15 and 16. *The Novels and Miscellaneous Works of Daniel Defoe.* London: 1840-41.

Dickens, Charles. *The Uncommercial Traveller and Reprinted Pieces.* London: Oxford Univ. Press, 1958.

————. *David Copperfield.* New York: Modern Library, 1934.

Dilworth, Ernest Nevin. *The Unsentimental Journey of Laurence Sterne.* New York: Kings Crown Press, 1948.

Dobrée, Bonamy. "Some Aspects of Defoe's Prose." In *Pope and His Contemporaries, Essays Presented To George Sherburn.* Ed. James L. Clifford and Louis A. Landa. Oxford: Clarendon Press, 1949, pp. 171-84.

Donovan, Robert Alan. *The Shaping Vision: Imagination in the Novel from Defoe to Dickens.* Ithaca: Cornell Univ. Press, 1966.

Doody, Margaret Anne. *A Natural Passion: A Study of the Novels of Samuel Richardson.* Oxford: Clarendon Press, 1974.

Drew, Elizabeth A. *The Novel: A Modern Guide to Fifteen English Masterpieces.* New York: Dell, 1963.

Duckworth, Alistair M. *Improvement of the Estate: A Study of Jane Austen's Novels.* Baltimore: The Johns Hopkins Univ. Press, 1971.

Durrell, Lawrence. *The Alexandria Quartet: Justine, Balthazar, Mountolive, Clea.* London: Faber & Faber, 1962.

Dussinger, John A. "Conscience and the Pattern of Christian Perfection in *Clarissa.*" *PMLA*, 81 (1966), 236-45.

Eagleton, Terry. *The Rape of* Clarissa. Oxford: Basil Blackwell, 1982.

Earle, Peter. *The World of Defoe.* New York: Atheneum, 1977.

Eaves, Duncan T. and Ben D. Kimpel. *Samuel Richardson: A Biography.* Oxford: Clarendon Press, 1971.

Edel, Leon. "Novel and Camera." In *The Theory of the Novel: New Essays.* Ed. John Halperin. New York: Oxford Univ. Press, 1974.

Edgeworth, Maria. *Belinda.* London: Dent, 1893.

Ehrenpreis, Irvin. *Fielding: Tom Jones.* London: Edward Arnold, 1964.

Eliot, George. *Middlemarch.* Ed. Gordon S. Haight. Riverside Edition. Boston: Houghton Mifflin, 1956.

Empson, William. "Tom Jones." *The Kenyon Review*, 20 (Spring 1958), 217–49.

Evans, David L. " 'Humphry Clinker': Smollett's Tempered Augustanism." *Criticism*, 9 (1967), 257–74.

Farrell, William J. "Fielding's Familiar Style." *ELH*, 34 (1967), 65–77.

———. "The Style and the Action in *Clarissa.*" *Studies in English Literature, 1500–1900,* 3 (1963), 365–75.

Faulkner, William. *As I Lay Dying.* New York: Modern Library, 1967.

———. *The Sound and the Fury.* New York: Modern Library, 1966.

———. *Absalom, Absalom!* New York: Modern Library, 1961.

Fielding, Henry. *Tom Jones.* Ed. Sheridan Baker. New York: Norton, 1973.

———. *Joseph Andrews and Shamela.* Ed. Martin C. Battestin. Riverside Edition. Boston: Houghton Mifflin, 1961.

———. *The Covent-Garden Journal.* Ed. Gerard E. Jensen. 2 vols. New Haven: Yale Univ. Press, 1915.

———. *Works.* Ed. William Ernest Henley. New York: Croscus and Sterling, 1902.

Fish, Stanley. *Is There a Text in this Class?* Cambridge, Mass.: Harvard Univ. Press, 1980.

Flanders, W. Austin. *Structures of Experience: History, Society, and Personal Life in the Eighteenth-Century British Novel.* Columbia: Univ.. of South Carolina Press, 1984.

Fluchère, Henri. *Laurence Sterne: From Tristram to Yorick: An Interpretation of* Tristram Shandy. Trans. and abr. Barbara Bray. London: Oxford Univ. press, 1965.

Folkenflik, Robert. "Self and Society: Comic Union in *Humphry Clinker.*" *Philological Quarterly,* 53 (1974), 195–204.

Forster, E. M. *Aspects of the Novel.* New York: Harcourt, Brace, 1927.

Frank, Joseph. "Spatial Form in Modern Literature." *Sewanee Review,* 53 (Spring Summer Autumn 1945), 221–40, 433–56, 643–53.

Freud, Anna. *The Ego and the Mechanisms of Defense.* Trans. Cecil Baines. New York: International Univ. Press, 1946.

Freud, Sigmund. *The Ego and the Id.* Trans. James Strachey. New York: Norton, 1962.

Friedman, Norman. "Point of View in Fiction: The Development of a Critical Concept." *PMLA,* 70 (December 1955), 1160–84.

Frye, Northrop. *Anatomy of Criticism.* Princeton: Princeton Univ. Press, 1957.

Goldberg, Homer. *The Art of* Joseph Andrews. Chicago: Univ. of Chicago Press, 1969.

Goldberg, M. A. *Smollett and the Scottish School.* Albuquerque: Univ. of New Mexico Press, 1959.

Golden, Morris. *Fielding's Moral Psychology.* Amherst: Univ. of Massachusetts Press, 1966.

———. *Richardson's Characters.* Ann Arbor: Univ. of Michigan Press, 1963.

Goldknopf, David. *The Life of the Novel.* Chicago: Univ. of Chicago Press, 1973.

Gombrich, E. H. *Art and Illusion: A Study in the Psychology of Pictorial Representation.* 2nd ed. 1961; rpt. Princeton: Princeton Univ. Press, 1969.

Gray, Thomas. *The Complete Poems of Thomas Grey*. Ed. H. W. Starr and J. R. Hendrickson. Oxford: Clarendon Press, 1966.

Halliday, E. M. "Narrative Perspective in *Pride and Prejudice*." *Nineteenth-Century Fiction*, 15 (1960), 65–71.

Halperin, John, ed. *Jane Austen Bicentenary Essays*. Cambridge, Eng.: Cambridge Univ. Press, 1975.

——. *The Theory of the Novel: New Essays*. New York: Oxford Univ. Press, 1974.

Harding, D. W. "Psychological Processes in the Reading of Fiction." *British Journal of Aesthetics*, 2 (1962), 133–47.

——. "Regulated Hatred: An Aspect of the Works of Jane Austen." *Scrutiny*, 8 (1940), 346–62.

Harmsel, Henrietta ten. *Jane Austen: A Study in Fictional Conventions*. The Hague: Mouton, 1964.

Hart, Francis Russell. *The Scottish Novel: From Smollett to Spark*. Cambridge, Mass.: Harvard Univ. Press, 1978.

Hartley, David. *Observations on Man, His Frame, His Duty, His Expectations*. 1749; rpt. Hildesheim: George Olms, 1967.

Harvey, W. J. *Character and the Novel*. London: Chatto & Windus, 1965.

Hatfield, Glenn W. *Henry Fielding and the Language of Irony*. Chicago: Univ. of Chicago Press, 1968.

Heilman, Robert B. "E Pluribus Unum: Parts and Whole in *Pride and Prejudice*." In *Jane Austen Bicentenary Essays*. Ed. John Halperin. Cambridge, Eng.: Cambridge Univ. Press, 1975, pp. 123–42.

Hill, Aaron. *The Art of Acting*. London: 1746.

Hill, Christopher. "Clarissa Harlowe and Her Times." *Essays in Criticism*, 5 (1955), 315–40.

Hilles, Frederick W. "The Plan of *Clarissa*." *Philological Quarterly*, 45 (1966), 236–48.

Holland, Norman. *Five Readers Readings*. New Haven: Yale Univ. Press, 1975.

——. *The Dynamics of Literary Response*. New York: Oxford Univ. Press, 1968.

Holtz, William V. "Typography, *Tristram Shandy*, Aposiopesis, etc." In *The Winged Skull: Papers from the Laurence Sterne Bicentenary Conference*. Ed. Arthur H. Cash and John M. Stedmond. London: Methuen, 1971.

——. *Image and Imortality: A Study of* Tristram Shandy. Providence: Brown Univ. press, 1970.

Homer, *The Odyssey*. Trans. Albert Cook. New York: Norton, 1967.

Hopkins, Robert. "The Function of the Grotesque in *Humphry Clinker*." *Huntington Library Quarterly*, 32 (1969), 163–77.

Horace, *The Art of Poetry*. Verse trans. Burton Raffel, prose trans. James Hynd. Albany: State Univ. of New York Press, 1974.

Hornbeak, Katherine. "Richardson's Familiar Letters and the Domestic Conduct Book." *Smith College Studies in Modern Languages*, 19 (1938), 1–29.

——. "The Complete Letter-Writer in English, 1560–1800." *Smith College Studies in Modern Languages*, 15 (1934), 50–76.

Hughes, Leo. "Theatrical Convention in Richardson: Some Observations on a Novelist's Technique." In *Restoration and Eighteenth-Century Literature:*

Essays in Honor of Alan Dugald McKillop. Ed. Carrol Camden. Chicago: Univ. of Chicago Press, 1963, pp. 239-50.

Hume, David. *An Inquiry Concerning the Principles of Morals* (1751). Ed. Charles H. Hendel. The Library of Liberal Arts. Indianapolis: Bobbs-Merrill, 1957.

_____. *A Treatise of Human Nature.* Ed. L. A. Selby-Bigge. Oxford: Clarendon Press, 1888.

Humphreys, A. R. "Richardson's Novels: Words and the 'Movements Within.' " *Essays and Studies by Members of the English Association,* 23 (1970), 34-50.

Hunter, J. Paul. *Occasional Form: Henry Fielding and the Chain of Circumstance.* Baltimore: The Johns Hopkins Univ. Press, 1975.

Hutchens, Eleanor Newman. *Irony in* Tom Jones. University: Univ. of Alabama Press, 1965.

Ingarden, Roman. *The Cognition of the Literary Work of Art.* Trans. Ruth Ann Crowley and Kenneth R. Olson. Evanston: Northwestern Univ. Press, 1973.

Iser, Wolfgang. *The Act of Reading: A Theory of Aesthetic Response.* Baltimore: The Johns Hopkins Univ. Press, 1979.

_____. *The Implied Reader: Patterns of Communication from Bunyan to Beckett.* Baltimore: The Johns Hopkins Univ. Press, 1974.

Jack, Ian. "The Epistolary Element in Jane Austen." *English Studies Today, Second Series.* Ed. G. A. Bonnard. Bern: A. Francke, 1961, pp. 173-86.

James, Henry. "The Art of Fiction." In *The Future of the Novel.* Ed. Leon Edel. New York: Vintage Books, 1961.

Jauss, Hans Robert. "Literary History as a Challenge to Literary Theory." In *Toward an Aesthetic of Response.* Trans. Timothy Bahti. Minneapolis: Univ. of Minnesota Press, 1982, pp. 3-45.

Jefferson, D. W. "*Tristram Shandy* and the Tradition of Learned Wit." *Essays in Criticism,* I (1951), 225-48.

Johnson, Samuel. *Johnson on Shakespeare.* Ed. Arthur Sherbo. Vol. VII, *The Yale Edition of the Works of Samuel Johnson.* New Haven: Yale Univ. Press, 1969.

_____. *The Rambler.* Ed. W. J. Bate and Albrecht B. Strauss. Vol. III, *The Yale Edition of the Works of Samuel Johnson.* New Haven: Yale Univ. Press, 1969.

Kahrl, George M. "Smollett as a Caricaturist." In *Tobias Smollett: Bicentennial Essays Presented to Lewis M. Knapp.* Ed. G. S. Rousseau and P. G. Boucé. New York: Oxford Univ. Press, 1971, pp. 169-200.

_____. *Tobias Smollett: Traveler-Novelist.* Chicago: Univ. of Chicago Press, 1945.

Kaminsky, Alice R. "On Literary Realism." In *The Theory of the Novel: New Essays.* Ed. John Halperin. New York: Oxford Univ. Press, 1974, pp. 213-32.

Kaplan, Fred. " 'Our Short Story': The Narrative Devices of *Clarissa.*" *Studies in English Literature, 1500-1900,* 11 (1971), 549-62.

Karl, Frederick R. *A Reader's Guide to the Eighteenth-Century English Novel.* New York: Noonday Press, 1974.

Kearney, Anthony M. "*Clarissa* and the Epistolary Form." *Essays in Criticism,* 16 (1966), 44-56.

Kermode, Frank. "Richardson and Fielding." *Cambridge Journal,* 4 (1950-51), 106-14.

WORKS CITED

Kettle, Arnold. *An Introduction to the English Novel.* 2 vols. 1951; rpt. London: Hutchinson, 1973.

Kinkead-Weekes, Mark. *Samuel Richardson: Dramatic Novelist.* Ithaca: Cornell Univ. Press, 1973.

Kirkman, Francis. *The Counterfeit Lady Unveiled.* In *The Counterfeit Lady Unveiled and Other Criminal Fiction of Seventeenth Century England.* Ed. Spiro Peterson. New York: Doubleday, 1961.

Knapp, Lewis Mansfield. *Tobias Smollett: Doctor of Men and Manners.* Princeton: Princeton Univ. Press, 1949.

Köhler, Wolfgang. *Gestalt Psychology.* 1947; rpt. New York: Liveright, 1970.

Konigsberg, Ira. *Samuel Richardson and the Dramatic Novel.* Lexington: Univ. of Kentucky Press, 1968.

Koonce, Howard L. "Moll's Muddle: Defoe's Use of Irony in *Moll Flanders.*" *ELH*, 30 (1963), 377-94.

Kroeber, Karl. "*Pride and Prejudice*: Fiction's Lasting Novelty." *Jane Austen Bicentenary Essays.* Ed. John Halperin. Cambridge, Eng.: Cambridge Univ. Press, 1975.

———. *Styles in Fictional Structure: The Art of Jane Austen, Charlotte Brontë, and George Eliot.* Princeton: Princeton Univ. Press, 1971.

Krutch, Joseph Wood. "*Modernism*" *in the Modern Drama.* Ithaca: Cornell Univ. Press, 1953.

Laclos, Chaderlos de. *Les Liaisons dangereuses.* Trans. Richard Aldington. New York: Dutton, 1924.

Lanham, Richard A. Tristram Shandy: *The Games of Pleasure.* Berkeley: Univ. of California Press, 1973.

Lascelles, Mary. *Jane Austen and her Art.* 1939; rpt. London: Oxford Univ. Press, 1963.

Leavis, Q. D. *Fiction and the Reading Public.* 1932; rpt. London: Chatto & Windus, 1965.

———. "A Critical Theory of Jane Austen's Writings." *Scrutiny*, 10 (1941), 61-87.

Lee, Nathaniel. *Mithridates.* From Vol. 1, *The Works of Nathaniel Lee.* Ed. Thomas B. Stroup and Arthur L. Cooke. New Brunswick, N.J.: Scarecrow Press, 1954.

———. *Rival Queens.* From Vol. 1, *The Works of Nathaniel Lee.* Ed. Thomas B. Stroup and Arthur L. Cooke. New Brunswick, N.J.: Scarecrow Press, 1954.

Lehman, B. H. "Of Time, Personality, and Author, A Study of *Tristram Shandy*: Comedy." *University of California Publications in English*, 8 (1941), 233-50.

Le Sage, Alain René. *The Adventures of Gil Blas of Santillane.* Trans. B. H. Malkin. New York: Brentano's, 1922(?).

Lewis, C. S. "A Note on Jane Austen." In *Selected Literary Essays by C. S. Lewis.* Ed. Walter Hooper. Cambridge, Eng.: Cambridge Univ. Press, 1969, pp. 175-86.

———. "Addison." In *Essays on the Eighteenth Century, Presented to David Nichol Smith in Honor of his Seventieth Birthday.* Oxford: Clarendon Press, 1945, pp. 1-14.

Liddell, Robert. *The Novels of Jane Austen.* London: Longmans, 1963.

Litz, A. Walton. *Jane Austen: A Study of her Artistic Development.* New York: Oxford Univ. Press, 1965.

Locke, John. *An Essay Concerning Human Understanding.* Ed. John W. Yolton. Everyman's Library 332 and 984. London: Dent, 1961.

Longinus, Cassius. *Longinus on the Sublime.* Trans. A. O. Prickard. Oxford: Clarendon Press, 1954.

Longus. *Daphnis and Chloe.* Trans. Paul Turner. Harmondsworth, Eng.: Penguin Books, 1956.

Lovejoy, Arthur O. *Essays in the History of Ideas.* 1948; rpt. New York: Putnam's, 1960.

Loveridge, Mark. *Laurence Sterne and the Argument about Design.* London: Macmillan, 1982.

Lubbock, Percy. *The Craft of Fiction.* London: Cape, 1921.

MacLean, Kenneth. *John Locke and English Literature of the Eighteenth Century.* New Haven: Yale Univ. Press, 1936.

Maresca, Thomas E. *Epic to Novel.* Columbus: Ohio State Univ. Press, 1974.

Marivaux, Pierre Carlet de Chamblain de. *Le Paisan Parvenu: or The Fortunate Peasant.* London: 1735.

Martz, Louis L. *The Later Career of Tobias Smollett.* New Haven: Yale Univ. Press, 1942.

McCann, Charles J. "Setting and Character in *Pride and Prejudice.*" *Nineteenth-Century Fiction,* 19 (1965), 65–75.

McKillop, Alan Dugald. *Samuel Richardson: Printer and Novelist.* 1936; rpt. Chapel Hill: Univ. of North Carolina Press, 1960.

———. *The Early Masters of English Fiction.* Lawrence: Univ. of Kansas Press, 1956.

———. "Samuel Richardson's Advice to an Apprentice." *Journal of English and Germanic Philology,* 53 (1954), 40–54.

———. "Richardson's Early Writings—Another Pamphlet." *Journal of English and Germanic Philology,* 53 (1954), 72–75.

———. "Epistolary Technique in Richardson's Novels." *Rice Institute Pamphlets,* 38 (1951), 36–54.

Melville, Herman. *Moby-Dick or The Whale.* Ed. Charles Fiedelson, Jr. Indianapolis: Bobbs-Merrill, 1976.

Mendilow, A. A. *Time and the Novel.* London: P. Nevill, 1952.

Miller, Henry Knight. "Henry Fielding's *Tom Jones* and the Romantic Tradition." *English Literary Studies Monograph Series,* No. 6. Victoria: Univ. of Victoria, 1976.

———. "The Voices of Henry Fielding: Style in *Tom Jones.*" In *The Augustan Milieu: Essays Presented to Louis Landa.* Ed. Henry Knight Miller, Eric Rothstein, and G. S. Rousseau. Oxford: Clarendon Press, 1970, pp. 262–88.

———. "Some Functions of Rhetoric in *Tom Jones.*" *Philological Quarterly,* 45 (1966), 209–35.

Miller, Nancy K. *The Heroine's Text: Readings in the French and English Novel, 1722–1782.* New York: Columbia Univ. Press, 1980.

Milton, John. *Paradise Lost.* Ed. Merritt Y. Hughes. New York: Odyssey Press, 1962.

Moglen, Helene. *The Philosophical Irony of Laurence Sterne.* Gainesville: Univ. Presses of Florida, 1975.

Moler, Kenneth L. *Jane Austen's Art of Allusion.* Lincoln: Univ. of Nebraska Press, 1968.

Monaghan, David. *Jane Austen, Structure and Social Vision.* London: Macmillan, 1980.

Monk, Samuel H. *The Sublime: A Study of Critical Theory in XVIII-Century England.* 1935; rpt. Ann Arbor: Univ. of Michigan Press, 1960.

Moore, John Robert. *Daniel Defoe, Citizen of the Modern World.* Chicago: Univ. of Chicago Press, 1958.

Morgan, Susan. *In the Meantime: Character and Perception in Jane Austen's Fiction.* Chicago: Univ. of Chicago Press, 1980.

Mudrick, Marvin. *Jane Austen: Irony as Defense and Discovery.* Princeton: Princeton Univ. Press, 1952.

New, Melvyn. *Laurence Sterne as Satirist: A Reading of* Tristram Shandy. Gainesville: Univ. Presses of Florida, 1969.

Newton, Sir Isaac. *Opticks; or, A Treatise of the Reflections, Refractions, Inflections and Colours of Light.* London: G. Bell and Sons, 1931.

Novak, Maximillian E. "Conscious Irony in *Moll Flanders.*" *College English,* 25 (1964), 198–204.

———. "Defoe's Theory of Fiction." *Studies in Philology,* 61 (1964), 650–68.

———. *Defoe and the Nature of Man.* New York: Oxford Univ. Press, 1963.

———. *Economics and the Fiction of Daniel Defoe.* Berkeley: Univ. of California press, 1962.

Odmark, John. *An Understanding of Jane Austen's Novels.* Oxford: Basil Blackwell, 1981.

Ortega y Gasset, José. "Notes on the Novel." In *The Dehumanization of Art and Other Writings on Art and Culture.* New York: Doubleday, 1916, pp. 53–95.

Page, Norman. *The Language of Jane Austen.* Oxford: Basil Blackwell, 1972.

Paulson, Ronald. *Emblem and Expression: Meaning in English Art of the Eighteenth Century.* Cambridge, Mass.: Harvard Univ. Press, 1975.

———. *Satire and the Novel in Eighteenth-Century England.* New Haven: Yale Univ. Press, 1967.

Phillipp, K. C. *Jane Austen's English.* London: Deutsch, 1970.

Pinion, F. B. *A Jane Austen Companion.* London: Macmillan, 1973.

Pope, Alexander, *Poems.* Twickenham Text. Ed. John Butt. New Haven: Yale Univ. Press, 1963.

Pope, Alexander, et al. *Memoirs of the Extraordinary Life, Works, and Discoveries of Martinus Scriblerus.* Ed. Charles Kerby-Miller. New York: Russell and Russell, 1966.

Poulet, Georges. "Phenomenology of Reading." *New Literary History,* 1 (October 1969), 53–68.

Preston, John. *The Created Self: The Reader's Role in Eighteenth-Century Fiction.* London: Heinemann, 1970.

Preston, Thomas R. "Smollett and the Benevolent Misanthrope Type." *PMLA,* 79 (March 1964), 51–57.

Price, Martin. *To the Palace of Wisdom: Studies in Order and Energy from Dryden to Blake.* Carbondale: Southern Illinois Univ. Press, 1964.

Pritchett, V. S. *The Living Novel.* London: Chatto & Windus, 1946.

Pufendorf, Samuel. *The Whole Duty of Man According to the Law of Nature.* English trans. 5th ed. London: 1735.

Rabkin, Eric S. *Narrative Suspense: "When Slim Turns Sideways."* Ann Arbor: Univ. of Michigan Press, 1973.

Rabkin, Norman. "*Clarissa*: A Study in the Nature of Convention." *ELH*, 23 (1956), 204–17.

Rawson, C. J. *Henry Fielding and the Augustan Ideal under Stress.* London: Routledge, 1972.

Reeve, Clara. *The Progress of Romance through Times, Countries and Manners.* 1785; facsimile rpt. New York: Facsimile Text Soc., 1930.

Richardson, Samuel. *Selected Letters.* Ed. John Carroll. Oxford: Clarendon Press, 1974.

———. *The History of Sir Charles Grandison.* Ed. Jocelyn Harris. 3 vols. London: Oxford Univ. Press, 1972.

———. *Pamela.* Everyman's Library 683 and 684. London: Dent, 1957.

———. *Clarissa.* Everyman's Library 882–85. London: Dent, 1932.

———. *Clarissa.* Shakespeare Head Edition. 7 vols. Oxford: Basil Blackwell, 1930.

———. *Familiar Letters on Important Occasions.* Ed. Brian W. Downs. London: G. Routledge, 1928.

———. *Correspondence.* Forster MS XII. Victoria and Albert Museum, London.

Richetti, John. *Defoe's Narratives: Situations and Structures.* Oxford: Clarendon Press, 1975.

———. *Popular Fiction before Richardson: Narrative Patterns, 1700–1739.* Oxford: Clarendon Press, 1969.

Rothstein, Eric. *Systems of Order and Inquiry in Later Eighteenth-Century Fiction.* Berkeley: Univ. of California Press, 1975.

Rubinstein, E. "Jane Austen's Novels: The Metaphor of Rank." *Literary Monographs*, Vol. 2. Ed. Eric Rothstein and Richard N. Ringler. Madison: Univ. of Wisconsin Press, 1969.

Russell, H. K. "*Tristram Shandy* and the Technique of the Novel." *Studies in Philology*, 42 (1945), 581–93.

Sacks, Sheldon. *Fiction and the Shape of Belief.* Berkeley: Univ. of California Press, 1964.

Scarron, Paul. *The Comical Romance.* Trans. Tom Brown, et al. 1700; rpt. New York: B. Blom, 1968.

Scholes, Robert. *Structuralism in Literature: An Introduction.* New Haven: Yale Univ. Press, 1974.

Scholes, Robert, and Robert Kellogg. *The Nature of Narrative.* New York: Oxford Univ. Press, 1966.

Shelley, Mary. *Frankenstein; or The Modern Prometheus.* Ed. M. K. Joseph. London: Oxford Univ. Press, 1969.

Sherbo, Arthur. *Studies in the Eighteenth-Century English Novel.* Lansing: Michigan State Univ. Press, 1969.

Sherburn, George. " 'Writing to the Moment': One Aspect." In *Restoration and Eighteenth-Century Literature: Essays in Honor of Alan Dugald McKillop.* Ed. Carrol Camden. Chicago: Univ. of Chicago Press, 1963, pp. 201–9.

———. "Fielding's Social Outlook." *Philological Quarterly*, 35 (1956), 1–23.

Sherwood, Irma Z. "The Novelists as Commentators." In *The Age of Johnson; Essays Presented to Chauncey Brewster Tinker.* New Haven: Yale Univ. Press, 1949, pp. 113–25.

WORKS CITED

Shinagel, Michael. *Daniel Defoe and Middle-Class Gentility.* Cambridge, Mass.: Harvard Univ. Press, 1968.

Shklovsky, Victor. "Art as Technique." In *Russian Formalist Criticism: Four Essays.* Trans. Lee T. Lemon and Marion J. Reis. Lincoln: Univ. of Nebraska Press, 1965, pp. 3-24.

————. "Sterne's *Tristram Shandy*: Stylistic Commentary." In *Russian Formalist Criticism: Four Essays.* Trans. Lee T. Lemon and Marion J. Reis. Lincoln: Univ. of Nebraska Press, 1965, pp. 25-57.

Shugrue, Michael F., ed. *Foundations of the Novel: Representative Early Eighteenth-Century Fiction, 1700-1739.* New York: Garland, 1972-73.

Singer, Godfrey Frank. *The Epistolary Novel.* Philadelphia: Univ. of Pennsylvania Press, 1933.

Smith, John Harrington. *The Gay Couple in Restoration Comedy.* Cambridge, Mass.: Harvard Univ. Press, 1948.

Smith, R. Dr. *A Compleat System of Opticks.* London: 1738.

Smollett, Tobias. *The Expedition of Humphry Clinker.* Ed. Angus Ross. Harmondsworth, Eng.: Penguin Books, 1961.

Spacks, Patricia Meyer. *Imagining a Self: Autobiography and Novel in Eighteenth-Century England.* Cambridge, Mass.: Harvard Univ. Press, 1976.

Spector, Robert Donald. *Tobias George Smollett.* New York: Twayne, 1968.

Sprat, Thomas. *The History of the Royal Society of London for the Improving of Natural Knowledge.* 4th ed. London: 1734.

Stamm, Rudolf G. "Daniel Defoe: An Artist in the Puritan Tradition." *Philological Quarterly*, 15 (1936), 225-46.

Starr, G. A. *Defoe and Casuistry.* Princeton: Princeton Univ. Press, 1971.

————. *Defoe and Spiritual Autobiography.* Princeton: Princeton Univ. Press, 1965.

Stedmond, John M. *The Comic Art of Laurence Sterne.* Toronto: Univ. of Toronto Press, 1967.

Sternberg, Meir. *Expositional Modes and Temporal Ordering in Fiction.* Baltimore: The Johns Hopkins Univ. Press, 1978.

Sterne, Laurence. *The Life and Opinions of Tristram Shandy, Gentleman.* Ed. James Aiken Work. New York: Odyssey Press, 1940.

Stevick, Philip. *The Chapter in Fiction: Theories of Narrative Division.* Syracuse: Syracuse Univ. Press, 1970.

Suleiman, Susan R. and Crosman, Inge, eds. *The Reader in the Text: Essays on Audience and Interpretation.* Princeton: Princeton Univ. Press, 1980.

Swearinger, James E. *Reflexivity in* Tristram Shandy. New Haven: Yale Univ. Press, 1977.

Swift, Jonathan. *Gulliver's Travels.* Ed. Robert A. Greenberg. New York: Norton, 1961.

————. *A Tale of a Tub to Which is Added the Battle of the Books and the Mechanical Operation of the Spirit.* Ed. A. C. Guthkelch and D. Nichol Smith. 2nd ed. Oxford: Clarendon Press, 1958.

Tave, Stuart. *Some Words of Jane Austen.* Chicago: Univ. of Chicago Press, 1973.

Tawney, R. H. *Religion and the Rise of Capitalism.* London: J. Murray, 1926.

Thomson, James. *The Seasons.* Ed. James Sambrook. Oxford: Clarendon Press, 1981.

Thornbury, Margaret. *Henry Fielding's Theory of the Comic Prose Epic.* 1931; rpt. New York: Russell and Russell, 1966.

Tillyard, E.M.W. *The Epic Strain in the English Novel.* London: Chatto & Windus, 1958.

Tolstoi, Lev Nikolaevich. *War and Peace.* Trans. Louise and Aylmer Maude. New York: Oxford Univ. Press, 1941.

Tomashevsky, Boris. "Thematics." In *Russian Formalist Criticism.* Trans. Lee T. Lemon and Marion J. Reis. Lincoln: Univ. of Nebraska Press, 1965, pp. 61-98.

Tompkins, Jane P., ed. *Reader-Response Criticism: From Formalism to Post-Structuralism.* Baltimore: The Johns Hopkins Univ. Press, 1980.

Tompkins, J.M.S. *The Popular Novel in England, 1770-1800.* 1932; rpt. Lincoln: Univ. of Nebraska Press, 1961.

Towers, A. R. "Sterne's Cock and Bull Story." *ELH,* 24 (1957), 12-29.

Traugott, John. *Tristram Shandy's World: Sterne's Philosophical Rhetoric.* Berkeley: Univ. of California Press, 1954.

Tuveson, Ernest. "Locke and Sterne." In *Reason and the Imagination: Studies in the History of Ideas, 1600-1800.* Ed. J. A. Mazzeo. New York: Columbia Univ. Press, 1962, pp. 255-77.

_____. *The Imagination as a Means of Grace: Locke and the Aesthetics of Romanticism.* Berkeley: Univ. of California Press, 1960.

Uphaus, Robert W. *The Impossible Observer: Reason and the Reader in Eighteenth-Century Prose.* Lexington: Univ. Press of Kentucky, 1979.

_____. "Sentiment and Spleen: Travels with Sterne and Smollett." *Centennial Review of Arts and Sciences,* 15 (1971), 406-21.

Van Ghent, Dorothy. *The English Novel: Form and Function.* New York: Rinehart, 1953.

Virgil. *The Aeneid.* Trans. Robert Fitzgerald. New York: Random House, 1983.

Warner, William Beatty. *Reading Clarissa: The Struggles of Interpretation.* New Haven: Yale Univ. Press, 1979.

Watkins, Owen C. *The Puritan Experience.* London: Routledge, 1972.

Watt, Ian. "The Comic Syntax of *Tristram Shandy.*" In *Studies in Criticism and Aesthetics, 1660-1800: Essays in Honor of S. H. Monk.* Ed. Howard Anderson and John S. Shea. Minneapolis: Univ. of Minnesota Press, 1967, pp. 315-31.

_____. *The Rise of the Novel.* Berkeley: Univ. of California Press, 1957.

_____. "*Robinson Crusoe* as a Myth." *Essays in Criticism,* I (1951), 95-119.

Wendt, Allan. "Clarissa's Coffin." *Philological Quarterly,* 39 (1960), 481-95.

West, William A. "Matt Bramble's Journey to Health." *Texas Studies in Language and Literature,* 2 (1969), 1197-1208.

Willey, Basil. *The Seventeenth Century Background.* 1935; rpt. New York: Doubleday, 1953.

Williams, Aubrey. "Interpositions of Providence and the Design of Fielding's Novels." *The South Atlantic Quarterly,* 70 (1971), 265-86.

Williams, Ioan M., ed. *Novel and Romance, 1700-1800: A Documentary Record.* London: Routledge, 1970.

Wolff, Cynthia Griffin. *Samuel Richardson and the Eighteenth-Century Puritan Character.* Hamden, Conn.: Archon, 1972.

Wordsworth, William. *The Prelude; or Growth of a Poet's Mind.* Ed. Ernest De Selincourt. 2nd ed. Rev. Helen Darbishire. Oxford: Clarendon Press, 1959.

WORKS CITED

Wright, Andrew H. *Jane Austen's Novels: A Study in Structure*. London: Chatto & Windus, 1957.

Würzbach, Natascha, ed. *The Novel in Letters: Epistolary Fiction in the Early English Novel, 1678–1740*. London: Routledge, 1969.

Zimmerman, Everett. *Defoe and the Novel*. Berkeley: Univ. of California Press, 1975.

_____. "Pride and Prejudice in *Pride and Prejudice*." *Nineteenth-Century Fiction*, 23 (1968), 64–73.

Index

INDEX